LEISURE SERVICES LAW

LEISURE SERVICES LAW

By
Michael Scott, LL.M.

Second Edition

LONDON
SWEET & MAXWELL
1993

First Edition 1985

Published in 1993 by
Sweet & Maxwell Limited of
South Quay Plaza, 183 Marsh Wall, London E14 9FT
Computerset by Promenade Graphics Ltd.,
Cheltenham, Gloucestershire
Printed in England by Clays Ltd.,
St. Ives plc

British Library Cataloguing in Publication Data

A CIP catalogue record for
this book is available
from the British Library

ISBN 0–421–45520–9

Dedicated to

Frank Saunders

whose 50 years' leisure with

an allotment has enriched his own and

many others' lives.

Foreword to the First Edition

This book will fulfil a long-held need in local government. There was a time when local authority leisure facilities consisted simply of public walks and pleasure grounds and public libraries. The law was simply and shortly expressed in several statutes. Those concerned with practice and administration could, by reference to a few sections and a small body of case law, discover what were the powers and duties of public authorities and what were the rights of the public.

Those days are passed. Public authorities are no longer limited in their activities: they now provide a wide range of sports and leisure services and many of these services are commercial in nature. It is a well established principle that as a service expands, so the law relating to that service expands, but to a more than proportionate degree. Similarly, as a service becomes more complex, the law relating to that service becomes more complex, but to a greater degree.

This principle applies to the law of public leisure services. The manager and administrators of a modern sports and leisure complex are now involved in many areas of law—commercial, employment, liquor and other licensing, health and safety, public liability, public entertainment, sex discrimination, sale of goods, as well as the torts of nuisance, negligence and trespass, and the law of parks and libraries.

The author of this work, by diligence and much research, has provided an exposition of law on all these and many other related topics, and in so doing will provide much needed guidance and advice to all concerned with sport and leisure.

460 The Royal Exchange Charles Cross
Manchester
September 1985

Preface

The appetite of our society for a proliferation of leisure services of all kinds has shown no signs of abating in the eight years since the first edition of this book was published. That interest has been reflected in the legal dimension by Parliament in over 50 new statutes and by the courts in many more cases for the Law Reports.

A second edition was thus needed and it will be seen to take account of legislation which followed the Taylor Report on the Hillsborough disaster, the Environmental Protection Act 1990, water privatisation, the changes, still almost annual, in gambling and licensing law, copyright and cinema statute consolidation, to mention a few. Deer, badgers, salmon and other wildlife have been affected by legislation in this period; so have billiards, horserider's headgear and footpaths.

From the courts we have noted cases about football trainers, sex shops, pop festivals, library reading rooms, football matches, the cases in the European Court of Justice affecting race and sex discrimination law, valuations of works of art and the legal harness constraining the Jockey Club.

At the same time, the opportunity has been taken to relieve this book of the burden of trying to record ever more complex changes in local government finance and that has now gone. This has left room for new material on skiing, car races in towns, compulsory competitive tendering and a number of other items.

Finally we have tried to reflect, in the title and in the text, the significant swing in recent years to the private sector as a more important provider of leisure services. Whether that pendulum has swung to its limit, only time will tell.

It has been my good fortune to have helpful comments on the changing text from colleagues in the legal profession, especially Mr. P. Maxlow-Tomlinson of Exeter, Mr. C. G. Karger of the Corporation of London and Mr. D. V. Pullen of the National Trust legal department. I thank them warmly. My gratitude is also due to Heritage Division 5 of the Department of the Environment, the Office of Arts and Libraries, H.M. Customs and Excise in connection with works of art, Miss G. Grimond of the National Gallery, Dr. J. G. Parker of Public Lending Right, Mrs. M. Richardson of the Sir John Soanes Museum, the Broads Authority, Mr. P. J. Clarke, secretary to the Forestry Commissioners, Mr. S. Bilbe of the Home Office section concerned with the safety of sports grounds, Miss K. Hayes of the Department of Health in relation to food safety controls, Miss J. Hartshorne of the Films Branch of the Department of Trade and

ix

Industry, Gateshead Borough Council Parks and Recreation Department, Mr. D. Lucas of the Birmingham City superprix section, Mr. P. Taylor of the Sheffield City Finance Department and Mr A. Goodwin of the Calderdale Borough Finance Department.

The Tourist Authority, and Arts and Sports Councils were very helpful with updates on their activities and the Law Librarian and her staff at Leeds University were helpful at all times. These thanks expressed, responsibility for errors remains with the author.

Halifax   Michael Scott
August, 1992

Contents

CONTENTS

Table of Cases

References throughout are to paragraph numbers.

xix

Table of Statutes

References throughout are to paragraph numbers.

1

Table of Statutory Instruments

References throughout are to paragraph numbers.

CHAPTER 1

GENERAL LEGAL PRINCIPLES FOR THE PROVIDERS OF PUBLIC LEISURE SERVICES

"A bottle is a container and not a trade mark"

Lord Templeman in *Re Coca Cola Co.* [1986] 1 W.L.R 695.

INTRODUCTION

This book is designed as an outline of so much of the law of this country as **1.001** falls within the area of activity connoted by the public leisure services. Chapters 3 to 10 embrace some 45 areas of law selected with that gauge in mind. In this and the next chapter, an outline is given of those branches of the general law which affect the management, the practice and the legal problems associated with the public leisure services. Necessarily, in this chapter this involves some treatment of the torts of nuisance, negligence and trespass, the rule in *Rylands* v. *Fletcher* and the principles of remoteness of damage.

This chapter will also deal with the Health and Safety at Work Act, the Race and Sex Discrimination Acts, and those Acts embodying our laws concerning the sale of goods, and employment law. All these branches of law combine, in varying degrees, law based on cases in the courts and law primarily laid down in Parliament. The law of contract, also to be discussed, is now an admixture from these two sources. Occasionally, law deriving from custom is touched upon. The whole will be selected in the light of the subject of this work; only so can it be reasonably limited; but only so, it is hoped, can some unity emerge in place of what might otherwise be a miscellany of selections from that extensive library constituted by English law at the present time.[1]

The various branches of law can conveniently be grouped as those met **1.002** when the public leisure services authority is acting as property owner, secondly as employer and manager, and thirdly as business organiser.

"Public leisure services" is an expression intended to extend beyond local authorities to other public bodies which operate in this field. The Forestry Commission, with its holiday chalets, the new Water and Rivers Authorities, with their promotion of fishing and boating and the Country-

---

[1] *Halsbury's Statutes* currently extend to 56 volumes: *Halsburys Laws*, the library of textbooks, which range over the whole field of English law, contains 60 volumes.

1

side Commission are examples. If in the text local authorities are referred to more than the others, that is a matter of convenience and is not intended to be an exclusive term. The term "public authorities" was not used, since it would seem to suggest branches of government and as such it would be misleading, since those departments and their branches are not normally involved in the provision of leisure services.

THE LEISURE SERVICES AUTHORITY AS PROPERTY OWNER

A. THE DUTY TO VISITORS

1.003   The Occupiers' Liability Act 1957 was a watershed in the law of tort. It sought to create order where there was confusion. It stemmed from a report of the Law Reform Committee[2] and was thus a considered and in fact a considerable measure of codification. It was not a consolidating Act, since it repealed no earlier statutes. The previous law had been case law and that Act of 1957 gathered together compactly what hitherto had been diffused. Its subject-matter is of importance for all in the public leisure services, since nearly all are occupiers of property to which visitors resort throughout the year. The Act of 1957 deals with the variety of situations created in law by the status of those visitors, the variety of those premises and the occasions which bring them together.

1. The Common Duty of Care

1.004   "The common duty of care is a duty to take such care as in all the circumstances of the case is reasonable, to see that the visitor will be reasonably safe in using the premises for the purposes for which he is invited or permitted by the occupier to be there."[3]

This duty, it will be observed, is owed to *visitors* and that term gives rise to the first of seven glosses upon expressions in this foundation definition:

1.005   The persons who are to be treated as visitors in relation to the occupier are the same as the persons who would, at common law, be treated as his invitees or licensees.[4]

Invitees and licensees were visitors lawfully on the premises. Whilst invitees were present for a purpose in which the occupier had a material interest, such as a customer in a cafe, in the case of licensees no such material interest existed. People taking a stroll in the local public park would be licensees of the local authority for this purpose.[5] There were different legal duties owed by the occupier to these two classes and these have now been united in "the common duty of care."

1.006   Secondly, this duty arises in respect of "dangers due to the state of the

---

[2] Law Reform Committee, Third Report *Occupiers' Liability to Invitees, Licencees and Tres- passers*, Cmd. 9305 (1954).
[3] Occupiers Liability Act 1957, s.2(2).
[4] *Ibid.* s.1(2).
[5] *Phipps* v. *Rochester Corporation* [1955] 1 Q.B. 450.

premises or to things done or omitted to be done on them."[6] As the word "premises" is not defined in the Act, difficulties oblige litigants to turn to the courts for assistance. Earlier, in 1943, Lord Wright said that the word "premises" embraces "places and structures of all sorts on which persons may be invited to come."[7] O'Connor J., in 1968, said that the word includes "fixed and moveable structures."[8] In the context of such words, it would seem that in a recreation ground, whilst a slide would be a fixed structure, a swing would not, in the normal use of the words, be a "moveable structure." It is a piece of playground equipment.

Thirdly, the common duty of care, the Act further provides, rests upon the same persons as at common law.[9] These arise out of a person's occupation or control of premises. This can mean that if, say, a museum was closed for a month for stone-cleaning, then the cleaning contractor could legally be in occupation of the premises for that period and accordingly bear the common duty of care in relation to visitors.[10] **1.007**

Fourthly, this common duty of care does not, moreover, impose on an occupier "any obligation to a visitor in respect of risks willingly accepted as his by the visitor."[11] **1.008**

The Act says that the question whether that risk has been willingly accepted is to be settled on the same principles as in other cases where one person owes a duty of care to another. For instance, a player in a rugby match accepts a risk of being thrown in a tackle[12] and a swimmer who uses a diving board over the sea accepts risks resulting from different depths of water caused by the ebb and flow of the tide.[13]

Fifthly, a person who enters premises under rights conferred by an access agreement under the National Parks and Access to the Countryside Act 1949, is not to be treated as a visitor of the occupier of those premises, for the purposes of the Act of 1957.[14] **1.009**

Sixthly, on the other hand, a person who visits premises pursuant to a contract with the occupier, as a spectator at a sports ground, is entitled to the benefit of the common duty of care. This provision is included to remove the old distinctions, which were somewhat fine, about the respective duties owed to such visitors compared with others who did not have a **1.010**

---

[6] Occupiers' Liability Act 1957, s.1(1).
[7] *Glasgow Corporation* v. *Muir* [1943] A.C. 448 at p. 461.
[8] *Bunker* v. *Brand (Charles) and Son Ltd.* [1969] 2 Q.B. 480 at p. 486.
[9] Occupiers' Liability Act 1957, s.1(2).
[10] *Kearney* v. *Waller (Eric) Ltd.* [1967] 1 Q.B. 29. Though in contrast an occupation of a Site of Special Scientific Interest for dredging by a Water Authority, held insufficient occupancy, within a strict criminal offence definition in the Wildlife & Countryside Act 1981, s.28: *S.W.A.* v. *Nature Conservancy Council, The Times,* June 17, 1991.
[11] Occupiers' Liability Act 1957, s.2(5).
[12] *Simms* v. *Leigh Rugby F.C. Ltd.* [1969] 2 All E.R. 923.
[13] *Pertiouski* v. *Wellington Corporation* [1959] A.C. 53.
[14] Occupiers Liability Act 1957, s.1(4). The Act of 1949 says that a person going on to land for open air recreation, while an access agreement is in force, is not, by reason only of such entry, to be treated as a trespasser (s.60 of the 1949 Act). Being neither a trespasser, nor a visitor, he must, one infers, be "another," as that expression is euphemistically used in the Occupiers Liability Act 1984, s.1(3).

contract.[15] (The Act says that the common duty of care is to be a term implied in a contract which is silent on this point.)

1.011   The last and by no means least important of these seven glosses on the common duty of care, is the provision that the occupier can "extend, restrict, modify or exclude his duty to any visitor or visitors by agreement or otherwise."[16]

Those last two words "or otherwise" import ways in which, before 1957, occupiers would limit their legal duty to visitors by warning notices. So in *Ashdown* v. *Samuel Williams and Sons Ltd.*[17] where a visitor to land was injured by a railway truck engaged in shunting work, a claim for damages failed since a notice warning visitors of this type of danger was on the land and of a nature and in a situation which would be reasonable to achieve its aim.

The Unfair Contracts Terms Act 1977

1.012   The Unfair Contracts Terms Act 1977 prohibits the use of contract terms and warning notices to limit liability in relation to death or personal injury due to negligence. The term or notice must pass the test of reasonableness for other loss or damage.[18]

2. The Common Duty of Care in Relation to Special Classes

(1) *Children*

1.013   The Act of 1957 expressly deals with an occupier's duty to visitors who are children: "an occupier must be prepared for children to be less careful than adults."[19]

The courts look for dangers known to the occupier and for which he is liable and which would be alluring, or even traps, for children. There are cases which relate to glass in a paddling pool,[20] poisonous berries in a public park,[21] a hillside used for children's slides,[22] a finger injury on a swing in a recreation ground,[23] and a head injury against a school playground flint wall.[24]

---

[15] Occupiers' Liability Act 1957, s.5(1).

[16] *Ibid.* s.2(1).

[17] [1957] 1 Q.B. 409.

[18] Note the definition of "business" liability in s.1(3) of the Act of 1977, as the prohibition is limited to this class.

[19] Occupiers' Liability Act 1957, s.2(3).

[20] [1938] 1 K.B. 212.

[21] [1922] 1 A.C. 44.

[22] (1983) 81 L.G.R. 460.

[23] [1947] 1 K.B. 359.

[24] *British Railways Board* v. *Herrington* [1972] A.C. 877. Two mischievous acts which made an adventure playground dangerous were not foreseeable and so did not render the owning local authority liable to injured children. The acts were to untie ropes fastening the gates and leaving a car with rubbish smouldering against it, from which an explosion ensued. This was so even though the defendants were in breach of their duty under the Act of 1957, by leaving the playground unsecure and unsupervised: *Morgan* v. *Blunden*; *Reilly* v. *Blunden* (1986) 83 L.S.Gaz. 705, C.A.

(2) *Trespassers*[25]

This group of persons, unlawfully on land, has recently been the subject of **1.014** Parliamentary attention. The Act of 1957 did not deal with trespassers but the Occupiers' Liability Act 1984 is devoted to the subject. The code laid out in section 1 of the Act of 1984 embodies the following principles:

(1) The occupier owes a duty to "persons other than his visitors," *i.e.* trespassers.

(2) The duty is to take such care as is reasonable, in all the circumstances of the case, to see that the trespasser does not suffer injury on the premises by reason of the danger concerned.

(3) And what is the "danger"? It is the risk of suffering injury by reason of any danger due to the state of the premises or to things done or omitted to be done on them.

(4) The occupier's duty arises "if he is aware of the danger or has reasonable grounds to believe that it exists," and if "he knows, or has reasonable grounds to believe, that the other is in the vicinity of the danger concerned or that he may come into the vicinity of the danger." Both these crucial new prerequisites are to be satisfied before the new duty exists. So also is a third condition, that the risk must be "one against which, in all the circumstances of the case, he may reasonably be expected to offer the other some protection." This is presumed to connote dangers akin to traps, known to the occupier, but indiscernible, even to a wide awake nocturnal prowler.

(5) How is the duty discharged? The Act continues that this can be **1.015** done, in an appropriate case, by giving warning of the danger or "taking steps to discourage the persons from incurring the risk."

(6) Lastly, by way of clarification, the section states that the duty is not in relation to persons using a highway, or to risks willingly accepted by the trespasser, or to loss or damage to property but only to personal injury.

The aim of the new Act of 1984 is to offer the non-visitor some protec- **1.016** tion, and obviously cases will develop this guideline. It will be of the greatest interest to occupiers and their advisers to see whether the law has been changed from that embodied in the common law. In the House of Lords debates on the Bill, the Lord Chancellor said: "This is not a charter for trespassers."[26] From those debates and the wording of the Act, it is at least clear that one avenue opened by the last leading case of *British Railways Board* v. *Herrington*[27] has been closed. That was the suggestion in one judgment that the duty to trespassers, who still entered land of others at their peril, might best be described as taking such steps "as common sense or common humanity would dictate."[28]

The facts of *Herrington's* case are worth recapitulating. An electrified **1.017**

---

[25] After the subject was referred to the Law Commission which reported (No. 75) in March 1976 and suggested a statutory duty to "unwanted entrants" in a draft Occupiers Liability Act. The case of *Pannett* v. *McGuinness* [1972] 2 Q.B. 599 still merits study.
[26] Second Reading, July 12, 1983, H.L.
[27] [1972] A.C. 877.
[28] *Ibid.* at p. 767*d.*

railway line ran through property of the National Trust, to which the public had access. Because of the poor state of the fencing, it was possible to gain access to the track and there was evidence that visitors to the National Trust properties did cross the track. The infant plaintiff was injured when crossing the line. At first instance, in the Court of Appeal and finally in the House of Lords, British Rail were held liable. They had allowed the fence to fall into disrepair, knowing that children were in the habit of trespassing on the line. Whilst none of the courts suggested that the occupier had an obligation to ensure that trespassers could not enter, the salient elements in the local circumstances which led to the finding for the plaintiff were the proximity of a public path, the land being open to the public, the ease with which a child could pass through the fence and the fact that a child would not appreciate the danger of a live rail.

It is pure conjecture what steps British Rail might have taken in the above circumstances in order to discharge the newly defined occupier's duty in the Occupiers' Liability Act 1984. It seems evident that, at the least, the plainest and boldest warning notice would not suffice.

(3) *Persons Enjoying Easements over Land*

1.018 This group of persons are not "visitors" and the case of *Greenhalgh* v. *British Railways Board*[29] exemplifies this distinction. It concerned a lady injured whilst exercising a right of way over a railway bridge.

(4) *People Exercising their Calling*

1.019 "An occupier may expect that a person, in the exercise of his calling, will appreciate and guard against any special risks ordinarily incident to it, so far as the occupier leaves him free to do so."[30]

The principle embodied in this provison may be exemplified in a case relating to an injured factory inspector and another case involving a window cleaner who was injured whilst traversing parts of premises outside his usual route and knowledge.[31]

(5) *Warning Notices under the Unfair Contract Terms Act 1977*

1.020 This important Act of 1977 has been mentioned as the location for statutory provisions about the nature of disclaimers of legal liability. The subsections mentioned above raise questions from time to time about the form and content of warning notices and their effectiveness in limiting an occupier's legal liability to persons injured on his land.[32]

---

[29] [1969] 2 Q.B. 286.
[30] Occupiers' Liability Act 1957, s.2(3)(*b*).
[31] *Read* v. *J. Lyons and Co. Ltd.* [1947] A.C. 156; *Christmas* v. *General Cleaning Contractors Ltd.* [1953] A.C. 180. *Ogwo* v. *Taylor* [1987] 1 All E.R. 668 is the latest authoritative fireman's case. The 1957 Act was pleaded though not critical in the decision in favour of the injured fireman. The case has interesting references to the USA approach.
[32] *Hartley* v. *Mayoh* [1954] 1 Q.B. 383, is instructive.

Attention is therefore drawn to the recent Occupiers' Liability Act 1984, where a modification of the Act of 1977 is effected. Parliament wishes to achieve two objectives:

(1) Encourage, *e.g.* farmers to permit ramblers to cross their lands. To do this, farmers had not to be subject to some new liability to those persons for natural and obvious risks, like rocks, lakes, "pots" for pot-holing. They should continue to be able to exclude any liability for that sort of feature of their land.[33]

(2) Retain within the general control of the Act of 1977 all terms restricting liability as regards business premises, where recreational facilities are part of a commercial proposition, to use the words of Lord Hailsham when explaining the new measure in the House of Lords. Holiday camps and safari parks were the two examples he gave.[34] Perhaps the final comment on this change of law should be that it is about the state of the premises and not about dangerous activities carried out there.

3. Other Aspects of the Common Duty of Care

(1) *The Common Law Liability for Negligence*

"If a landowner is driving his car down his private drive and meets **1.021** somebody lawfully walking upon it, then he is under a duty to take reasonable care so as not to injure the walker; and his duty is the same, no matter whether it is his gardener coming up with his plants, a tradesman delivering goods, a friend coming to tea or a flag seller seeking a charitable gift."[35]

As Lord Denning's utterance, above, was in a case in 1956, it may be reasonably treated as a last minute protest at undue niceties in the law about visitors, before the first Occupiers' Liability Act reached the statute book. But, nearly 30 years later, it is not universally accepted that the Act of 1957 embodies the total existing common law of duties to lawful visitors. The position is, indeed, rather the reverse. Cases come before the courts where the choice between two or more bases of claim is canvassed, and that under the Act of 1957 is regarded as only one option. Useful examples are found in cases relating to a fall on the Queen Elizabeth liner[36] and an injury on a toboggan slide in Canada.[37] This arises because the Act lays down the rules discussed in the previous subsections:

"in place of the rules of the common law, to regulate the duty which

---

[33] Since our last edition, public debate has sharpened on the extent to which and limits within which hunting, in its various forms, can be accepted in our society as a leisure pursuit. The Courts made it clear, in one prominent case, that landowners can still maintain actions for trespass, and secure injunctions and damages: *League Against Cruel Sports Ltd.* v. *Scott* [1985] 3 W.L.R. 400.

[34] Occupiers' Liability Act 1984, s.2.

[35] Lord Denning M.R. in *Slater* v. *Clay Cross Ltd.* [1956] 2 Q.B. 264, 269.

[36] [1969] 1 Lloyd's Rep. 150.

[37] [1969] 3 D.L.R. 649.

an occupier of premises owes to his visitors in respect of dangers due to the state of the premises or to things done or omitted to be done on them."[38]

But the Act proceeds to state that the new rules:

"regulate the nature of the duty imposed by law in consequence of a person's occupation or control of premises."[39]

1.022 The view is taken by some textbook writers, that the Act of 1957 does not deal with claims arising out of an occupier's neglect towards his visitor in doing something like shunting an engine, or riding a horse or putting a bull into a field: what have been called "activity duties."[40]

One can only conclude that those responsible for the public leisure services, with premises open to the public, have to guard also against this second limb of liability, based on negligence.

(2) *The Common Duty of Care in Relation to the Intervention of the Independent Contractor*

1.023 The Act of 1957 contains a provision about the occupier's duty to the visitor when the accident occurred due to the intervention of an independent contractor engaged by the occupier.[41] Examples which may be studied relate to a lift[42] and a snow-covered step at a school.[43]

(3) *The Common Duty of Care in Relation to the Limitation Acts*

1.024 The law governing the limits on the time within which legal action in the courts can be commenced is, unfortunately, technical and complex. It is nonetheless vital and as a possible pitfall for litigants, can give rise, rightly, to charges of negligence against their advisers if its provisions are overlooked.

Public property owners are at risk from injured claimants for a basic period of three years from the time when the action could be brought. This is sometimes described as the time when the breach of duty took place.

Unhappily, from the point of view of those seeking certainty, the above statement is clouded by recent statutory provisions which seek to allow latitude to plaintiffs when latent damage prevents their taking prompt

---

[38] Occupiers' Liability Act 1957, s.1(1).
[39] *Ibid.* s.1(2). See *Cunningham* v. *Reading Football Club, The Independent*, March 20, 1991, where the football club was held liable for injuries to police officers, lawfully at a match, caused by hurled missiles of concrete broken from the structures on the premises by opposing team supporters. The club, said the Court, should on the evidence have known of this likelihood and had failed to maintain the concrete structure adequately for its lawful visitors.
[40] "Not one which would have been encountered in the normal use of the premises," is the Law Reform Committee's wording for what they wished the Act to cover in this situation.
[41] s.2(4)(b).
[42] *Haseldine* v. *Daw* [1941] 2 K.B. 343.
[43] *Woodward* v. *Hastings Corporation* [1945] K.B. 174.

action on some injury or accident. The statutory provisions must, in these circumstances, be consulted.[44]

B. The Duty to Neighbours

1. **Nuisance**

(1) *Private Nuisance*

The Occupiers' Liability Acts 1957 and 1984 have given a pattern to the law about a property owner's duty to his lawful and unlawful visitors. There is, as yet, no comparable statute for this section of our survey, relating to the occupier's duty to his neighbours. It is the law of nuisance which embodies the legal principles to be applied to that situation.   **1.025**

Nuisance is a tort with the prestige of antiquity and experience. Unfortunately, the pressure it has come under, from the chemical and other industrial nuisances of our society, on the one hand, and on the other, from the inroads made by statutes dealing with public nuisances, have left a misshapen body of case law and an ill-assorted set of rules for litigants.

By way of entry into this territory, from the point of view of the public leisure services, we shall take the subjects of cricket matches and trees. This is partly because they happen to have some special relevance to the subject but also because they are areas where the benefit of recent significant court decisions, provides a modern conspectus of the law, as it responds to social changes and pressures.

The law of nuisance is, indeed, very much a matter of balance. It is in essence concerned with that use of one's own property to an extent which constitutes an unacceptable interference with the use and enjoyment of his land by the neighbour. Thus the interference suffered by the neighbour must be appreciable. Whether the nuisance consists of smell,[45] vibration,[46] noise,[47] subsidence,[48] flooding,[49] or other ways in which the use and enjoyment of one's own property can be impaired, the courts only intervene when "damage of a material kind" is suffered, to take a phrase from a typical case.[50]

Cricket matches

In the case of *Miller* v. *Jackson*[51] an action was brought by a householder against a cricket club. This alleged (*inter alia*) nuisance, and it was said   **1.026**

---

[44] See now the Limitation Act 1980; also the Law Reform (Limitation of Actions) Act 1954, the Fatal Accidents Act 1976 and the Limitation Amendment Act 1980, and see para. 1.130.
[45] *St. Helen's Smelting Co.* v. *Tipping* (1865) 11 H.L.C. 642.
[46] *Meux's Brewery Co.* v. *City of London Electric Lighting Co.* [1895] 1 Ch. 287.
[47] *Shelfer* v. *City of London Electric Lighting Co.* [1895] 1 Ch. 187.
[48] *Bognuda* v. *Upton and Shearer* (1972) N.Z.L.R. 74.
[49] *Bartlett* v. *Tottenham* [1932] 1 Ch. 114.
[50] *Nobilo* v. *Waitemata County* (1961) N.Z.L.R. 1064.
[51] [1977] Q.B. 966.

that the frequent hitting of cricket balls into the garden of the house and against the house and its roof, interfered with the householder's use and enjoyment of the house and its curtilage. The club had offered various forms of physical protection for the house, as well as the 14 feet 9 inch boundary wall and surmounting fence. What the club could not do was to guarantee that balls would not be hit on this residential property, which was only 34 yards from the square in the centre of the cricket pitch. At a first hearing, an injunction against the playing of cricket was granted but on appeal the Court of Appeal did not maintain the injunction. The Court of Appeal decision comprised:

(1) Agreement (by two of the three judges) that the club's activities amounted to an actionable nuisance.

(2) It was no defence to the complaint that the cricket club has been active for 70 years and the plaintiffs had moved into a new house a few years before the court case was begun. The case of *Sturges* v. *Bridgman*[52] should be followed on that point.

(3) The borderline between the tort of nuisance and the tort of negligence is not always easy to see but at least in the remedies available to a successful plaintiff, there is a difference. An injunction is possible for nuisance, though not for negligence.

(4) However, an injunction to stop the cricket was not held to be the appropriate remedy. A payment of damages in respect of past and future damage to the plaintiff's property was held to be the right remedy.

(5) In considering whether the cricket club's activity was an unreasonable interference with the plaintiff's enjoyment of his house and garden, a balance had to be maintained between the right of the individual to enjoy his house and garden without the threat of damage and the rights of the public in general or a neighbour to engage in lawful pastimes. There was, in the view of the majority in the Court of Appeal, a real risk of serious injury.

This case usefully illustrates certain basic principles in the tort of nuisance:

(a) The interference has to be significant.[53]

(b) The question of the remedy for the nuisance is crucial. An injunction to restrain the nuisance is not automatic: damages may be appropriate.

(c) The principle of *Sturges* v. *Bridgman*,[54] a leading case, 100 years old, is still important. It is no defence to say: you came to the nuisance.

1.027   (d) It was the continuing cricket activity which precipitated the case and led the court to concentrate on the tort of nuisance. This provides a contrast between this case and another one where a person was hit by a cricket ball struck by a batsman 100 yards from the highway where the injured plaintiff was walking. That

---

[52] (1879) 11 Ch.D. 852.
[53] See, *e.g. Att.-Gen.* v. *Hastings Corporation* (1950) 94 S.J. 225, where the Court of Appeal upheld an injunction to stop organised speedway racing.
[54] (1879) 11 Ch.D. 852.

case[55] turned on negligence and, in particular, the reasonable foresight of the reasonable man that such damage as ensued might occur.

Trees

If games of cricket exemplify the approach of the courts to activities on land, then the spread of tree roots and branches illustrates, in relation the law of nuisance, the perils possible from the natural state and condition of the land. Two cases are of particular interest.

1.028

Masters v. London Borough of Brent[56]

The roots of a lime tree spread beneath the plaintiff's land and caused subsidence of his house. The Corporation as owners of the tree, were held responsible for the cost of remedying that damage.

Solloway v. Hampshire County Council[57]

The roots of a horsechestnut tree, standing in the highway, spread under the plaintiff's house and caused subsidence. Though the house stood, for the most part, on plateau gravel with clay beneath, there were pockets or outcrops of clay in the gravel beneath the house. These were dehydrated by the roots and thus subsidence occurred earlier than might otherwise have happened.

As the risks to the plaintiff's house were not found to be such that the Corporation should reasonably have foreseen them, the plaintiff lost his case. The case of *Leakey* v. *National Trust*,[58] a year previously, had developed this area of the law by providing a definition of the duty of the property owner in relation to the foreseeable risks of damage to his neighbour's property. These cases about trees thus illustrate important principles in the law of nuisance:

1.029

(a) A continuing nuisance carries continuing liability.
(b) Things naturally on the land still carry liability in nuisance, if consequential danger to adjoining land is foreseeable and can reasonably be averted.

General

It remains to outline the other main points affecting the public leisure services in relation to the law of nuisance:

1.030

(1) A property owner who engages in otherwise reasonable use of his land, does not thereby become liable in nuisance merely because a neighbour embarks upon an extraordinary or specialised use of adjoining land. So when mink farmers wished their neighbours to desist from allegedly

---

[55] *Bolton* v. *Stone* [1951] A.C. 850.
[56] [1978] Q.B. 841.
[57] (1981) 79 L.G.R. 449.
[58] [1980] Q.B. 485.

noisy activities during the whelping season, the tort of nuisance did not avail the mink traders.[59]

(2) Malice by a property owner in relation to some activity on his land, which provokes an action for nuisance by his neighbour, is not relevant to liability. However it can stop a defendant in such an action alleging that his use of his land is reasonable.[60]

1.031   (3) The plaintiff in an action for nuisance must "occupy" the land allegedly affected. However, this occupation may be as freeholder, lessee, ordinary licensee or as a licensee in exclusive occupation.

(4) There must be a legal link between the defendant and the alleged nuisance on his land. Thus gypsies were legally on land of the local authority[61] against whom a nuisance action was brought on account of the activities of the gypsies. Again, a landlord from whose property a slate fell and caused injury, had a legal right in his tenancy agreement to enter that property and carry out repairs.

(5) The three legal remedies for a nuisance suffered to land are:
  (i) damages.
  (ii) injunction.
  (iii) abatement, without legal process. This is the justification for lopping overhanging branches. It is not a recourse to be taken except with care and reasonableness. It is a privilege and its use precludes an action for damages.[62]

(2) *Public and Statutory Nuisances*

1.032   The main discussion hitherto has been devoted to what are called private nuisances. That is the "unlawful" interference with a person's use and enjoyment of his property. In the interests of completeness, we add a short note on these two other legal areas where the word nuisance is also used.

Statutory nuisances

This is a criminal offence, created by statute. The Public Health Acts create such offences for foul deposits, noises and odours which are of such consequence that they call for abatement or other control: local authorities as public health authorities exercise these powers in the public interest.

Public nuisances

1.033   These too are criminal offences which "materially affect the reasonable comfort and convenience of life of a class of Her Majesty's subjects."[63]

---

[59] *Grandel* v. *Mason* (1953) 3 D.L.R. 65. *Home Brewery Co. Ltd.* v. *William Davis & Co. (Leicester) Ltd.* [1987] 1 All E.R. 637 gives a nice differentiation by the Court of reasonable and unreasonable use of his land by a builder. To fill in two clay pits was reasonable, to fill in an osier bed was not, though both had the effect of flooding neighbouring land.
[60] *Christie* v. *Davey* [1893] 1 Ch. 316.
[61] *Page Motors* v. *Epsom and Ewell B.C.* (1982) 80 L.G.R. 337.
[62] *Lagan Navigation* v. *Lamkeg Bleaching Co.* [1927] A.C. 226, 244.
[63] *Att.-Gen.* v. *PYA Quarries Ltd.* [1957] 2 Q.B. 169, 184.

The sphere of the nuisance is said, in one case, to be "the neighbourhood" and the class of persons affected is a question of fact in each case.

Examples of public nuisance are quarrying to the discomfort of a neighbouring village,[64] a pop festival,[65] obstructing public highways and allowing oil to wash onto the shore.[66]

To prevent a multiplicity of legal actions, it is normal for legal process for a public nuisance to be in the hands of a local authority or the Attorney-General. Only when special damage is suffered by the individual can he sue.[67]

2. **The Rule in Rylands v. Fletcher**

This subsection has considered those situations where a property owner **1.034** can be liable in nuisance due to unreasonable behaviour on his part. For a hundred years, these cases have been complemented by a special group of situations where the property owner's liability is strict, *i.e.* not dependent upon his negligence. They all involved a non-natural use of land and an "escape" to the neighbour's land. The series began with a bursting reservoir in the case of *Rylands* v. *Fletcher*[68] and was extended to "escapes" of methane gas from a refuse tip and yew tree leaves[69] which harmed a neighbour's cattle. The rule has been less and less used. It was always subject to exceptions for an act of God, an act of a stranger, the consent of the plaintiff and the case of the default of the plaintiff.

C. THE DUTY TO TENANTS AND TIED COTTAGES

1. **Introduction**

A public leisure services authority from time to time finds itself, legally, **1.035** not only an occupier in relation to visitors and a property owner in relation to neighbours, but also a landlord in relation to tenants.

This role may well be slight, compared with those so far considered. There would indeed seem to be three groups of such tenants in normal experience. The first will be those town flats that Victorian forefathers or thoughtful successors have built in out of the way corners of civic theatres, libraries or museums. These premises call for residential tenancies, perhaps slightly specialised. Secondly, most parks and recreation authorities will have cottages hidden away in some of the large Victorian parks, for-

---

[64] *Att.-Gen.* v. *PYA Quarries Ltd.* [1957] 2 Q.B. 169.
[65] See Department of the Environment Report, "Pop Festivals and their Problems." (HMSO, 1978).
[66] *Southport Corporation* v. *Esso Petroleum Co. Ltd.* [1954] 2 Q.B. 182 at p. 196.
[67] There are full discussions of this subject in the standard textbooks on the Law of Torts; *e.g. Winfield and Jolowicz* (13th ed., 1989) and *Salmond and Heuston* (20th ed., 1992).
[68] (1868) L.R. 3 H.L. 330.
[69] *Crowhurst* v. *Amersham Burial Board* (1878) 4 Ex.D. 5. A judge declined to describe as "non-natural" a tannery factory with its storage of necessary solvent, when such use went back 300–400 years in an industrial community. *Cambridge Water Co.* v. *Eastern Counties Leather, The Times*, October 23, 1991.

mer lodges perhaps of town estates. Similar cottages will be found in woods and forests laid out with tourist attractions, such as nature trails or orienteering activities. Thirdly, non-residential lettings will proliferate, not least with the catering facilities that accompany leisure services. Of course, many of these may be licences, franchises, tenuous legal permits to provide or use kiosks, hoardings, piers, seaside entertainment of all sorts. The aim on the one side is to achieve security, so that money can be committed by an entrepreneur. On the local authority side, whilst acknowledging the reasonableness of this object, is a desire to retain some scope for manoeuvre should future policy call for early repossession of the property in question.[70]

1.036 The important feature of the first two groups of lettings described, is that they are lettings to employees of the authority. Their work will be so related to the location of the cottage or flat that the dwelling is "tied" to the work.[71] When the work ends, so should the tenancy. Whilst the law now contains elaborate restraints on the landlords of both residential and agricultural tenancies, on the general market, the local authority will be seen to be in a different position.

1.037 Non-residential lettings and licences on the other hand, call into play the law relating to business tenancies, contained in the Landlord and Tenant Acts of 1927 and 1954, for the greater part.

In both fields, common law and custom and practice fill in the interstices left by the series of statutes, though it must be emphasised that this whole area of the law is now very much one of statute law.[72]

2. Residential Lettings

1.038 On the basis that the residential lettings in which we are interested will be confined to individual houses, cottages or flats, away from the municipal housing estates, we turn to consider them in two groups. The first is where an employee is *required* to occupy a particular house or flat, to enable him to perform his job effectively. This arrangement is appropriate for the lodge in the forest, the flat in the sports centre—anywhere, indeed, where location is vital. The agreement is a licence to occupy the residence, whilst the employment continues. It will deal with payments for the occupancy, rates, repairs, alterations to the premises, nuisances, non-assignment and any other special terms. The main legal provision, however, will be that when the employment ends, the right to occupy that property ends too. This is on the reasoning that the real occupation is that of the employer, not the employee. The employer arranges the occupancy, so that his work

---

[70] Though *R.* v. *Wear Valley District Council, ex p. Binks* [1985] 2 All E.R. 699 is a warning that the occupant, in that case, a caravan selling take away food in the market place, is entitled to natural justice when the site is repossessed.

[71] "House with job," as a former Archbishop of Canterbury is alleged to have said of the episcopal situation.

[72] The account given here has been designedly kept free of the various complex statutory systems which do not apply to the properties with which this book is primarily concerned.

can be done effectively by his employee. This means that, in the final analysis, the authority[73] could resort to the County Court and secure an order for possession. They would have to give evidence of the background as above and also satisfy the court that their attitude and their action had been reasonable. They would be expected to show that they had allowed some time for the existing employee to vacate the premises and that there was a real need for the incoming employee to occupy it.

On the other hand, when a house is *made available* to an employee as an **1.039** emolument and so is part of the benefits of the employment, but its location is not vital in order to carry out that employment, then the agreement is a tenancy.[74] This means that it is an agreement which will deal with the items mentioned above. It will also refer to the employment which the tenant provides for the landlord and will then set out the rent, the period of notice to terminate the agreement and other terms common to tenancies. These will include a covenant for quiet enjoyment, given by the landlord, a covenant to permit the landlord to enter and inspect and terms about painting and about the permitted use of the premises. These are to regulate the occupation so that both parties understand what is expected of them. If the situation alters and the landlord needs possession for another person, he will have to give the proper notice to quit and if necessary satisfy a court that he had reasonable grounds for requiring possession.

The difference between the employee's licence to occupy and the ordin- **1.040** ary tenancy is heightened by the terms of the Housing Act 1980, and the right of a tenant to buy his property from his landlord. The Housing and Building Control Act 1984 extends that line of legislation. By the Act of 1980, and later amendments, such a right to buy is given to large numbers of local authority tenants but these are precisely those houses which are held by the council in question under Part V of the Housing Act 1957. This provides the powers and duties for a local authority to provide housing accommodation. All municipal housing estate houses and flats are normally held on that legal basis.

However, the houses and flats for public leisure services will not normally be so held. They will be held, perhaps, under the Public Health Act 1875 and its successors or the Museums and Libraries Acts and a variety of other Acts. What the Housing Act 1980 does is to confer on the Part V tenants, as explained above, the status of "a secure tenancy," and it is

---

[73] *Thompsons (Funeral Furnishers) Ltd.* v. *Phillips* [1945] 2 All E.R. 49. A chauffeur was placed in occupation of a residence, to be available for orders. The money allowance by his employers was a complicating factor but the court agreed that it was a licence rather than a tenancy they were construing. Fifty years ago, terminology was a problem. The first judge called it a "service occupancy" (Lawrence L.J. at p. 51A); the second "a service licence" (Mackinnon L.J. at p. 51F); and the third, "a mere service occupation" (Morton L.J. at p. 52D). See *Halsbury's Laws of England* (4th ed., 1981) Vol. 27, para. 14. The editor of this volume of Halsbury appeals to practitioners to abstain from the ambiguous "service tenancy" and stay with licence and tenancy as the alternatives.

[74] *Dover* v. *Prosser* [1904] 1 K.B. 94. And the landmark decision of Street v. Mountford [1985] A.C. 809.

from this status that the right to buy stems. The Act schedules local authority employees with others as not coming into that class.[75]

Though the Secretary of State in 1983 exercised a power under the Housing Act 1980 to extend the right to buy to houses of local authorities held otherwise than under the Housing Act 1957, Pt. V, he qualified that extension. It was limited to "secure tenants" and thus still leaves untouched by that legislation the employees with which we are currently dealing.[76]

1.041   Another relevant provision in the Housing Act 1980 must be mentioned. Section 28 and Schedule 3 define tenancies which are not "secure tenancies," as mentioned above, in terms which restrict the provision to employee's licences rather than tenancies. In other words, the provision is only about those "required" to occupy "for the better performance of his duties," to quote the statute. This phrase was used to define only "strictly tied accommodation"[77] and the case of *Gray* v. *Holmes* may be referred to for an indication of the implications of that concept.[78]

Whilst section 48 of the Housing Act 1980 confers on the holder of a licence to occupy a dwellinghouse the status of secure tenancy, the Schedule 3 to that Act clearly leaves such occupants where they were before the Act. This is reassuring but it emphasises the difference between the employee's licence and the general tenant with which this discussion began.[79]

The difference between these two types of agreement, *i.e.* the licence and the tenancy, is important, mainly in relation to recovering possession: it is easier in the case of the licence. The difference has been put in the form of the test: "Has the employee exclusive occupation for his own purposes or does he occupy the premises in order to carry out his employment obligations on the premises?"

3. Agricultural Tenancies

1.042   It was pointed out above that some of the lettings of houses and cottages will be in rural locations. Whilst the above basic distinction in house lettings applies also to these houses, the legal provisions relating to agricultural tenancies are covered by different legislation.

---

[75] s.1 deals with "secure tenants"; s.28 and Sched. 3 with exempted tenancies.

[76] Housing (Extension of the Right to Buy) Order 1983 (S.I. 1983 No. 672). This Order in terms defines a group of tenant employees of local authorities, *i.e.* those with tenancy agreements dated before October 3, 1980. But it does not affect the exclusion from the right to buy, of this group of employees on licence, conferred by the Housing Act 1980 Sched. 3. The Housing and Building Control Act 1984, s.31, is relevant in so far as it releases from the public trust status, the lands held under s.164 of the Public Health Act 1975 and s.10 of the Open Spaces Act 1906 (see Chap. 4, on these groups of land holdings). But the Act of 1984 does not change the position of employees occupying houses or flats under licence, as discussed in para. 1.038 above.

[77] H.L.Deb., Vol. 412.

[78] [1949] T.R. 71.

[79] See also *Hirst* v. *Sargent* (1967) 65 L.G.R. 127; *Glasgow Corporation* v. *Johnstone* [1965] A.C. 609; and *Chapman* v. *Freeman* [1978] 1 W.L.R. 1298.

Farm labourers' cottages are the archetype of the tied cottage and there are several statutes on that subject. Basically, local authority houses are outside that area of law but it is desirable to indicate briefly what that area of law comprises.

"Agriculture" is defined in the Agricultural Holdings Act 1986 as including[80]:

> "Horticulture, fruit growing, seed growing, dairy farming, livestock breeding and keeping, the use of land as grazing land, meadow land, osier land, market gardens and nursery grounds and the use of land for woodlands where that use is ancillary to the farming of land for other agricultural purposes."

This Act affords protection to the tenant of an agricultural holding for a **1.043** term of years or from year to year, and an agricultural holding is the aggregate of land used commercially for agriculture for such a letting.[81] The definition has given rise to interesting borderline problems about the inclusion of cottages and buildings. The courts take a broad view: is it in substance a tenancy of agricultural land?

The protection begins with a restriction; legal termination can be achieved only by notices to quit of 12 months duration. The Act then makes essential the adjudication of the Agricultural Land Tribunal, to safeguard continuity in the cultivation and husbandry of agricultural holdings. There are elaborate codes to encourage improvements and guard against the division of viable farms.[82]

Recovery of possession of houses used by persons employed in agriculture is the only topic on which it is proposed to embark in detail. Section 1(1) of the Agricultural Holdings Act 1986 excludes "a contract under which the said land is let to the tenant during his continuance in any office, appointment or employment held under the landlord," from being an agricultural holding. This excludes that class of tenancy agreement from the provisions mentioned above.

Again the Rent (Agriculture) Act 1976 contains a detailed pattern of **1.044** law by which agricultural workers are given in relation to their houses the same sort of protection as has been conferred for many years on urban houses under the Rent Acts.[83] But where the landlord's interest belongs to a local authority and a number of other public bodies, the tenants do not acquire statutory tenancies[84] and thus the Act is not relevant from that point of view. (Local authorities as housing authorities were given new duties but that falls outside the purview of this book.)

---

[80] Agricultural Holdings Act 1986, s.96.
[81] *Ibid.* s.1. By the Housing Act 1988, s.34, the legal occupations occurring after January 1989 are governed by Pt. I, Chap. III of that Act of 1988, as assured agricultural tenancies.
[82] See Muir-Watt, *Agricultural Holdings* (13th ed., 1987). Also Yates and Hawkins, *Landlord and Tenant Law* 1981 (2nd ed., 1986). Agricultural Holdings Act 1986, Pts. II and IV.
[83] See now the Rent Act 1977 as the latest consolidating Act.
[84] Rent (Agriculture) Act 1976, s.5(3).

1.045   However, section 4 of the Protection from Eviction Act 1977, contains a provision which does affect the agricultural tenants of local authorities.[85] The effect is as follows:

(1) The house is occupied under the terms of his employment as a person employed in agriculture.

(2) Procedure to recover possession of such a dwelling begins with service of the appropriate notice to quit. The court which hears a subsequent application for an order of possession, has a general power to suspend such an order. However, that court, under the above Act, must suspend the order unless satisfied:

(3) (i) Other suitable accommodation will be available or

    (ii) Efficient management of agricultural land or the efficient carrying on of any agricultural operations[86] will be seriously prejudiced unless the premises are available to be occupied by a person employed by the owner or that greater hardship will be caused by suspending the order than by executing it in the period in question or that the occupier has been causing damage to the property or been a nuisance to neighbours and also that it would be reasonable not to suspend the order for possession.

(4) The section contains 10 subsections in all, which elaborate the main provisions summarised above. It will be evident that it is at the commencement and the termination of their occupancies that the legal position of employees in agricultural and forestry tied cottages is particularly critical.

4. Business Tenancies

1.046   The Landlord and Tenant Act 1954 introduced a code to regulate the legal management of business tenancies which has operated without significant amendment for 35 years. It affects local authority lettings. An outline of the framework created by the Act of 1954 is set out below.[87]

(1) *Businesses Affected*

The Act excludes the following:
(a) Agricultural holdings.[88]
(b) Mining leases.[89]

---

[85] It is the current re-enactment of a provision first in the Rent Act 1965, s.33, as amended by the Agriculture Act 1970, s.99.

[86] The definition from the Rent (Agriculture) Act 1976, s.1, includes forestry.

[87] Lord Denning said it should be called "the Business Tenancy Act" (*Cheryl Investments Ltd.* v. *Saldanha* [1978] 1 W.L.R. 1329, 1332B. For a detailed study see *Woodfall's Law of Landlord and Tenant* and others). Also a compact study is Yates and Hawkins, *Landlord and Tenant Law*, (2nd ed., 1986).

[88] Landlord and Tenant Act 1954, s.43.

[89] *Ibid.*

(c) Part-residential use.[90]
(d) Licenced premises.[91]
(e) Service tenancies.[92]
(f) Public interest tenancies, where the landlord is a government department, a local authority, a development corporation, statutory undertaker or certain health service authorities. But this exclusion applies only when a certificate of the relevant government department, under section 57 of the Act of 1954, has been given that a change of use from business is requisite for the body concerned.[93] This provision, whilst no doubt a necessary safeguard for occasional critical situations, does not appear to be used very much.
(g) National security cases.
(h) Extended leases.[94]
(i) Short leases.[95]
(j) Commercial licences, where the licence is genuine and the ramifications of a legal business tenancy are not appropriate for the wishes of the parties, *e.g.* a tea kiosk, in a park, or sometimes a franchise for deckchairs perhaps, on the promenade at the seaside.

Whilst contracting out of the Act is forbidden, a joint application to the court to exclude the Act is in order.[96]

The Act itself applies to "any tenancy where the property comprised in the tenancy is or includes premises which are occupied by the tenant and are so occupied for the purposes of a business carried on by him or for those and other purposes." The definition of "business" is wide:

"a trade, profession or employment and includes any activity carried on by a body of persons."[97]

The business to be within the Act must not be:
(a) unlawful[98]; or
(b) sporadic[99]; or
(c) on premises convenient, though not necessary, for the conduct of the business.[1]

---

[90] This exclusion was introduced by the Rent Act 1968, s.9(3).
[91] *Ibid.*
[92] For an example of one identified by the court as a sham, see *Teasdale* v. *Walker* [1958] 1 W.L.R. 1076.
[93] These s.57 certificates are, in practice, not greatly used, so that exclusion, apparently maximal, is minimal.
[94] Leasehold Reform Act 1967, s.16(1).
[95] See n.88, *supra.*
[96] Landlord and Tenant Act 1954, s.38.
[97] *Ibid.* s.23. The word "activity" gave rise to *Addiscombe Garden Estates Ltd.* v. *Crabbe* [1958] 1 Q.B. 513, where a members' tennis club was held to be a business within the Act.
[98] Landlord and Tenant Act 1954, s.23(4), *e.g. Daimar Investments Ltd.* v. *Jones* (1962) 112 L.J. 424, where a tenancy was held to be under a "prohibition" when it lacked planning permission for business use.
[99] *Cheryl Investments Ltd.* v. *Saldanha* [1978] 1 W.L.R. 1329.
[1] *Chapman* v. *Freeman* [1978] 1 W.L.R. 1298.

(2) *Excluded Tenants*

1.047 If the tenant sub-lets the whole of his tenancy he loses the protection of the Act; though his sub-tenant may acquire that protection.[2]

Where several persons are tenants but only one or two run the business, then those only are identified for the purposes of the Act of 1954.[3]

A series of subsidiary companies gives rise to another situation where the statute provides a formula to resolve the question: who is now the tenant?[4]

(3) *The Protection of the Act*

1.048 The main provision of the Act of 1954 is to give the lawful tenant of the lawful business the right to a new tenancy on the expiry of the existing one, unless that renewal is successfully resisted by the landlord on one of the following seven grounds[5]:

(a) The state of repair of the premises due to the tenant's failure to fulfil his repairing obligations.

(b) Persistent delay in paying the rent.

(c) Other substantial breaches of the tenant's obligations.

(d) Suitable alternative accommodation is available.

(e) Possession is required of the whole of the premises, of which this is only a subletting.

(f) The landlord intends to demolish or reconstruct the property.

(g) The landlord wishes to occupy the property himself.[6]

This list serves to focus the court case on the central issue between the parties: who should have possession? That stage is not reached without other procedural steps. For instance, the landlord will normally terminate the tenancy, it will continue as the tenant serves notice requesting a new tenancy. This in turn obliges the landlord to state if he will do so and, if not, on which of the above seven grounds he is resisting the tenant's request.

The timetable for these exchanges is very important. The landlord has to give six months' notice, the timing of which is critical; but ultimately it is the attitude of the landlord on the request for renewal which is decisive.

(4) *Assignments*

1.049 This is another feature of the Act of 1954 which requires comment. Many tenants wish to assign their tenancy and the agreement may be expected

---

[2] *Lee Verhulst (Investments) Ltd.* v. *Harwood Trust* [1972] 1 Q.B. 204.

[3] An amendment to the Landlord and Tenant Act 1954 by the Law of Property Act 1969 achieved this situation, which was unclear hitherto. S.41A of the 1954 Act, now covers the matter.

[4] Landlord and Tenant Act 1954, s.42(1).

[5] *Ibid.* s.30.

[6] The Act refers to the landlord's intention. Proof that this is firm is sometimes difficult, *e.g.* Asquith L.J.: "It must have moved out of the zone of contemplation, out of the sphere of the tentative, the provisional and the exploratory, into the valley of decision." (*Cunliffe* v. *Goodman* [1950] 2 K.B. 237).

to contain a term which forbids this outright or, in the alternative, says that consent to an assignment should not be unreasonably withheld. The strict position on assignments in the first form may have been agreed only at the expense of a reduced rent and other terms favourable to the tenant, who has accepted this major imposition. The latter alternative is more common and has been the subject of interpretation in the courts. What might the word "unreasonably" mean? The courts have said that the word limits an enforceable objection to assignments by the landlord to one objectively related to the proposed assignee or to the premises. What is not acceptable, the courts have said, is a refusal of a quixotic character, say, in relation to the race or sex of the proposed assigneee.[7] Nor can the request for consent be made the occasion for the landlord to demand a premium.[8]

(5) *New Tenancies*

Where a new tenancy has been sought by a tenant, refused by the land- **1.050** lord, taken to court and resolved in the tenant's favour, that court is empowered to lay down not only the term and rent of the new tenancy but also other relevant terms.[9]

(6) *Conclusion*

Attention has been drawn to those areas in operating the Landlord and **1.051** Tenant Acts of 1927 and 1954 which, in practice, often prove contentious. The machinery and indeed the text of the Acts allow for these disputes to be resolved. For a local authority with possibly hundreds of business tenancies, the use of the procedure of the Acts is constant. It can only be emphasised that, despite these remarks, it behoves managers of public leisure services to ensure that their commercial lettings do not come within the procedures of the Acts if the lettings are inherently unsuitable for that tight control, whether because of the mixed property content, the slight amount of property involved or possibly the ephemeral nature of the letting.

D. LISTED BUILDINGS AND THE NATIONAL HERITAGE FUND

Most public leisure service authorities own some listed buildings and **1.052** ancient monuments, whether they are Victorian libraries or museums with statues in the forecourts, former town houses, country houses in parkland or recent buildings displaying "technological innovation," or virtuosity (for instance cast iron, prefabrication or the early use of concrete) to quote a recent circular.[10]

---

[7] Landlord and Tenant Act 1927, s.19.
[8] See Yates and Hawkins, *supra*, n.89, footnotes at p. 482.
[9] Landlord and Tenant Act 1954, s.35.
[10] D.O.E. Circular 8/87, Historic Buildings and Conservation Areas—Policy and Procedures.

The law about these edifices has been developed since 1882[11] and the last major Act was in 1990.[12] At the start of the century, 29 monuments were the subject of legal protection in England and Wales: now there are some 450,000 listed buildings and 12,000 scheduled ancient monuments.[13] The legal aspects of this subject to which attention is drawn here are:

    (a) The scheduling of ancient monuments.

    (b) The listing of buildings.

    (c) The designation of areas of archeological importance.

These provide the basic legal framework within which property owners have to work. This outline does not attempt to move into detail: it seeks only to help the owners of the buildings and monuments in question when changes affecting that property have to be made. *The Scheduling of Ancient Monuments* and *The Designation of Areas of Archeological Importance* will be found in Chapter 3 in relation to the law for museums authorities, being the service most closely affected.

1. Listed Buildings

1.053   "Buildings," for this purpose, range from lampposts and horse troughs to railway viaducts and textile mills, bandstands, and model villages, market crosses and stocks, caves and archways, towers and stables and the Tower of London. The definition in the Town and Country Planning Act 1971 states that it includes "any structure or erection and any part of a building, structure or erection, but does not include plant or machinery comprised in a building."[14]

In addition to the building is its curtilege and its setting. Curtilege is a word used in many conveyances of buildings: it connotes land associated with the occupation or use of a building or needed for its comfortable enjoyment.[15] The "setting" of a building is also now referred to in the statute when planning applications are made for development which is thought to affect a listed building.[16]

1.054   "The List" is the list kept by the Department of the Environment of all listed buildings. It grades buildings into I "of exceptional interest" and II "of special architectural or historic interest which warrant every effort

---

[11] Ancient Monuments Protection Act 1882.

[12] Planning (Listed Buildings and Conservation Areas) Act 1990.

[13] A comprehensive outline of this subject by R. W. Suddards, *Listed Buildings: The Law and Practice of Historic Buildings, Ancient Monuments and Conservation Areas* (2nd ed., 1988), is recommended for detail on all aspects of this subject. It instances 1985 as a year when 23,000 new listings were made.

[14] Planning (Listed Buildings and Conservation Areas) Act of 1990, s.91 and the Town and Country Planning Act 1990, s.336.

[15] *Att.-Gen. ex rel. Sutcliffe* v. *Calderdale Borough Council* [1983] 46 P. & C.R. 399, C.A. But see cautious note on this in C.A. in *Debenhams plc* v. *Westminster City Council* [1987] 1 All E.R. 51, 60. The case illustrated a broad approach to s.54 of the Town and Country Planning Act 1971 in construing "curtilage," so that the effective decision about demolition of a building connected to the main listed building rests with the Department of Environment on a Listed Building Consent application and not with the courts on construction of a word.

[16] Planning (Listed Buildings & Conservation Areas) Act 1990, s.67.

being made to save them."[17] The List is compiled both by systematic geographic survey and also by spot-listing. Listing is not appealable but the List can be amended.

Once a building is listed, then before works of demolition, alteration or extension can be carried out, listed building consent must be obtained.[18] This gives rise to public notice, occasional objection, public enquiry and final decision from the Department of the Environment. It may be an episode of considerable public interest and even furore. It is sometimes important that financial considerations are taken into account in deciding whether to give listed building consent, though not, it is emphasised, in deciding to list a building. It is now possible to seek immunity from listing for five years, but such a course of action is by no means easy to recommend to a property owner: delicate considerations affect both advantages and disadvantages.[19]

The criteria currently in use for selecting buildings built between 1914 and 1939 cover a range of buildings and of nine classes, the second is "cinemas, theatres, hotels and other places of public entertainment" and the seventh class is "municipal and other public buildings."[20]

A building preservation notice can be made by a local authority as an emergency procedure to prevent works of demolition or alteration.[21] The notice delays those works until the Department of the Environment has considered whether the building should be listed. It is designed to freeze the situation for six months whilst that consideration takes place.

In conclusion, it is emphasised that the listing of a building, whilst it has important legal consequences—and, indeed, criminal sanctions for breaking the law, is intended as a control mechanism. It does not represent a final or considered judgment on the architectural or other merits of the building. It allows, to quote Sir H. Casson, at a public enquiry, "time for study and second thoughts."[22]

1.055

2. The National Heritage Fund

Public leisure service authorities need to know of this national fund, which can sometimes assist projects which have national tourist attraction. Part I of the Act of 1980 contains the following provisions:

1.056

[17] Circular 8/87, *supra*, gives criteria for listing buildings by reference to their age; *e.g.* before 1700 all are listed if in anything like their original condition. Then most buildings of the 1700–1840 range are to be listed.
[18] Listed Buildings Act 1990, ss.7 and 8.
[19] The immunity certificate is dealt with in s.6 of the 1990 Act. Application to the Department of the Environment can be made on condition that planning permission has been given or sought. The certificate is the recognition that expenditure can safely take place; for five years there will be no listing nor any Building Preservation notice. A copy of the application has to be served upon the local planning authority.
[20] D.O.E. Circular 8/87.
[21] Listed Buildings Act 1990, s.3.
[22] R. W. Suddards, n.13, *supra*. The text does not attempt to embark on a description of Conservation Areas. These, too, lead to the need to seek consent to demolish a building in such areas. They differ from Listed Building and Building Preservation procedures described above in referring to areas rather than individual buildings.

The National Heritage Act 1980 sets up the National Heritage Memorial Fund. "Memorial" refers to its memorial nature in relation to those who have died for the United Kingdom. The fund is managed by trustees.[23] Grants and loans are made from the fund:

(1) To acquire, maintain or preserve any land building or structure of outstanding scenic, historic, aesthetic, architectural or scientific interest.

(2) Similarly, to acquire, maintain or preserve any object or collection or group of objects of outstanding artistic, historic or scientific interest and

(3) Similar powers in relation to lands or objects connected with (1) or (2) and also for rights over land being rights considered desirable for the benefit of the land mentioned above.[24]

In each case of a grant or loan, the supported object has to be "of importance to the national heritage."[25]

The securing of public access or public display, as the case may be, is an aspect to which the trustees are required to have regard.[26]

There are wide powers about the conditions which the trustees can impose on their advances, including if necessary, repayment in the event of a breach.

A grant can be made to an existing trust, if it will advance one of the stated objects of the fund.[27]

Eligible recipients for payments from the fund are listed in the Act, *i.e.*

(1) a museum, an art gallery or some institution having the purpose of preserving for the public benefit a collection of historic, artistic or scientific interest;

(2) some body with the purpose of providing, improving or preserving amenities or land to be enjoyed by the public or acquiring land to be used by the public;

(3) any body whose purpose is or includes nature conservation,[28]

(4) the Secretary of State, when acting under section 5 of the Historic Buildings and Ancient Monuments Act 1953 or section 11 or 13 of the Ancient Monuments and Archeological Areas Act 1979.[29]

Trustees can use monies from the fund on related expenses other than grants, *e.g.* transport or repairs. They are expressly forbidden to hold property without the consent of the Minister. In other words, they are not to build themselves into a holding company. They can accept gifts for the fund; they can make investments from the fund when prudent to do so; they are required to present annual reports.

---

[23] It succeeded the National Land Fund, which was set up in 1946 as a "public war memorial" and which had been operated under the auspices of the Treasury.

[24] s.3. This is supported by a useful provision in s.16. This allows the Secretary of State to give an indemnity to a museum for a collection maintained for the public benefit, whilst it is on loan to another similar museum.

[25] s.3(2).

[26] s.3(3).

[27] s.3(5).

[28] s.3(6).

[29] *i.e.* respectively, buildings or objects of outstanding historic or architectural interest, and acquiring or maintaining ancient monuments.

The above summarises those parts of the Act relevant to the subject of this book and does not embark upon the remainder.[30]

THE LEISURE SERVICES AUTHORITY AS EMPLOYER AND MANAGER

Introduction

Public leisure services gather into their ranks many who can be described as employers and managers. An essential element in services which use artistes, advertisers, and enterprise of all sorts, are those persons who engage and dismiss staff, who arrange for the payment of the large labour force, deal with its health, safety and general welfare, its mischief and misconduct and determine the legal implications of its activities. **1.057**

The legal aspects of taking people into employment have never been more complex. It has been estimated that over 100 statutes on aspects of employment law have come onto the statute book in the last century. But collective bargaining, by national agreements of employers and employees, has transformed the pattern and the content of the contract of employment, especially for the individual employee. His contract will often incorporate terms from such a national agreement; their enforcement may be complicated. **1.058**

Again the European Economic Community dimension of this subject has to be taken into account. Some of the British employment laws have been enacted to give effect to standards embodied in international charters or conventions, to which the British government is a party.[31] Provisions about closed shops in the European Convention on Human Rights and Fundamental Freedoms were the subject of litigation before the European Court. The Treaty of Rome, Article 118, states that the aim of members is to produce close collaboration in relation to "employment, labour law and working conditions . . . and collective bargaining between workers and employers." Provisions in the Employment Protection Act 1975 gave effect to the Directive of the EEC on collective redundancies, but the overlap between the two documents is not always complete.[32] **1.059**

These comments will indicate the growth of this branch of law in recent years. For the purposes of this book, the outline will necessarily be limited **1.060**

---

[30] National Heritage Act 1980 is not linked with the National Heritage Act 1983, which set up trustees for Kew Royal Botanic Gardens, and for the Victoria and Albert Museum, and also dissolved the Historic Buildings Council and replaced it by the Historic Buildings and Monuments Commission for England.

[31] See, *e.g.* the right of disabled persons to rehabilitation and resettlement in the European Social Charter (1965).

[32] See *Johnson* v. *Nottinghamshire Combined Police Authority* [1974] 1 W.L.R. 358. Leisure services cases in European Law Reports are rare. But one decided that a Belgian coach was entitled to reasons when not recognised as qualified by the French football body, though duly qualified in Beligum. Thus EEC law impinges on domestic employment law—*Union Nationales des Entraineurs et Cadres Techniques Professionels du Football* v. *Heylens* (No. 222/86), *The Times*, October 26, 1987, European Ct.

in the first place to the basic elements in the general contract of employment to which employers and managers should be alert.[33]

A. THE CONTRACT OF EMPLOYMENT

1.061   A convenient starting point is the Employment Protection (Consolidation) Act 1978 (the Act of 1978). This requires an employer within 13
weeks of the start of a person's employment, to give his employee a written
statement containing basic facts about the terms of his contract of employment. These are:
  (a) The wage or salary, how it is calculated and when it will be paid.
  (b) Terms and conditions about the hours of work, and also about
       holidays, sickness, injury and pensions.
  (c) Particulars of the notice required to terminate the contract.
  (d) The title of the job.[34]

Common law requirements

1.062   The common law has evolved a number of conditions in a normal contract of employment, which help to fill out the terms listed above. These
include the following:

Duties on the employee

The employee is to serve faithfully and obey instructions. The employee
is prohibited from working for a trade competitor, whilst in the employment in question.[35]

The employee is responsible to his employer for the consequences of his
negligence, whilst engaged in his employer's work.[36]

An employee is to show loyalty to his employer[37] and not, for instance,
canvass his employer's customers to induce them to become his customers
if and when he should end his existing employment.[38]

The employer's secrets

Leisure services can be an area of work where it is important that an
employer's secrets are preserved, *e.g.* about negotiated terms for artistes or
sports teams to appear or commercial companies to provide goods in the

---

[33] The provisions in the Treaty of Rome about the free movement of workers (Articles
48–50) have continuing implications for contracts of employment.

[34] s.1. Some jobs are excluded and not relevant to this book. There are also some exempted
short-time jobs, *i.e.* some less than 16 hours per week and others subject to another rule
when 16 to 26 hours per week.

[35] *Hivac Ltd.* v. *Park Royal Scientific Instruments Ltd.* [1946] Ch. 169.

[36] *Lister* v. *Romford Ice & Cold Storage Co. Ltd.* [1957] A.C. 555 at p. 572. For interesting
modern limits on misuse of phone by phone-cleaner, see *Heasmans* v. *Clarity Cleaning Co.
Ltd.* [1987] I.C.R. 949.

[37] *Bents Brewery Co. Ltd.* v. *Hogan* [1945] 2 All E.R. 570. Job mobility is important these days
and the Courts have considered many cases. A recent authoritative one is *United Bank Ltd.*
v. *Akhtar* (1989) I.R.L.R. 507.

[38] *Wessex Dairies Ltd.* v. *Smith* [1935] 2 K.B. 80 at p. 85.

locality. A term in a contract of employment which seeks to restrain an employee from competing against the employer for a stated period and in a defined area, after the employment in question ends, is one which needs careful drafting if it is to be effective in the courts. The general view taken currently is that such covenants are an undue restraint on a man's freedom in the market place, unless the covenant is reasonable both between the two parties and also reasonable in the public interest.[39]

Duties on the employer

The employer's general duty, apart from any arising from statute and **1.063** discussed below, is to provide competent staff, adequate materials, a proper system of work and effective supervision.[40] This statement is meant to define a duty lower than that of an insurer of his employee's safety. An employee is expected to accept the reasonable risks of his employment and this limits the employer's obligations.[41]

On the other hand, this is not a duty which the employer can delegate to an independent contractor. Where a kiosk was the place in which a workman had to work close to live electrical equipment, his employer was liable for his death, since it was no defence to say that he had entrusted the manufacture of the inadequate kiosk to another person. The employer had the primary duty and also had the opportunity to examine the kiosk and decide if it was safe for his workman.[42]

Lastly, from the employer-employee relationship is implied a term that the employer will indemnify the employee against losses incurred in carrying out the duties of his employment reasonably.[43] This obligation of the employer does not, however, extend to any consequences of the employee's misconduct.[44]

Dismissal

Dismissal has become legally complex, coupled as it is with redundancy **1.064** law, compensation and numerous statutory provisions.

The Employment Protection (Consolidation) Act 1978, amended in part by the Employment Act 1982, stipulates periods of notice related to the term of years served as an employee, *e.g.* one week of notice for every

---

[39] *Mason* v. *Provident Clothing and Supply Co. Ltd.* [1913] A.C. 724, 733. See also for a void contract due to unreasonableness. *A Schroeder Music Publishing Co. Ltd.* v. *Macaulay* [1974] 3 All E.R. 616. See more recently *Spencer* v. *Marchington* [1988] I.R.L.R. 392 and *Office Angels Ltd.* v. *Rainer-Thomas, Financial Times*, March 27, 1991, C.A. where a carefully drawn covenant was held invalid.
[40] *Wilsons and Clyde Coal Co. Ltd.* v. *English* [1938] A.C. 78.
[41] *Smith* v. *Baker* [1891] A.C. 325, 360.
[42] *Paine* v. *Colne Valley Supply Co. Ltd. and British Insulated Cables Ltd.* [1938] 4 All E.R. 803.
[43] *Adamson* v. *Jarvis* (1827) 4 Bing. 66, and, more recently, in *re Ready Mixed Concrete* (1991) I.C.R. 52.
[44] *Lister* v. *Romford Ice Cold Storage Co. Ltd.* (*supra*). A significant contribution of the Courts—not Parliament—to this topic in the last 15 years has been the deliberate addition to the normal implied terms in a contract of employment of one of mutual trust and confidence. This is particularly important in providing a basis for a claim of constructive dismissal—*Wood* v. *W.M. Car Services (Peterborough) Ltd.* [1981] I.C.R. 666.

year served between two and 12 years, and 12 weeks' notice if more than
12 years has been served. The calculation of the period of continuous
employment for the above formula is itself intricate and the cases upon it
must be studied. Changes of employer complicate that issue.[45]

A written statement of reasons for the dismissal is to be given if
requested.[46]

Unfair dismissal in relation to trade union activities

1.065   An employee must not be dismissed unfairly. To do so gives rise to the
right of the employee to seek redress, including, possibly, reinstatement,
from an Industrial Tribunal.[47] The reasons given in the amended Act of
1978 which are stated to make the dismissal "unfair" are:

    (a) that the employee was or proposed to become a member of an inde-
pendent trade union; or

    (b) that the employee had taken or proposed to take part at any appro-
priate time in the activities of an independent trade union; or

    (c) that the employee was not a member of any trade union.

These reason are elaborated in the Act; so also are the various circumstances in which they are not to apply, so that the Act has to be looked at
carefully if this situation is relevant.[48]

Fair dismissal in relation to trade union activities

1.066   The new section 58 provides that a dismissal is fair if, in brief:

    (a) it is the practice, within the closed shop at the establishment in
question, to join a specified independent trade union; and

    (b) a principal or substantial reason for the dismissal is that the
employee was not a member of such a trade union; and

    (c) the closed shop had the status of having been approved by a postal
ballot, complying with the Act and held within five years preceding
the dismissal.[49]

(The Act sets out the various percentages for the ballot in question to be
acceptable for this purpose.)

1.067   The Act of 1978, as amended, then provides that the above shall not
apply if one of the following five conditions is met:

    (a) The employee was a non-trade union member for the stated five-
year period[50]; or

    (b) the employee objects on conscientiously held grounds to joining a
trade union[51]; or

---

[45] Employment Protection (Consolidation) Act 1978, s.49.
[46] *Ibid.* s.53.
[47] *Ibid.* s.54.
[48] *Ibid.* s.58. This is an amended s.58; see Employment Act 1982, s.3. Also Employment Acts
of 1989 and 1990.
[49] *Ibid.* s.58(3A).
[50] *Ibid.* s.58(5).
[51] *Ibid.* s.58(4).

(c) the employee participated in the ballot by which the closed shop agreement at this establishment came into existence after August 14, 1980, and has not been a member of a trade union since that time; or

(d) an employee's declaration of unreasonable expulsion from a trade union existed or was the subject of proceedings before an industrial tribunal at the time of the dismissal[52]; or

(e) the employee's refusal to take part in a strike (giving rise to his expulsion) or to join a trade union was due to the terms of a written code of conduct for employees of his qualifications and (b) or (d) do not apply.

This is admittedly complex and no attempt is made here to summarise the ballot provisions. The inclusion of this subject-matter is intended to alert employers and managers in the public leisure services to the points that will be relevant in a dismissal situation with which they may have to deal.

Unfair dismissal in relation to redundancy

After these three reasons relating to an employee's trade union membership, the Act turns to the question of redundancy.[53] It says that the dismissal shall be unfair if, though the principal reason for the dismissal is that the employee was redundant, the employer has not dismissed other employees who were in virtually the same situation as the one dismissed. In addition it has to be shown that the employer either was departing from an agreed practice governing redundancy (without special reasons for so doing) or that his real reason was the trade union membership one outlined above. The employer has the option to provide evidence that the employee could only have been in contravention of some enactment if he had been retained at work, as a driving disqualification when he has to drive at work. Finally the employer may show some other "substantial reason" for the dismissal.[54] This is wide-ranging, covering the deliberate misleading of the employer about a material fact when applying for the job and an irreconcilable conflict of personalities mainly caused by the dismissed employee. Two statutory "substantial reasons" may also be adduced by the employer:

1.068

(a) The person being dismissed is the temporary replacement of a permanent employee and he was told this would happen when appointed;

(b) the person being dismissed was a temporary replacement for a pregnant employee and, again, was told at the time of appointment what would happen.

---

[52] Employment Act 1980, s.4.

[53] Employment Protection (Consolidation) Act 1978, s.59. Attention is drawn to the leading case of *Williams* v. *Compair Maxim Ltd.* [1980] 1 I.R.L.R. 83, for guidelines in dealing with this situation. These relate to warnings, consultation, objective criteria for selection, considering suggestions by the union on selection and offering alternative employment.

[54] *Ibid.* s.57(2).

Unfair reasons for dismissal—pregnancy

1.069   The last of the statutory situations dealt with in detail in the Act of 1978 is a dismissal related to an employee's pregnancy.[55] Such a dismissal is unfair, unless:

(a) at the time in question, the employee will, because of her pregnancy, have become unable to do her work adequately; or

(b) some statutory provision would be contravened if she continued in work when pregnant.

Even if able to substantiate one of the above reasons, the employer must still be in a position to show that he is offering the lady in question a new and equivalent job, in circumstances detailed in the Act.

Valid reasons for dismissal

1.070   In assessing the merits of the employer's reasons in the situations described above, the tribunal also has to comply with the following general provisions:

(a) The employer has to show the reason for the dismissal.[56]

(b) He does this by showing that the reason related to the conduct of the employee or his capability or qualifications in relation to his particular job. Alternatively he can show that it was because the employee was redundant or could only continue in work if in conflict with some enactment; or fifthly, was some other substantive reason of a kind such as to justify that particular dismissal.[57]

(c) Lastly, "the determination of the question whether the dismissal was fair or unfair, having regard to the reason shown by the employer, shall depend on whether, in the circumstances (including the size and administrative resources of the employer's undertaking) the employer acted reasonably or unreasonably in treating it as a sufficient reason for dismissing the employee; and that question shall be determined in accordance with equity and the substantial merits of the case."[58]

Exceptions

1.071   There are eight classes of employees outside the above provisions:

(a) Employees who at the time of termination had not been employed for at least two years.[59]

---

[55] Employment Protection (Consolidation) Act 1978, s.60. These dismissals have in recent years been inter-related with Sex Discrimination and thus EEC law. Most recently, see, *e.g. Webb* v. *EMO Air Cargo (UK) Ltd., The Times*, December 30, 1991, C.A.

[56] *Ibid.* s.57(1).

[57] *Ibid.* s.57(2). Recently misconduct outside employment has been recognised as a valid ground for a fair dismissal if, *e.g.* theft or use of drugs, reflects on the employee's fitness to perform his work satisfactorily.

[58] *Ibid.* s.57(3), as amended by the Employment Act 1980, s.6. Currently these are all looked at in the light of authoritative guidance from the House of Lords in *Polkey* v. *Dayton Services Ltd.* [1988] I.C.R. 142.

[59] *Ibid.* s.64(1)(*a*) and Unfair Dismissal (Variation of Qualifying Period) Order (S.I. 1985 No. 782).

(b) An employee who at the time of termination has reached his normal retiring age.[60]

(c) Where there is no prescribed retiring age, that he has reached pensionable age, *i.e.* 65 for men and 60 for women.[61]

(d) Persons employed by their husbands or wives.[62]

(e) Dockworkers.[63]

(f) Persons working in fishing vessels as non-profit sharers.[64]

(g) Persons working under contracts which normally involve their working outside the United Kingdom.[65]

(h) Persons employed on ships registered in Great Britain but whose employment is normally outside Great Britain, or who are not normally resident in Great Britain.[66]

General

A general exemption is also prescribed for a case where a dismissal is certified by a Minister that it was required for the purpose of safeguarding national security.[67]

The pressure upon an employer by a strike or other industrial action is to be ignored when a tribunal is considering whether a dismissal was fair or unfair.[68]

The Employment Protection (Consolidation) Act 1978 has a series of provisions about strikes and lock-outs. One of these gave rise to a case in the Court of Appeal concerning 30 employees at the National Theatre who went on strike, for reasons worth noting. **1.072**

The case is *Williams* v. *National Theatre Board*.[69] At the conclusion of a damaging strike, which involved the cancellation of eight performances, there was a claim for unfair dismissal. The employers succeeded in their defence by showing that the employees had been offered re-engagement in the same jobs as before. It was that word "jobs" which engaged the main attention of the court. The only real difference in the situation was that the

---

[60] Employment Protection (Consolidation) Act 1978, s.64(1)(*b*) This, as we go to press, is still much litigated since in this provision Sex Discrimination law and EEC law are both involved. See, *e.g. Barker* v. *Thames Television plc* [1991] I.C.R. 253, E.A.T.

[61] Employment Protection (Consolidation) Act 1978, s.64 (1)(*b*).

[62] *Ibid.* s.146(1).

[63] *Ibid.* s.145(2).

[64] *Ibid.* s.144(2).

[65] *Ibid.* s.141(2).

[66] *Ibid.* s.141(5).

[67] *Ibid.* Sched. 9, para. 2(1).

[68] *Ibid.* s.63. Generally, attention is drawn to recent remarks of the President of the Employment Appeals Tribunal, Waite J. in the case of *Amandarajah* v. *Lord Chancellor's Department* (1984) 1 I.R.L.R. 131. A warning was given against "pre-occupation with guideline authority" by Industrial Tribunals in unfair dismissal cases. "Industrial Tribunals are not required . . . to subject the authorities to the same analysis as a court of law searching in a plethora of precedent for binding or persuasive authority." The aim of Parliament had been "to banish legalism" in the Industrial Tribunals, the statement continued. This is itself a guideline and as time passes seems to gather or lose strength like waves on the seashore, dependent on the impetus from the centre.

[69] [1982] I.R.L.R. 377.

employees were told that they would be regarded as being in a second warning situation. The question for the court was whether this feature altered the "jobs" done by the men, so that they were not the same as before. Lord Denning M.R. giving the leading judgment, studied the definition of "job" in the Act of 1978.[70] This referred to place, nature and capacity and as place and nature were the same, without argument, the critical question was whether the "capacity" had altered. Shaw L.J. summed up the view which supported the employers: "Capacity," he said, "goes to conduct in his position and not performance in his task."[71]

B. CONDITIONS OF WORK

1. The Health and Safety at Work, etc., Act 1974

1.073 This Act contains a comprehensive legal code for the health, welfare and safety of persons at work. The code is regularly updated and with the associated regulations, and codes of practice, provides a flexible system for inspecting, repairing and improving the physical environment of employees. Its scope extends to the protection of non-employees against risks to their health and safety arising from the activities of persons at work.

It contains one unusual feature. It schedules over 30 statutes which it is planned to have progressively replaced by a system of regulations and approved codes of practice, operating in conjunction with the other provisions of the Act.[72] The main provisions are as follows.

(1) Duties of Employers

1.074 A general duty is laid down to ensure the health, safety and welfare of all their employees, so far as is reasonably practicable.[73]

This is, in particular, to cover plant and systems of work, the use, storage and transport of substances, health education and work training, safe working conditions and facilities for welfare at work for the employees.[74]

Employers must prepare and bring to the notice of employees a written statement of their general policy in relation to health and safety at work.[75]

---

[70] Employment (Protection) Consolidation Act 1978, s.62(4).

[71] para. 47.

[72] s.1(2). Reference should be made to the treatment of the Act in relation to work in theatres (Chap. 6, s.1).

[73] s.2(1). This well worn phrase came under useful scrutiny by the House of Lords in *Austin Rover Group Ltd.* v. *H.M. Inspector of Factories* [1990] 1 A.C. 619. Responsibility is to be limited, said that Court, by the amount of the employer's control, knowledge and reasonable foresight.

[74] s.2(2).

[75] s.2(3). The Health and Safety at Work etc. Act 1974 includes a definition of the contract of employment, in s.82, and cases go to the Tribunals on this issue. The case *Quinnen* v. *Hovell* [1984] I.C.R. 525, in allowing an appeal from an Industrial Tribunal, decided that self-employed persons were within the definition, in s.82, of a "contract to execute any work or labour."

Employers must consult safety representatives of the employees and set up a safety committee, if requested.[76]

They must ensure that substances used at work are safe, so far as possible, by testing and examining them.[77]

(2) *Duties of Employees*

They must take reasonable care for the health and safety of themselves **1.075** and others affected by their acts or omissions at work.

They must co-operate with the employer, in relation to the duties under the Act.

(3) *Breach of Duties*

Breach of these duties gives rise to liability for a fine in the criminal courts but not to civil liability.[78]

(4) *Codes of Practice*

The Health and Safety Commission can promulgate codes of practice. Consultation is necessary and ministerial approval obtained before that is done. The codes are, however, an integral part of the legal framework for this comprehensive legislation. They can, indeed, be used as support for prosecutions for dereliction of duties under the Act.[79]

2. Discrimination

There are currently three statutes embodying, respectively, the principle **1.076** of equal pay for men and women doing equal work, and prohibiting discrimination in terms and conditions of employment in relation to sex and race. They are:

(a) The Equal Pay Act 1970.
(b) The Sex Discrimination Act 1975.
(c) The Race Relations Act 1976.

The first two are the measures by which Article 119 of the Treaty of Rome and associated Directives have been implemented in this country, in relation to the principle of equal pay for equal work.[80] The Race Relations Act, on the other hand, stems from an earlier Act of 1968 and represents the stance of Parliament on a social problem considered to need legislative aid.

---

[76] s.2(7).
[77] s.6(4)(*a*).
[78] *Ibid.* ss.33 and 47.
[79] *Ibid.* s.17.
[80] EEC Directives 75/117 and 76/207.

(1) *Equal Pay for Men and Women*

1.077   The Equal Pay Act of 1970 provides that an equality clause shall be deemed to be included in every contract of employment, at an establishment in Great Britain, where a woman is employed.[81]

An equality clause is then defined as being to ensure that existing terms shall be modified so that they are no less favourable to a woman than a term of a similar kind in the contract under which a man is employed on like work in the same employment.[82]

This is to operate in a situation where a woman is employed on like work with a man in the same employment or on work rated as equivalent with that of a man in the same employment.

It is not to apply when the employer can show that the different treatment of men and women is "due to a material difference" other than sex.[83] The Act proceeds to elaborate ways of checking that a "like work" situation exists, or a "work rated as equivalent" situation exists.[84]

Recourse to an industrial tribunal is then prescribed to resolve problems created by the Act.[85]

Other principles are designed to implement the equal pay principle in the fields of collective pay agreements,[86] the armed forces[87] and existing wages regulation orders.[88]

From the point of view of providers of leisure services, the principle of equal pay for equal work between men and women has received parliamentary approval and is to be applied in all matters relating to terms and conditions of employment.

(2) *The Sex Discrimination Act 1975*

1.078   The Act makes unlawful certain acts of discrimination against either men or women on grounds of sex. It sets up an Equal Opportunities Commission, which is to promote equality of opportunity for men and women generally and work towards the elimination of discrimination as mentioned.

Basic principles

1.079   These are contained in Parts I and II of the Act of 1975 and are as follows:

It is discrimination against a woman when, for the purposes of circumstances relevant to any provision in the Act, she is treated "on the ground of her sex" less favourably than a man. If a condition or requirement is

---

[81] Equal Pay Act 1970, s.1.
[82] *Ibid.* s.1(1).
[83] *Ibid.* s.1(2)–(5).
[84] *Ibid.* s.2.
[85] *Ibid.* s.2.
[86] *Ibid.* s.3.
[87] *Ibid.* s.7.
[88] *Ibid.* ss.4 and 5.

applied to a woman which is to her detriment, then again that is discrimination for the purposes of the Act of 1975.[89] In the case, for example, of *Gill* v. *El Vino Co. Ltd.*, it was held to be unlawful discrimination when ladies were not served drinks at the bar, as men were, but restricted to service at tables. The Court of Appeal said: "This is not a technical statute, and, therefore, is not of a kind where one should or need go for the meaning of words to other decided cases. It is a simple statute seeking to deal with ordinary everyday behaviour and the relative positions of men and women."[90] The decision was that there had been a breach of section 29 of the Act of 1975.

In the earlier case of *Peake* v. *Automotive Products Ltd.*[91] the Court of Appeal said it was not discrimination to allow women to leave a factory five minutes before men, in order to avoid being hurt in the rush through the factory gates, when work finished for the day.

In *Jeremiah's Case*,[92] the Court of Appeal said that certain expressions in *Peake's Case* (above) were "too forceful." *Jeremiah's Case* is very useful in understanding the Act.

The underlying principle is to apply to men, as it does to women, with such verbal modifications as are needed to make it read correctly.[93]

Special treatment of a woman in relation to pregnancy or child birth is not to be taken into account, when looking for discriminatory practices.[94]

It is unlawful discrimination within the Act of 1975 to treat a married person of either sex, in the circumstances of Part II of the Act relating to employment, less favourably than an unmarried person of the same sex.[95]

It is unlawful discrimination to victimise a person who has brought legal proceedings against the victimiser, given evidence or otherwise exercised his or her legal rights and powers under the Equal Pay Act 1970.[96]

In relation to employment by himself, at an establishment in Great Britain, it is unlawful for a person to discriminate against a woman in either the arrangements for filling a vacant post or in relation to the conditions on which the post is offered or, indeed, by refusing or deliberately omitting to offer her employment.[97]

---

[89] Sex Discrimination Act 1975, s.1.

[90] [1983] 1 All E.R. 398 and Eveleigh L.J. at p. 401e.

[91] [1978] 1 All E.R. 106.

[92] *Ministry of Defence* v. *Jeremiah* [1979] 3 All E.R. 833. This case has important comments on the principles embodied in s.1 of this Act of 1975. The Court found a "detriment," adverse to men examiners, existing in an ordnance factory. Their work conditions, in relation to colour bursting shells, were different from those of women inspectors. Lord Denning M.R. said "Equality is the order of the day. In both directions. For both sexes." (at p. 836a).

[93] Sex Discrimination Act 1975, s.2. *James* v. *Eastleigh Borough Council* [1990] 2 All E.R. 607, H.L. tries to cut through subtleties by asking: Would he have received the same treatment but for his sex? The applicant, aged 61, had to pay for entry to the swimming pool whilst his wife, also 61, entered free. The pension ages were the critical factor. Mr. James won his case.

[94] *Ibid.*

[95] *Ibid.* s.3.

[96] *Ibid.* s.4.

[97] *Ibid.* s.6. *Webb* v. *EMO Air Cargo (UK) Ltd.* [1989] I.R.L.R. 124 is a pregnancy case and *Baker* v. *Cornwall County Council* [1990] I.C.R. 452 is another useful recent case.

(3) Specific Exclusions by the Nature of the Job

1.080   Certain areas of employment and social life are excluded from the operation of the Act. Some of these, like mining, are outside the ambit of this
book. Some are specifically within it, *e.g.* where being a man is a genuine
occupational qualification for a job, then it is not unlawful to discriminate.
The eight areas thus excluded from the operation of the Act are as follows:

(1) Where the essential nature of the job calls for a man for reasons of
physiology (excluding physical strength or stamina), or in dramatic performances or other entertainments for reasons of authenticity, so that the
essential nature of the job would be materially different, if carried out by a
woman;

(2) where it is necessary to preserve decency or privacy and physical
contact or the circumstances are such that men might reasonably object to
the job being done by a woman;

(3) where the nature or location of the place of work makes it impracticable for the employee to live elsewhere than on the employer's premises
and it would be unreasonable to expect the employer to provide sleeping
accommodation and sanitary conveniences for both men and women in
privacy from each other;

(4) where the job is part of a prison or hospital or other establishment
for persons requiring personal care and attention and all the persons are
men and it is reasonable, "having regard to the essential character of the
establishment," that the job should not be held by a woman;

(5) where the holder of the job provides personal services for individuals, which promote their welfare or education or other similar personal
services and those services can most effectively be provided by a man;

(6) where the job needs to be held by a man, because of restrictions
imposed by the laws regulating the employment of women;

(7) where the job involves work in a country whose laws or customs preclude easy discharge by a woman;

(8) where the job is one of two to be held by a married couple.

In respect of items (1) to (7) above it is stipulated that the Act is not to
preclude an employer from filling the post with a man in his employment
if he can reasonably do so, having regard to the number of available men
and the switch can be made without undue inconvenience.[98]

(4) Unlawful Acts of Sex Discrimination

1.081   Persons engaged in the public leisure services should be aware of certain
other actions rendered unlawful by the Act of 1975, *i.e.*

(1) Discrimination against a woman by a person providing goods, facilities or services to the public, when that woman seeks to obtain or use those

---

[98] Sex Discrimination Act 1975, s.7. The Act is to apply to both men and women, though it
does not print "or men" every time after the word "women" (s.2).

goods, facilities or services. This discrimination, to constitute an unlawful act under the Act of 1975, involves:

    (i) refusing or deliberately omitting to provide the woman with them; or

    (ii) refusing or deliberately omitting to provide the woman with goods facilities or services of the like quality manner or terms normal for men.[99]

Examples of these discriminatory acts, given in the section, include:

    (i) "Access to and use of any place which members of the public or a section of the public are permitted to enter." This could be relevant to many leisure facilities.[1]

    (ii) Accommodation in an hotel, boarding house, or other similar establishment.[2]

    (iii) Facilities for entertainment, recreation or refreshment.[3]

    (iv) Facilities for transport or travel.[4]

    (v) "The services of any profession or trade or of any local or other public authority."[5]

(2) The Act also prohibits discrimination against a woman when engaged in disposing of premises or affording to a woman in premises occupied by her any benefits or facilities.[6]

(3) An exception to the offences contained in sections 29 and 30 of the Act (*i.e.* (i) and (ii) above), is given in favour of a voluntary body where its membership or facilities are restricted to one sex.[7]

(4) A further exception, of importance to managers of bathing pools or similar facilities, is provided where "the facilities or services are provided for, or are likely to be used by, two or more persons at the same time, and **1.082**

    (i) the facilities or services are such that male users are likely to suffer serious embarrassment at the presence of a woman, or

    (ii) the facilities or services are such that a user is likely to be in a state of undress and a male user might reasonably object to the presence of a female user."[8]

(5) *General Unlawful Practices*

Part IV of the Sex Discrimination Act 1975 deals with a number of unlawful practices which can be found in specific areas of employment and commerce. These are: **1.083**

---

[99] Sex Discrimination Act 1975, s.29(1).

[1] *Ibid.* s.29(2).

[2] *Ibid.* s.29(2)(*b*).

[3] *Ibid.* s.29(2)(*e*).

[4] *Ibid.* s.29(2)(*f*).

[5] *Ibid.* s.29(2)(*g*) "profession" has been spelt out in detail in relation to barristers in the Courts & Legal Services Act 1990, s.64.

[6] *Ibid.* s.34.

[7] *Ibid.*

[8] *Ibid.* s.35(1)(*c*) and s.35(2).

(1) Advertisements indicating a discrimination against women. The examples given in the Act of 1975 are postman, waiter, sales girl and stewardess "unless the advertisement contains an indication to the contrary."[9]

(2) Instructing another person to do an action unlawful under the Act of 1975.[10]

(3) Putting pressure on a person to carry out a discriminating act by offering some benefit or threatening some detriment to make him do so.[11]

(4) An employer is equally guilty with his employee of an unlawful action, under the Act of 1975, when that action is done in the course of employment by his employee "whether or not it is done with the employer's knowledge or approval." The statutory defence available to the employer is that he took such steps as were reasonably practicable to prevent the employee doing the act in question.

A principal is equally guilty with his agent under the Act of 1975 of an unlawful action done with his authority.[12]

Training

1.084　(5) Every manager in the public leisure services becomes involved in training recruits to the service from time to time. It is important to take note of an exception contained in the Act of 1975 for what would otherwise be discriminatory training. Section 48 deals with this activity and the exemption is described as limited to the situation where there was a shortage of persons of the sex in question for the job or activity in question.[13]

Enforcement

1.085　(6) Part VII of the Act of 1975 deals with enforcement of its provisions. This rests generally upon action through industrial tribunals. When satisfied that a complaint brought before them is well founded, such a tribunal may take such of the following as it considers just and equitable:

(i) Declare the rights of the parties before it.

(ii) Order payment of compensation, as if it were damages in the County Court.[14]

---

[9] Sex Discrimination Act 1975, s.38. The unlawful act is the publication of an advertisement which indicates "an intention by a person to do an act which is, or might be, unlawful, by virtue of Part II, or Part III of the Act of 1975." By reference, this lists all the general acts of discrimination in ss.1, 2, 3, and 4 of the Act, as outlined at para. 1.079 above, and also refers to the specific field of employment.

[10] *Ibid.* s.39.

[11] *Ibid.* s.40.

[12] *Ibid.* s.41. This authority can be express or implied and can be given before or after the act in question.

[13] The words in the Act are that, in the preceding 12 months, there were either no persons "of the sex in question" among those doing that work, or the number of that sex was "comparatively small."

[14] The present limit is £10,000 (Unfair Dismissal (Increase of Compensatory Limit) Order 1991 (S.I. 1991 No. 466)).

(iii) Recommend action the respondent should take to obviate the damage he has caused.

The High Court may still be approached for orders of prohibition, mandamus and certiorari.[15]

Acts of discrimination under Part III of the Act may be the subject of civil proceedings like any other claim in tort but only in the County Court, which in this instance may give the same remedies as the High Court might do.[16] Such remedies, if including damages, may include an item for injury to feelings, in addition to any other head of claim.

The Equal Opportunities Commission is constituted in Part VI of the Act of 1975, to secure enforcement of the Act.

A term in a contract is void under the Act of 1975, if it embodies an action rendered unlawful by this Act. Also a term is unenforceable if it purports to limit or exclude any provision in this Act, or the Equal Pay Act of 1970. These principles can be taken to the length of a County Court Order if desired; such an order could, for example, have the offending clause removed from the contract in question.[17]

EEC law

Since the first edition, a rapid growth of case law at the interface of United Kingdom and Community law has had various implications for equal pay and sex discrimination law. Some of this new law has strongly emphasised the primacy of Community law in detail after detail of our legal processes.[18] Some Community law has applied directly to the United Kingdom applicants.[19] Some is the reaction of United Kingdom courts to the new principles of Community law, apparently to avoid the delay and loss of face from adverse EEC decisions.[20] This field of law is extremely fluid.

3. **Disabled Persons**

Providers of leisure services constantly have to meet the special needs of **1.086** disabled persons. This relates to access to entertainments, personal needs, ramps rather than stairs, physical dangers on premises to which the public resort, the use of lifts and numerous other situations. The legislation on the subject is slight: common sense and humanity govern the approach to most situations. It may be useful to itemise such legislative guidance as exists.

---

[15] For details, see Chap. 2. Further, the Employment Act 1989, s.2, contains a very wide power for the Secretary of State for Employment to repeal provisions in earlier Statutes which require discrimination in relation to employment and training.

[16] Sex Discrimination Act 1975, s.66.

[17] *Ibid.* s.77. (This is a large Act of 87 sections and 4 Schedules. It is outlined in the text to the extent considered suitable for those engaged in or with the public leisure services).

[18] See *R.* v. *Secretary of State for Transport ex p. Factortame Ltd. (No. 2)* [1990] 3 W.L.R. 818.

[19] *Dekker* v. *Stichting Vormingscentrum voor Jong Volwassen Plus* [1991] I.R.L.R. 27.

[20] *O'Brien* v. *Sim-Chem Ltd.* [1980] I.C.R. 573.

1.087   This is centred upon the Disabled Persons (Employment) Acts 1944 and 1958, in which the main points of interest are as follows:

(1) Employers of a substantial number of persons are obliged to give employment to a quota of disabled persons from the official register.[21] This quota is currently 3 per cent.[22]

(2) The two additional obligations imposed by the Acts upon employers are:

    (i) not to dismiss such a disabled person from his employment without a permit from the Minister, if such action would take him below his statutory quota[23]; and

    (ii) not to engage a non-disabled person if a vacancy arises when he is still below his legal quota[24];

    (iii) to keep suitable records.[25]

(3) The Secretary of State for Employment may authorise criminal proceedings for breaches of the Act.[26]

(4) Under his power to designate suitable employments for disabled persons, the Secretary of State has so designated passenger electric lift attendant and car park attendant.[27]

(5) District Advisory Committees ("Disablement Advisory Committees" in practice) are set up by the Secretary of State and provide a point of contact for the employer, together with the Employment office.[28]

(6) A person suffering from mental disorder can be "disabled" for the purposes of these Acts.[29] Like others, he has to be registered.[30]

4. Race Relations Act 1976

1.088   An outline of the Race Relations Act 1976 is easier in the light of the above outline of the Sex Discrimination Act 1975. This is because the drafting of the 1976 Act followed the framing of the 1975 Act. There had been a Race Relations Act 1968 but the Act of 1976 makes what its preamble calls "fresh provision" and the shape of the Act of 1976 is remarkably similar to that of the Sex Discrimination Act.[31]

It may assist the reader to identify those parts of the Act of 1976 in which the wording follows the Act of 1975 and then to turn to those differences which are important for the providers of public leisure services.

---

[21] Disabled Persons (Employment) Act 1944, s.9.

[22] Disabled Persons (Standard Percentage) Order 1946 (S.R.O. 1946 No. 1268).

[23] s.11. Figures published in May 1983 showed only one in 10 of district councils were meeting their quota. The figures were no better for larger authorities.

[24] s.9(2).

[25] s.14.

[26] s.19.

[27] Disabled Persons (Designated Employments) Order 1946 (S.R.O. 1946 No. 1257). The Disabled Persons (General) Regulations 1945 (S.R.O. 1945 No. 1558) are also important.

[28] Disabled Persons (Employment) Act 1944, s.17.

[29] *Ibid.* s.1. (Definition of disabled person.)

[30] *Ibid.* s.6.

[31] Introducing the Race Relations Bill the Home Secretary said it was "closely modelled" on the Sex Discrimination Act 1975 (*Hansard*, March 4, 1976).

(1) *The Acts of 1975 and 1976—Common Features*

(1) Discrimination by employers is defined in similar terms in both Acts **1.089** by reference to applications, appointments and dismissals (paragraph 1.079 above).

(2) Contract workers are dealt with in the same way in both Acts.[32]

(3) Discriminatory practices are defined in similar terms relating to advertisements, giving instructions,[33] exerting pressure, aiding unlawful acts and liability as employer or as principal (paragraph 1.083 above).

(4) Charities are given a similar exemption in both Acts (paragraph 1.081 above).

(5) Education, training and welfare by an employer (paragraph 1.084 above).

(6) The composition and powers of the Commission for Racial Equality set up under the Act of 1976 are very similar to those of the Equal Opportunities Commission (paragraph 1.085 above).

(7) Enforcement of the Act of 1976 follows a pattern very similar to that in the Act of 1975 in relation to county courts, industrial tribunals, non-discrimination notices and assistance for persons whether aggrieved in fact or as prospective claimants.[34]

(2) *Distinctive Features of the Act of 1976*

Definition of discrimination

Whilst the basic definition of discrimination is identical, the Act of 1976 **1.090** has two necessarily distinctive points:

(1) The social ill against which the Act is directed is discrimination "on racial grounds," a term defined as connoting "colour, race, nationality, or ethnic or national origins."[35]

(2) The term "racial group" is used in the basic definitions of discrimination, *i.e.* treating a person differently from those of another racial group. This term is defined as "a group of persons defined by reference to colour, race, nationality or ethnic or national origins and references to a person's racial group refer to any racial group into which he falls." The fact that a racial group comprises two or more distinct racial groups does not prevent it from constituting a particular racial group for the purposes of this Act."[36]

Again it is laid down that a comparison of the case of a person of a particular racial group with that of a person not of that group must be such

---

[32] Sex Discrimination Act 1975, s.9; Race Relations Act 1976, s.7.

[33] See *Showboat Entertainment Centre Ltd.* v. *Owens* [1984] 1 W.L.R. 384, for a case on unlawful instructions to discriminate, *i.e.* to exclude black persons from an entertainment centre.

[34] It is often vital to obtain sight of documents in the possession of the other side in these cases.

[35] Race Relations Act 1976, s.3.

[36] *Ibid.* Cases since our first edition have examined whether gypsies, Sikhs and Rastafarians constitute such groups, *e.g. Crown Suppliers (PSA)* v. *Dawkins* [1991] I.C.R. 583.

that the relevant circumstances in the one case are the same, or not materially different, in the other.

Exclusions

1.091   There are fewer exclusions in the Act of 1976, but they are interesting:

(1) A dramatic performance or entertainment, where a person of that racial group is required as a matter of authenticity.

(2) Being an artist's or photographer's model and needed on account of authenticity.

(3) Where the setting for the provision of food and drink requires persons of that racial group in the interests of authenticity.

(4) "The holder of the job provides persons of that particular group with personal services promoting their welfare and those services can most effectively be provided by a person of that racial group."[37]

Codes of practice

1.092   The Code for Race Relations[38] published by the Commission for Racial Equality in 1984 is an example of an exercise of one of the Commission's powers in the field of education and public relations. The wording for this section of the Act of 1976 has been adapted from the Act of 1975.

Local authorities

Local authorities are required to promote equality of opportunity and the elimination of discrimination.[39]

5. **Bribery and Corruption; Theft**

(1) *Bribery and Corruption*

1.093   The public leisure services involve large commercial contracts; sometimes in catering, sometimes in entertainment in all its forms, sometimes in relation to gambling. An extensive licensing system is also integral to the public leisure services. Furthermore, building contracts often involve large sums of money. In all these spheres human frailty can give rise to situations where this small but vital branch of the law is involved.

The Acts

1.094   The Acts are the Public Bodies Corrupt Practices Act 1889, the Prevention of Corruption Act 1906, and the Prevention of Corruption Act 1916.

---

[37] Race Relations Act 1976, s.5.

[38] *Ibid.* s.47. The new publication provides a useful summary, directed to employers, employees, trade unions and employment agencies. The latest annual report of the Commission for Racial Equality shows that there were three times more settlements than tribunal awards, and 10 times more cases in the employment sector than other sectors of social life.

[39] *Ibid.* s.71.

Main offences

(a) Members of public bodies receiving corrupt gifts.[40]   **1.095**
(b) Giving or offering corrupt gifts to members of a public body.[41]
(c) Corrupt acceptance of gifts by an agent in relation to his principal's affairs.[42]
(d) Giving or offering corrupt gifts to an agent in relation to his principal's affairs.[43]
(e) Giving to an agent, or using as an agent, a false receipt, account or other document in order to mislead the principal.[44]

"Public body" means the council of a county or of a town or city—and   **1.096**
generally the body which has power to administer money raised by rates.[45]

"Public office" means any office or employment of a person as a member, officer or servant of such public body.[46]

"Consideration" includes "valuable consideration of any kind."

"Agent" includes any person acting for another and "principal" includes an employer.[47]

The current sanction for these offences is imprisonment for not more than two years or a fine of £500, or both, when tried on indictment: if tried summarily, four months' imprisonment or a fine of £200 or both. These punishments relate to offences (c), (d) and (e) above.[48]

For the two offences (a) and (b), the punishment is imprisonment for not more than two years, or £500 fine, or both. In addition, a person convicted of either of these two offences may be ordered to restore the gift and forfeit[49] the office in question for five years.

If the offence is committed in connection with a contract with a government department, then the maximum period of imprisonment is increased, for a conviction on indictment, to not less than three years and not more than seven years.[50]

There is a very important provision about onus of proof in the Act of   **1.097**
1916. Where the money, gift or other consideration is proved to have been given, it is deemed to have been given and received corruptly, unless the contrary is proved.[51]

In the light of these provisions, it would be normal for those responsible to insert in appropriate contracts a clause providing for the avoidance of the contract if found to have been tainted by corruption.

---

[40] Public Bodies Corrupt Practices Act 1889, s.1(1).
[41] *Ibid.* s.1(2).
[42] Prevention of Corruption Act 1906, s.1.
[43] *Ibid.*
[44] *Ibid.*
[45] Public Bodies Corrupt Practices Act 1889, s.7.
[46] *Ibid.*
[47] Prevention of Corruption Act 1906, s.1(2).
[48] *Ibid.* s.1.
[49] Public Bodies Corrupt Practices Act 1889, s.2.
[50] Prevention of Corruption Act 1916, s.1.
[51] *Ibid.* s.2.

An example of the onus provision in practice is *R.* v. *Mills*,[52] where a person was convicted of accepting free holidays in connection with a lucrative contract. He sought to show an intention to double-cross the donor for the future, but did not discharge the statutory onus of proof which lay upon him when the acceptance of the holidays had been proved.

(2) *Theft*

1.098 Theft is universal; it is, in law, simple and yet may be complicated in the extreme.

Theft from the employer or fellow-worker, at work, is normally a justification for summary dismissal, as constituting gross misconduct.

The discovery of a thief, red-handed, is not the most difficult situation for an employer but the loss of bar takings at a sports centre, where several employees are under suspicion; the probability that two employees are involved in the theft of an expensive grass mower, though only one has confessed; the quiet young man who spends long hours in a corner of the reference library and provides no tangible evidence to justify an allegation that he is connected with the disappearance of valuable books, whose subject-matter is unconnected with travel—these are all serious employer problems. The courts have met them all.

The employer should have a published disciplinary code which covers theft and the existence of which is known to all employees.[53]

He must act reasonably at all times. He should bear in mind a test suggested by the court in the case of *Rolls Royce Ltd.* v. *Walpole*[54]: Was dismissal within the reasonable range of responses open to a reasonable employer in those circumstances?

1.099 Employment law differs from criminal law. The employer is entitled to take account of the feelings of other employees when theft is discovered and thus is entitled to take action when police might not take a case to court. A test in the case of *British Home Stores Ltd.* v. *Burchell*[55] is important:

    (a) The employer must honestly believe in the guilt of the employee.

    (b) The employer must have in his mind reasonable grounds to support that belief.

    (c) At the final stage when he formed that belief, the employer must have carried out as much investigation into the matter as was reasonable in all the circumstances of the case.

This reasonable investigation must include hearing the employee's account of the situation, as well as carrying out his own code of discipline.[56]

---

[52] (1978) 68 Cr.App.R. 154.
[53] See ACAS Code of Practice on Disciplinary Practice and Procedures.
[54] [1980] I.R.L.R. 343.
[55] [1978] I.R.L.R. 379.
[56] *Moore* v. *C. and A. Modes* [1981] I.R.L.R. 71, was a case where the "reasonable belief" of the employer was critical.

Conclusion

This is not comprehensive. It endeavours to indicate the approach to the problem of theft in its various forms, which Industrial Tribunals have been encouraging in recent years.[57]

C. NEGLIGENCE

1. Introduction

The tort of negligence is of great importance to the providers of leisure ser- **1.100** vices. It can arise when a cricket ball injures a passer-by after being struck in the adjoining cricket ground[58]; or where a spectator is injured at a hockey match[59]; or a consumer of ginger beer finds her drink tainted with a foreign body.[60] It is at once simple and yet subtle. It consists in the breach of a duty of care and consequent injury, not necessarily physical, suffered by an aggrieved person. Yet the duty is not universal, the breach is not always easy to agree and the injury is sometimes complex and has to be dissected into that within and that outside the duty in law. A working definition comes from the leading case of *Donoghue* v. *Stevenson*, in the judgment of Lord Atkin:

> "The rule that you are to love your neighbour becomes, in law, you must not injure your neighbour, and the lawyer's question: Who is my neighbour? receives a restricted reply.
> You must take reasonable care to avoid acts and omissions which you can reasonably foresee would be likely to injure your neighbour. Who then, in law, is my neighbour? The answer seems to be—persons who are so closely and directly affected by my act, that I ought reasonably to have them in contemplation as being so affected, when I am directing my mind to the acts or omissions which are called in question."[61]

It is convenient to consider the subject of negligence under the following **1.101** headings:
1. The duty.
2. The breach.
3. Special situations:
    (1) Negligent statements and economic loss.
    (2) Liability of professional advisers.
    (3) Defective premises.
4. Consequences of the breach.
5. The burden of proof.

---

[57] A difficult area not discussed above is that of offences not connected with the work situation but which render the employee less suitable for his work or unacceptable to his fellow employees. The author is indebted to an article in (1983) L.S.Gaz. by Mr. M. Edwards at p. 892, which considers this further problem.
[58] *Bolton* v. *Stone* [1951] 1 All E.R. 1078.
[59] *Klyne* v. *Bellegarde* [1978] 6 W.W.R. 734.
[60] *Donoghue* v. *Stevenson* [1932] A.C. 562.
[61] *Ibid.* at p. 580.

2. **The Duty**

1.102   This is a duty to exercise care to avoid acts and omissions which can be reasonably foreseen to be likely to cause damage, as later discussed.

The degree of care varies according to the circumstances. In *Paris* v. *Stepney Borough Council*[62] a one-eyed garage mechanic suffered injury to his eye whilst working. The House of Lords held that the special risk of injury was part of the matters the employer should consider and the failure to provide goggles was negligent, so that damages should be paid to the workman. "The test is what precautions would the ordinary, reasonable and prudent man take?"[63] "These included the foreseeable consequences of an accident and their seriousness for the person to whom that duty was owed."[64] *Donoghue's* case came into the argument before the court in that case. In another case, the knowledge of the link between asbestos dust inhalation and a lung disease was clear only at a time too late to provide a legal link between employer and employee's wife, who was exposed to the danger when washing family clothes.[65]

1.103   The degree of care also results from keeping abreast of current knowledge. The recent case of *Thompson* v. *Smiths Shiprepairers Ltd.*[66] was a test case on the extent of an employer's duty, and consequential damages, for avoiding deafness to labourers in ship repair yards. The period of work extended over 40 years and knowledge of the growth of deafness due to that work had increased due to certain publications and events in that period.

A second recent case, *Rimmer* v. *Liverpool City Council*,[67] usefully illustrates a third aspect of the duty of care, namely knowledge of the materials and potential danger in a building. The council let a flat to the tenant, which included a glass panel 3mm thick as part of an internal wall opposite to the lounge door. A panel twice as thick was initially specified by the project architect. The plaintiff suffered serious injury when his hand went through the glass panel. The landlord's duty was defined by the court as being "to take reasonable steps to see that the premises were reasonably safe."[68] They had failed and were thus held liable in negligence. A local leisure services authority might be involved in litigation if harm befell young persons they had in good faith entrusted to specialist trainers and who then suffered assaults. *P.* v. *Harrow London Borough Council*[69] exonerated an education authority in such circumstances since the prime requisite, the duty of care, was absent. "Foreseeability, proximity and the justice of imposing liability" were the main criteria, said Potter J.

---

[62] [1951] A.C. 367.
[63] *Ibid.* Lord Normand at p. 380.
[64] *Ibid.* p. 381.
[65] *Gunn* v. *Wallsend Slipway & Engineering Ltd.*, *The Times*, January 23, 1989.
[66] [1984] Q.B. 405. It was said to be the test case for 20,000 others. See especially Mustill J. at p. 531.
[67] [1984] 2 W.L.R. 426.
[68] *Ibid.* at p. 431.
[69] *The Times*, April 22, 1992.

3. **The Breach**

The test was put a century ago by Baron Alderson: "Negligence is the **1.104** omission to do something which a reasonable man, guided by those considerations which ordinarily regulate the conduct of human affairs, would do or doing something which a prudent and reasonable man would not do."[70]

The reasonable man, the man on the Clapham omnibus, is a creation of law and is used as a yardstick in many legal problems. What would he do? Of course, the question is hypothetical but it helps to focus the problem on a person who is detached from those in the case before the court.

In *Bolton* v. *Stone*,[71] the possibility of injury to a lady in the adjacent highway was not a risk a reasonable man would have contemplated. The attitude of the cricket club was upheld and the plaintiff lost her case.

In *Hilder* v. *Associated Portland Cement Manufacturers Ltd.*,[72] a football kicked into a road from adjoining ground where youngsters were allowed to play struck a passing motor-cyclist, who suffered injury. The likelihood of injury in this way was real and, said the court, should have been foreseen and the plaintiff won his case. Vandalism of goods in the custody of a leisure services authority is a current hazard. The principles from which failure to discharge a duty of care can be found by the court are usefully discussed in the Australian case *Pitt Son & Badgery* v. *Proulefco S.A.* where stored wool was set ablaze by vandals.[73]

4. **Special Situations**

The law of negligence has the capacity to develop to meet new customs **1.105** and social pressures. There are three particular areas of social life where the growth of this tort in recent years has been marked and should be noted briefly here. They relate to negligent statements causing economic loss, negligent professional loss and, lastly, the situation now covered by the Defective Premises Act 1972.

(1) *Negligent Statements and Economic Loss*

This is an interesting development of the principle in *Donoghue's* case. It **1.106** shows the courts as ready to uphold a claim for damages due to a negligent statement.

Hedley Byrne and Co. Ltd. v. *Heller and Partners Ltd.*[74] has proved a watershed in cases of its kind. It was a decision of the House of Lords on a claim for £17,000 lost by the plaintiffs in reliance on negligent statements of the defendants. There was no physical injury and there was no contract. It was a case where the plaintiffs sought references at second hand from

[70] *Blyth* v. *Birmingham Waterworks Co.* [1856] 11 Ex. 781 at p. 784.
[71] [1951] 1 All E.R. 1078.
[72] [1961] 1 W.L.R. 1434.
[73] [1984] 153 C.L.R. 644, High Court of Australia.
[74] [1964] A.C. 465.

the defendants, who were bankers, about a company with whom the plaintiffs were having business dealings. There was no doubt that the defendants' advice was crucial and would be relied upon. In that situation, favourable references were given carelessly. The decision of the court, although the actual claim was dismissed, was important because it showed acceptance of this principle, namely that in order to be liable at law for a false statement which gives rise to economic loss, the defendant must be shown to have assumed some responsibility to those who will act on his information or advice. "This creates a duty of care towards them,"[75] said the court.

1.107   The court cases on this subject are generally from the business and commercial world: mortgages, debentures, architect's certificates, hire-purchase agreements. In the leisure services field, if a significant block booking of seats for a football match or a play were made on the basis of a statement by the defendant that a particular player or actor would be appearing in that match or play, without disclaimer, then the duty of care would arise, with the consequences indicated above.

(2) *Liability of Professional Advisers*

1.108   Since our first edition, the case of *Anns* v. *Merton London Borough Council*[76] has been overruled. But this is because the duty of care of professional advisers, be they doctors, architects, leisure service directors or otherwise, has been developed rapidly and stated more precisely. Such advice is still a rigorous duty, breach of which can give rise to a claim of damages for negligence. An effort to dissect the duty somewhat subtly, in the case of doctors, into components to which different levels of legal responsibility attached was not acceptable to the Court of Appeal.[77]

The duty of a local authority in appraising and approving plans for development is now to be limited to acting within the purposes set out in the legislation under which that approval is given—perhaps just health and safety of occupiers, not the economic loss of speculative builders. This emerges from the cases which laid the *Anns* decision aside.[78] This could have implications for a leisure services director who gave advice to his town planning authority about someone else's plans to build a golf course, swimming pool or sports centre.

(3) *Defective Premises*

1.109   This is noted as a signal instance of the principle in *Donoghue's* case, being embodied in a statute in relation to one special social and legal problem.

Under the Defective Premises Act 1972, where work of construction, repair, maintenance or demolition or any other work is done on or in relation to premises, then any duty of care owed, because of that work, to per-

---

[75] [1964] A.C. 465. Lord Devlin at p. 529.
[76] [1978] A.C. 728.
[77] *Gold* v. *Haringey Health Authority* [1988] Q.B. 481.
[78] *Murphy* v. *Brentwood District Council* [1990] 2 All E.R. 908, H.L.

sons who might reasonably be expected to be affected by the doing of that work, is not ended when the premises are subsequently disposed of to another owner or occupier.

A plaintiff, in other words, can still base his claim on the negligence of the builder.[79]

The Act has a number of other provisions which are not of relevance to this section.

5. **Consequences of the Breach**

The consequence, in the tort of negligence, of breach of the duty of care is liability for a claim for damages. As indicated above, this comprises monetary compensation for the physical injury suffered by the plaintiff, as well as the economic consequences of that injury in loss of wages and other expenses directly associated with the act which gives rise to the claim. There are three aspects of damages and they can be critical. They are the question of remoteness, the question of nervous shock and finally, the question of the special characteristics of the plaintiff.   **1.110**

(1) *Remoteness*

What damage is too remote to be attributed to the defendant's breach of duty? There are two classic cases. An American one concerned a person on a railway station, injured when an explosion caused scales to fall and injure her. The explosion was caused by a parcel which fell from a passenger who was boarding a train: a railway company employee had negligently dislodged the parcel, which was believed to contain fireworks. The plaintiff's injury was held to be too remote.[80]   **1.111**

In the second case, a Greek ship in Casablanca harbour was a total loss after a fire had been started by a spark from a falling plank, which ignited petrol vapour in the hold.[81]

Both cases demonstrate a sequence of totally unexpected events.

For a century, two views have been canvassed: **1.112**
   (a) Consequences are too remote if a reasonable man could not have foreseen them.
   (b) A man is responsible for all the direct consequences of his action, whether a reasonable man would have foreseen them or not.

The above shipping case, *Re Polemis*, was settled in 1921 on the basis of the second principle above. But in 1967, another shipping case, known as *The Wagon Mound*, caused the Judicial Committee of the House of Lords to lay down the first principle above as the one to be followed. This time the accident occurred in Sydney harbour, involving heavy damage to two ships and the adjacent wharf. Oil had gathered on the water near the ves-

---

[79] s.3.
[80] *Palsgraf* v. *Long Island Railway Co.* (1928) 284 N.Y. 339.
[81] In *Re Polemis and Furness Withy & Co.* [1921] 3 K.B. 560.

sels, due to carelessness while bunkering oil was loaded. Repairs on one boat by oxy-acetylene welding led to hot pieces of metal flying out over the water and igniting the oil.

1.113   "It is the foresight of the reasonable man which alone can determine responsibility. The *Polemis* rule, by substituting 'direct' for 'reasonably foreseeable' consequences, leads to a conclusion equally illogical and unjust,"

said one of the judges in the *Wagon Mound* case. One merit of "reasonable foreseeability" as a test of remoteness of damages is that this is also the test used when considering the first question of breach of duty.[82]

(2) *Nervous Shock*

1.114   It has been established for some years that damages available to a successful plaintiff in a negligence action can include an item for nervous shock. In the leading case of *Bourhill* v. *Young*,[83] a motor-cyclist in Edinburgh, driving at an excessive speed, collided with a motor car and was killed. The plaintiff, a fishwife standing 45 feet away, was unloading her basket. She heard the noise, suffered nervous shock and, being eight months pregnant, her child was still-born a month later. She failed in an action against the driver's estate for, the court said, she was outside the area of those the motor-cyclist should reasonably have foreseen would be affected by his actions.

1.115   The case is, however, a focus for the law and various cases on either side of success or failure have turned on the formulations it contains. In brief, the plaintiff may recover when the fear for his own safety is reasonable, in the light of the foreseeability test. This has been extended to a fear also for the safety of his close relatives.[84]

(3) *Taking the Plaintiff as He Is*

1.116   The defendant in an action for damages for negligence may be surprised to discover that the injured plaintiff had an egg-shell skull and died from a fall which would have bruised a robust person. But the law is that the defendant takes the plaintiff as he finds him. Whatever the physical frailty of the plaintiff, that is part of the situation. In other words, the law looks for a real person. This aspect of a claim is treated in practice as part of the process of assessing damages. Likewise, when turning to that part of a

---

[82] *The Wagon Mound* [1961] A.C. 388 (P.C.) *No. 1 case* at p. 424; [1967] A.C. 617, *No. 2 case.*
[83] [1943] A.C. 92.
[84] The House of Lords in the claims arising from the Hillsborough stadium disaster (*Alcock* v. *Chief Constable of South Yorkshire Police* [1991] 3 W.L.R. 1057) discussed this important topic at length. Both foreseeability and appropriate relationship were involved, they said, approving a Court of Appeal dismissal of 10 claims. Six similar claims had been dismissed at first instance.

claim that relates to loss of earnings and loss of expectation of life, the discovery by the defendant that the plaintiff is a pop star or a professor or a cleaner or a canteen assistant is all part of the situation for which he has responsibility.[85]

6. The Burden of Proof

A plaintiff in a claim for damages for negligence has to prove the duty of **1.117**
care, the breach and the consequent damages.

Sometimes the facts encourage the plaintiff to invite the court to say that the negligence is clear. This step is associated with the maxim *res ipsa loquitur*.[86] Even so, the courts have emphasised that this maxim is just a neat way of summarising the plaintiff's case: these are the facts; can the defendant rebut the inference of negligence which the court is invited to draw? The defendant may well be able to do so.

As a recent example in a commercial setting, see *Ward* v. *Tesco Stores*.[87] A **1.118**
lady slipped on spilt yoghurt in a supermarket and was injured. She sued the owners who gave evidence that they cleaned the floor five or six times a day, so the yoghurt could not have been there long. They claimed that they exercised reasonable care for their customers. The case turned on whether the owners had left the spillage for an unreasonable period of time. In the absence of more cogent evidence from the owners, they lost.

The burden of proof is at all times upon the plaintiff.

D. DEFENCES

The defences available for an action in tort may be conveniently con- **1.119**
sidered under four headings:
  1. Contributory negligence.
  2. The plaintiff voluntarily accepted all the risks involved in the action of which he complains: *volenti non fit injuria*. Contributory negligence presupposes a breach of duty by the defendant. *Volenti* does not. It alleges that because the plaintiff saw and accepted what was happening and what might happen, the defendant had no duty to protect the plaintiff.
  3. The statutory powers of the defendant.
  4. The Limitation Acts.

These defences are those generally available. This does not alter what **1.120**
has been said above about the *Rylands* v. *Fletcher* defences, *i.e.* the unforeseeable act of a stranger, an Act of God and default of the plaintiff. Nor, indeed, nuisance, where 20 years' prescription may legalise a private nuisance, though not a public one.

---

[85] See further discussion in Chapter 7.

[86] *i.e.* the facts speak for themselves: *Scott* v. *London and St. Katherine's Docks Co.* [1865] 3 H. & C. 596.

[87] [1976] 1 All E.R. 219.

1. Contributory Negligence

1.121 This defence is available when it can be established that the plaintiff is partly at fault when sustaining his injury. The "contribution" of the plaintiff is not to the negligence of the defendant (since that has to be settled on the principle of breach of the duty of care) but to the injury or damage he has suffered. For example, the plaintiff may have been partly responsible for the accident which caused the injury (perhaps a traffic accident at a cross-roads) or his injury may be more serious than it need have been because of his own conduct (not wearing a seatbelt).

1.122 The Law Reform (Contributory Negligence) Act 1945 provides that where a person suffers damage, as the result partly of his own fault and partly of the fault of any other person, the damages recovered shall be reduced as the court thinks fit, having regard to the claimant's share in the responsibility for the damage. Where several parties are involved in the accident, the damages are apportioned among them according to their respective faults. The assessment of relative fault will take into account all relevant factors, including the age or disability of the claimant.

Contributory negligence is not only a defence to an action based on negligence. It is also available as a defence to actions brought for nuisance, under *Rylands* v. *Fletcher* and for occupier's liability.

2. Volenti Non Fit Injuria

1.123 A person who assents to an injury cannot sue for it. The defence is also known as the voluntary assumption of risk by the plaintiff. In normal circumstances whether or not the defence will apply is to be judged from the surrounding facts of the case, but some decisions of the courts are of assistance in stating the general principles underlying the defence. Participants in games are expected to accept the normal risks inherent in the playing of the games and spectators at sporting events assume the risk of injury caused by the playing of the game they are watching. The occupier of premises on which games are being played can thus avail himself of the defence both as against the players and the spectators.

Examples from three cases about different sports may be helpful.

1.124 A rugby player failed in an action based on his injury when thrown against a boundary wall in a tackle.[88] A spectator at a motor race failed when injured by a car that crashed through a boundary railing.[89] A boy, injured by an ice hockey puck, failed after being struck when the puck came through boundary netting. All three claimants were met by the *volenti* defence.[90]

1.125 There may be circumstances when the voluntary assumption of the risk of injury does not disentitle the plaintiff from his remedy. The cases in which this applies are usually called the "rescue cases." They arise when the plaintiff has voluntarily responded to a moral duty to go to the assist-

[88] *Simms* v. *Leigh Rugby Club* [1969] 2 All E.R. 923.
[89] *Hall* v. *Brooklands Auto-Racing Club* [1933] 1 K.B. 205.
[90] *Murray* v. *Harringay Arena* [1951] 2 All E.R. 320.

ance of another person who has been injured or is in danger of being injured as a result of the negligence of a third party. There are cases which illustrate this principle.

In one (*Haynes* v. *Harwood*), the plaintiff was a policeman who was **1.126** injured when he grabbed a bolting horse of the defendant as it was heading for a crowded street. He succeeded in an action, the court holding that he had responded reasonably to an emergency created by the defendant's negligence.[91] But another claimant failed when injured after helping to hold a bolting horse in a field. The emergency was over, and the plaintiff had voluntarily accepted a risk of injury.[92]

It should be noted that the defence can only be used when it is estab- **1.127** lished that the plaintiff has voluntarily assumed the risk of injury. Knowledge of the danger is not by itself the equivalent of the assumption of the risk of injury; knowledge of a potential danger may be relevant to the defence of contributory negligence but mere knowledge will not constitute a total defence.

For the effect of the Unfair Contract Terms Act 1977 on exclusion clauses, as one aspect of the *volenti* defence, see paragraph 1.155 of this chapter.

3. **Statutory Powers**

Public providers of leisure services include local authorities, who will **1.128** invariably be acting under statutory powers. It may be that these afford a good defence to some of the claims in tort brought against them. That defence would bear upon liability; even though it were successful, the plaintiff could conceivably be entitled to statutory compensation—outside his claim in tort—for injury or damage suffered due to the exercise of the powers in question. There are two associated points which bear upon the defence that statutory powers have been employed:

(1) The courts lean towards the citizen, in the sense that they will not impute to the legislature an intention to take away private rights without clear language.[93] Being satisfied on the point, the courts, of course, do not put obstacles in the way of a duly authorised activity.[94]

(2) Many of these cases arise in the field of nuisance.[95] The statutory powers may exonerate the authority from a claim in nuisance[96]; they do not exempt the authority for the consequences of using those powers negligently.[97] One or two examples will assist.

(a) Blackburn J. in the leading case of *Geddis* v. *Proprietors of Bann Reservoir*[98] said:

"No action will lie for doing that which the legislature has author-

---

[91] *Haynes* v. *Harwood* [1935] 1 K.B. 146.
[92] *Cutler* v. *United Dairies (London) Ltd.* [1933] 2 K.B. 297.
[93] *Farnworth* v. *Manchester Corporation* [1929] 1 K.B. 533.
[94] *Att.-Gen.* v. *Nissan* [1970] A.C. 179 at p. 229, *per* Lord Pearce.
[95] *Marriage* v. *East Norfolk Rivers Catchment Board* [1950] 1 K.B. 284.
[96] *Manchester Corporation* v. *Farnworth* [1930] A.C. 171, (*supra*, on appeal).
[97] *Dunne* v. *N.W. Gas Board* [1964] 2 Q.B. 806.
[98] [1873] 3 A.C. 430 at p. 455.

ised, if it be done without negligence, although it does occasion damage to anyone; but an action does lie for doing that which the legislature has authorised, if it be done negligently.''

(b) In the case of *Home Office* v. *Dorset Yacht Co.*[99] the court was able to review these principles. Seven boys had escaped from Borstal custody, seized a yacht and damaged a boat of the plaintiff's in a collision. The main issue, considered by the House of Lords, was whether the Home Office owed a duty of care to the plaintiffs, and the answer was in the affirmative. Lord Reid rested his argument on *Donoghue* v. *Stevenson* in an authoritative judgment.[1]

(3) Naturally a defence of statutory powers has to be supported by evidence that those powers have been correctly exercised. The aggrieved party will, reasonably, seek evidence of any weak link in the long chain which runs from the Act of Parliament, through assignment of the duty of decision, a minute of a properly constituted committee, to the way in which the work, perhaps, was authorised to be put in hand.[2] Finally, the court will often be invited to scrutinise whether the action taken comes within the four corners of the parent statute.

4. The Limitation Acts

1.129   The facts sometimes give a defendant the opportunity to plead the Limitation Acts; the plaintiff, he can say, has not come to the courts soon enough.[3] It is not a popular plea but it is legal. With regard to actions in tort, these Acts lay down:

(a) A basic period of six years from the date when the right of action arose.[4]

(b) A reduction in the basic period to three years in cases of personal injuries. The wording is important:

"This section applies to any action for damages for negligence, nuisance or breach of duty (whether the duty exists by virtue of a contract or of provision made by or under a statute or independently of any contract or any such provision) where the damages claimed by the plaintiff for negligence, nuisance or breach of duty consist of or include damages in respect of personal injuries to the plaintiff or any other person."[5]

---

[99] [1970] A.C. 1004.

[1] Further instances of local authorities' negligence in carrying out statutory duties are *Dawson & Co.* v. *Bingley Urban District Council* [1911] 2 K.B. 149, *Manchester Corporation* v. *Markland* [1936] A.C. 360.

[2] *Radstock Co-op. and Ind. Society* v. *Norton-Radstock Urban District Council* (1968) Ch. 605; *Allen* v. *Gulf Oil Refining Co. Ltd.* [1981] 2 W.L.R. 188.

[3] The main consolidating Act is now the Limitation Act 1980.

[4] Limitation Act 1980, s.2.

[5] *Ibid.* s.11(1). *Stephen* v. *Riverside Health Authority* (1990) 1 Med L.R. 261 illustrates the subtlety of this area of law. The court said that the plaintiff's "knowledge" of the facts on which he would base a claim of say negligence, and which is critical in fixing the point from which the limitation period runs, is to be distinguished from mere "believing" or "suspecting."

The Act must be pleaded if it is to be relied on.

The period of six or three years above runs from the date when the **1.130** cause of action accrued. This is sometimes a matter of difficulty. For instance, if the cause of action for defective house foundations is the negligent inspection by a building inspector, it would be unfair to make the date of that inspection the start of the limitation period if the defect in question did not become apparent for more than six years.[6] The expression in section 32 of the Limitation Act 1980 is "discovered or might with reasonable diligence have discovered it," in relation to periods of limitation which have a starting date delayed by fraud, mistake or concealment of facts. A comparable formula seems to be emerging for this other situation—the latent defect.[7]

If, as sometimes in nuisance, the tort is of a continuing nature, a limitation period is not relevant since, while the nuisance continues, each day can found a new period.[8]

There are special rules for persons under a disability due to infancy or mental illness, or for the case of the death of the plaintiff.[9]

There is also a power available to the court to override the starting time **1.131** limits, if it appears equitable to do so in the light of prejudice to the parties if the ordinary rules were enforced.[10] For the purposes of this Act any damage for which a person is liable under the Environmental Protection Act 1990, section 73 is to be treated as due to a person's fault.

THE LEISURE SERVICES AUTHORITY AS BUSINESS ORGANISER

A. Contract

Introduction

This is a subject that runs through the whole of public leisure services. **1.132** There is a basic framework for the English law on the subject which is not difficult. How is a legal contract formed? What are its essential elements? How can it be terminated? What residue of responsibility remains when that is done? Are some contracts forbidden? What effect on the formation of a contract have mistake, misrepresentation, duress or fraud? Are there some people who cannot make a legal contract?

Like a number of other branches of the law, however, the law of con-

---

[6] *Anns* v. *Merton* [1978] A.C. 728.
[7] *Ibid. Anns* was overruled by the House of Lords in *Murphy* v. *Brentwood District Council* [1990] 2 All E.R. 908 for its creation of a cause of action for economic loss resulting from latent damage. It is physical damage to a person or other property that is now to be shown by a plaintiff in such circumstances.
[8] *O'Connor* v. *Isaacs* [1956] 2 Q.B. 288.
[9] Limitation Act 1980, ss.22, 28 and 38.
[10] Limitation Act 1980, s.33. And see *T. McCafferty* v. *Metropolitan Police Receiver* [1977] 2 All E.R. 756. Any inaction by the plaintiff prior to the expiration of the limitation period may be taken into account by the court in assessing the balance of prejudice—*Donovan* v. *Gwentoys Ltd.* [1990] 1 W.L.R. 472, H.L. An amending Act, the Latent Damage Act 1986, refined the *Anns* case. As that foundation was decided to be unsure, the 1986 Act is regarded as having little use now.

tract has become increasingly subtle. This may be looked on in one sense with satisfaction; the law should meet the needs of society and if those needs have changed, the law can do so too, by grafting on exceptions and nuances. In a real sense, nevertheless, it is regrettable if the law to be applied to a new set of facts is not easily predictable by legal advisers. That has become the case in more and more fields of contract law in the last 40 years.

1.133   It will be convenient to divide this subject into the following sections:
1. Formation.
2. Deviations—Mistake, Misrepresentation, Duress.
3. Void and Illegal Contracts.
4. Capacity to Contract.
5. Limits of the Lawful Contract.
6. Performance.
7. Breach and Remedies.

1. **Formation**

1.134   A contract has been defined as "a promise or set of promises which the law will enforce."[11] It is complete when a valid offer has been matched by a valid acceptance and the two are bonded together by valid consideration. Offer and acceptance take place in many ways. In a recent Manchester City Council case,[12] there was a series of letters between the council and a tenant about a possible sale to him of the house he occupied. The House of Lords was called upon to analyse the legal effect of the correspondence at the critical moment when political control of the council changed and the new council wished to stop this sale. The House ruled that a contract had not then been concluded, after applying the classic principles for contract formation.

1.135   **Acceptance** may be made in the form appropriate to the nature of the offer. Both use of the post and oral communication have in the past given rise to difficulties. Acceptance must be reasonably prompt or the offer may lapse. Again, the offer may be withdrawn before acceptance has occurred. Death of the offerer cancels the offer.

Consideration has been defined as the price paid by the plaintiff for the defendant's promise. It is fundamental for a legal contract. It can take many forms, as well as money, *e.g.* giving employment, withholding opposition to a sale, and others.[13]

The courts do not audit the value of consideration but, if slight, the consideration may indicate lack of serious intent in the agreement. Moral

---

[11] Sir F. Pollock.

[12] *Gibson* v. *Manchester C.C.* [1979] 1 All E.R. 972. It was a test case for 350 others and the House overruled the two lower courts. In *Butler Machine Tool Co. Ltd.* v. *Ex-Cell-O Corporation Ltd.* [1979] 1 W.L.R. 401, another case about the effect of letters, the approach which seeks "the area of consensus," to avoid too mechanical an attitude, is usefully discussed.

[13] *Williams* v. *Roffey & Nichols (Contractors) Ltd.* [1990] 1 All E.R. 512 is a realistic recent case of interest to managers pressing to complete building work. New terms were held to be adequate consideration for an enforceable revised contract.

considerations and past consideration do not rank as adequate legal consideration.

A valid agreement under seal does, however, rank as a valid legal contract without the need for consideration.

Legally enforceable relations

An agreement is sometimes made without any intention thereby to enter into legally enforceable relations. The law respects this position and examples from the reports include football pools,[14] family arrangements and even an industrial compact, which, said the court, embodied "undertakings binding in honour."[15]

Two classes of contract formation must comply with statutory requirements. In this respect they differ from the general principles for contract formation under common law as described above. The two cases are as follows:

(a) The sale or other disposition of land is to be in writing and signed by the party to be charged. See the Law of Property Act 1925, section 40, which has widespread and detailed implications.

(b) The Statute of Frauds 1677, section 4, relates to a promise to answer for "the debt default or miscarriage" of another person. In one case, a man promised the owner to reimburse him for the horse injured by his son. Under this Act, he was held to his promise by the court.[16]

2. **Deviations**

(1) *Mistake*

Many of the cases of contract law taken to court turn on a mistake by one   **1.136**
or both of the parties. We now consider:

(a) Mutual mistake.
(b) Unilateral mistake.
(c) Documents mistakenly signed.

(a) **Mutual mistake**

This can arise in connection with the subject-matter of the contract, *e.g.* who was the artist of the painting being sold[17] or whether the flat being let was outside the Rent Acts.[18] Such a contract, being voidable in equity, can be set aside or rectified to achieve the real agreement between the parties.

Sometimes the mistake concerns the intentions of the parties and

---

[14] *Jones* v. *Vernons Pools Ltd.* [1938] 2 All E.R. 626.

[15] *Balfour* v. *Balfour* [1919] 2 K.B. 571.

[16] *Kirkham* v. *Marter* (1819) 2 B. & A. 619.

[17] *Leaf* v. *International Galleries* [1950] 2 K.B. 86. *Associated Japanese Bank (International) Ltd.* v. *Crédit du Nord S.A.* [1988] 3 All E.R. 902 is a recent classic where £1m changed hands due to belief in four precision textile machines which simply did not exist.

[18] *Solle* v. *Butcher* [1950] 1 K.B. 671.

neither is aware of the misunderstanding. The courts start with the aim of upholding the agreement if possible. Secondly, if one party has made a mistake, he must abide by it and pay for it. The principle applied is to ask what agreement the reasonable man would infer from the evidence of the circumstances relating to the formation placed before the court.

(b) **Unilateral mistake**

1.137   Here the mistake by one party is known to the other. Most cases in the reports on this topic stem from mistaken identity of the parties. The principle here is that the concluded agreement can only be upset if the aggrieved party satisfies the court that he intended to agree with M, that the identity of M was important to him, that the other party knew this and, finally, that he took reasonable steps to verify the identity of the other party.

Cases of trickery in the reports concern false letterheads,[19] disguises when valuable jewellery is purchased[20] and false names when a letting of premises is obtained for immoral use by the tenant and her customers.[21]

(c) **Documents mistakenly signed**

1.138   When a person has signed a document by mistake, thinking it was something else, the general approach of the courts is to uphold the signature. He must have been careless, say the courts, and we cannot relieve him on that account.

In the House of Lords 21 years ago, the test applied in this situation was: What was the object of the exercise?[22] When the document signed was so different from the one intended that it would be inequitable to hold a man to it, the courts will give equitable relief.

(2) *Misrepresentation*

1.139   Under the Misrepresentation Act 1967, section 2, liability in damages can follow misrepresentation which leads to a contract and consequential loss. The misrepresentation does not have to be fraudulent and the defendant is relieved of his penalty only if he believed in its truth on reasonable grounds up to the time when the contract was made.

This is intended to allow an aggrieved party to obtain damages for a misrepresentation negligently made, which led him to enter into the contract. A misrepresentation is a statement, or conduct, or even silence at a critical juncture in pre-contract discussion, which induces a party to go forward and enter into the contract. The relevant legal principles are:

1.140   (1) If it was made fraudulently, the aggrieved party can sue for

---

[19] *Kings Norton Metal Co.Ltd.* v. *Eldridge Merritt & Co.Ltd.* (1897) 14 T.L.R. 98.

[20] *Phillips* v. *Brooks Ltd.* [1919] 2 K.B. 243.

[21] *Sowler* v. *Potter* [1940] 1 K.B. 271. As a recent decision see also *Lewis* v. *Averay* (No. 2) [1973] 1 W.L.R. 510. A useful article on unilateral mistake is S. Tromans, "Careless Slips and Greedy Snaps" [1984] L.S.Gaz., October 18.

[22] *Saunders* v. *Anglia Building Society* [1971] A.C. 1004, H.L.

rescission of the contract and compensation in the form of consequential damages.[23]

(2) Under section 2 of the Act of 1967, he can now take the same step for negligent misrepresentation.

(3) But an undue delay in seeking his legal remedy can limit that remedy. Where, in *Leaf* v. *International Galleries*, a man bought a fake, believing the picture to be Constable's Salisbury Cathedral, and delayed five years before taking legal process to rescind the contract, he was denied that remedy and limited to damages only. As they were not claimed, the plaintiff lost his case.[24]

(4) The contract is only voidable and not void where there has been misrepresentation.

(5) A condition is a statement which, as well as inducing the contract, is embodied in it. "That car has only done 20,000 miles," may induce a sale. But if it is no condition in the contract, it is a warranty only. For a false warranty, the legal remedy is damages only and not rescission; with a broken condition, both are available.

(6) Rescission is not granted by the court, if (i) there has been an undue lapse of time or (ii) restoration to the pre-contract situation is impossible or (iii) it would adversely deprive an innocent third party of the subject-matter of the contract or, finally, (iv) if the aggrieved party has effectively affirmed the contract.

It is the view of many commentators that the Act of 1967, making only a partial reform, has made the existing law more complex.

(3) *Duress*

A contract induced by duress can be set aside. Whilst physical duress is **1.141** encountered infrequently, it is, nevertheless, some pressure of a physical nature that the courts look for if this extreme situation is to give rise to rescission.[25]

3. **Void and Illegal Contracts**

Certain contracts are not enforceable in the courts: **1.142**

(1) Wagering contracts, *e.g.* about a greyhound race or other uncertain event. Under the Gaming Act 1845, these are void, though not illegal. No legal rights derive from them.[26]

(2) Restrictive trading agreements. These are, under the Restrictive Trade Practices Act 1976, in the realm of agreements for both goods and services, where two or more parties agree about restrictions on prices, charges, terms or conditions or other matters. These agreements must be

---

[23] *Derry* v. *Peek* (1889) 14 A.C. 337 is the leading case.
[24] [1950] 1 All E.R. 693.
[25] Undue influence, short of duress, was found in a recent popular music publishing case— *O'Sullivan* v. *Management Agency and Music Ltd.* [1985] Q.B. 428. The plaintiff recovered moneys resulting from that feature.
[26] See *Hill* v. *William Hill (Park Lane) Ltd.* [1949] A.C. 530.

duly registered and if that is not done, the agreements are not enforceable in the courts.

(3) The Treaty of Rome, Article 85 deals with trade restrictions embodied in agreements and affecting trade between states.[27]

1.143   (4) There are six classes of contract which, on account of public policy, are illegal. These are contracts:

   (i) prejudicial to the administration of justice;

  (ii) to defraud the Revenue;

 (iii) which tend to corruption in public life;

 (iv) to the prejudice of public safety;

  (v) to commit a crime[28];

 (vi) that are sexually immoral.

1.144   (5) Then there is an important group of three which may be described as void, since the courts will not enforce them:

   (i) Contracts to oust the jurisdiction of the courts.[29]

  (ii) Those to the prejudice of marriage.

 (iii) Those in restraint of trade. This is the most complex of the three groups. It was illuminated by a recent case that went to the House of Lords, *Esso Petroleum Co. Ltd.* v. *Harper's Garage (Stourport) Ltd.*[30] This emphasises that two separate questions must not be confused. First is the question: Is the contract void because the restraint is so restrictive? Then, secondly, can the restrictive clause be thought reasonable? This case is a store of information and guidance on these points.

1.145   (6) A last group is of interest to those in the leisure services, where it is inevitable that staff will acquire great knowledge about commercial customs and negotiating practices. They can thus be made subject to contracts seeking to restrain them from working in the immediate area when they change their work.

The courts, it must be emphasised, are not sympathetic to such agreements, unless there is clear evidence that they are needed to protect some trade secret or the employer's business connection. There are cases in the reports about professional footballers and cricketers, as well as the Jockey Club. A recent one concerned a boxer who signed a standard Boxing Board of Control agreement with a man who was both promoter and manager. The conflict between these two roles led to the court deciding that the agreement could not be enforced.[31]

---

[27] As examples see *Esso Petroleum Co.* v. *Kingswood Motors (Addlestone)* [1974] Q.B. 142; *Lerose* v. *Hawick Jersey International* [1973] C.M.L.R. 83. A high-water mark in this area is *R.* v. *Secretary of State for Transport, ex p. Factortame Ltd.* [1991] 1 All E.R. 70. A national law can be suspended if it will impair a decision to enforce Community law.

[28] *Howard* v. *Shirlstar Container Transport Ltd.* [1990] 3 All E.R. 366 shows "crime" redeemed by fear of personal safety.

[29] A cinema case is *R.* v. *London County Council, ex p. The London Entertainments Protection Association* [1931] 2 K.B. 215.

[30] [1968] A.C. 269.

[31] *Watson* v. *Prager* [1991] 1 W.L.R. 724. A long and useful case. The essence is that there were terms in the contract which were unduly restrictive and unreasonable.

In the background, as creatures of statute, are the Monopolies and Mergers Commission and the Restrictive Trade Practices Court. These exercise a specialised role.

4. **Capacity to Contract**

(1) *Minors*

The Minors' Contracts Act 1987 has helped to clarify the law. It supplements the common law and replaces the Infants Relief Act 1874 which had been a source of confusion. **1.146**

Under 18s can now be liable for their contracts of service, *e.g.* as an apprentice snooker player, secondly for goods regarded as "necessaries," *i.e.* appropriate to their way of life, and thirdly, if they relate to say a flat, as being something of a "permanent nature."

These are exceptions to the normal rule that contracts by minors are not legally binding.

Further, the new Act of 1987 has conferred power on the court to order restitution of property acquired by the minor, even under an unenforceable contract, if "it is just and equitable to do so." This Act is designed to restore the balance, which previously had been too much in favour of minors.

(2) *Corporations*

The capacity of a statutory corporation to enter into contracts is governed by its powers. Local authorities, being now creatures of statute, are governed by the relevant statute. **1.147**

Functions such as providing swimming pools, country parks or libraries are dealt with in empowering statutes about those subjects.

The power to take action to achieve those objects is then supplemented by the Local Government Act 1972, or similar general Act. This not only authorises all action "reasonably incidental to the discharge of their functions" by local authorities, it also widens what might seem tightly drawn legal powers to cover expenditure when it is, in the opinion of the authority, in the interests of their area or part of it or all or some of its inhabitants.

The challenge relating to the powers of the local authority may not, initially, relate to a contract; it would be strange, however, if, in the train of a policy decision, some contract was not eventually needed.

(3) *Commercial Companies*

The capacity to contract by a limited liability company is governed by the terms of its memorandum of association. This can often be widely drawn so that there need not in practice be great risk of challenge on the ground of its *vires* when contracting for trade or business. **1.148**

5. **Limits of the Lawful Contract**

1.149 We note next three legal limits placed on the making and dealing in contracts.

(1) *Privity of Contract*

Only a party to a contract can sue upon it and be bound by it.[32] This does not gainsay the ability to assign powers under a contract, nor the ability to appoint or become an agent. An assignee steps into the shoes of the party from whom he took his assignment; an agent exercises such powers as are conferred upon him in the agency agreement.

(2) *Assignments*

1.150 A party to a contract may assign his interest in whole or in part to a third party. Thus a party due to receive £1,000 under an insurance policy could assign the right to receive all or part of that sum to a third party. It is sometimes obligatory but always wise to notify the other party to the initial contract that an assignment has taken place. Such notification may indeed be a compliance with a term in the original contract. Failure to give notice would prejudice the assignee in respect of payments made to his assignor after the assignment and in ignorance of it.

(3) *Contracts of a Personal Nature*

1.151 It is not permitted to assign contractual rights that depend on personal skill and confidence, nor certain rights to pensions and alimony. The main bar on assignment is the right to litigate, sometimes called the "bare right of action."[33] This distinguishes it from a right to litigate that arises from and goes with some right in property. In that situation the right to litigate would go with the property without restraint.

6. **Performance**

1.152 When has a contract been "substantially performed?" When has a contract been frustrated, so that performance is not possible? These are the two most common legal problems associated with performance.

(1) *Substantial Performance*

It is common practice in building contracts to refer to the point of substantial performance. It is not to be expected that every screw and grum-

---

[32] *Tweddle* v. *Atkinson* (1861) 1 B. & S. 393. So an action against a sub-contractor failed (his workmen had caused a fire in a swimming pool extension) because it was only with the main contractor that the property owner's contract was made—*Norwich City Council* v. *Harvey* [1989] 1 All E.R. 1180.
[33] *Trendtex Trading Corporation* v. *Crédit Suisse* [1980] Q.B. 629.

met will then be in position. It means that the purpose of the building is substantially achieved, so that the major payment to the builder can be completed and the customer take possession and start shop-fitting or whatever it might be. Substantial performance is a desirable and important milestone in the execution of a contract.

(2) *Frustration*

Sometimes a contract, though well-intentioned and well-made, simply cannot be performed. The ship sinks, the procession is cancelled, the weather is so bad that the match is postponed, the concert hall is burned down.

Before 1943, the courts handled this situation by seeking to define that which was essential to the performance of the contract or, as said in one case, "the state of things going to the root of the contract."

Under the Law Reform (Frustrated Contracts) Act 1943, moneys paid before the date when the frustration occurred may be recovered, with a set-off for agreed expenses incurred by the other party. A *quantum meruit* calculation is then allowed for the benefit of the work done up to the time of discharge of the contract. This Act has created the climate in which the courts now seek a reasonable solution to the new situation created by the unexpected happening.[34]

7. **Breach and Remedies**

There are three principal legal remedies for breach of contract. **1.153**

(1) **Quantum meruit** is "as much as he deserves." One may sue for the value of the benefit conferred, or money expended, under the contract before the breach occurred.

(2) **Damages** are the normal remedy. The classic measure for damages for the aggrieved party is:

(a) those which may fairly be considered to arise naturally from the breach. A nice case on this point concerned racehorse purchase: *Naughton* v. *O'Callaghan* [1990] 3 All E.R. 191. The breeding was hopelessly adrift at the sale, *i.e.* not *ex Nomalco ex Habanna ex Habitat* but *ex Moon Min ex First Landing ex Capelet*. But (i) the price would still have been the same and (ii) performance was lamentable. The award to the buyer took account of the catalogue of misfortunes and is a useful practical guide to the law; and

(b) that which may reasonably be supposed as having been envisaged by the parties as the probable result of the breach, at the time when they entered into the contract.

(3) **Specific performance** is the equitable remedy, to be pursued when damages are considered to be inadequate. Whilst damages are a right, specific performance is discretionary. It is not allowed by the court if it

---

[34] There are three excluded contracts, *viz.* shipping, insurance and, strangely, one "for the sale and delivery of specific goods where the contract is frustrated by reason . . . that the goods have perished" s.2(5)(*c*).

would be complex to carry out, such as the supervision of a contract involving personal service. But it is available, if practicable, in a situation where damages are simply not an adequate recompense for the injury caused by the breach.

Limitation Acts

1.154   It has always been a principle that persons seeking legal remedies in the courts should do so in a reasonable time. Statute has codified practice and currently the Limitation Act 1980 sets out the limitation periods for various types of action.

(1) For an action based on breach of contract, the action must be commenced within six years of the date when the right of action accrued.[35]

(2) If the action is based on a "speciality," *i.e.* a document under seal, the comparable period is 12 years.[36]

(3) An action based on an account is subject to the same period of limitation as the subject-matter of the account.[37]

(4) In addition:

 (i) In the case of an action for a specific sum of money, like a debt, the period runs from the date of the last part-payment, as a visible acknowledgment, or the date of a document constituting a valid acknowledgment. This means that it is in writing, signed by the debtor and admits liability to pay the sum in question.[38]

 (ii) Where the plaintiff has a disability when his cause of action accrues, the period of limitation does not start to run until the disability is removed, possibly even by death.[39]

 (iii) Since specific performance, and sometimes injunctions, are historically equitable remedies, these statutory limitations do not apply to them.[40] Nonetheless, courts of equity always took a firm line against undue delay in coming to court—*laches* was the old word—and at the present day the courts maintain that principle when equitable remedies are sought. The doctrine of laches, as it is called, is preserved in the Limitation Act 1980.[41]

B. The Unfair Contracts Terms Act 1977

1.155   Restraints upon the use of unfair contract terms are to be found in the Act of 1977 of that name, passed to carry into legislation recommendations of the Law Commission. The terms in question form a somewhat untidy group; the Act itself is in the nature of an interim one; and it is arguable that the piecemeal nature of its reforms has left the body of contract law more complex. Managers in the public leisure services can only be guided,

[35] Limitation Act 1980, s.5.
[36] *Ibid.* s.8.
[37] *Ibid.* s.23.
[38] *Ibid.* s.29.
[39] *Ibid.* s.28.
[40] *Ibid.* s.26.
[41] *Ibid.* s.36.

in this work, to the items with which the Act of 1977 deals. These are as follows:

(1) Notices and contract terms cannot be used to exclude or limit a person's business liability for death or injury due to negligence, *e.g.* on recreation ground equipment or from the diving board of a swimming pool.

(2) A test of reasonableness is applied to similar terms or notices relating to loss or damage[42]; also to contract terms which seek to limit a person's obligations to a consumer or in a situation where his written terms of business are used; and to indemnity clauses in a contract with a consumer.

(3) Specious guarantees are prohibited. These are the ones which take away a customer's statutory or common law rights whilst offering to remedy defects in the goods sold.

C. Sale of Goods

The Sale of Goods Act 1979, and associated cases in the courts, govern this subject. It can conveniently be considered as follows: **1.156**

1. The Contract; Definitions and Formation

(1) The contract of sale of goods is a contract by which the seller transfers, or agrees to transfer, the property in the goods to the buyer for the price, *i.e.* the money consideration.

(2) If the transfer is to take place in the future, it is an agreement to sell.[43]

(3) The contract may be valid, whether made in writing or by word of mouth or may be part written and part oral; it may indeed be inferred from conduct.[44]

(4) The "goods" may exist or be planned to come into existence after the contract is made, when they are known as "future goods." A present contract for the sale of future goods takes effect as an agreement to sell.[45]

(5) If the goods have perished at the time the contract is made, the parties being ignorant of this, the contract is void.[46] Likewise, with an agreement to sell, if the specific goods perish before a transfer of the risk to the buyer, the agreement is at an end.

(6) The price may be fixed but if it is not, guidelines in this Act are that the price be simply "reasonable" and "according to the circumstances." Other statutes have increasingly been used to determine prices in particular areas of commerce, such as the Prices Acts 1974–1975, the Resale Prices Act 1976 and the Consumer Credit Act 1974.[47]

---

[42] A useful recent case concerned terms for a contract when someone borrowed transparencies to browse through for the purpose of commissioning an advert. *Interfoto Picture Library Ltd.* v. *Stiletto Visual Programmes Ltd.* [1988] 1 All E.R. 348.

[43] Sale of Goods Act 1979, s.2.

[44] *Ibid.* s.4.

[45] *Ibid.* s.5(3).

[46] *Ibid.* s.6.

[47] Consumer Credit Act 1974, ss.137–140 on extortionate credit bargains, permits the court to reopen a credit agreement.

Conditions and warranties

1.157   (7) When the parties wish time to be a condition of the contract—default in which can give rise to action for breach—they must state that time is of the essence of the contract.[48]

(8) A condition in a contract is an important term, breach of which gives rise to a right to reject the contract and ask for the return of the price paid. A warranty is collateral, often about quality, and gives rise only to a claim for the appropriate damages.[49] The buyer is empowered to waive a condition or to treat a breach of condition as a breach of warranty.[50] The fact that a term is called a warranty in the contract is not to be regarded as conclusive: it may be still found, on analysis, to be a condition.[51]

The goods

1.158   (9) Section 12 of the Act defines legal implications about the title which the seller possesses and is able to pass to the buyer.

(10) Goods are to correspond with the description of them in the terms of sale. The correspondence of the bulk of the goods with a sample used in the bargaining does not relieve the seller of this condition in relation to the description.[52]

(11) The goods are deemed to be of "merchantable quality" when sold in the course of business. The statute makes this an implied condition in the contract.[53] The expression "merchantable quality" means as fit for the purpose for which goods of that kind are bought as it is reasonable to expect having regard to the circumstances.[54]

(12) Sale by sample is a method which is the subject of an express or implied term in the contract.[55] Conditions are implied in three elements of such a sale, namely that the bulk corresponds with the sample, that reasonable examination of the sample will reveal any defect of a nature that would render the goods unmerchantable, and, thirdly, that the buyer will be able to compare the bulk with the sample.[56]

2. Effect of the Contract

1.159   The Act of 1979 has four rules for the passing of the property under a contract for the sale of goods:

[48] Sale of Goods Act 1979, s.10.
[49] *Ibid.* s.11 Two of the leading cases on the distinction are: *Wallis Son & Wells* v. *Pratt & Haynes* [1911] A.C. 394; *Cehave N.V.* v. *Bremer Handelsgesellschaft mbh* [1975] 3 All E.R. 739.
[50] Sale of Goods Act 1979, s.11(2).
[51] *Ibid.* s.11(3).
[52] *Ibid.* s.13.
[53] *Ibid.* s.14(2). "Goods" includes not only the packaging but also the instructions: *Wormell* v. *RHM Agricultural (East) Ltd.* (1987) 3 All E.R. 75.
[54] *Ibid.* s.14(6). The Unfair Contract Terms Act 1977, s.6, forbids any exclusion or restriction of liability for this obligation, as against a person dealing as a consumer. The subsection (6) is from the Supply of Goods (Implied Terms) Act 1973, s.7(2). The same prohibition applies to ss.12 and 13 of the 1979 Act relating to the title and description of goods sold.
[55] Sale of Goods Act 1979, s.15(1).
[56] *Ibid.* s.15(2).

(1) No property passes until the goods are ascertained. (With a large quantity of goods, ascertainment occurs when part is allocated to the contract.)[57]

(2) In other cases, property passes when the parties intend it to pass.[58] The Act then sets out rules for ascertaining that intention.[59] In sum, they provide for the immediate passing, in the case of "deliverable goods," on the making of the contract; transfer on completion of acts of the vendor, where the contract depends on such acts[60]; and transfer on the buyer notifying his approval or acceptance of the goods, where, *e.g.* they were in his possession "on approval" or "on sale or return."

(3) Even if the property is in the possession of the buyer, the property will not pass if the seller has reserved the right of disposal on conditions and that fetter has not been removed.[61]

(4) The risk passes with the property.[62]

Transfer of title

The Act then turns to the subject of the transfer of title. This is complex **1.160** and moves into the questions of theft and fraud cases, where goods which are not legally owned are disposed of. The Act deals with sales in the open market, being one of the means by which a person without a title of his own can confer a good title on the buyer[63]; goods retained in the possession of the seller after the sale is complete and then coming into the possession of a third party[64]; the purchase of goods under a voidable title, when a buyer in good faith can acquire a title[65]; or the difficult case when the buyer acquires premature possession and then parts with the goods, but again in certain circumstances a third person can obtain a good title if he is acting in good faith.[66] All these are cases where legal advice would of necessity be sought and fuller inquiry made than can be embarked upon in this work.

3. **Performance**

Rights on delivery

The seller is under a duty to deliver the goods and the buyer to accept **1.161** and pay for them, under the normal contract for the sale of goods.[67] Vari-

---

[57] Sale of Goods Act 1979, s.16.
[58] *Ibid.* s.17.
[59] *Ibid.* s.18.
[60] This could be the allocation of goods to the contract or testing them.
[61] *e.g.* payment of only part of the purchase price did not entitle the property to pass: *Mitsui & Co. Ltd.* v. *Flota Mercante Grancolumbiana S.A.* [1989] 1 All E.R. 951, C.A.
[62] Sale of Goods Act 1979, s.20.
[63] s.22. The goods have to be purchased in good faith and without notice of the defect or want of title on the part of the seller.
[64] Sale of Goods Act 1979, s.24.
[65] *Ibid.* s.23.
[66] *Ibid.* s.25. See useful discussion in *National Employer's Mutual General Insurance Association* v. *Jones* [1988] 2 All E.R. 425.
[67] *Ibid.* s.27.

ations from normal expectancy are for the parties in their contract, *e.g.* if delivery is to be elsewhere than the normal place of the seller's place of business.

When wrong quantities are delivered, the contract rate obtains if the buyer decides to accept larger or smaller quantities than those covered by the original contract.[68]

Unless agreed, the buyer is not bound to accept delivery by instalments.[69]

Delivery by the seller to a carrier, if contracted, is deemed delivery to the buyer.[70]

Acceptance normally follows inspection by the buyer; he should be afforded a reasonable opportunity to do so.[71] Acceptance is inferred from the buyer's conduct if he does not communicate with the seller.[72] If the buyer rejects the goods for a reason stated and tells the seller, he is not obliged to return the goods.[73]

On the other hand, if the buyer is told that the seller is ready and willing to deliver and he declines to take delivery, the buyer is responsible for the deterioration in the goods due to his so acting.[74] In addition the seller can treat the buyer as having put an end to the contract and then sue him for damages.

4. Rights of the Unpaid Seller

1.162   The Act of 1979 sets out three rights of the unpaid seller:
   (1) He has a lien on the goods, *i.e.* a right of retention until paid.[75]
   (2) He has a right to stop the goods in transit if the buyer becomes insolvent.[76]
   (3) He has a right of resale if he has notified the buyer of his intention to do so, because he has not been paid. If he exercises this right of resale, the seller may recover any resulting loss from the buyer.[77]

5. Breach of Contract

1.163   (1) Once the property has passed and no due payment is made, the seller can sue for the price.[78]

---

[68] Sale of Goods Act 1979, s.30.
[69] *Ibid.* s.31.
[70] *Ibid.* s.32.
[71] *Ibid.* s.34.
[72] *Ibid.* s.35. The occasional conflict of s.35 with s.14 is illustrated in *Bernstein* v. *Pamson Motors (Golders Green) Ltd.* [1987] 2 All E.R. 220. The Nissan car was unmerchantable the court held, due to one blob of sealant in the lubrication system which made the engine seize up. But since the owner had delayed three weeks he had "accepted" the car within s.35 and could not repudiate and recover his £8,000: he only got damages of £232.
[73] *Ibid.* s.36.
[74] *Ibid.* s.37.
[75] *Ibid.* s.41.
[76] *Ibid.* ss.44–46.
[77] *Ibid.* s.48.
[78] *Ibid.* s.49(1).

(2) If the buyer refuses to accept the goods, he may be sued for damages for non-acceptance.[79] The Act provides that such damages are to be "the estimated loss directly and naturally resulting in the ordinary course of events from the buyer's breach of contract." This can prima facie be the difference between the contract price and the market price—if there is one—at the time when the goods should have been accepted.[80]

(3) Likewise, the buyer can sue for non-delivery if the seller declines to do so; the basis of damages will be as in (2) above.[81]

(4) Specific performance may be ordered by the court, in either of the situations in (2) and (3) above, if "specific or ascertained goods were involved,"[82] as an alternative to damages.

(5) An action for damages for breach of warranty is a final legal resource for parties facing a breach of contract situation.[83]

D. CONSUMER PROTECTION

Consumer Protection law has had a major revamp by Parliament in the Consumer Protection Act 1987. This consolidates law on consumer safety and trade descriptions and provides new law on product liability to conform with an EEC Directive. **1.164**

These are the main areas of law in which leisure service managers are interested. We do not embark on the great related speciality areas of hire-purchase and consumer credit nor the macro topics of mergers and monopolies.

1. **The Fair Trading Act 1973**

This Act can conveniently be considered in relation to: **1.165**
  (1) The Director General and the Consumer Protection Advisory Committee.
  (2) Current activities.

(1) *The Director General and the Consumer Protection Advisory Committee*

A Director General of Fair Trading is appointed under the Fair Trading Act of 1973.[84] His duties are to:
  (1) keep under surveillance commercial activities in the United Kingdom in relation to goods supplied to consumers, goods produced in order to be so supplied and services provided for consumers;

---

[79] Sale of Goods Act 1979, s.50.
[80] s.50. See *Lazenby Garages* v. *Wright* [1976] 1 W.L.R. 459.
[81] *Ibid.* s.51.
[82] *Ibid.* s.52.
[83] *Ibid.* s.53.
[84] s.1. The 1st Schedule sets out the main terms of the appointment.

(2) collect information about these activities in order to be aware of circumstances about "Practices which may adversely affect the economic interests of consumers in the United Kingdom." He is to receive and collate "evidence" about both the economic interests of consumers and "interests with respect to health safety or other matters" concerning consumers. This remit could hardly be wider[85];

(3) inform the Secretary of State regularly on the above matters; submit to him an annual report and receive his directions on work priorities[86];

(4) consider action under Part III of the Act of 1973 against any person "in relation to any course of conduct on the part of a person carrying on a business, which appears to be conduct detrimental to the interests of consumers in the United Kingdom and to be regarded as unfair to them"[87];

(5) take general and detailed directions from the Secretary of State on priorities for his work and otherwise.[88]

The Consumer Protection Advisory Committee

1.166   Though active for four years, this appointed committee has had no references about undesirable trade practices, from Ministers or the Director General, since 1977. Consequently, since 1982, its membership has been allowed to lapse.

(2) *Current Activities*

1.167   These stem from Part II of the Act of 1973 and it is evident, from the disbandment of the Consumer Protection Advisory Committee and the latest annual report of the Director General, that this is the field for fruitful activity under the Act at the present time. Part II allows the Director General to take action, not against trade practices, but against individual traders. His annual reports now regularly list such persons who have been called to give legally binding assurances to desist from adverse practices or who have been prosecuted (*e.g.* 22 assurances taken in 1988 and 43 convictions—only one for leisure service goods).[89]

The cases go to the Restrictive Practices Court[90]: an appeal can be taken to the Court of Appeal.[91]

These steps are under section 34, which calls on the Director General to deal with traders who "persist in a course of conduct which is detrimental to the interests of consumers" and is to be regarded as "unfair to consumers."

---

[85] Fair Trading Act 1973, s.2(1).

[86] *Ibid.* s.2(3).

[87] *Ibid.* s.2(4).

[88] *Ibid.* s.12.

[89] Annual Report, Office of Fair Trading 1989.

[90] s.35. ss.36–38 relate to evidence, Orders of the Court and corporate bodies in these procedures.

[91] *Ibid.* s.42.

As well as action in the courts, the Office of Fair Trading continues to promulgate information about the best trading practices.[92] A Code of Practice about travel agents is part of this work.

2. **Product Liability**

This law is in Part I of the consolidating measure, the Consumer Protec- **1.168** tion Act 1987.[93] The main provision is that strict liability for a defect in a product attaches to the producer, brand-owner or importer into the EEC when that defect causes personal injury or damage to property.[94] Qualifications to note are:

(a) The product must be intended for private use or consumption, or in the case of property damage, private occupation.

(b) Liability attaches only to manufactured products. Thus game or agricultural products are exempt unless they have undergone such a process.

(c) The product could, it seems, be a plant or an entire building.

(d) A defence is that the product:
   (i) was within another product and the defect arose from the design or manufacturer's directions about that other product;
   (ii) another defence, sometimes called "the state of the art" defence, is that scientific and technical knowledge at the relevant time "was not such that a producer of products of the same description as the product in question might be expected to have discovered the defect if it had existed in his products while they were under his control."[95]

(e) Damages which would total less than £275 are excluded.[96]

3. **Consumer Safety**

The Consumer Protection Act 1987, Part II, reproduces and reforms law **1.169** formerly contained in the Consumer Safety Act 1978. It authorises legal action to safeguard consumers from dangerous goods. It is now a criminal offence for a trader to supply unsafe consumer goods.[97] The action takes the following forms:

---

[92] This gives legal backing to the voluntary standards hitherto embodied in the Codes of Practice.

[93] It is the U.K. response to EEC Directive 85/374 on Product Liability.

[94] ss.2 & 5. "Strict" means that negligence does not have to be proved by the plaintiff. The Thalidomide tragedy is considered to have been the mainspring for this law. It is an addition to existing law which allows claims for breach of contract or damage suffered by negligence.

[95] *Ibid.* s.4.

[96] *Ibid.* s.5.

[97] This unvarnished précis is to be found in a section (s.10) hedged about with a huge array of qualifications on every word. Parliament now presents us with "the get-up of the goods" (s.2(*a*)).

(1) Prohibition Notices.[98]

These measures, of unlimited duration, place a ban on one trader in respect of listed products. The Secretary of State issues these. Suspension Notices for a maximum of six months are also available. A local authority can issue these.[99]

(2) Safety Regulations.[1]

These are designed to be permanent.

(3) Notices to Warn.[2]

These are the fourth type of stricture available against dangerous goods. They are used when the goods are in circulation and their receipt obliges a trader to take all reasonable steps to alert all persons in his trade outlets about the deemed danger of named goods.

Contravention of the above Regulations, Orders and Notices gives rise to offences which can be the subject in the courts of fines or six months' imprisonment.[3] The offences are created by the Act and not by the subordinate legal documents described above.[4]

A statutory defence is "that the accused took all reasonable steps and exercised all due diligence to avoid continuing the offence."[5] If the accused blames another person for the essential offence, he must notify the prosecutor at least seven days before the relevant court hearing.[6]

Enforcement of this Part II lies with the inspectors of the weights and measures authority.[7] A defence of due diligence is generally available (section 39).

1.170   Lastly, what area of commerce comes within this Act, and is there anything in the field of public leisure services which is outside its purview?

(a) Part II of this Act of 1987 covers all goods except food, animal feed, fertiliser, medicines and drugs.[8]

(b) The goods have to be ordinarily intended for private use or consumption and also supplied or in possession for supply. The word "supply" is defined to limit it to an action "in the course of carrying on a business. A qualification is included to include a business if it is selling manufactured or imported goods which have not previously been supplied in the United Kingdom and provided also that they do not form a significant extent of the business.

The "dangerous" element in this class of goods is defined as "not reasonably safe having regard to all the circumstances," but the Act details other qualifications and should be consulted.[9]

---

[98] s.13 and Sched. 2.

[99] *Ibid.* s.14. An interesting recent case, *Regina* v. *Birmingham City Council, ex p. Ferrero Ltd.* (1991) Tr.L.R. 129, C.A. discussed the limits of this procedure.

[1] s.12.

[2] *Ibid.* s.13.

[3] *Ibid.*

[4] *Ibid.*

[5] *Ibid.* s.2(6).

[6] *Ibid.*

[7] *Ibid.* ss.27 & 45.

[8] *Ibid.* s.10.

[9] *Ibid.*

E. Trade Descriptions

Introduction

Trade Description is the title used for recent statutes containing offences for fraudulent trade practices.[10] The consolidating and reforming Act of 1987 on Consumer Protection has left intact the general law which is found in the Trade Descriptions Act 1968. But responding to the argument that the law about misleading prices was unsatisfactory, it repealed the Trade Descriptions Act 1972 and the associated section in the Act of 1968.[11] **1.171**

Offences

The Trade Descriptions Act 1968 initially created two main offences: **1.172**
  (a) A person who in the course of a trade or business applies a false trade description to any goods; and
  (b) A person who in the course of a trade or business supplies or offers to supply any goods to which a false trade description is applied.[12]
There are a number of comments to be made on these offences:
  (1) "Offering to supply" has been held to include not only having available for sale in a shop but also having goods in store on the premises and available for supply.[13]
  (2) If it transpires that the offence is due to some other person than, *e.g.* the salesman, then the Act also allows the prosecution of that other person.[14]

Definition

  (3) A trade description is defined as "an indication direct or indirect and by whatever means given of any of the following matters with respect to any goods." "These matters" then include quantity, size, suitability, performance, behaviour, accuracy, tests and the results of such tests, method of manufacture, date of manufacture, and other history about the ownership or use of the goods.[15] **1.173**
  (4) "Applying" the trade description is defined comprehensively to include the various ways in which a trade description of the nature mentioned can be understood by a customer as referring to the goods in question. Thus the description has been "applied," if it is not only on the goods themselves but on a container, or if the goods in question are with other goods which bear a trade description.[16]
If the handing over of the goods, from seller to customer, is in response

---

[10] Acts of 1968 and 1972 had replaced six earlier Merchandise Acts on the same topic.
[11] s.11. The reform in the law is discussed below in the paragraph about False Prices, *i.e.* 1.180. It comprises Part III of the Act of 1987.
[12] Trade Descriptions Act 1968, s.1(1)(*a*) and (*b*).
[13] *Ibid.* s.6. But see *Ben Worsley* v. *Harvey* [1967] 2 All E.R. 507.
[14] *Ibid.* s.23, and *Havering B.C.* v. *Stevenson* [1970] 3 All E.R. 609.
[15] *Ibid.* s.2.
[16] *Ibid.* s.4(3).

to a request which embodies a trade description, then the law infers that the conduct of the supplier amounts to the application of that trade description to those goods.

Falsity

1.174   (5) It is the "false" trade description that breaks the law. When is it false? The Act of 1968 states that the description must be false "to a material degree."[17]

False prices

1.175   The definition of trade description did not include price. That element in a trade description is dealt with separately in the Consumer Protection Act 1987, Part III.[18]

In place of earlier provisions defining precisely certain items of falsity, *e.g.* suggesting that the price offered is less than the one actually charged, the reform concentrates initially on defining as an offence the giving of "misleading" information about the price of goods for sale, *viz.*: "in the course of . . . business . . . gives (by any means whatsoever) to any consumers an indication which is misleading as to the price at which any goods, services, accommodation or facilities are available."[19]

Persons in the leisure services should note that "services" here includes car parks and caravan sites.

The Act follows with an elaborate section on the meaning of "misleading" which we do not reproduce. It is comprehensive, seeking to cover every aspect of a sale.[20]

A Code of Practice supports this provision.[21]

Defences

1.176   There are some new statutory defences. These tend to be detailed, elaborate and only an indication is appropriate for this work[22]:

   (a) That Regulations authorise the defendant's action.[23]
   (b) A specific defence about acting in the ordinary course of business for a person in an advertising business.
   (c) That a recommendation about price had been followed and recom-

---

[17] Trade Descriptions Act 1968, s.3.
[18] *Heron Service Stations* v. *Hunter* (1981) 79 L.G.R. 679, shows that an actual sale is not necessary in order to complete this offence.
[19] Consumer Protection Act 1987, s.20.
[20] See a recent case on "misleading": *Director General of Fair Trading* v. *Tobyward Ltd.* [1989] 1 W.L.R. 517. The Act elaborates the reference to services, facilities and accommodation: ss.22 and 23.
[21] See Consumer Protection (Code of Practice for Traders on Price Indications) Approval Order 1988 (S.I. 1988 No. 2078).
[22] See Consumer Protection Act 1987, s.24.
[23] *Ibid.* s.26.

mended reasonably and any misleading of a purchaser was due to failure to follow that recommendation.

(d) That the defendant took all reasonable precautions and exercised all due diligence to avoid the commission of the offence by himself or by any person under his control.[24]

If part of a defence is to draw attention to the act or default of a person other than the defendant, the defence must give to the prosecution in writing such notice, at least seven clear days before the hearing, as will identify that person or help to identify that person.

If the offence charged should relate to a false trade description in an advertisement, then it is a defence for the defendant to show that he received it in the course of ordinary business and did not know or have reason to suspect that the publication would amount to an offence.

Enforcing authorities

The Trading Standards authorities are charged with enforcing the Acts. **1.177** These are the county councils, district councils and, in London, the Common Council and the London borough councils.[25]

Their powers include entry for spot-checks, seizure when an offence is suspected, and entry and seizure under warrant when they have reason to expect to be refused entry.[26]

The practice of making Compensation Orders is common in Trade Descriptions cases, under the Powers of Criminal Courts Act 1973, section 35.

If, when a case is taken before the courts the owner of goods is not convicted, the authority or government department which brought the case is liable to compensate the owner if those goods are lost, damaged or deteriorate.[27]

Limitation periods

No prosecution for an offence under these Acts may be started more **1.178** than three years after the commission of the offence.[28] The alternative period is one year from the discovery of the offence by the prosecutor and the earlier of these two periods is the effective one, in any particular case.

There is a 12 months' limit, rather than the usual six months, on laying an information in a magistrates' court.

This Act is designed to catch foreign goods which are given names or trademarks which are likely to be taken as United Kingdom ones. An offence is committed by the supplier unless he ensures that the real place of production is conspicuously indicated on the goods or, at the other extreme, the offending name is so inconspicuous that a purchaser is unlikely to be aware of it or be influenced by it. There are various forms of defence and relief provided in the Act.

[24] Trade Descriptions Act 1968, s.24 and as to prices, see Consumer Protection Act 1987, s.39.
[25] Weights and Measures Act 1985, s.69.
[26] *Ibid.* s.28. There are associated offences for obstructing such officers (s.29).
[27] Trade Descriptions Act 1968, s.33.
[28] *Ibid.* s.19.

1. **Supply of Goods and Services Act 1982**

1.179   Managers in the public leisure services may well be involved in contracts for the provision of a new tennis court, the construction and equipment of a new trim trail, or the building of a new swimming pool, with its diving boards, seating, lockers and associated equipment.

The common feature of these contracts is that they arrange for both goods and work to be provided by the contractor. The type of contract is of frequent occurrence but the Law Commission found a gap in the law in relation to such contracts. The Sale of Goods Act 1979 dealt with the goods. This Act of 1982 deals with the combined agreements for both goods and services, as well as one or two other items.[29]

(1) *The Framework of the Act*

1.180   These goods and services contracts are made subject to four provisions almost identical with corresponding terms in the Sale of Goods Act 1979, discussed above. They require sound title to the goods, their conformity with any contracted description and their compliance with any standard of merchantable quality and fourthly, if supplied with a sample, their compliance with the three Sale of Goods Act stipulations for that situation. (See paragraph 159.)

1.181   These four terms are implied conditions. The same four terms, about good title, reliability of the description, merchantable quality and correspondence of bulk with sample, are applied in the Act of 1982 to a second type of contract, *i.e.* for the hiring of goods.[30] This was because the Law Commission had found considerable difference of view among judges in earlier cases about the legal obligations laid upon a hirer where the contract is silent on that point.

The third class of contracts dealt with in this Act relates purely to services. Instances which might be met by leisure service managers and which have been before the courts in the past include: transporting goods on land[31] or water,[32] erecting scaffolding,[33] inoculating cattle,[34] or repairing motor vehicles.[35] There are, of course, many more.

In these contracts to perform a service, the Act of 1982 now implies three terms:

> (a) The supplier will carry out the service with reasonable care and skill.[36]
> (b) The service will be carried out within a reasonable time.[37]

[29] Law Commission Report No. 95. Implied Terms in Contracts for the Supply of Goods, July 17, 1979.
[30] Trade Descriptions Act 1968, ss.7, 8, 9 and 10.
[31] *Lally & Weller* v. *George Bird*, May 23, 1980, Q.B.D., unrep.
[32] *McCutcheon* v. *MacBrayne* [1964] 1 W.L.R. 125.
[33] *Sims* v. *Foster Wheeler* [1966] 1 W.L.R. 769.
[34] *Dodd & Dodd* v. *Wilson & McWilliam* [1946] 2 All E.R. 691.
[35] *Stewart* v. *Leavell's Garage* [1952] 2 Q.B. 545.
[36] Supply of Goods and Services Act 1982, s.13.
[37] *Ibid.* s.14.

(c) A reasonable charge will be paid for the service.[38]
What is "reasonable" in (b) and (c) is "a question of fact."

(2) *Significant Detail*

We turn now to a little greater detail about some of the provisions.   **1.182**

Excluded contracts

To define the group of contracts for work and materials with which Part
I of the Act of 1982 is concerned, it is necessary to exclude contracts for
the sale of goods, hire-purchase agreements, contracts with no consideration but which, being sealed, are enforceable, and trading stamp transfer
agreements.[39]

Title

The section about the implied condition of a good title also refers to the
case where a transferor wishes to give only a qualified, or cautiously
guarded, assurance of his title, perhaps because of the continuing interest
in the goods of a third party.[40] The Act gives the transferee the benefit of a
warranty, rather than a condition, and holds the transferor to a full disclosure of the charges or incumbrances affecting the property.

The new implied term about the merchantable quality of the goods is
not to commit the transferor to liability for defects to which he draws
attention, or those to which an inspection, reasonably carried out, should
have alerted the transferee.[41]

The terms implied in a contract for the transfer of goods or the hire of
goods are not to be exclusive, with the exception of those about quality
and fitness.[42] The same principle applies to a contract for a service.[43]

Excluded services

Excluded from Part II of the Act of 1982 concerning the supply of ser-   **1.183**
vices are:
(a) An apprenticeship.
(b) A contract of service, *i.e.* a contract of employment.[44]
(c) Any services subsequently excluded by Orders made by the Secretary of State.[45]

---

[38] Supply of Goods and Services Act 1982, s.15.
[39] *Ibid.* s.1. The Law Commission called the Part I contracts "analogous to sale." G. F.
Woodroffe in his book on the 1982 Act, *Goods and Services—The New Law* calls them "quasi-
sales" (para. 2.01).
[40] *Ibid.* s.2(3), (4) and (5). This section and ss. 3, 4 and 5 can also apply to a contract of bar-
ter. The law reports contain a case on portrait painting, which nicely illustrates the difficulties which this section is designed to eliminate, *i.e. Robinson* v. *Graves* (1935) 1 K.B. 79.
[41] *Ibid.* s.9.
[42] *Ibid.* s.11.
[43] *Ibid.* s.16.
[44] *Ibid.* s.12(2).
[45] *i.e.* the Secretary of State for Trade and Industry.

The definition of a contract of service for the purposes of this Act is simply: "a contract under which a person agrees to carry out a service."[46]

The Act contains a provision to harmonise its main provisions about implied terms with the Unfair Contract Terms Act 1977.

A new Act, the Consumer Arbitration Agreements Act 1988, allows recourse to arbitration rather than the courts, when the "consumer" so submits or agrees in writing, or is so ordered by a court. It means looking at the small print even more carefully to see if a supplier is using this Act.

[46] Supply of Goods and Services Act 1982, s.12.

CHAPTER 2

LOCAL AUTHORITIES—MAJOR LEISURE SERVICE PROVIDERS

"It is unthinkable that the Panel (on Take Overs and Mergers) should go on its way cocooned from the attention of the Courts in defence of the citizenry"

Lord Donaldson (*R. v. Panel on Take-overs and Mergers, ex p. Datafin plc* [1987] Q.B. 815 at p. 839)

INTRODUCTION

This chapter leaves the general legal background, against which the pub- **2.01** lic leisure services operate. Local authorities are responsible for many of those services and this chapter looks at certain branches of the law which affect their role in this field.

Initially we shall consider the statutory framework within which they must work. This includes recognition of the innovation of the 1980s, Compulsory Competitive Tendering, which has significantly affected some of the leisure services run by local authorities. The domestic law connoted by local Acts and by-laws is the subject of the following section. There follow three sections about the large specialist territories in which there are laws for local authorities. These are commons, open space land and the slightly vaguer but very important subject of land purchase, appropriation and disposal.

A. Creatures of Statute

Many former local authorities were the creations of charters; all are now **2.02** creatures of statute.[1] The great reorganisation of 1974 saw a rationalisation of the functions of local authorities. There was a considerable effort made to regulate practice and function more effectively. Then and thereafter a large number of unnecessary statutes were repealed. The Local Government Act 1985 comprehensively abolished the Greater London Council and six Metropolitan County Councils and led to further drastic transfer of their powers to the surviving authorities.

Yet amid this reshaping and reform, the central legal core of local authority activity remained. It is the powers conferred by Parliament which

---

[1] The Local Government Act 1972, s.245, is the authority under which district councils have petitioned for charters to acquire borough status.

determine the powers of local government. "Without those powers, it has no power."[2]

1. **Powers and Duties**

2.03   Local authorities are managers of legal functions, some of which are duties and some powers. For instance, in the Public Libraries and Museums Act 1964: "It shall be the duty of every library authority to provide a comprehensive and efficient library service. . . . " But: "A library authority may make a charge for notifying a person that a book . . . (is) . . . available for borrowing."[3] The difference is traditional and necessary.

A simple example of the difference between the statute which prescribes and the statute which permits relates to the statutory timetable for the application for a bingo club licence in the Gaming Act 1968. The case is *R.* v. *Pontypool Gaming Licensing Committee.*[4] The Act requires a copy of the newspaper advertisement about the application to be sent to the clerk of the licensing committee within seven days of publication. In the event, it was 13 days before it was sent, 15 before it was received. All else was in order. The authority did not object in principle to the application. But it was declined because the mandatory requirements of the Act of 1968 had not been fulfilled. On appeal it was argued that a mere administrative inconvenience had occurred. The High Court held otherwise: "Parliament has laid down the entire procedure, with specific limits of time." The court refused an application for an order that the licensing committee should hear and determine the licence application. This could not be done: the application was not lawful.[5]

2.04   In exercising both powers and duties, local authorities come under scrutiny in the courts if they depart from the principle that in exercising those statutory functions, they must not inflict on others damage that might, with reasonable care, be avoided. Provided that they carry out the functions Parliament has entrusted to them, without negligence, they incur no liability. In the well-known words of Lord Blackburn in the case of *Geddis* v. *Proprietors of Bann Reservoir,* "No action will lie for doing that which the legislature has authorised if it be done without negligence but an action does lie . . . if it be done negligently."[6]

---

[2] Watkins L.J. in *Bromley London Borough Council* v. *Greater London Council* [1983] 1 A.C. 768 at p. 768.

[3] ss.7 and 8(2).

[4] [1970] 1 W.L.R. 1299.

[5] In other cases on the same Schedule, a court has excused the printing of ABE for ABC as an obvious error (*R.* v. *Dacorum Gaming Licensing Committee, ex p. EMI Cinemas & Leisure Ltd.* [1971] 3 All E.R. 666), but another court declined to uphold another notice, which whilst containing the correct items, added several superfluous ones. It was an invalid public notice, said the court. The Schedule is mandatory on these matters (*R.* v. *Leicester Gaming Licensing Committee, ex p. Shine* [1971] 1 W.L.R. 1648. Depending on the context, courts have held time requirements to be directory only, and thus a mistake in that respect has not been fatal to the statutory procedure. See *R.* v. *Inspector of Taxes, ex p. Clarke* [1974] Q.B. 220. A recent Court of Appeal case is *R.* v. *Lambeth London Borough Council, ex p. Sharp* [1987] J.P.L. 440.

[6] [1878] A.C. 430 at p. 455.

There are two other principles established by the cases, which under- **2.05**
line this prime duty of local authorities to operate competently within the
statutes:
   (a) They cannot by deed or contract limit themselves not to fulfil their
       obligations under the statutory functions.[7]
   (b) They may make internal rules to guide themselves in executing
       those functions, provided that those rules are not arbitrary but are
       relevant and consistent with the enabling legislation.[8]

2. **Constraints**

The main sanctions against local authorities which depart from these **2.06**
principles, have emerged over the years. They include:
   (1) Breach of Statutory Duty
   (2) Judicial Review
   (3) Ministerial Oversight
   (4) The Ombudsman
   (5) Audit
   (6) The Monitoring Officer
   (7) Compulsory Competitive Tendering

(1) *Breach of Statutory Duty*

This is a sanction which has often received acceptance in the courts, para- **2.07**
doxically, by the claims based upon it which are dismissed, rather than
those which succeed. It was, however, upheld in *Thornton* v. *Kirklees Metropolitan Borough Council*[9] The Court of Appeal supported a claim for
damages for breach of the statutory duty to secure housing accommodation for the plaintiff, which arises under the Housing (Homeless Persons) Act 1977, section 3(4). They rested their decision on being satisfied
with the application to the facts of that case of three tests, which emerge
from a House of Lords decision in 1949 (*Cutler* v. *Wandsworth Stadium*)[10]:
   (a) Is this claim for the kind of harm the statute was intended to pre-
       vent?
   (b) Was the plaintiff one of the class of those for whom the protection
       of the statute was intended?
   (c) Was the special remedy provided by the statute adequate for the
       protection of the person injured?
The general principle is that where a statute imposes a duty on a public

---

[7] See *Blake* v. *Hendon Corporation* [1962] 1 Q.B. 283, for an illuminating discussion by Devlin
   J. of this principle in relation to s.164 of the Public Health Act 1975. To dedicate land for a
   public park was not, said the court, binding themselves to flout a statutory duty. It was
   compatible with the main objects for which the land was acquired.
[8] See, *Kennedy* v. *Birmingham Licensing Committee* [1972] 2 Q.B. 140, where it was held that an
   "equation of barrelage" required by the Committee from an applicant for a new on-
   licence was invalid because it was unreasonable.
[9] [1979] Q.B. 626.
[10] [1949] A.C. 398.

authority, for the benefit of a specified category of persons, but prescribes no special remedy for breach of that duty, it is to be assumed that a civil action for damages will lie for such a breach.

(2) *Judicial Review*

2.08 An application for judicial review is a general form of appeal to the High Court against alleged breach of some duty in law, by any body of persons granted legal authority to determine questions affecting the rights of subjects. This somewhat general description certainly brings many of the decisions taken by local authorities into the category of those which can be brought before the courts for examination and possible corrective action. It arises precisely under the terms of Order 53 of the Rules of the Supreme Court and for detail that Order should be consulted.[11] It originated in 1977 and has been described as providing a uniform, flexible and comprehensive code of procedure for the exercise by the High Court of its supervisory jurisdiction over the proceedings and decisions of other bodies of persons charged with the performance of public acts and duties.[12]

2.09 There have been many cases when this procedure has been employed, for example:

In *O'Reilly* v. *Mackman*,[13] certain prisoners brought an ordinary action for damages against the Board of Visitors for Hull Prison. The defendant raised the question of appropriate procedure and succeeded in the House of Lords. That House said that Order 53 should have been used, due to the nature of the case. "It would be contrary to public policy and, as such, an abuse of the process of the court, to permit a person seeking to establish that a decision of a public authority infringed rights to which he was entitled to protection under public law, to proceed by way of ordinary action and by this means to evade the provisions of Order 53 for the protection of such authorities."

The case of *R.* v. *Bromley London Borough Council, ex p. Lambeth London Borough Council*,[14] was important in showing that the Order 53 powers and procedures were available for litigants when a declaration was sought, even though no decision was being challenged and none of the three prerogative orders was being sought. The subject of the declaration sought in that case was whether a subscription to the Association of London

---

[11] This came into operation under the Supreme Court Act 1981, s.31.

[12] The extent of this procedure is indicated in *R.* v. *Electricity Commissioners* [1924] 1 K.B. 171 at p. 205.

[13] [1983] 2 A.C. 237. There were 2129 applications for judicial review in 1990 of which 902 were allowed. Almost one-third concerned immigration problems.

[14] *The Times*, June 16, 1984 D.C. The three prerogative orders, formerly known as writs, are *mandamus*, which commands the body or person to do that which is his legal duty to do; *prohibition*, which forbids, *e.g.* a lower court from doing that which it should not do; and *certiorari*, which brings into the High Court in order to quash them, judicial (in its widest sense) proceedings which have gone wrong, or are going wrong, because, *e.g.* fair trial is not likely due to bias, or jurisdiction is exceeded. More than one of these orders may issue for a particular complaint.

Authorities was lawful. Before ruling in the affirmative on this question, the High Court required to be satisfied that:

(a) The plaintiff council had a real and not simply an academic interest in the matter,[15] and

(b) There was a real "contender," (*i.e.* in the person of Lambeth L.B.C.), "a proper contradictor," as Lord Dunedin had once said.[16]

(3) *Ministerial Control*

Local authorities have always been subject to the control of a Minister of **2.10** the Crown for some of the many services they administer. For dereliction of duty by a local education authority, the Secretary of State has the clearest reserve default power:

"If the Secretary of State is satisfied that they . . . have failed to discharge the duty imposed upon them, the Secretary of State may make an Order declaring . . . to be in default and giving such directions as may be expedient for enforcing that duty."[17]

For general local government oversight, there are still a variety of controls, such as inspection, obtaining information, consenting to appointments, giving directions,[18] making regulations, not to mention the extensive areas of local government decisions, *e.g.* for large urban redevelopment where development plans and compulsory purchase orders go to one Minister or another for confirmation.

Whether used rarely or frequently, these controls and reserve powers create the climate of opinion in which local authorities work.

(4) *The Local Government Commissioners*

The Ombudsman, to use the popular term, was introduced to local **2.11** government by the Local Government Act 1974. England has three and Wales one. Each Local Commissioner has a territorial responsibility.

---

[15] The status of being an "aggrieved person," and thus entitled to pursue litigation, received a further refinement in *R.* v. *Secretary of State for Social Services, ex p. Greater London Council, The Times,* August 16, 1984, before Woolf J. The court held that the local authority, *i.e.* the G.L.C., had no standing but the Child Poverty Action Group did have sufficient standing to seek and obtain a Declaration under Order 53 procedure against the Secretary of State and his chief Supplementary Benefits officer, on behalf of unidentified claimants for arrears of Supplementay Benefit. A local authority could not simply assume this role, under s.222 of the Local Government Act 1972.

[16] *Russian Commercial and Industrial Bank* v. *British Bank for Foreign Trade Ltd.* [1921] 2 A.C. 438 at p. 447.

[17] s.68 of the Education Act 1944, gives even stronger control over actual or potential failure by an education authority to carry out its duties in a reasonable manner.

[18] *e.g.* Local Government Planning and Land Act 1980, ss.71, 98 and 116 about the restriction on capital expenditure, the disposal of land not put to good use and the assessment of land suitable for residential development.

These Ombudsmen investigate complaints, duly lodged, into "injustice in consequence of maladministration."[19] The decision to investigate is discretionary, so that, for instance, an Order of Mandamus by the High Court to a Local Commissioner requiring him to investigate a particular matter would be inapt.[20] (This discretionary element is fortified by section 34 of the Act of 1974: "It is hereby declared that nothing in this Part of this Act authorises or requires a Local Commissioner to question the merits of a decision taken without maladministration by an authority in the exercise of a discretion vested in that authority.")

The Ombudsman affords to the local authority, against which the complaint is levelled, a chance to comment, even to try to negotiate a local settlement of the grievance. The annual report is a useful record of the scale and effectiveness of this new control over local government.[21]

2.12   The emphasis is on the *way* in which the local authority handled the problem, whether it be housing, or town planning (which still head the list of subject areas calling for investigation), or compensation, or a variety of others. Lord Donaldson M.R. has underlined this by stating "Administration and maladministration have nothing to do with the nature, quality or reasonableness of the decision itself."[22]

The Ombudsman is likely to find maladministration if he finds evidence of unfairness, neglect, bias, unreasonable delay, failure to follow prescribed procedures, or arbitrariness.[23]

2.13   An Ombudsman can recommend a culpable authority to take action to remedy their failure, perhaps pay compensation, repair a house, rehouse someone, and the findings are given the pressure of publicity to induce some favourable, positive, response. The local authority is required to inform the Local Commissioner of the action they have taken on his report. On receiving this, the Commissioner may decide to issue a second report.[24]

2.14   After nearly 20 years' experience of this system, one or two points have

---

[19] These reports are submitted to "representative bodies," being committees with representatives from the local authority associations and the National Water Council. They in turn circulate reports throughout the country: s.24 Local Government Act 1974. Whilst the Act of 1974 says that the maladministration is to have occurred "in the exercise of the administrative functions of the authority," (s.26), any exclusion of, *e.g.* law-making activities such as by-laws, or executive functions, seems in practice difficult to discern.

[20] *Re Fletchers' Application* [1990] 2 All E.R. 527. This is about the Parliamentary Commissioner but the wording is the same and is thus relevant.

[21] In the latest annual report "The Local Government Ombudsmen" covering 1990–91, it is said that 9169 complaints were received. This is three times the 1984 figure. Housing and planning still accounted for 67% of the complaints. Only 103 of the total related to leisure and recreation. 254 reports found maladministration.

[22] *R.* v. *Local Commissioner for Administration for the South, the West, the West Midlands, Leicestershire, Lincolnshire and Cambridgeshire, ex p. Eastleigh Borough Council* [1988] Q.B. 855.

[23] H.C. Debates, (1966) Vol. 754, c. 51; Mr. R. Crossman in Second Reading debate on the Bill. It is important to note that the maladministration is one of two elements to be looked at by the Ombusdman. The other is that the complainant has "sustained injustice" (Local Government Act 1974, s.26).

[24] Local Government Act 1974, s.31(1). The annual report calls this stage "Accepting the Umpire's Decision" and says 35 further reports had to be issued in that year.

been ventilated in the courts and additional legal provisions in the code of practice followed by the Ombudsmen are worth emphasis.

(a) Communications to and from an Ombudsman as part of an investigation are, for the purposes of the law of defamation, absolutely privileged.[25]

(b) The case of *R.* v. *Local Commissioner for Administration for the North and East Area of England, ex p. Bradford Metropolitan Borough Council*[26] illuminates the selection by an Ombudsman of complaints for investigation, in the light of a restriction in section 26 of the Act of 1974 that this is not to cover:

  (i) an action in relation to which a person has a right of appeal to a tribunal under an enactment, or to a Minister of the Crown;

  (ii) likewise, an action in which a person has a remedy by way of process in a court of law.

(c) The case of *Re A Complaint against Liverpool City Council*[27] is a useful test of the effect of the statutory notice served by a local authority, under investigation, under section 32(3) of the Act of 1974, that the production of certain papers to the Ombudsman would be contrary to the public interest. In that case, the papers related to the fostering of a child. Under the Act of 1974, the Secretary of State has power to "discharge" such a notice by a local authority but he had not done so. In these circumstances the refusal of the council was upheld in the Divisional Court.

(d) Obstruction of an investigation gives rise to an Ombudsman's certificate to the High Court, which is empowered to deal with the offender as if he were before that Court. The offence has to be "such that it would constitute contempt of court" if the Ombudsman's investigations were a proceeding in the High Court.

(e) An Ombudsman can call in expert advice.[28] The whole approach of the Ombudsman to his task, not least the tightrope he must walk in avoiding an area where the courts have concurrent jurisdiction, is illuminated by a Croydon Council case.[29]

(5) *Audit*

The increased scrutiny of local government finances by central government, and the whole ethos of central government involvement with those monies connoted by the practice of rate capping, have not surprisingly led to a more elaborate auditing of local authority accounts. We mention here the main elements in the present system briefly, as a fifth constraint affecting local authorities at the present time.[30]

---

[25] Local Government Act 1974, s.32.

[26] [1979] 1 Q.B. 287.

[27] [1977] 2 All E.R. 650.

[28] Local Government Act 1974, s.29(6).

[29] *R.* v. *Commissioner for Local Administration, ex p. Croydon London Borough Council* [1989] 1 All E.R. 1033.

[30] A further account for the professional can be found in *Encyclopedia of Local Government Law* (Sweet & Maxwell).

The Audit Commission for Local Authorities in England and Wales was set up by the Local Government Finance Act 1982. It appoints an auditor for each authority, after consultation. The scope of the auditor's duties is indicated in the phrase "economy, efficiency and effectiveness in its use of resources" as part of his duty under the Act of 1982.[31] He is also to see that "proper practices" have been used in preparing the accounts.[32] These crucial terms are amplified in the Code of Practice, a comprehensive document of 85 paragraphs and eight specimen certificates.[33]

The auditor is thus interested in the lawful exercise of its discretion by the local authority.[34] He is never to overlook his duty to the public and he is expected to look out for and recognise unfamiliar situations. He can comment on the effectiveness of management arrangements. He has guidelines in the Code for handling fraud, irregularities and corruption. The Code and Statute amplify his duties in presenting his Certificate at the end of an audit.

(6) *The Monitoring Officer*

The Local Government and Housing Act 1989, section 5 requires each local authority under the Act—generally county and district councils, London borough councils, the Common Council and a number of joint authorities[35]—to appoint this new officer. His duty is to keep an eye on decisions taken, or contemplated or even not taken, which are likely to bring the authority into trouble in one of two ways.

The first is with the Ombudsman, which we discussed above. The second is more generally in breaking the law or breaching a Code of Practice. This can be at officer level as well as Committee level. The Monitoring Officer is to present a report on that matter to the authority. We await court decisions about the interpretation of this novel and interesting provision.

(7) *Compulsory Competitive Tendering*

Local authorities have been employing their own staff since the day they came into existence. There must be a day in history when the first one employed the first handyman, and then a painter and a joiner and a plumber. Small drops of rain become rivers. Likewise tenders have been accepted from the earliest days of local government, and thus competitive tendering has a long history.

But in the Local Government Act of 1988 the two elements came together under a legal framework which created obligations. Direct Labour Organisations, for building maintenance work in the main, had

---

[31] s.15.
[32] For a definition of "proper practices" see Local Government and Housing Act 1989, s.66.
[33] November 28, 1990, under s.14 of Local Government (Miscellaneous Provisions) Act 1982.
[34] *Anns* v. *Merton London Borough Council* [1978] A.C. 728, 754.
[35] Local Government and Housing Act 1989, s.21.

been known since legislation of 1980 but now a universal duty has been created. Since some of this wave has washed up on the leisure services shore we must summarise the main elements.

(a) Defined services have to be managed within the framework of the tendering procedure laid down in the Act of 1988. The first six were refuse collection, building cleaning, other cleaning, catering for schools, welfare and other catering, ground maintenance and vehicle maintenance. Catering and ground and vehicle maintenance had potential impact on leisure services.

(b) Strict accounting for each separate service is required. This is associated with an annual report to be produced within six months of the year end and copied to the Government.

(c) Tenders are invited by pubic notice and an in-house bid can take its chance with the outside ones. Evaluation of tenders is complex. Each tender will be assessed for resources and management to undertake the contract, ability to recruit and retain labour and references, apart from detailed technical and financial appraisals.

(d) One has seen in-house papers of enormous volume assembled for leisure services management tenders, a service which soon followed the six above. A list of 51 check list steps is in another publication. The scale of the exercise is registered by the fact that the initial de minimis figure below which this procedure was excused, was £100,000 per annum.

(e) The Government has default powers when an authority falters at one of the hurdles or tries to by-pass an obstacle. These have been used. We are beginning to see the first cases appearing in the law reports.[36]

In conclusion, the subject, only four years old, has already assumed a technical complexity, size and finesse that rivals local government financial controls from Government, and is already creating its own literature, seminars and experts. It will be soon enough to gauge its abiding impact on those leisure services still provided by public authorities by the time of our next edition.

3. Ultra Vires

As local authorities are creatures of statute, they are not allowed to act **2.15** outside the powers conferred by those statutes. To do so is *ultra vires* (beyond the powers). The application of the doctrine of *ultra vires* provides a particular example of circumstances in which actions and decisions of local authorities may become subject to judicial review, which is referred to above.

The territory

If a local authority seeks to spend money outside its own area, it is likely **2.16** to be acting *ultra vires*. The Public Libraries and Museums Act 1964

---

[36] *e.g. R.* v. *Islington London Borough, ex p. Building Employers Confederation* [1989] I.R.L.R. 382.

empowers the authority to provide a service for people resident in the area or in full time education there. This is the normal situation—a service for the rate payers. It has been modified to the extent, *e.g.* that the Local Authorities (Goods and Services) Act 1970 allows agreements between adjoining authorities for the provision of a joint service, joint use of plant or the carrying out of maintenance. As social development has reduced the likelihood that any authority will be selfcontained, this is an area of risk to be kept under review.

The money

2.17   The local authority by law works within its annual budget. Differing political opinions can lead to an *ultra vires* decision in the field of staff payments or contracts to be made. This happens if prudence is stretched to breaking point, as in *Roberts* v. *Hopwood*[37] when the courts held *ultra vires* wages paid to a class of employees of a London borough which went significantly beyond nationally negotiated levels.

An acceptance by a local authority of a tender for goods or services which is not the lowest has normally to be justified by giving "special reasons," within the authority's standing orders. This kind of internal ruling is a good way of starting to meet an *ultra vires* challenge to such expenditure: it evidences an intent to act with financial prudence.

For the approach of the courts in the field of education policy to such internal guidelines, see *Cumings* v. *Birkenhead Corporation*.[38]

Easing the ultra vires rule

2.18   A number of statutory provisions should be noted which enlarge an authority's powers at points where the *ultra vires* rule would have applied.

By the Local Government Act 1972, section 111, "a local authority shall have power to do any thing . . . which is calculated to facilitate, or is conducive or incidental to, the discharge of any of their functions." The words "conducive or incidental to" can give rise to keen debate.

By the same Act of 1972 the power in section 137 to spend money, up to the product of a two penny rate, "in the interests of their area or of all or some of its inhabitants" on purposes not specified or authorised in any other enactment, gives a measure of leeway to members frustrated by the limits of their portfolio of enabling statutes.[39]

The Local Government (Miscellaneous Provisions) Act 1982 has extended two earlier powers:

  (a) The power above in section 137 of the main Act of 1972 is widened
      to include "power to incur expenditure in giving financial assist-

---

[37] [1925] A.C. 578.

[38] [1971] 2 All E.R. 881.

[39] This was the power under which Hackney London Borough Council successfully resisted a challenge to their action in giving financial help to the costs of the British Olympic team in Moscow in 1980. The Council said that their action was based on the involvement of local inhabitants in the Olympics.

ance to persons carrying on commercial and industrial undertakings."[40]

(b) A power in the Local Authorities (Land) Act 1963 is extended so that the local authority can advance money to enable a person to acquire land or erect buildings or carry out work on land.[41] (The former provision was limited to land sold or let by the local authority or to land where the council was a party to a building agreement.[42])

Abuse of statutory powers

In addition to the primary question, have the powers been exceeded?, **2.19**
there is a more general and searching question: have the powers been abused?[43]

Though the House of Lords has held that bad faith as such is not a ground for a challenge to a decision as being *ultra vires*, the jurisdiction of the courts in the face of an abuse of legal powers, is evidenced by *London and Westcliff Properties Ltd.* v. *Ministry of Housing and Local Government.*[44] The local authority came to an arrangement with the freeholders of a site to dispose of the leasehold interest in that site to them, when the authority's compulsory purchase order on that leasehold interest had been confirmed. The financial arrangements to achieve this destination of the valuable leasehold interest were agreed before the public enquiry into an objection by the leaseholders to the order. The order was confirmed by the Ministry but quashed by the High Court as *ultra vires*. Ashworth J. said: "The proposal and the agreement involved the council in as plain a contravention of section 47(2) of the Housing Act 1957 as can be imagined. This was a bargain which . . . the Minister's officials should at once have detected as improper . . . it was acting ultra vires."[45]

Ultra vires and estoppel

There is a final point to be made, illustratrated by *Rhyl Urban District* **2.20**
Council v. *Rhyl Amusements Ltd.*[46] A local authority granted a 31 year lease of a marine lake and pleasure grounds to a company, without taking the necessary first step of obtaining consent from the Ministry for the trans-

[40] Local Government (Miscellaneous Provisions) Act 1982, s.44.
[41] *Read* v. *J. Lyons & Co. Ltd.* [1947] A.C. 156; *Christmas* v. *General Cleaning Contractors Ltd.* [1952] 1 All E.R. 39.
[42] Local Authorities (Land) Act 1963, s.32.
[43] *Smith* v. *East Elloe R.D.C.* [1956] A.C. 736, a compulsory purchase order case.
[44] [1961] 1 W.L.R. 519.
[45] *Ibid.* at p. 529. S.47, referred to by the court, requires the best price to be obtained for land thus bought. The arrangement with the freeholders breached this requirement. *R.* v. *Manchester City Council, ex p. Donald King* (1991) 89 L.G.R. 696 is another good instance. To increase fees for street traders' licences excessively was an abuse and unlawful. Likewise the making of a charge for pre-application advice about planning controls in relation to development had no statutory basis and was *ultra vires* (*R.* v. *Richmond-upon-Thames London Borough Council, ex p. McCarthy & Stone (Developments) Ltd., The Times*, November 15, 1991, H.L.
[46] [1959] 1 All E.R. 257.

action, as the lease was longer than seven years. Some 20 years later, desiring to renegotiate terms, the Council advanced the argument that the original lease was void, for the reason explained above. In court, the company lessee sought to hold the council estopped from presenting that point, having by conduct honoured the lease for many years. The court did not agree with the company. Harman J. said that to allow that argument would be to gloss over the *ultra vires* act. "Otherwise such a body," he said, "could by this means confer on itself a power which it had not got and the *ultra vires* doctrine would be reduced to a nullity."

As indicated at the start of this Chapter, local authorities, as creatures of statute, are subject to certain resulting restraints. The *ultra vires* rule enshrines one of these and it is evident from recent decisions in the courts that it is still being regularly exercised.[47]

4. Statutory Interpretation

2.21   "A judge should ask himself this question. If the makers of this Act had themselves come across this ruck in the texture, how would they have straightened it out? A judge must not alter the material of which it is woven but he can and should iron out the creases."

This is an extract from the judgment of Denning J. in *Seaford Court Estates* v. *Asher*.[48] It is not a view held by all courts. There have clearly been different approaches to statutory interpretation and only a small part of the topic has been codified into statute. When one text book has some 75 rules for different problems raised by this subject,[49] clearly all that can be collected here is a series of some of the main ones.

(1) The making of law is for the legislature, not the courts.

"There is one course the courts cannot take; they cannot fill the gaps. They cannot, by asking the question 'What would Parliament have done in this case?—one not contemplated—if the facts had been before it?' attempt themselves to supply the answer, if the answer is not in the terms of the Act itself."[50]

(2) Many Acts of Parliament have their own interpretation section. In addition there is an Interpretation Act of 1978. These often help.

(3) Where a statute is ambiguous, the court should seek the intention of Parliament:

　　(a) in the statute itself;
　　(b) in other related legislation;

---

[47] *Hazell* v. *Hammersmith & Fulham London Borough Council* [1990] 2 W.L.R. 17 is a full review by the courts on rate swaps and *ultra vires*.

[48] [1950] A.C. 508.

[49] *Halsbury* (4th ed.), Vol. 44, Statutes, paras. 840–915 incl.

[50] *Royal College of Nursing* v. *D.H.S.S.* [1981] A.C. 800 at p. 822E, *per* Lord Wilberforce. Though, for a possibly perilous step down this slope, see *Pickstone* v. *Freemans plc* (1988) 2 All E.R. 803 H.L. and *Litster* v. *Forth Dry Dock and Engineering Co. Ltd.* [1990] 1 A.C. 546. 1134 H.L. when "we are in Europe now" was the occasion for making a judicial interpolation in an Act.

(c) in contemporaneous circumstances;
(d) then in the rules of law:
  (i) What was the common law before this Act?
  (ii) What was the defect or mischief for which the common law did not provide?
  (iii) What remedy had Parliament resolved upon?
  (iv) What was the purpose—the aim—of the remedy?[51]

(4) The words of the statute should be construed to give them a sensible meaning.

(5) Words should be given their ordinary meaning if there is nothing to alter or modify the language.

(6) Where general words follow specific words, the general words ought to be confined to things of the same kind as those specified.[52]

(7) When construing a consolidating Act, there is a presumption that it was not intended to alter the law. This must give way to a contrary intention.

If this subsection began with a challenging point of view of Denning J., it may end with an equally searching one from Templeman J. in *Halifax Building Society* v. *Registrar of Friendly Societies*[53]

> "There are no reasons why I should officiously strive to limit the scope of section 43 in order perversely to forbid that to be done which plainly must and ought to be done, namely, the safeguard of the investors in a building society from loss."

B. LOCAL LAW MAKERS

Local authorities operate within a framework of legal powers and duties; **2.22** hence the reality of *intra vires* and *ultra vires* discussed above. For the most part, that framework is contained in the general law of the land, *i.e.* Acts of Parliament: Housing Acts, Finance Acts, Town and Country Planning Acts, Public Health Acts, Local Government Acts and others.

A local authority can acquire more legal powers in the following ways: (1) adoptive Acts, (2) provisional Orders, (3) by-laws and (4) local Acts. These are the classic methods and this subsection considers their present usefulness.

1. Adoptive Acts

These are important Acts of Parliament which are operative only in those **2.23** parts of the country where, by the prescribed method, they are "adopted."[54] Examples are the Private Places of Entertainment (Licens-

---

[51] Cited in *Universal Corporation* v. *Five Ways Properties Ltd.* [1978] 3 All E.R. 1131 at p. 1136.
[52] *Beswick* v. *Beswick* [1968] A.C. 58 at p. 87.
[53] [1978] 1 W.L.R. 1549 at p. 1550.
[54] The Adoptive Act itself prescribes the procedure for adoption. Sometimes it is a vote of the local authority but, instead, it might be a majority vote of the inhabitants. For the first Libraries and Museums Act 1850, a two-thirds vote of the voting burgesses in favour of the Act was stipulated.

ing) Act 1967 and Local Government (Miscellaneous Provisions) Act 1982, namely the control of sex establishments (section 2) or the licensing of public entertainments (section 1(2)). Whilst this class of legislation was used from time to time in the nineteenth century, and allowed for some flexibility in the application of special laws, it has now ceased to fulfil any ongoing useful purpose, as general law has become comprehensive. Its use is infrequent.

2. **Provisional Orders**

2.24   These are Orders employed to give legal authority for a special and limited activity, *e.g.* adjusting a harbour, or local authority boundaries, or arranging for joint local authority functions, perhaps for a regional art gallery or sports centre, in a boundary area. They are akin to Orders subject to special parliamentary procedure, both being within the same section of the Local Government Act 1972.[55] They are procedures used occasionally, for "special" occasions, and an example from the public leisure services relates to the disposal of land within a public park. By section 123 of the Act of 1972, only 250 square yards of such land could be disposed of and this special procedure was then necessary. (That particular stipulation has now been amended.) By the use of a Provisional Order a disposal of land in excess of that ceiling could be achieved, in special circumstances, which would have to satisfy Parliament. Nowadays, Orders subject to Special Parliamentary Procedure have largely superseded Provisional Orders. Section 240 of the 1972 Act covers these Orders also.

3. **By-Laws**

2.25   These have been mentioned above. They provide detailed powers of control in a limited area of legal activity. To that extent only, they enhance a local authority's powers. They are in regular use by all local authorities. A full discussion will be found in Chapter 4 in the context of public parks.

4. **Local Acts**

2.26   This form of local law is in decreasing use. There are good reasons for this situation:

(1) The scope for Local Acts has been greatly reduced because of the vast range of public and general Acts. In 1990, 32 were completed, relating to harbours, charities, problem properties, rapid transit systems, a lighthouse and a wavescreen to improve a marina. In 1991, 17 finished the Parliamentary course, relating to similar subjects but adding a bank, a life assurance company, a market and an express railway from Paddington to Heathrow.

(2) The Government, after the local government reorganisation of 1974, stimulated a close scrutiny of Local Acts, as part of the consolidation of the new authorities by amalgamating their Local Acts. This exercise was

---

[55] s.240, especially subs. (1)(*c*).

demanding and rigorous but worthwhile and necessary. It called for a certain amount of legal spring cleaning and when the exercise was complete, the calls for new Local Act powers were few.[56]

(3) A Local Act is still an expensive venture for a local authority and thus not embarked upon lightly.

Procedure

The essential procedure for obtaining a Local Act is contained in the **2.27** standing orders of each House of Parliament:

(1) A petition for the Bill is presented. This is supported by special resolutions of the authority passed before and after the deposit of the Bill.

(2) The procedure in Parliament then, as Erskine May says:

> "partakes of a judicial character. The persons who are applying for powers or benefits appear as suitors for the Bill, while those who apprehend injury are admitted as adverse parties in the suit. Many of the formalities of a court of justice are maintained . . . if the parties do not sustain the Bill in its progress, by following every regulation and form prescribed, it is not forwarded by the House in which it is pending."[57]

This is in a section headed: "Distinctive character of Private Bills."

(3) As an adjunct of this judicial character, private bills were subject for some time to a jurisdiction exercised in the Chancery Court, to restrain persons from petitioning for or against them.[58]

A full examination of the position of the courts in relation to private bills took place in the recent case of *British Railway Board* v. *Pickin*[59] and the House of Lords ultimately decided that Parliament, and not the courts, was responsible for rectifying any irregularity in procedure in relation to an Act passed by Parliament.[60]

(4) Even though this examination of Private Bills takes on a judicial atmosphere, with counsel and witnesses and cross-examination, the essential procedure corresponds to that for Public Bills. They have their First and Second Readings, and the important scrutiny takes place in Committee. Two committees are available, one when the Bill is opposed and the other when unopposed. The preamble and each clause of the Bill are

---

[56] Local Government Act 1972, s.262.

[57] *Parliamentary Practice* (20th ed.), p. 893.

[58] See this asserted as recently as 1942 in *Bilston Corporation* v. *Wolverhampton Corporation* [1942] 1 Ch. 391. Though the court there found Wolverhampton Corporation acting in breach of an agreement in opposing a Private Bill, the court declined to grant an injunction, as being outside its proper jurisdiction. The remedy lay with Parliament, said the court, not with the courts.

[59] [1974] 1 A.C. 765, where the House of Lords, overruling the Court of Appeal, held that the courts have no power to examine proceedings in parliament in order to see whether the passing of an Act had been obtained by means of an irregularity or fraud. This was followed by the important case on the Canada Act—*Manuel* v. *Att.-Gen.* [1982] Ch. 77.

[60] Erskine May, *ibid.* at p. 895.

considered, particularly in the light of any petitions also before Parliament, from interested pressure groups or formal objectors in the country.

The Bill is then reported to the House and given its Third Reading. Then the other House embarks upon the same procedure leading in due course to the Royal Assent. By convention between the two Houses, the major scrutiny takes place in the first House: this serves to share out the Private Bill work between the two Houses.[61]

(5) The general power to oppose or promote Private Bills, in the interests of the area in question, is now contained in section 239 of the Local Government Act 1972.

C. LAND TRANSACTIONS

2.28   The statutory provisions relating to the land transactions of local authorities are to be found in the Local Government Act 1972, as amended by the Local Government, Planning and Land Act 1980. Supplementary powers in connection with town and country planning are contained in Part IX of the Town and Country Planning Act 1990 (the 1990 Act).

1. **Acquisition**

2.29   Very wide powers to acquire land are given by the 1972 Act.[62] These powers for acquiring land inside or outside their areas are given to principal councils (local authorities other than parishes) for the purposes of any of their functions under the 1972 or any other Act and for the benefit, improvement or development of their areas. Land may be acquired in advance of requirements and until required for the purpose for which it was intended, the land may be used for any of the Council's functions.[63] Two or more Councils acting together can arrange for one of them to acquire land required for the joint project.[64]

2.30   Principal councils are empowered to acquire land compulsorily, with the approval of the Minister concerned with the function for which the land is required.[65] The power of acquisition by compulsory purchase exists where there is a power to acquire by agreement except in three cases, namely (i) where in any case the power to acquire land is limited to acquisition by agreement, (ii) purchases under the Local Authorities (Land) Act 1963 and (iii) where the land is to be acquired for the benefit, improvement or development of their area.[66] Two or more councils can act together through one of them being nominated for the purpose. The procedure to be followed in the compulsory purchase of land is prescribed by the Acquisition of Land Act 1981.[67]

---

[61] *Ibid.* especially Chap. 38.
[62] Part VII.
[63] s.120(2).
[64] s.120(4).
[65] s.121.
[66] s.121(2).
[67] s.121(4). A useful full treatment of compulsory purchase procedure is in the *Encyclopedia of Compulsory Purchase and Compensation* (Sweet and Maxwell).

The 1990 Act enables county, London Borough and district councils   **2.31**
and Joint Planning Boards (Peak Park Joint Planning Board and Lake
District Special Planning Board) to acquire compulsorily any land which
they require, for certain purposes[68]:

  (a) land in their area which is suitable for and is required in order to
      secure the carrying out of one or more of the following activities,
      namely development, re-development and improvement;

  (b) any land in their area which is required for a purpose which it is
      necessary to achieve in the interests of the proper planning of an
      area in which the land is situated.

In deciding what land is suitable for development, redevelopment or
improvement, account has to be taken of the provisions of the development plan, any planning permissions in force and any considerations
which would be material in dealing with a planning application.[69] The
power to acquire compulsorily extends to any adjoining land which is
required for facilitating the development of the former land and to any
land required for the purpose of being given in exchange for any common
land or open space required for development.[70]

The Secretary of State for the Environment has power under the 1990
Act to acquire compulsorily land "necessary for the public service."[71]
"Public service" is not defined and the power appears to have the widest
scope. Section 122 of the 1980 Act extends this power by authorising the
acquisition of other land which in the Minister's opinion should be
acquired in the interests of the proper planning of the area concerned, for
the better or most economic development of the other land, or for
exchange for common or open space land. "Public service" is to be construed as including activities of international bodies.

2. Appropriation

Land belonging to a principal council which is no longer required for the   **2.32**
purpose for which it is held, may be appropriated for any purpose for
which the council may acquire land by agreement and the appropriation
takes effect, subject to the rights of any person with an interest in the
land.[72] Land forming part of a common (for which a procedure is described under section 229 of the 1990 Act) may not be appropriated unless
its area does not exceed 250 square yards and a notice of the intention to
appropriate is advertised for two weeks in a local paper, after which the
council consider any objections to the proposed appropriation. In the case
of open space land, a similar procedure has to be followed and where the

---

[68] ss.226 and 244.
[69] s.226(2).
[70] s.226(3).
[71] s.228.
[72] L.G.A. 1972, s.112. Appropriation is the change of the legal purpose for which the land is
   held. It is effected by resolution of the council, and is, normally, subject to confirmation by
   a Government department. The Birmingham City Council Act 1991 is an instance of a
   local authority clearing its legal hurdles for an appropriation and disposal by a Local Act.

land appropriated is held for the purposes of section 164 of the Public Health Act 1875, or under section 10 of the Open Spaces Act 1906, the land ceases to be subject to the trusts which arise by reason of those statutory provisions.[73]

2.33 The appropriation of commons open space and fuel and field garden allotments, (other than green belt land within the meaning of the Green Belt (London and Home Counties) Act 1938), is dealt with under section 229 of the 1990 Act. The procedure requires the Order of the local authority, which is confirmed by the Secretary of State. The special provisions of the Acquisition of Land Act 1981, relating to the compulsory purchase of commons, are applied to Orders under section 229.

2.34 Land for the time being held for planning purposes, may be appropriated under section 232 of the 1990 Act. The consent of the Secretary of State is required for the appropriation of land which consists of a common, part of a common or which formerly consisted of a common or part thereof. The advertisement procedure of the Act has to be followed where the land in question consists of or forms part of an open space.

3. **Disposal**

2.35 Principal councils may dispose of land in any way they wish but unless the consent of the Secretary of State has been obtained or the disposal is by way of the grant of a lease not exceeding seven years or the assignment of a lease with not more than seven years to run, the authority must obtain the best consideration that can reasonably be obtained.[74] In the case of land which consists of, or forms part of, an open space, the advertisement procedure described above has to be followed and when the land is sold, any trusts which arise solely by reason of the statutory power under which the land was held, cease to be applicable.[75] Land held for planning purposes, which consists or forms part of an open space, is subject to the same constraints as to disposal as are described above in relation to land whose disposal is governed by the 1972 Act. The 1990 Act specifically authorises the disposal of planning land in such manner and subject to such conditions as appear to be expedient in order to secure the best use of that and other land or to secure the construction of buildings needed for the proper planning of the area.[76]

2.36 The phrase "for a consideration less than the best that can reasonably be obtained" does not necessarily mean the highest price that can be obtained.[77] Local authorities can often attain their purposes by arrangements with other persons and one particular means of achieving this

---

[73] Town and Country Planning Act 1990, s.229. See Chap. 4.
[74] Local Government Act 1972, s.123. For a case where a lease was *ultra vires* because for the veiled purpose of evicting caravans and not simply an open space lease, see *Costello* v. *Dacorum District Council* (1980) 79 L.G.R. 133.
[75] *Ibid.* This was the critical issue in *R.* v. *Doncaster Metropolitan Borough Council, ex p. Braim* [1987] 85 L.G.R. 233.
[76] s.233.
[77] Local Government Act 1972, s.123(2).

objective is by the sale or lease of land, subject to covenants requiring the execution of specified works or restricting the use to a specified one. The imposition of covenants of this nature can in themselves reduce the value of land, especially where the commercial prospects of a proposed venture are diminished and the land has to be valued subject to the restrictions on the use or the requirements imposed by the authority. It is a matter of policy for the authority to determine whether such a course of action is justified in the particular circumstances. Statutory recognition of this principle is given in the case of the disposal of land which has been acquired or appropriated for planning purposes involving the development, redevelopment or improvement of an area.[78] Land may be disposed of to its former owners living in the area or carrying on businesses there, who wish to return there on terms which reflect the price at which the land had been acquired from them.[79]

Parish councils

The provisions of the 1972 Act are applied to parish and community **2.37** councils with certain adaptations which allow for their relationship with the district councils covering their areas, and their different constitutional position.[80] Their powers of acquisition by agreement parallel those of principal councils, but in the case of compulsory purchase, a special procedure is provided involving the intervention of the district council which, if the proposal is approved by the Secretary of State, carries into effect the provisions of the order.[81] A particular feature of the procedure is the need to give consideration to the land holdings of certain owners and to the avoidance, so far as possible, of taking an undue or inconvenient quantity of land from any one owner. The powers of appropriation and disposal by a parish or community council closely follow those applicable to principal councils under the 1972 codes, including the requirements relating to commons and open spaces.[82]

Church land and burial grounds

Most useful powers which enable consecrated land and burial grounds **2.38** to be developed or used for other purposes are contained in sections 238 and 239 of the 1990 Act, which apply to purchases by a Minister, local authority or statutory undertaker. For the purposes of the sections "land" includes a building. The sections apply to land acquired under Part IX of the 1990 Act or compulsorily under any Act and to land appropriated by a local authority for planning purposes. Or, for completeness to acquisitions under another of the quartet of 1990 Planning Acts: the Planning (Listed Buildings and Conservation Areas) Act 1990, Part I Chapter V. In the

---

[78] Town and Country Planning Act 1990, s.233.
[79] The so called Crichel Downs rules, from the case which established the principle currently set out in DOE Circular 18/84.
[80] Local Government Act 1972, s.125.
[81] *Ibid.* s.125(5).
[82] *Ibid.* s.126

case of burial grounds, (defined as including any churchyard of consecrated land or land, including buildings, used for religious worship or a cemetery or other ground, whether consecrated or not, which has at any time been set apart for the purposes of interment) the powers do not have effect in respect of land which has been used for burial of the dead, until the prescribed requirements relating to the removal and reinterment of human remains and the disposal of monuments have been complied with. This means obtaining the faculty of the bishop of the diocese, in respect of consecrated ground or a licence of the Home Secretary under the Burial Act 1857 in other instances.[83] Subject to the procedural requirements of the section and the Regulations made thereunder, the land acquired may be used by a Minister in any manner by him or on his behalf, for any purpose for which he acquired it. In the case of purchase by any other body under the section, the land may be used in accordance with planning permission.

Commons and open spaces

2.39   A similar power is contained in section 241 of the 1990 Act enabling land consisting of or forming part of a common, open space, or fuel or field garden allotment to be used by a Minister or another person on his behalf for any purpose for which the land was acquired or by a local authority or statutory undertaker in accordance with planning permission. As mentioned above, the power applies to land which has been acquired under Part VI of the 1971 Act or compulsorily under any other Act, or which has been appropriated for planning purposes. This provision avoids any difficulty which might otherwise arise in the use of commons or open space which are subject to strict limitations in their use.

Reference was made in the previous Chapter to the powers of local and other authorities to make land available for use by other persons. Apart from outright disposal, as described earlier in this Chapter, the choice in making land available for use by others is by licence or by lease.

Licences

2.40   A licence constitutes the permission of the owner or occupier of land to another person to enter the land. A licence is granted for the personal benefit of the person or group of persons intended to enter the land, as opposed to a lease, the effect of which is to create an interest in the land, giving a right of possession to the lessee to the exclusion of the person granting it (the lessor). Licences should normally be the vehicle for granting the use of land or buildings where the use is of a transient kind or for a limited period. Examples are:

    (a) the hire of a hall for a few days for a flower show or concert,

    (b) a seasonal franchise to sell refreshments in a theatre or park;

---

[83] Town and Country Planning Act 1990, s.239(2). See the Town & Country Planning (Churches, Places of Religious Worship and Burial Grounds) Regulations 1950, S.I. 1950 No. 792.

(c) the use of a sports facility (bowls, tennis, football) on a seasonal basis or for one day per week;

(d) an agreement to place boats on a boating lake or on a canal;

(e) stationing an ice-cream kiosk or van on the foreshore or at a picnic site or in a country park.

Licences of these types are normally incorporated in agreements which **2.41** contain relevant conditions in respect of usage, provision for termination at a specified date or on notice being given, safety of the public or users, restrictions on works having an effect on the land or building, indemnity for damage to land and building or injury to third parties, avoidance of nuisance, and compliance with any licensing requirements. Because licences are matters of agreement between the parties, there is no limitation on their content: it is for the parties to agree on the relevant terms. The grant of a licence may follow an advertisement seeking tenders for the operation of a facility and the licence will normally embody the advertised terms which are central to the agreement.

Leases

Whilst licences have the advantage of flexibility, leases tend to be more **2.42** formal in structure and are subject to the applicability of a number of statutes. Contravention of any term of a licence can usually be remedied quickly or the licence can be terminated in the more serious cases. Any contravention of a covenant in a lease (with limited exceptions) will normally require the service of a formal notice on the lessee, who may have the right to serve a counter notice resulting in the intervention of a court, which can be a costly and lengthy process.

The grant of a lease for premises or land, which the tenant occupies for the purpose of a business carried on by him, is subject to the provisions of Part II of the Landlord and Tenant Act 1954. This has been considered in the last Chapter.

D. OPEN SPACE

1. **Introduction**

The Open Spaces Act 1906 (the Act of 1906) is the statutory foundation of **2.43** a group of powers and duties of local authorities. The Act of 1906 provided a badly needed code of law, which allowed open space land, as it was called, to be taken into the ownership of municipal and other councils and maintained for the benefit of the community. This class of land supplemented the parks, which were usually fenced.

Previously, customary rights over open areas of land were only for the benefit of limited groups, such as "the inhabitants of the village of Ambridge," and not for the use of the public at large. Again, when a donor wished to ensure that his bequest of open space land was kept by a local authority for that ongoing use, he was able, by use of the Act of 1906, to escape from the restraints of the conveyancer's obstacle race, the Perpetuities Rule[84]; for a local authority, in 1906 at least, did not perish. Finally, a benefit of the Act of 1906 was the by-law making power. This helped to control nuisances and other unsocial conduct on the public open spaces.

2.44   It is true that, in the more affluent areas, houses were often built round squares, which were laid out as gardens for the benefit of the house owners. Unfortunately, as time passed, many of these areas became neglected, as interest in their upkeep waned or its cost became prohibitive. The Town Gardens Protection Act 1863, which is still in force, enabled local authorities to take remedial action in that situation. They could vest the garden land in management committees of the local residents or, ultimately, in themselves. By-laws could then be made to regulate these areas and penalties were available as a sanction against those who caused damage.

2. The Open Spaces Act 1906

2.45   It was the Open Spaces Act 1906, however, which marked a major advance in dealing with an issue much wider than town squares. The Act of 1906 defined "Open Space" as:

> "Any land, whether enclosed or not, on which there are not buildings or of which not more than one twentieth part is covered with buildings and the remainder of which is laid out as a garden or is used for purposes of recreation or lies waste and unoccupied."[85]

The powers in that Act are available to all local authorities,[86] including the new Broads Authority and the London Boroughs and to those powers we now turn. It will be convenient to consider them in relation to the acquisition of land, and the powers of management.

(1) *Acquisition*

2.46   A group of powers enables open spaces to be transferred to local authorities by various classes of trustees:

Statutory trustees

Trustees holding open space land under statutory[87] trusts with a view to its preservation as a garden, or some other open space, are empowered, with the consent of the occupiers of any houses fronting to the open space, or who are liable to be rated for its upkeep, to convey the land, with or

---

[84] This restricts the period during which the destiny of land can be controlled by will to the sum of 21 years plus the number of years actually lived by a selected living person.

[85] s.20.

[86] Open Spaces Act 1906 does not apply to the Royal Parks, Crown land, land owned by the Duchy of Lancaster, metropolitan commons, land belonging to the Societies of the Inner and Middle Temple, gardens managed by the Secretary of State for the Environment, or lands managed under the Crown Estate Act 1961, s.19.

[87] *Ibid.* s.2.

without consideration, to the local authority. Alternatively, they can transfer the right of management to the authority; again, they can make an agreement with the authority to open up the land to the public; a fourth option is to grant a lease or a lesser right to the local authority; lastly, they may themselves open up the land to persons not entitled to its use under the terms of their own holding statute. If the freehold of the land, or the greater part of the houses about the space, is held by the same person, his consent must be obtained. Any purchase money is to be held by the trustees for the benefit of the persons originally intended to benefit from the use of the open space.

Non-statutory trustees

Where land is held by trustees not appointed by statute, for the purpose **2.47** of public recreation, they may transfer it to the local authority or grant a lease of it to the local authority, which will then hold it subject to the same trusts, unless they should be legally varied by a scheme which has been approved by the procedure set out in the Act.[88]

Charitable trusts

Land held by trustees other than those described above, for any chari- **2.48** table purpose as an open space, may be conveyed or leased to the local authority, subject to such conditions as may be agreed. The Charity Commissioners and High Court or County Court might well be involved in the approvals needed for such a transfer and the details of such authorisations are described in the Act of 1906.[89]

Open space with adjoining houses

Where the right to use open space is limited to the owners or occupiers **2.49** of houses round or near the open space, the owner of the freehold in the open space may, with the consent, expressed in special resolution of those owners and occupiers, convey or lease the land to the local authority in trust for the enjoyment of the public. Alternatively, he can make an agreement with the authority to open up the land for use by the public, under the management of the local authority. If that is done then the freeholder is discharged from his obligations to those persons originally entitled to the rights of user.[90]

Sales by groups

Sections 7 and 8 of the Act of 1906 authorise groups of persons or indi- **2.50** viduals to sell land to local authorities, in order to enable it to be preserved as open space.

---

[88] Open Spaces Act 1906, s.3.
[89] *Ibid.* s.4. The court is the High Court or County Court.
[90] *Ibid.* s.5. Two meetings are needed, with a two-thirds majority for the resolution at each one.

In these ways the old difficulties were overcome and wide use, enduring and effective control were achieved, so that open spaces could be provided for everyone to enjoy.

(2) *Management of Open Space*

2.51   Having acquired the open space from the trustees, or a disused burial ground from the ecclesiastical authority,[91] the local authority has a clear, if broad, duty laid down in the Act of 1906 for keeping the land as "open space":

  (a) It is to be held in trust to allow, and with a view to, the enjoyment thereof by the public, as an open space and under proper control and regulation and for no other purpose.
  (b) It is to be kept in a good and decent state.
  (c) The authority may spend money on drainage, levelling the land, railings, plants, lights, ornaments, seats and improvements.[92]

By-laws

2.52   One of the principal powers given by the Act of 1906 is to allow local authorities, subject to the usual confirmation at the level of Government, to make by-laws, under section 15, to regulate the use of open spaces, ensure the maintenance of order and the prevention of nuisances, the removal of persons offending against the by-laws and finally, fixing the days and times of admission. Since these regulatory powers are similar to those normally used in relation to public parks and pleasure grounds provided under the Public Health Act 1875, it is not unusual for a common set of by-laws to be in force within a local authority's area for these two sorts of open space for the public. The same type of by-laws may also be made by the trustees or other owners of land to which the public have been given access under the earlier provisions of the Act of 1906 or under the Town Gardens Protection Act 1863.

3. **Other Acts**

(1) *Open Space on Housing Estates*

2.53   Recreation grounds are often provided by housing authorities on their larger housing estates. Power to make this provision is contained in the Housing Act 1985.[93] This is one of the "ancillary facilities" which the Secretary of State may approve in conjunction with housing projects; it may also be the subject of a direction by the Secretary of State, when consider-

---

[91] For local authority powers to hold on trust a disused burial ground for enjoyment by the public as an open space, see the Act of 1906, s.10.
[92] Open Spaces Act 1906, s.10.
[93] s.12 and see *Dunton* v. *Dover District Council* (1978) 76 L.G.R. 87.

ing such a project, that other statutory powers, appropriate to the facilities in question, should be used.

A specific power to make by-laws for such lands is now available.[94]

(2) *Open Space Land of Local Education Authorities*

Local education authorities are required, under the Education Act 1944, **2.54** to provide adequate facilities for recreation for pupils in their schools.[95]

Large areas of land have, in consequence, been acquired and laid out as school playing fields. These lands are often heavily used by the pupils and many local education authorities have been reluctant to see sports clubs and the general public add to the wear and tear suffered by the playing fields.

The arguments for and against such dual use have been well rehearsed over the years and the outcome turns on policy, rather than law.

The legally flexible ways for the discharge of a local authority's functions, introduced by section 101 of the Local Government Act 1972, permit a variety of ways to achieve co-operation between their interested departments.[96]

Some local education authorities, in permitting (or taking no steps to **2.55** prevent) the casual use of school playing fields, have found it difficult to establish a basis for regulating such use and indeed bringing it to an end, if that is desired. The employment of playing field wardens is expensive and the civil remedy of proceedings for trespass both heavy handed and ultimately ineffectual. There are problems of identifying the persons playing the games and the award of damages or even an injunction does not solve the real problem. The answer attempted in some local Acts, promoted during the consolidation of local legislation enjoined under the Local Government Act 1972, section 262,[97] has been to make it an offence to play games on school playing fields, when a notice prohibiting such use is displayed. Such notices need not be continuously displayed: they can be used in the above way from time to time and area to area, as a form of regulation dependent on the condition of the various playing fields.[98]

(3) *Open Space under the Town and Country Planning Acts*

Extensive powers of land acquisition are given to local authorities by the **2.56** Town and Country Planning Acts. These were noted earlier in this Chapter. These powers include one to purchase land required as exchange land for any part of a common, open space or field garden which is being acquired. The current series of Town and Country Planning Acts gives

---

[94] *Ibid.* s.23.

[95] s.53. These are "leisure-time facilities" within the Education (No. 2) Act 1986, s.50.

[96] The four methods set out in s.101 are discharged by a committee, by a sub-committee, by an officer or by another local authority.

[97] These joint authority Local Act promotions in metropolitan areas obliged each authority to consider which powers were of vital interest in the post-1974 regime.

[98] An instance is the Greater Manchester Act 1981, s.163.

considerable scope to local authorities to create open space land in urban areas as part of redevelopment schemes and elsewhere. Specific powers are now available to local authorities to establish country parks under the Countryside Act 1968[99] but even without going to that stage, local authorities can use their powers under these Acts to good advantage by acquiring and improving open land in their areas, clearing unsightly land, restoring derelict land and reclaiming waste or polluted land.

The final reference must be to the areas of open space which probably have the greatest popularity—the foreshore round our coasts. This particular subject is dealt with in Chapter 7.

E. Commons

1. Introduction

2.57   The creation of larger local government units by the Local Government Act 1972 brought commons from the purview of rural and county authorities into the management of district and urban councils. Furthermore, the pace engendered by the registration and thus the rationalisation of commons, under the Commons Registration Act 1965, has stimulated interest in and clarification of the legal problems associated with them. It is not surprising that volumes of collected law reports in recent years regularly include some on this subject.

It has to be admitted that the law relating to commons and the town and village greens, with which they are usually associated, is complex and it is not the purpose of this book to expound it in detail.[1] However, in order to understand the current position, it is desirable to give some historical background of the law relating to commons, their enclosure over the years and ultimately the rights now enjoyed by the public.

2. Historical

2.58   The nature and extent of the rights of villagers over common land can best be understood by reference to social history.[2] After many years in which the existence of much common land was an accepted part of the manorial

---

[99] See Chapter 8.

[1] Commons were originally for cropping grazing and turfing. The classic rights are pasture, turf (turbary), timber (estovers), beechmast and acorns for pigs (pannage) and fishing (piscary). Village greens, on the other hand, were for recreation. The two uses have in many areas dovetailed. Recreation as a desirable usage of commons is mentioned in the Commons Act 1876, s.7. The modern reader will think of "commons" as *areas of land* for the use of commoners and the public. In earlier days, commons were the *rights* over common land. The specialist book, *The Law Relating to Common Land* by B. Harris and G. Ryan (1967, Sweet and Maxwell) uses "common land" consistently but Parliament—the Commons Registration Act 1965—and law report editors stay with "commons" as both land and rights.

[2] G. M. Trevelyan, *English Social History* is a useful starting point.

system of land holding, improved agricultural methods in the seventeenth and eighteenth centuries led to an increasing speed of enclosing common land. No less than 4,000 Inclosure Acts were passed in the century before the general Inclosure Act of 1836.[3] The agricultural revolution saw many commons converted into rectangular fields, where scientific rotation of crops could be practised.

The extinguishment of common rights was possible by agreement with **2.59** the lord of the manor and those persons entitled to exercise rights of common. This was difficult because agreement had to be reached between many parties.

The lord of the manor could also exercise rights of approvement to terminate commons rights.[4] This meant taking superfluous manorial waste into his possession and use, leaving unenclosed sufficient common land for the owners of the common rights. In many cases the lord of the manor was able in this way to extinguish common rights physically, without agreement from those entitled to exercise rights of common.

However, the principal means of extinguishing common rights for a **2.60** lengthy period of time was by the use of Inclosure Acts. The Acts tended to be in common form and after the Inclosure Act 1845, a code of these clauses normally used was approved and this facilitated inclosures without the need for full individual statutes. That Act of 1845 generally made all land which was the subject of rights of common, available for inclosure; but whilst that Act remains the regulatory Act on the subject of inclosures, the procedure it lays down is nowadays regarded as obsolete.[5]

The pressure on commons is further evidenced by the practice of Inclosure Commissioners, when making their awards, in diverting land from its agricultural use to that of recreation for the local inhabitants, or public purposes such as roads or schools, individuals such as churchwardens or overseers and some land for field gardens for the labouring classes. Later in the nineteenth century, additional protection was afforded to commoners, particularly by the Inclosure Acts of 1852 and 1857. A range of offences was also created in relation to town and village greens, such as wilful damage to their fencing, driving animals onto the green or interfering with the enjoyment of people using the greens.

The metropolis

The first effective legal move to protect commons was taken in the **2.61** metropolitan police district, by the Metropolitan Commons Act 1866. As strengthened by later Acts in 1878 and 1893, the Act of 1866 effectively prevented any further inclosure of metropolitan commons. The first of those three Acts made it obligatory to obtain the consent of the Secretary

---

[3] *Halsbury's Statutes* (3rd ed.) Vol. 3, p. 679.

[4] *Nicholls* v. *Mitford* [1882] 20 Ch.D. 380 illuminates this practice.

[5] G. M. Trevelyan (*supra*) identifies the decade 1865–1875 as the time when this practice was halted. He ascribes it less to protests by commoners than to agitation, eventually via the Commons Preservation Society, by town dwellers who were loathe to lose these opportunities for air and exercise.

of the State for the Environment (to substitute the present ministerial counterpart) before either inclosures or approvements could be lawful.[6]

The Commons Act 1876

2.62   The Commons Act 1876, which marked the turning point in public attitudes to commons outside London, made provision for the regulation, inclosure and improvements of commons. The Act is still in force and the Secretary of State for the Environment exercises the powers it conferred upon the Inclosure Commissioners. He is required, in considering the expediency of any application for inclosure, to take into account the question whether the inclosure would be for the benefit of the neighbourhood. He is also empowered to include in any Order under the Act requirements about free access, reservation of recreation areas, safeguarding of trees or historical objects, the provision of roads, footpaths and bridleways and indeed any other matters deemed to be of advantage to the neighbourhood. It will be evident that this marked a significant break with earlier legislation.[7]

This policy guidance is supplemented in the Act of 1876 by detailed procedural conditions to be met before a Provisional Inclosure Order reached its final stage.[8] A Provisional Order under the Act of 1876 required the approval of Parliament and had no validity until the appropriate procedure had been completed.[9]

An interesting protection afforded to town and village greens by this Act was the section which said that any erection thereon or disturbance or interference with the land, otherwise than with a view to the improvement of the town or village green or recreation ground, was to be deemed a public nuisance.[10]

The Commons Act 1899

2.63   The Commons Act 1899 marked a further step towards the present position. It enables district councils to make Schemes and Provisional Orders for the regulation and management of commons in their area with a view to expenditure on the drainage, levelling and improvement of the common.[11] It also empowers those councils to make by-laws and regulations for the prevention of nuisances and preservation of order on the common.

After due public notice, deposit for inspection of the draft Scheme and consideration of objections made in a three month period, the Council may decide to make the Scheme. The need for ministerial approval was dispensed with by the Local Government, Planning and Land Act 1980.[12]

Having made the Scheme, the Council becomes responsible for the

---

[6] See Law of Commons Amendment Act 1893, s.2: "not valid unless . . . with the consent of the Board of Agriculture."
[7] Commons Act 1876, s.7.
[8] *Ibid.* ss.10 and 12.
[9] *Ibid.* s.12.
[10] *Ibid.* s.29.
[11] Commons Act 1899, s.1.
[12] ss.1 and 3 and Schedule 34.

management of the common. They can make by-laws[13] and take a contribution towards the costs of management from any neighbouring Council whose inhabitants benefit from the Scheme.[14]

An indication of the contents of a Scheme of Management under the **2.64** Act of 1899 is illuminating.[15] It has to cover the following:

(a) Any works of drainage, fencing, treeplanting, providing seats and otherwise improving the common as a place for exercise and recreation.

(b) Except as provided by the Scheme, the authority are forbidden to alter the natural features of the common or interfere with free access to any part thereof.

(c) In particular the authority are prevented from erecting any buildings or similar erections on the common without the consent of the landowner.

(d) The authority must deal with all problems associated with the prevention of trespass and the making of encroachments.

(e) A statement must be published of the rights of the local inhabitants to free access to all parts of the common and the privilege of playing games and enjoying other kinds of recreation thereon, subject to by-laws made by the Council.

(f) Any features on the common requiring preservation.

(g) The maintenance and construction of any paths or roads over the common.

(h) The provision of parking places on the common and making charges for parking.

(i) A statement about the purpose of by-laws is to be made by the Council. The by-laws would aim to prevent conduct or behaviour which interfered with the rights of enjoyment of the common by the public.

(j) Finally, the Scheme is to provide for protecting the rights of the landowner or any rights over or under the common for game, mines and minerals. The Scheme must not adversely affect the commoners' rights nor the lawful use of any highway over the common.

Definitions

All the powers in relation to commons considered above may give the **2.65** impression that it is easy to define common land. The two definitions now appended are taken from the last major Act of Parliament on this subject, the Commons Regulations Act 1965. They indicate how in this area of the law, definitions are built out of history:

---

[13] Commons Act 1899, s.10.

[14] *Ibid.* s.12.

[15] Local authorities are required in the Commons (Schemes) Regulations 1982 (S.I. 1982 No. 209) to ensure, when laying out games areas, that they are not so near any dwelling houses or road that they will create a nuisance or be an annoyance to the inhabitants of the houses or to persons using the road.

"**22.**—(1) In this Act, unless the context otherwise requires,—
"common land" means—
    (*a*) land subject to rights of common, (as defined in this Act)
    whether those rights are exercisable at all times or only during
    limited periods;
    (*b*) waste land of a manor not subject to rights of common; but
does not include a town or village green or land which forms part of
a highway; [. . .]
"town or village green" means land which has been allotted by or under
any Act for the exercise or recreation of the inhabitants of any locality
or on which the inhabitants of any locality have a customary right to
indulge in lawful sports and pastimes or on which the inhabitants of any
locality have indulged in such sports and pastimes as of right for not less
than twenty years."[16]

The Commons Registration Act 1965

2.66   The Act of 1965 requires the registration of common land, rights of
common and town and village greens in registers maintained by county
councils, metropolitan district councils, London Borough Councils and
the Common Council as registration authorities.

Two separate registers are kept, one being for common land and the
other for town and village greens.[17]

Periods for provisional registration of commons and greens are prescribed[18] and at the end of those periods, no land capable of being registered shall be common land or a town or village green, unless duly
registered and likewise, no rights of common shall be exercised over such
land unless those rights are duly registered under the Act of 1965 or, in
this instance, under the Land Registration Acts.[19]

2.67   When objections to provisional registration are resolved and registra-
tions are final, then if no person is duly registered as owner, the registration authority must refer the issue to the Commons Commissioner, unless
the land is registered under the Land Registration Acts. If the owner is
known or can be found, the land will be vested in him. If the land is town
or village green, with an unknown owner, the appropriate local authority
becomes the effective owner and can exercise powers of management
under the Open Spaces Act 1906.[20] Where the land is unclaimed common
land, again, local authorities are empowered to take steps to protect it.

2.68   The final registration of the land and the rights, as described above, is

---

[16] s.22. A decision of the Commons Commissioner was obtained that land acquired under
the Public Health Act 1975, s.164, for "pleasure grounds" was not "allotted for exercise
and recreation" under s.22. "Acquiring was not apt for 'allotting'," he said, *Re The Downs,
Herne Bay Kent* (Ref 219D/2) [1980] C.L.Y. 246.
[17] Commons Registration Act 1965, ss.1, 2 and 3.
[18] *Ibid.* s.1.
[19] Law of Property Act 1925, s.189(2).
[20] Commons Registration Act 1965, provides for ultimate vesting in the local authority, if no
owner is apparent to the Commissioner: s.8.

conclusive evidence of the matters so registered.[21] There is provision for due amendment of the two registers on change of circumstances.[22] Further, the High Court has a residual power to rectify the registers.[23]

The Act does not apply to the New Forest, Epping Forest or the Forest **2.69** of Dean or where it is exempted by Order of the Minister.[24] This power of the Minister is circumscribed. It is not to be exercised unless the land is regulated by a Scheme under the Commons Act 1899, or by the Metropolitan Commons Acts, or by a Local Act or by an Order made under the Commons Act 1876 and, in each case, no rights of common have been exercised there for at least 30 years and the landowner is known. (The Act allows for certain interruptions in that period of prescription, as it is called, and these can be ignored, *e.g.* where the land was requisitioned or where the land could not be used by those with rights due to steps taken in connection with animal health.)[25]

3. **Public Rights Over Commons**

Members of the public have the right of access for air and exercise to any **2.70** land which is a metropolitan common or is manorial waste[26] or a common which is wholly or partly situated in an area which, immediately before the major local government reorganisation at April 1, 1974, was a borough or an urban district. Lastly, the rights of access apply to land which on January 1, 1926, was subject to rights of common. It is a section of the Law of Property Act 1925 which confers these important rights of access and that section has to be formally applied to the last mentioned class of land by the deposit with the Minister of a deed to that effect, given by the lord of the manor or some other owner of that land over which the rights of common have been exercised.[27]

The above rights are subject to four qualifications: **2.71**
 (a) The provisions of any Act, Scheme, Provisional Order, By-law, Regulation or Order made under statutory authority.
 (b) Any conditions affecting access imposed by the Minister to prevent the land being injuriously affected, particularly in relation to any object of historical interest or other rights over that land.[28]
 (c) The rights do not include the right to draw or drive any carriage, cart, caravan, truck or other vehicle over the common or to camp there or to light a fire.
 (d) Those rights terminate if (i) the common rights are extinguished

[21] Commons Registration Act 1965, s.7. An objection to the registration of common land puts in issue its validity as a whole. When the Commons Commissioner has the issue referred to him, he should make the person who made the registration prove its validity: *Re Sutton Common, Wimborne* [1982] 1 W.L.R. 647.
[22] Act of 1965, s.13.
[23] *Ibid.* s.14.
[24] *Ibid.* s.11.
[25] *Ibid.* s.16.
[26] That part of the manor subject to the tenants' rights of common.
[27] Law of Property Act 1925, s.193.
[28] *Ibid.* s.193(1)(*b*).

under any statutory provision or (ii) if any land is excluded from public access by resolution of the local authority managing it, and that resolution is duly confirmed by the Minister.

2.72   The existence of public rights over commons does not affect the legal rights of any persons to win and remove mines and minerals.

These Law of Property Act rights of access do not apply if commons are being held for military purposes and the rights of common have been extinguished or otherwise cannot be exercised.[29]

Building on commons

The Law of Property Act 1925 also prohibits the erection of any building or fence whereby access to the commons is prevented or impeded, unless the consent of the Minister is obtained.[30] An exemption from this provision is granted for works carried out under the authority of an Act of Parliament or an Order having the force of an Act or in relation to the working of minerals or the placing of a telegraphic line.

Custom

2.73   The right of the public to use town and village greens was examined by the Court of Appeal in *New Windsor Corporation* v. *Mellor*.[31] The land in that case was owned by the local authority and had been registered in the register of town and village greens under the Commons Registration Act 1965. This was done on the basis of enjoyment of customary rights to indulge in lawful sports and pastimes on the site from the middle of the seventeenth century. From time to time, the land had become neglected but groups of inhabitants, including one known as the "Bachelors of Windsor," had joined together to improve it, so that it could be enjoyed by all local inhabitants. Attempts had been made a hundred years before to inclose the land but these had been successfully resisted by the inhabitants. The last local authority before 1964 had let the land for pasture, subject to the rights of "the Bachelors of Windsor who are entitled to use the land for all lawful recreations and amusements." Many other attempts over the years to use or sell the land had shown determination by local inhabitants to retain the rights quoted above. It was when the position as thus set out was affirmed by a Commons Commissioner, after registration under the Commons Registration Act 1965, that the local authority took the opportunity to test the matter in an appeal to the Court of Appeal. The legal ground taken by the local authority was that, in the light of earlier cases, the customary right was not lawful. It was not enjoyed by the residents of a specific locality. Being either for the Bachelors of Windsor or the inhabitants at large, it did not subsist for the inhabitants of a specific locality.

In its judgment the court said that Parliament was presumed to have intended that all registered greens should be available for sports and pas-

---

[29] Law of Property Act 1925, s.193(5).
[30] *Ibid.* s.194. The same restraint applies if "other work" will have the same effect.
[31] [1975] 3 All E.R. 44.

times for the local inhabitants and that all commons should be opened to the public, subject to the rights of the commoners. The decision was to uphold the registration by the Commons Commissioner of the land as a green; the court found that the right in question had been enjoyed for 300 years.

The foreshore

Difficulties in the definitions of commons and town and village greens, **2.74** have arisen where claims have been made for the registration of parts of the foreshore as commons or greens. (Rights over the foreshore are discussed in Chapter 7.) Sometimes the right to registration has been claimed on the basis of alleged public rights to fish or to collect wood. Rights of common have then to be distinguished from public rights at common law, which do include the rights of fishing and navigating in tidal waters.[32] In short, the legal position is that where the foreshore is owned by the Crown, the Crown Estate Office dispute the possibility of its being waste of the manor. Where the foreshore has been disposed of to a local authority or private owner, the position will fall to be determined by the terms of the conveyance or lease.

4. Caravan Sites and Commons

Finally there are two modern statutory provisions relating to commons **2.75** which should be noted.

The Caravan Sites and Control of Development Act 1960 contains a code for the regulation of caravan sites.[33] Under the Act, a District Council may make an Order which prohibits, either absolutely or subject to the terms of the Order, the stationing of caravans on common land for the purposes of human habitation. Contravention of the Order is punishable by fine. The making of exceptions to the Order does not in itself give a right as against the landowner to station caravans on the common.

The second and rather more important provision in recent years is in **2.76** the Countryside Act 1968.[34] Certain authorities are given powers to provide or improve opportunities for the enjoyment of the countryside and in the interests of people resorting to the common land. These include facilities for meals and refreshments, parking places, shelters and public conveniences. However, accommodation and refreshments are only to be provided by the authorities to the extent that existing facilities are inadequate.

To the extent also that the local authorities require land as sites for some of these facilities, they may be authorised by the Minister to acquire land and this can include parts of the common. If the common land should thus be needed, the authority will normally be expected to give

---

[32] See *Goodman* v. *Saltash Corporation* (1882) 7 App.Cas. 633. For a recent case see *Baxendale* v. *Instow Parish Church* [1982] Ch. 14.
[33] s.23 has certain exclusions, which need to be studied.
[34] s.9.

equal land by way of exchange; the Minister again may decide that in special circumstances this is not necessary.

The exercise of these powers by local authorities is not to be prevented by reason of general restrictions applying to common land or restrictions affecting particular land or by any trusts affecting common land.

It will be recalled that the acquisition, appropriation and disposal of land subject to common rights is subject to special rules, which were considered earlier in this chapter.[35]

[35] Para. 2.29.

CHAPTER 3

LIBRARIES AND MUSEUMS

"To a man possessed of the higher imaginative powers, the objection to legal studies is the amount of detail which they involve . . . Still it is a great pursuit"

(Mr. W. Micawber, *David Copperfield*, Chapter 39).

INTRODUCTION

If parks and recreation grounds are the oldest form of public leisure ser- **3.01** vice provided in this country, then libraries and museums must be ranked second. The first general Act was passed in 1850, though there were earlier local Acts. The Public Libraries Act 1850 was described in the preamble as being "for the Instruction and Recreation of the people," and it authorised the collection, though not the purchase, of books and maps and, in addition, specimens of art and science. This was so that both public libraries and public museums of art and science might be established.[1] The Act was adoptive in municipal boroughs having a population of more than 10,000. The money to be devoted to this new public service was not to be greater than the product of a halfpenny rate, though power to borrow moneys with Treasury consent was also contained in the Act.

From such tentative beginnings arose the present libraries and **3.02** museums services of this country. It is true that the expression "lending library" does not appear in a statute until the Public Libraries Consolidation (Scotland) Act 1887[2] but the principle of a collection of books in a library, to which public admission was obliged to be free, was established in the Act of 1850.

It will be convenient to consider libraries and museums law separately, and to turn first to libraries.

---

[1] There had first been parliamentary authority to set up public museums in the Museums Act 1845, which was consolidated and repealed by the Libraries Act 1850.

[2] It seems that three authorities, Canterbury, Salford and Warrington, were beginning to operate libraries under the Museums Act 1845. Mr R. J. B. Morris, in his perceptive study *Parliament and the Public Libraries* (1977), p. 18, offers the view that the three authorities took advantage of ambiguities in the scope of the terms of the Museums Act 1845 to establish combined museums and libraries and so made the Act of 1845 "a Libraries Act of a sort."

A. Libraries

1. Library Provision and Management

(1) *The Public Libraries and Museums Act 1964*

3.03 The Public Libraries and Museums Act 1964 now contains the basic law about this subject. It can be conveniently summarised as follows:—

(1) The Lord President of the Council is responsible for superintending and promoting the improvement of the public library service provided by local authorities in England. In Wales that duty rests on the Secretary of State for Wales.[3]

(2) The Library Advisory Councils, one for England and one for Wales, act under the above Minister to advise him.[4]

(3) The whole of England and Wales is divided into library region areas. A council is established for each such area and it operates under a Scheme made by the Lord President.[5] The primary duty of a council is to encourage co-operation between library authorities.

(4) The library service to the public is provided by library authorities who are, in England, non-metropolitan county councils, London borough councils and the City of London Common Council and metropolitan district councils.[6] In Wales it is the county and district councils who are the library authorities. These authorities operate under a duty set out in the Act of 1964, to "provide a comprehensive and efficient library service for all persons desiring to make use thereof and for that purpose to employ such officers, to provide and maintain such buildings and equipment, and such books and other materials, and to do such other things, as may be requisite."[7]

(5) This duty extends only to residents in the area of the library authority and persons undergoing full-time education in that area.[8]

3.04 (6) The general duty is then made specific in three fields:

(i) There should be sufficient books, pictures, films, gramophone

---

[3] Public Libraries and Museums Act 1964 designated the Secretary of State for Education and Science as the responsibile Minister. After a period when the Chancellor of the Duchy of Lancaster assumed these duties, they were passed to the Lord President by the Transfer of Functions (Arts Libraries and National Heritage) Order 1986 (S.I. 1986 No. 600). Functions about contributions and grants continue to be exercised jointly by the Education & Science Department and the Lord President. The Lord President also retains a duty for the Library Advisory Council in Wales.

[4] Public Libraries and Museums Act 1964, s.2.

[5] *Ibid.* s.3.

[6] *Ibid.* s.4 and Local Government Act 1972, ss.206 and 207.

[7] *Ibid.* s.7. Now that gramophone records have become an integral part of the library service, it is no longer necessary to show the fine ingenuity of counsel in a pre-1964 opinion. Basing himself on the Public Libraries Act 1892, which allowed collections of "specimens of art and science," he argued "As music is both a science and an art and a gramophone record is undoubtedly a specimen of music, the Council have power under s.15(1) of the Act of 1892 to form a lending library of gramophone records"!

[8] *Ibid.* s.7 (proviso). *Att.-Gen.* v. *The Observer* [1988] 1 All E.R. 385 contains recent interesting discussion on the extent of this duty. At the least it should not, said the Court, interfere with the due administration of justice. The case was about the legality of putting copies of *Spycatcher* by P. Wright in public libraries.

records and other materials to meet both general requirements and the special needs of adults and children.

(ii) There should be encouragement to both adults and children to use the service fully.

(iii) The library authority should ensure full co-operation with any other authority whose functions are exercisable in the library authority area.[9]

(7) The Act then provides some useful detail about the services for which it is lawful to make a charge.[10] These are: **3.05**

(i) When notifying the borrower that the book or any other article he has reserved is available.

(ii) When taking action for the non-return of a book or other article.

(iii) For borrowing any article except a book, journal, pamphlet or similar article or a reproduction thereof.

(iv) Supplying book catalogues and indexes.

(v) Generally, for providing a facility which "goes beyond those ordinarily provided by the authority as part of the library service."

(8) The library authority may make grants and contributions to other   **3.06**
library authorities or other persons who provide library facilities for members of the public.[11]

(9) The Lord President has default powers in the event of failure of a library authority to fulfil its duties.[12]

(10) The library authority has the power to make by-laws about its services. These are subject to confirmation by the Lord President.[13]

(11) The library authorities can be authorised by the Lord President to purchase land for their functions by compulsory purchase procedure.[14]

(12) There is a provision setting out the duties of the local authority under this Act in relation to any duties or powers the authority may possess under a local Act. The public Act is to prevail where the two are inconsistent with each other but otherwise the local Act is to continue in force.[15]

(13) The Lord President is placed under a duty to provide an annual report to Parliament upon the discharge of his duties under this Act.[16]

---

[9] Public Libraries and Museums Act 1964, s.7(2).

[10] *Ibid.* s.8. This law about charges for services has been elaborated, even complicated, by amendments to this section in s.154 of the Local Government and Housing Act 1989, and regulations made under it.

[11] *Ibid.* s.9.

[12] *Ibid.* s.10. In one case the Q.B.D. issued certiorari and injunctions in connection with the banning of newspapers from library reading rooms. This was because the court was satisfied that the terms were imposed for an improper purpose *viz.* not to discharge their duty to library users but to bring political pressure to bear in relation to an industrial dispute affecting the papers. The court in particular rejected a submission of the library authority that the default powers available to the Secretary of State under s.10 ousted the court's initiative under s.7 *supra.* (*R.* v. *Ealing London Borough Council, ex p. Times Newspapers* (1987) 85 L.G.R. 316.)

[13] *Ibid.* s.19.

[14] *Ibid.* s.18.

[15] *Ibid.* s.23.

[16] *Ibid.* s.17.

(14) A section empowers a library authority to use or allow the use of its premises for meetings, exhibitions or other events of an educational or cultural nature. This is in keeping with the trend to make libraries into attractive community buildings rather than simply quiet bookish retreats.[17]

(15) The Act repeals four earlier Library Acts from 1892 onwards.[18]

The Act of 1964 is thus comprehensive and consolidating. It was necessarily amended at the time of local government reorganisation in 1974 to take account of the new library authorities. Otherwise it has withstood well the wear and tear of nearly 30 years.

(2) *Legal Aspects of the Library Service*

3.07 (1) There are certain legal aspects of this service which are common to all who manage staff and buildings. These include the torts of nuisance and negligence, trespass and the legal defences to those issues, and also the subject of damages consequent upon breaches of the law. These have all been discussed in the first two chapters of this book. Those branches of the law deal with the situations which arise when visitors to premises suffer injury or persons enter premises without authority. Again, buildings may give rise to complaint from the occupier of a neighbouring building, perhaps because of damp from escaping rainwater or weakened foundations of a building due to the roots of a tree in the library curtilage. These are problems which lead into the general legal areas covered in Chapter 1. Again, the implications of the Health and Safety at Work legislation, and those statutes which embody terms to be built into the employer-employee contracts, have been discussed in the earlier chapters. In particular the engagement of staff and termination of their contracts of service is, in these days, very much a matter for legal expert advice.

3.08 (2) The basic service of lending books and other articles is free of legal worries for the greater part of its time. But there will be persons who keep books too long and they will sometimes have to be taken to the county court on claims to recover the property or damages in lieu. There will be other persons who damage the authority's property, both the personalty and the realty. The extreme case may call for reference to the police for prosecution. The extensions of the service to records and pictures and perhaps video cassettes will open up different problems for the staff of the authority, particularly relating to the causes of damage to goods borrowed, but experience will enable most of these to be handled satisfactorily.

---

[17] Public Libraries and Museums Act 1964, s.20. The case of *Att.-Gen.* v. *Westminster City Council* [1924] 2 Ch. 416, illustrates the perils of treating library premises as available for any use to which the local authority choose to put them. An injunction was issued to restrain their use for office purposes. In his judgment Sargant L.J. said:

"Their powers in respect of these premises are powers under the Public Libraries Act as the library authority and not as an authority having a whole number of other powers under other Acts, relating to other properties; otherwise, illimitable confusion may be caused." (p. 425).

[18] *Ibid.* Sched. 3.

(3) Librarians develop their own sensible custom and practice in relation to the inclusion among books for loan to the public of those in sensitive areas. The *Observer* case dealt specifically with *Spycatcher* as one falling in the category of "interfering with the due administration of justice." But the lengthy judicial survey in that case helpfully touched also on the categories of obscenity, breach of copyright, national security and breach of confidence. Each of these calls for its own prudent steps by librarians. The possibility of legal obscenity of written material can give rise to difference of opinion. Some further comfort to librarians is perhaps found in the stress on possession for gain in criminal law relating to that topic. That condition excludes the public library service from the peril of that particular literary land-mine.

(4) Parliament has retained the Library Offences Act 1898 for its power to deal with four troublesome areas of conduct. These are being disorderly, using violent, abusive or obscene language, gaming in the library or remaining after closing time, after proper warning. All four offences have as a constituent element "to the annoyance or disturbance of any person using the same." No doubt they are a weapon of last resort for the staff of our public libraries: it is nonetheless significant that the Act was not repealed when such major consolidating legislation was undertaken in 1964.

(5) By-laws supplement the Act of 1898. They cover the conduct of persons using libraries which, whilst falling short of the four specific acts mentioned above, is nonetheless to be discouraged. Remaining on the premises for an undue time or consuming food and drink on the premises are two simple examples. **3.09**

2. Public Lending Right

After several unsuccessful Bills and a campaign lasting more than 20 years, one Bill succeeded and became the Public Lending Right Act 1979. It represented the culmination of much public debate on the grievance of authors at the loss of royalties on the copies of their books read by the public after purchase by the public libraries. The Act has been set in motion: it is unusual in several ways but it depends for its effectiveness on the co-operation of the public libraries. As an adjunct of the public library service, it is of interest to append a short outline of the basic features of the Public Lending Right Scheme.[19] **3.10**

(1) *A Legal Right*

The Public Lending Right is a legal property right. It can be owned by a registered author of a book available for borrowing from public libraries. It is a right to receive payments "from time to time" out of a Central **3.11**

---

[19] The skeleton scheme in the Act is filled out by the Public Lending Right Scheme (Commencement) Order 1982 (S.I. 1982 No. 719), with 52 articles and four Schedules. The outline in the text combines the provisions of both Act and Order.

Fund.[20] This right can be assigned as personalty.[21] The document of transfer bears stamp duty and must be produced to the Registrar appointed under the Act. The right can also be bequeathed or otherwise pass on death. It lasts for 50 years from the year when the author died.[22] As a legal right, it can also be renounced.[23]

(2) *The Central Fund*

3.12   The Central Fund was created with a sum of £2 million and a current rule that the maximum annual or other periodic payment to an author for loans of his registered books is £6,000.[24] The payments are made by the Registrar. He operates the whole scheme set up by the Act.[25] The amount of an individual payment is proportional to the number of times the books of the author in question have been borrowed through the public libraries of this country.[26]

(3) *Registration*

Registration is effected by an author applying for registration, duly validated by a professional person. "Author" for the purposes of the Act can now include the illustrator, reviser, compiler or translator of a book, who may qualify for a share of the PLR arising from it. As a general rule, books with more than three authors are not eligible, but this may change. To qualify, books must be printed and bound but PLR is no longer restricted to books with 32 or more pages.

     A book can be removed from the Register by the Registrar if no sum under the Scheme has been due to an author for it for 10 years.[27]

(4) *The Library Authority's Role*

3.13   The part played by library authorities in the scheme is as follows. Thirty authorities at any one time are designated by the Registrar as sampling points. Either a single branch library or all the branches within that authority can represent that authority. They are selected in order to constitute a variety of library authorities.[28] The numbers of loans at those libraries are recorded and extrapolated by the Registrar in order to calculate his periodical payments. The costs incurred by the library authorities in acting as sampling points are reimbursed by the Registrar.[29]

---

[20] s.1., Public Lending Right Act 1979.

[21] S.I. 1982 No. 719, art.19.

[22] *Ibid.* art. 20.

[23] *Ibid.* art. 32.

[24] *Ibid.* art. 46. The Fund is currently £4¾ million.

[25] S.I. 1982 No. 719, art. 49.

[26] *Ibid.* art. 46. The formula to be used in calculating the periodic payment is set out in this article.

[27] Public Lending Right Act 1979, s.4(5).

[28] S.I. 1982 No. 719, art. 38 and the Public Lending Right Scheme 1982 (Commencement of Variations) Order 1990, art. 38 (S.I. 1990 No. 2360).

[29] *Ibid.* art. 44.

There is an offence, for which a maximum fine of £1,000 is the present sanction, for making false statements in connection with an entry in the register.[30]

The Minister for the Arts is to report annually to Parliament on the working of the scheme.[31]

3. **Copyright**

(1) *Introduction*

An action by Charles Dickens to restrain the breach of his copyright in his story "The Christmas Carol" provides a suitable introduction to this section.[32] Dickens's classic was published by Messrs. Chapman and Hall on December 19, 1843, six days before Christmas. On January 6, 1844, a fraudulent imitation of half of the book was published as "A Christmas Ghost Story—re-originated from the original, by Charles Dickens Esq. and analytically condensed expressly for this work." It was in a series called *Purley's Illuminated Library*. The story and characters were the same as in the Dickens book, except that "Fizziwig" became "Fuzziwig." It sold for 1d. instead of 5s. The case was heard before Knight-Bruce V.-C. and the argument for the defendant is of interest since it is still relevant whenever the question of plagiarism or pirating arises. Although Lee, the defendant, got his ideas and names from Charles Dickens, it was said he had bestowed "so much mental labour" on the story for the weekly library, "that it is not a colourable imitation nor a piracy" but "a fair abridgement." Using principles established in an earlier case,[33] it was argued that it had become a new work, since "a fair application of mind and talent has been made to the labours of another." The defendant said further that Charles Dickens had acquiesced in similar treatment of his earlier works in the same publication.

The judge did not find the defendant's publication "deserving the character of an original work" nor did it exhibit a "fair exercise of mental operation." Dickens won his case.

3.14

(2) *The Ames Case*

Librarians are now expected to hire out pictures, gramophone records, video cassettes as well as books. The law of copyright is thus part of the legal framework within which they work. A modern writer on library legislation says: "The problem of copyright runs like a thread throughout the whole modern history of the distribution of literature."[34] The rel-

3.15

---

[30] Public Lending Right Act 1979, s.4(7).

[31] *Ibid.* s.3(8). The first annual report published in July 1984 states that 7,750 authors and 66,000 books were registered for the scheme. The maximum payment of £5,000 was attained by 46 authors. (*The Public Lending Right Scheme*, Cmnd. 9303, (1983/84). The latest such report says that 41% of all library borrowings were of books on the PLR Register.

[32] *Dickens* v. *Lee* (1843) 8 *The Jurist*, 183.

[33] *Dodsley* v. *Kinnersley* (1761) 1 Amb. 403.

[34] R. J. Morris, *Parliament and Library Law*, p. 175.

evance of this branch of the law is well indicated by a recent authoritative case in the High Court: *C.B.S. Inc.* v. *Ames Records and Tapes Ltd.*[35] A record lending library was established by the defendant in his shops in Burnley and Blackburn. It resembled the record lending schemes of the public libraries apart from two respects: first, in the *Ames* scheme, the hirer had a right to purchase the records borrowed; secondly, the proportion of "pop" records was somewhat greater than might be found in a public record library.

The case put by the plaintiffs was that the defendant had infringed the copyright held by the plaintiffs in the records, by authorising home taping of those records whilst on hire from his shops. By the Copyright Act 1956, only the owner of the copyright had the right "to make a record embodying the recording."[36] Hence during the hearing and in his judgment the judge, Whitford J., considered the evidence about the knowledge of the shopkeeper that persons hiring his records might tape-record the music from them. The shopkeeper had given evidence that his sales of records had increased, in order to counter any inference that his businesses were solely devoted to pushing the hiring of records. With regard to tape-recording, the defendant said that he could not stop it but did not encourage it. "Can it be said," asked the judge, "that Ames have 'authorised' such home taping? I cannot believe that anybody other than a lawyer would have any difficulty in saying No."

3.16   Whitford J. mentioned the various sources from which records for home taping might be acquired—including public libraries—and declined to say that the shopkeeper "authorised" home taping by running his record-lending library. (Evidence had been given that, at the time of the trial, warning notices existed in the libraries and on the record sleeves to dissuade hirers from breaching copyright in the music.)

(3) *The Earlier Cases*

3.17   In the *Ames* case, the judge reviewed a number of cases which had raised the same question that he had to determine, *i.e.* had the act which constituted an infringement of the copyright in the music been "authorised" by the defendant? The copyright "thread" can usefully be followed through a number of these cases:

(1) When an infringing performance of music was given by a band engaged by a company, then the managing director of that company, being abroad and unaware that the music in question would be performed, was not liable for a breach of copyright.[37]

(2) The above case was considered by the Supreme Court of Victoria in

---

[35] [1981] 2 W.L.R. 973.

[36] Copyright Act 1956, ss.1, 12.

[37] *Performing Rights Society Ltd.* v. *Ciryl Theatrical Syndicate Ltd.* [1924] 1 K.B. 1, C.A.. The company was liable and the band was liable but the case is important in allowing a distinction to be made about the position of the managing director. One of the defendant's letters to the plaintiff said: "I engage an orchestra who provide their own music; if they are infringing any copyright, you must look to them and not to me."

Winstone v. *Wurlitzer Automatic Phonograph Co. of Australia Ltd.*[38] A jukebox in
a coffee bar played the tune "Pony Express" composed by the plaintiff.
The court held that the coffee bar proprietor had "authorised" the performance. There were no relevant circumstances to distance him in law from
the simple operation of the jukebox, and the playing of the music. The
defendant indeed provided the jukebox, and selected the records to be
placed in it. He did everything except place the coin in the jukebox and
the Court did not consider that this one element relieved the proprietor of
his legal responsibility for copyright infringement.

(3) *Moorhouse and Angus & Robertson (Publishers) Pty.* v. *University of New* **3.18**
South Wales,[39] an Australian case, was then examined by Whitford J. in the
Ames case, since it was strongly urged upon him by the plaintiffs that it
supported their case. It concerned not a record-player but a photocopying
machine in the University. It was available for use by students. Not only
the machine but also all necessary materials to photocopy their own
scripts were provided by the University. The incident which gave rise to
the case was the photocopying by a graduate on the machine, not of his
thesis or other legitimate work, but of a published book of short stories.
This act infringed the copyright of the author. Had the University "authorised" the infringement? In that case, the court said: Yes. The word
"authorise" was treated as meaning "sanction, approve, countenance," as
in the other cases in this series. The judge, Hutley J.A., was not prepared
to exclude authorisation when the evidence indicated mere passivity by
the University. On appeal, his decision was upheld. McTiernan A.C.J.
said:

> " 'authorise' connoted a mental element and so, in addition to having
> the power to prevent the copyright infringement, it was necessary to
> be able to infer from the circumstances that the University knew or
> had reason to anticipate or suspect that the particular act is or is
> likely to be done."

That judge's own summing up of the principle involved is helpful:

> "A person who has under his control the means by which an infringe-
> ment may be committed,—such as a photo-copying machine—and
> who makes it available to other persons, knowing, or having reason to
> suspect that it is likely to be used, for the purpose of committing an
> infringement and omitting to take reasonable steps to limit its use to
> legitimate purposes, would authorise an infringement that resulted
> from its use."[40]

In the *Ames* case, Whitford J. concluded that the shopkeeper had not **3.19**
authorised the infringement of copyright. Apart from the gloss on "authorised" established by the above cases, it would seem that the judge was
influenced by the fact that the plaintiffs had sold their records to the

[38] [1946] V.L.R. 338.
[39] [1976] R.P.C. 151.
[40] *Ibid.* at p. 487 (quoting Knox C.J. in the case of *Adelaide Corporation* v. *Australasia P.R. Society* [1928] 40 C.L.R. 481).

defendant "who was then perfectly entitled to sell them, give them away, hire them or destroy them."[41] Thus the limit of legal control residing with the plaintiffs over the defendant's use of the records lay in the Copyright Act protection.

The normal lending activities of public libraries relate to goods which they own—books, records, pictures and cassettes—and the above cases show that, provided the library stays short of authorising a breach of copyright when engaging in that lending activity, its activities are not at risk of legal challenge.

(4) *Libraries: The Legal Copying Categories*

3.20   We turn now to some important provisions in the Copyright, Designs and Patents Act 1988, which prescribe classes of copying of documents which are within the law for library authorities, provided that the relevant conditions are honoured.

Periodicals

The librarian of a library falling within the current Regulations made under the earlier Act of 1956 is entitled to supply a copy of a periodical publication, subject to the following conditions:

    (a) The copies are supplied for the purposes of private study or research and a declaration to that effect is completed by the person taking the copy.[42]

    (b) Only one copy is supplied.

    (c) The copy should not extend to more than one article in the same issue of the publication.

    (d) Payment in respect of the cost is made for the copy supplied.[43]

Parts of published works

3.21   A librarian of the class of library mentioned in (a) above may supply a copy of part of a published literary, dramatic or musical work, any illustrations accompanying the work or of the typographical arrangement.[44]

The three conditions (a), (b) and (d) above apply.[45]

---

[41] *Ames* case, *supra.* no. 38 at p. 830. The *cri de coeur* of the House of Lords for reform of this home copying anomaly in *CBS Songs Ltd.* v. *Amstrad Consumer Electronics* [1988] A.C. 1013, has not yet secured action in Parliament.

[42] The form of Declaration is contained in the Copyright (Librarians and Archivists) (Copying of Copyright Material) Regulations 1989 (S.I. 1989 No. 1212).

[43] Copyright, Designs and Patents Act 1988, s.38. The libraries and archives which enjoy the benefit of this exemption are described in the Copyright (Copying by Librarians and Archivists) Regulations 1989 (S.I. 1989 No. 1009) with amendment in the 1989 Regulations (S.I. 1989 No. 1212) *supra*.

[44] *Ibid.* s.39.

[45] s.40 now strengthens the sanction against multiple copies of the same material being sought from libraries by concerted requests.

Complete works for other libraries

A copy of a literary, musical or dramatic work may be supplied to the **3.22** librarian of another library if it is in the classes covered by the above Regulations. Also an article in a periodical can be supplied. However, the first exemption above, concerning full works, does not apply if the librarian knows or could by reasonable inquiry ascertain the name and address of the copyright holder.[46]

Replacement copies of works

A new section in the Act of 1988 grants a right to librarians in respect of **3.23** the four classes set out in section 3.20 if necessary to provide working copies of fragile or irreplaceable books, or to supply replacements for such books in the permanent collection of another prescribed library where their own copies have been lost, destroyed or damaged. The condition is that it is not reasonably possible to purchase a copy of the item in question to fulfil that purpose.[47]

Copying by librarians of unpublished works

The fifth and final exception in favour of librarians making copies is inter- **3.24** esting and exceptional. Libraries and archive authorities often act as the repository of literary, dramatic or musical works which have not been published. Conditions attached to the transfer into the custody of the library may touch on the question of use for private study or research. The Act of 1988 deals with this situation. Though the finer details are not reproduced here, the basic procedure cannot begin until 50 years have elapsed from the death of the author. Due notice of intention to publish has then to be given on two occasions in newspapers with national circulations, so that copyright owners, if existing, have an opportunity to come forward.[48]

Copy required as condition of export

If an article of cultural or historical importance or interest cannot law- **3.25** fully be exported from the United Kingdom unless a copy of it is made and deposited in an appropriate library or archive, it is not an infringement of copyright to make that copy.

(5) *The Framework of the Copyright, Designs and Patents Act 1988*

The law of copyright is here outlined only to the extent that those seeking **3.26** to work with or within the public leisure services will need to understand its extent and structure.[49] The framework of the Act of 1988 itself gives a

---

[46] Copyright, Designs and Patents Act 1988, s.41.

[47] *Ibid.* s.42.

[48] The Copyright (Librarians and Archivists) (Copying of Copyright Material) Regulations 1989 (S.I. 1989 No. 1212).

[49] A practitioner's textbook of over 2,000 pages such as *Copinger and Skone James on Copyright* (12th ed., 1980, Sweet and Maxwell) is an indication of the depth and range of the full subject.

useful perspective within which to set the important provisions contained in the previous subsections of this chapter.[50]

The definition

The Act of 1988 makes a bold attempt at a new definition of copyright. The last Act of 1956 had merely referred to rights in relation to a work. The new Act says copyright is a property right and that it subsists in the nine types of "work" there listed. These are original literary, dramatic, musical and artistic works, sound recordings, films, broadcasts and cable programmes as well as typographical arrangements of published editions.[51]

3.27 The important word "original" has been considered at the highest legal level.[52] It is regarded as connoting, originating from an author as distinct from being copied. It does not in this context mean a novel or inventive idea. Copyright is concerned with the expression rather than the thought itself. In essence, the object of copyright law is to protect the writer, composer and artist against the unlawful reproduction of his material.[53] The purpose of the above statutory definition is to allow its adaptation to all the above areas of artistic creation. The Act indeed provides some elaboration of each of those nine areas but the section 1 definition is the starting point.

The statutory prohibitions

The Act of 1988 sets out the four activities which the copyright owner has exclusive right to do, and these acts carried out by anyone else become infringements of the copyright. The acts are copying, issuing copies to the public, performing, showing or playing the work in public and broadcasting it or including it in a cable programme service.[54]

3.28 The Act then goes into detail about the way in which these various areas of copyright protection are to be looked at to see if infringement has taken place. There is a special provision controlling adaptation of works.[55] A number of secondary infringements, as they are called, are then described. These are importing infringing copy,[56] possessing or dealing with

---

[50] The Copyright, Designs and Patents Act 1988 is a landmark. It not only replaced the consolidating Copyright Act of 1956 but also several other Acts: it was wider in subject-matter and was also designed to express more helpfully some of the provisions in earlier copyright law. It went so far as to reassure its readers: "A provision which corresponds to the previous law shall not be construed as departing from (it) merely because of a change of expression" (s.172). The Act came in the wake of many technical changes and also the Report of the Whitford Committee, Cmnd. 6732 (1977).

[51] S. 1.

[52] See *Interlego AG* v. *Tyco Industries Inc.* [1988] 3 W.L.R. 678, P.C., 702–706.

[53] In the case of *George Hensher Ltd.* v. *Restawhile Upholstery (Lancs) Ltd.* [1976] A.C. 64 at p. 98, there is approval for this definition, found in Copinger and Skone James, (n. 49 *supra*) at p. 3.

[54] Copyright, Designs and Patents Act 1988, ss.16–21.

[55] *Ibid.* s.21.

[56] *Ibid.* s.22.

infringing copy,[57] providing means for making infringing copies, permitting premises to be used for an infringing performance and providing apparatus for an infringing performance.

Permitted Acts

Part I, Chapter III is a major part of the Act of 1988 and in over 40 sections deals in detail with a considerable range of permitted acts. Confining our attention to librarians, we can only mention "fair dealing" with certain of the works for the purposes of private study or research,[58] reproduction for the purposes of judicial proceedings,[59] and fair dealing for the purposes of criticism, review or news reporting.[60] Public reading and use for educational purposes are permitted if the proper legal steps are taken.[61]   **3.29**

Fair dealing

"Fair dealing" is again protected and this expression is clearly important; it emphasises in this field how important are the judicial interpretations that have gathered about some of the other key expressions above.[62]   **3.30**

The copyright provisions in relation to cinematograph films, sound recordings, TV and sound broadcasts must be studied in detail by those particularly involved in those areas.[63]

Litigation

Part I, Chapter VI of the Act contains the legal rights of copyright owners in protecting their copyright and also the defences that can be raised to their claims.   **3.31**

Damages, an injunction and the taking of accounts are three of the remedies that can be secured by a justifiably aggrieved copyright owner.

The flagrancy of the infringement can lead to increased damages.[64]

Proof by a defendant, on the other hand, of his ignorance that he was breaching a copyright can limit an otherwise successful plaintiff to an account for profits rather than damages.[65]

Miscellaneous copyright

Finally the Act of 1988 has several miscellaneous points to which attention is drawn: **3.32**

---

[57] Copyright, Designs and Patents Act 1988, s.23.
[58] *Ibid.* s.29 and see *Discount Inter-Shopping Co. Ltd.* v. *Micrometro* [1984] Ch. 369.
[59] *Ibid.* s.45.
[60] *Ibid.* s.30.
[61] *Ibid.* ss.32–36 and s.59.
[62] *Ibid.* ss.29 and 30. Two interesting cases in which interpretation of "fair dealing" was involved are *Hubbard* v. *Vosper* [1972] 2 Q.B. 84 and *Beloff* v. *Pressdram Ltd.* [1973] 1 All E.R. 241. The term is not defined in the Act.
[63] See ss.61 to 76 in Part I, Chapter III of the Act of 1988.
[64] Copyright, Designs and Patents Act 1988, s.97.
[65] *Ibid.* s.97(1).

(a) Copyright can be transmitted by assignment, by will or otherwise as personal property.[66]

(b) The BBC and ITV possess copyright in TV and sound broadcasts but can deal with the performing rights in those broadcasts only strictly in accordance with a procedure laid down in the Act.[67]

(c) A saving provision protects the use of copyright material in schools. Such use, including the performance of literary, dramatic or musical work "if in the course of the activities of school," is not to be deemed to be in public.[68]

(d) The normal term for copyright extends from the date of publication until 50 years after the author's death.[69] There are some fine modifications to this general provision, relating to photography, sound recordings, cinematograph films, broadcasts and others for which the Act should be consulted.

Other legal action

3.33   The Act sets out legal presumptions relating to the author, joint authors, lack of an author's name and other technical problems that arise when legal action is taken in copyright cases[70]; lays down penalties for various offences, in each of which knowledge of the copyright infringement in question is an important ingredient[71]; and prescribes steps available to a copyright owner in literary, dramatic or musical works, to secure the prohibition, by the Commissioners of Customs and Excise, of printed copies of his work, being copies which, if printed in the United Kingdom, would be infringing copies.[72]

The Copyright Tribunal

3.34   The old Performing Rights Tribunal is renamed and its membership and jurisdiction expanded.[73] It is basically able to adjudicate on the licensing schemes of, *e.g.* the Performing Rights Society or similar licensing bodies, as the Act calls them. It now deals also with artistic as well as literary, dramatic and musical works and has added to that portfolio films, broadcasts and cable programmes. This jurisdiction is not only about public performances. Royalties can be referred to the Tribunal, as can rentals of sound recordings and films.[74]

The decisions of the Tribunal are subject to appeal to the High Court or in Scotland to the Court of Session.[75]

The Tribunal, constituted of a legal Chairman, two deputies and two to

---

[66] Copyright, Designs and Patents Act 1988, Pt. I, Chap. V.

[67] *Ibid.* s.91.

[68] *Ibid.* s.34. But contraventions of this permission for, *e.g.* school orchestra scores, have led to enforcement of their legal rights by the Music Publishers Association.

[69] *Ibid.* s.12.

[70] *Ibid.* ss.104–105.

[71] *Ibid.* s.107.

[72] *Ibid.* ss.111 and 112.

[73] *Ibid.* s.145.

[74] *Ibid.*, s.149.

[75] *Ibid.* s.152.

eight ordinary members.[76] is to determine questions arising under 13 statutory provisions and touching generally on licences, royalties, consents by performers and rentals for recordings and films.[77] For the finer points about the Tribunal and the licence schemes upon which it can adjudicate, the interested reader must be referred to the text of the Act.[78]

(6) *EEC and Foreign Aspects*

Copyright is a branch of British law in which the law of the European **3.35** Economic Community is integrated.[79] It is therefore necessary to take account of any decisions of the European Court of Justice in this field in so far as they have a bearing upon the practice of those engaged with the law of the public leisure services. EEC law is a specialist area, as is the other international aspect, *i.e.* the impact of the Berne and other Conventions upon the operation of the British copyright law.[80]

One instance only is given of a copyright case dealt with under EEC law, as a pointer to a developing situation.[81]

Treaty of Rome

The law of copyright makes its appearance in the foundation document of the EEC, the Treaty of Rome, where it refers to "the protection of industrial property," in Article 36. This is part of a complex section of the Treaty which places qualifications upon the broad declaration of Article 30:

> "Quantitative restrictions on imports and all measures having equivalent effect shall, without prejudice to the following provisions, be prohibited between the member states."

The Gema case

The case in question raised the interpretation of these Articles in con- **3.36** nection with the import of gramophone records to Germany. It was the German *Gema*[82] case of 1981 where 100,000 records had been placed in free circulation in the United Kingdom, and the Performing Rights Society or its equivalent had collected royalties when that took place. The records had been manufactured in the United Kingdom and the rate of royalty was based upon that fact. The records were then imported into Germany and that circumstance led *Gema*—the German counterpart of the Performing Rights Society in this country—to claim an additional

---

[76] Copyright, Designs and Patents Act 1988, s.148.

[77] *Ibid.* s.149.

[78] Pt. I, Chap. VIII.

[79] European Communities Act 1972, s.2(1).

[80] See, *e.g. Halsbury's Laws of England* (4th ed.), Vol. 9, § 965. Our copyright law has the distinction of having been linked to international conventions for its main provisions for over a century.

[81] But see also a U.K. case where the court allowed defences to be added, based on Arts.85 and 86 in the EEC Treaty, concerning undue restriction of competition and abuse of dominant position. (*Application des Gaz S.A.* v. *Falks Veritas Ltd.* [1974] Ch. 381).

[82] *Musik-Vertrieb GmbH and K Tel International* v. *GEMA* [1981] E.C.R. 147.

royalty. In so far as this could be regarded as a financial restriction within Article 30, it led to *Gema* going before the EEC Court of Justice. The German national court, which first heard the case, had raised the point whether such an exercise of copyright, being lawful under German domestic law, was compatible with the requirements of the EEC Treaty on the free movement of goods.

In the event, the claim of *Gema* was not upheld by the Court of Justice. The court held that copyright raised the same question as any other industrial or commercial property right. The case law of the EEC Court showed that the holder of such a right, which was protected by the law of a Member State, might not rely on that law to prevent the marketing of a product on the market of another Member State when that marketing results from a lawful distribution of the product. The product here was the gramophone record and the final conclusion of the European Court of Justice was that this lawful distribution was either by the proprietor of the right or, alternatively, with his consent. *Gema* argued that its claim was not a restriction on marketing but only the collection of the balance of licences paid for all such distribution on the German market. This case is mentioned as a cameo of EEC legal complications for British leisure service staff involved in, *e.g.* gramophone record commercial dealings with the Continent.[83]

4. Rights in Performances

3.37 Part II of the Copyright, Designs and Patents Act 1988 re-enacts and re-inforces provisions formerly contained in the Performers Protection Acts 1958–72. They are an important adjunct of copyright law.[84] They are designed to protect performers from having records made of their performances and distributed commercially without their consent. Thus a literary, dramatic, musical or variety artiste or artistic performance, whilst not itself having the benefit of copyright, is given a degree of protection against others benefiting commercially from it without payment or other consent from the performers. The Act spells out a civil right conferred on performers and those with recording rights. An outline of these provisions is set out below[85]:

    (a) There are three offences, namely, making the record, selling or distributing the record commercially and, thirdly, using the record for a public performance.

[83] The EEC Court is developing the continental concept in copyright of distinguishing between the existence or substance of the right and the exercise of the right. This has been described in a leading case in that court by saying that Art.36 permits restrictions on freedom of trade only to the extent that they are justified "for the protection of the rights that form the specific object of that property." Clearly this concept has to be developed further in U.K. terms. (*Deutsche Grammophon Case* 78/70 *Grammophon GmbH* v. *Metro etc.* [1971] E.C.R. 487).

[84] There are 32 sections now compared with 18 in the three earlier Acts.

[85] Copyright, Designs and Patents Act 1988, s.180. The Court of Appeal decision in *Rickless* v. *United Artists Corporation* [1988] Q.B. 40 had clarified the law and the statute now accepts that timely clarification.

(b) In relation to the first of the above offences, it is a defence to prove that the record was made only for private or domestic use.

(c) A similar set of three offences is then applied to the making of a cinematograph film of a musical or dramatic work without consent. For these the defence of non-commercial use, as in (2) above, is available.[86]

(d) The variety of offences has been increased since 1985 and the whole net cast for offenders is an effort to keep pace with technology in the video and recording industries.[87]

(e) A court dealing with one of these offences is empowered to order the destruction of files or records made in contravention of the Acts of 1958–1972.[88]

(f) Schedule 2 to the Act of 1988 lists no less than 21 types of recording which do not infringe the Act. These are modelled on the copyright defence provisions and include archival use, free public showings and special treatment of folk songs.[89]

(g) Consent is not dealt with as deliberately as under the former statutes but is likely to continue to provide a field for argument.[90] A recent case has underlined the difference that might arise between the nature of the consent needed merely to tape a performance and that required to make and sell commercial records based upon that tape.[91]

5. **Archives**

The archives of a locality have been recognised as a suitable accompaniment to the collection of books to be found in public libraries, since Parliament began to interest itself in the matter in the mid-nineteenth century. Plans, muniments, documents of all sorts, collections of family and estate papers, newspapers—all were part of the public heritage which some members of the community in each generation would wish to study. The public library has come to be regarded as a natural centre for the storing and inspection of this specialised collection.[92]   **3.38**

Legally, a period of concurrent powers for county and district councils in the metropolitan counties followed local government reorganisation.[93] The demise of those counties will leave the metropolitan district councils

---

[86] Copyright, Designs and Patents Act 1988, s.2.
[87] *Ibid.* ss.182–185.
[88] *Ibid.* s.5.
[89] *Ibid.* s.6
[90] See, *e.g.* s.7 of the Dramatic & Musical Performers Protection Act 1958.
[91] See *Apple Corps Ltd.* v. *Lingasong Ltd.* (1977) 121 S.J. 692, a colourful and instructive case. But see, *e.g.* s.182(2) which introduces "belief on reasonable grounds that consent has been given."
[92] The Local Government (Records) Act 1962 deals specifically with the subject of archives. It describes them, identifies the various tasks needed to keep them available for study and exhibition to the public, and empowers local authorities to accept and store them (ss.1, 2).
[93] Whilst the Act gave this last power to counties and London boroughs, it was available only to such county districts as are approved by the Secretary of State for the Environment. (Local Government Act 1972, ss.206–208.)

as archive authorities. Elsewhere, the service goes with the library service.[94]

6. **Art Galleries**

(1) *Provision*

3.39 Local authorities are empowered by the Public Libraries and Museums Act 1964 to provide art galleries.[95] These are an important feature of any public leisure service and have featured in legislation since 1845.[96]

By agreement of the Secretary of State, a local authority may transfer an art gallery and its collections to another local authority.[97]

(2) *Finance*

A charge for admission may be made by the managing local authority, on condition that, before imposing such a charge, the authority has taken into account the position of its school children and students and also the need for itself, as the local authority, to take its full part in the promotion of education in the area.[98]

Local authorities maintaining art galleries may make financial contributions to persons who are maintaining art galleries in England and Wales or who are providing an advisory service, or some other service, for the benefit of an art gallery. Thus public money could provide support for a private art gallery.

There is a further financial power for library authorities. This is to establish an Art Fund. With the Secretary of State's consent, such a Fund may be amalgamated with an existing Local Act fund.[99]

(3) *Art Gallery Liaison*

Since art collections are frequently on loan from gallery to gallery, with a view to exhibition, co-operation between local authorities and also with the national galleries is an essential feature of this public leisure service.[1]

---

[94] A repository provided by a local authority under the above Act of 1962 may be designated as a diocesan record office by virtue of the Parochial Registers and Records Measure 1978, s.7(4).

[95] In England the authorities are shire counties, metropolitan districts, London Boroughs and the Common Council and in Wales, county and district councils and joint boards, if constituted. See Act of 1964, ss.4, 25, and the Local Government Act 1972.

[96] Whipping thrice and hard labour were deemed to be suitable penalties for persons damaging pictures or other works of art, whether the damage was done out of malice or not. (Protection of Works of Art, etc., Act 1845)

[97] Public Libraries and Museums Act 1964, s.12.

[98] *Ibid.* s.13. Under the Sunday Entertainment Act 1932, s.4, there is exemption from Sunday closing requirements for art galleries.

[99] The second Schedule to the Act of 1964 sets out the procedures for managing such a fund.

[1] Handling collections involves the law of bailment, on which see Museums, *post*, paras. 3.44 *et seq.*

It will be useful, accordingly, to note the legal background of some of the major national galleries.[2]

The National Gallery

This houses the collection of over 2,000 old master paintings of estab- **3.40**
lished merit or significance, representative of Western European painting
from the thirteenth century to the early part of this century.

This is the gallery which initially receives pictures or other works of art
which have been given or bequeathed to the nation for public benefit and
in the absence of any direction to the contrary by the donor. The management is in the hands of a director, working with 12 to 14 trustees. The
trustees have a power of selection in the case of bequests: they select only
those deemed fit for a national collection; the rest fall back into the residu-
ary estate of a testator.[3] The Minister of Arts has a power, rarely exercised
in practice, to direct that a picture or work of art which would otherwise
have gone to the National Gallery trustees, shall go the the Tate Gallery
trustees or some other specified institution.[4] The Act of 1956 directs regular consultation between the trustees of the National Gallery and the
Tate Gallery, in order to facilitate decisions on the making of loans or
transfers. It was the National Gallery and Tate Gallery Act 1954 which
had given independent legal status to the Tate Gallery and that Act contained three important guiding principles[5]:

(a) To maintain at the National Gallery a collection of pictures of
established merit or significance.

(b) To maintain at the Tate a collection of British pictures and a collection of modern pictures.[6]

(c) To ensure that each picture is in that collection where it will be
available and on view in the best context.

Before agreeing to let a picture go on loan from the National Gallery,
the trustees are to satisfy themselves that it is proper to expose the picture
to the incidents of the journey and also that it will not be exposed to
special risks.

A picture appearing to have been painted by a foreign artist before 1700
cannot be loaned for exhibition outside the United Kingdom without parliamentary procedure. There is also a 15-year period[7] to run before a
recent bequest can be loaned at all, save with the consent of the owner's

---

[2] The general approach in this book is to deal with features of the London situation separately, see Chap. 10, *post.*

[3] See the National Gallery Act 1856 and the National Gallery and Tate Gallery Act 1954,
Sched. 2.

[4] See the Transfer of Functions (Cultural Institutions) Order 1965 (S.I. 1965 No. 603), art.
2(1). Since 1983 he has worked through the Office of Arts and Libraries. Thirteen major
museums are listed in the Schedule to the Act of 1954. These include the National Portrait
Gallery and the National Gallery of Scotland.

[5] National Gallery and Tate Gallery Act 1954, s.2.

[6] *Ibid.* s.4(5). Speaking on the second reading debate (October 29, 1954) Mr. Henry Brooke
said it was designed to "start the Tate Gallery on a new life, give it new status and new
strength."

[7] *Ibid.* s.4.

representatives.[8] In this situation, if the proposed transfer outside the country involves some departure from conditions laid down by the donor, then the above 15-year period becomes a qualifying period of 25 years. Again, the owner's representatives can give consent, as above.[9]

Finally, the Act of 1954 requires the trustees to give students and others engaged in research reasonable opportunities to view pictures and works of art whilst on public display.

The Tate Gallery

3.41 This gallery dovetails with the National Gallery in a number of ways, as indicated above. Now established with its own trustees and director, the Tate is maintained as a gallery for modern foreign art and British paintings, as well as modern sculpture.

The powers available to its trustees for loans are subject to similar constraints to those laid upon the National Gallery in relation to physical hazards to the pictures, the justification for releasing them on loan, meeting the claims of students and researchers, and other matters. The proportion of the number of their pictures and works of art which the trustees can lend for display is one-tenth of the total in their charge.[10]

Sir John Soane's Museum

By way of contrast with the restrictions on the movement of art treasures described above is the permission granted by statute for the famous Hogarth and other pictures kept at Sir John Soane's museum in Lincoln's Inn Fields, London, to be moved for display near Hampstead Heath, at Kenwood, the former estate and mansion of Lord Iveagh, which is now maintained as a period home for public viewing.[11]

(4) *Works of Art—Customs, Excise and Tax*

3.42 The legal provisions to which attention is drawn are those associated with the potential high value of certain works of art. The current legal framework is found in the Customs and Excise and Finance Acts, as follows:

Import and export control

Under the Import Export and Customs Powers (Defence) Act 1939, section 1, the Board of Trade was authorised to make orders to prohibit or regulate the importation into or exportation from the United Kingdom of "all goods or goods of any specified description."

Since 1945, a series of Export of Goods (Control) Orders has been used by the Government to maintain control over (*inter alia*) the export of works of art. The current Order is S.I. 1989 No. 2376.

[8] National Gallery and Tate Gallery Act 1954.
[9] *Ibid.* s.4.
[10] *Ibid.* s.5. For the National Gallery the comparable figure is one-twentieth.
[11] London County Council (General Powers) Act 1952, s.20(3). The Minister for the Arts has general oversight of this Museum under a Scheme of 1969.

The actual legal control is:

(a) Goods[12] as scheduled are prohibited to be exported to any destination (article 2) unless a licence has been given by the Secretary of State (article 4a).

(b) There are severe penalties for fraud or any other contravention of this procedure (article 6).

EEC Regulations also relate to this subject. They permit collector's pieces, and works of art not intended for resale, to be imported without payment of duties under Commission Customs Tariff. Galleries, museums and other institutions seeking this relief have to obtain approval as institutions from the Department of Trade and Industry, after which relief from the duty is granted by H.M. Customs and Excise.[13]

Gifts

Library and museum authorities are sometimes offered gifts or bequests **3.43** of works of art. In certain circumstances donors can obtain tax exemptions.[14] In the Finance Acts, the relevant category of "goods" is "works of national, scientific, historic or artistic interest."

Under the Capital Gains Tax Act 1979, a gift can be made of a work of art, as above, if the Board of Inland Revenue direct that it falls into the above category. The consequence is that a gain accruing on the disposal is not a chargeable gain on which the donor would pay Capital Gains Tax. As a matter of practice, the Board of Inland Revenue will expect an undertaking from the recipient that the item will remain in the United Kingdom.

The same approach is made by the Board of Inland Revenue in the case of a bequest.

B. MUSEUMS

1. **Introduction**

The modern museums service demonstrates the immense expansion in the **3.44** concept of the museum since that first tentative Public Libraries Act of 1850. Wrecks and folk museums, metal detectors and treasure trove, natu-

---

[12] Whilst earlier Orders said "works of art," a recent assimilation of the Schedule of "goods" to EEC categories led the Export of Goods (Control) Order 1970 (S.I. 1970 No. 1288) to use the expression "Articles not elsewhere specified, manufactured or produced more than 100 years before the date of exportation, including works of art but not including postage stamps of philatelic interest and similar articles." The Export of Goods (Control) Order 1981 (S.I. 1981 No. 1641) goes a stage further in elliptical reference to Old Masters. Its wording is "Any goods manufactured or produced more than 50 years before the date of exportation" (with certain exceptions not relevant to the subject), Pt. 1, Sched. 1, Group B. Thus the expression "works of art" is no longer in the Order, though the control described above continues in force.

[13] Such goods may only be lent, hired out or transferred to other institutions if those are themselves approved institutions and prior permission for the loan has been obtained from the D.T.I., Notice 361 (1988).

[14] The current statutes are the Capital Gains Tax Act 1979, s.147: the Capital Transfer Tax Act 1984, s.26 and the Inheritance Tax Act 1984, s.25. V.A.T. is dealt with currently in H.M. Customs & Excise Notice No. 712 (1990).

ral history and regimental museums, as well as national monuments and memorials, are all within its accepted range. Art galleries move a little arbitrarily from museums to libraries as one moves from town to town; on this occasion we have dealt with them in the Libraries section.

2. **The Legal Framework for the Public Museum Service**

(1) *The Local Authority Service*

3.45 The museums service provided by local authorities in this country works within a legal framework contained in the Public Libraries and Museums Act 1964 (the Act of 1964). There is no national directive on policy or provision, as with the library service. Instead, the Act of 1964 simply enjoins a local authority "to provide and maintain museums . . . within its administrative area or elsewhere, in England and Wales . . . and to do all such things as may be necessary or expedient in connection with the maintenance or provision thereof."[15]

Local authorities, in England, for the purposes of the museums service, means London Boroughs and the Common Council, county councils, district councils and the Council of the Isles of Scilly. In Wales, the relevant local authorities are the county and district councils.[16]

(2) *Finance*

3.46 Charges may be made for admission to a museum.[17] At one time, it was the practice to obtain local Act powers in order to charge for such admissions. In those days, it was thought that charges should be made only for special museums and not, generally, for all municipal museums.[18] Even now, though the general power of charging is available, it is discretionary. A local authority is required, nonetheless, before using those powers, to consider how far it can be said that the museum in question plays its full part in the promotion of education for the people in the area. The local authority is, secondly, to have particular regard to the interests of children and students when determining to impose museum entrance charges.[19] Education is one aspect of museum provision; the above section in the Act of 1964 does not rule out consideration of leisure service aspects of the service when charging is under review.

The local authority is empowered to make contributions to the expenses of "some other person" in providing a museum.[20] Those expenses can include the cost of advisory and financial help in running that museum.

[15] Public Libraries and Museums Act 1964, s.12.
[16] Local Government Act 1972, s.206.
[17] Public Libraries and Museums Act 1964, s.13.
[18] See, *e.g.* Halifax Corporation Act 1959, s.24, where only Shibden Hall Folk Museum was deemed suitable for such a step.
[19] Public Libraries and Museums Act 1964, s.13(2).
[20] *Ibid.* s.14.

(3) *Specimens fund*

A fund can be set up to purchase objects to exhibit in the museum. Guidelines, additional to those in the Act, will normally be laid down by a council for such a fund.[21]

(4) *By-Laws*

By-laws can be made about the use of the facilities provided in museums. **3.47** The Lord President of the Council has to confirm these.[22] The conduct of visitors and maintenance of good order in the premises will normally feature in such by-laws, together with the avoidance of nuisances in and around the premises.[23]

(5) *Community Activities*

A local authority can permit its museums to be used for community events of a cultural or educational nature.[24] If a museum shop is provided, the Trades Description Acts, discussed in Chapter 1, are relevant.

(6) *External Grants*

Many public museums will qualify to be considered as recipients of grants **3.48** or loans from the National Heritage Memorial Fund.[25] Within the context of an Act passed to preserve property of importance to the national heritage, the trustees of the fund thereby created are authorised to make grants or loans to "eligible recipients." These advances will be to secure the preservation of collections or groups of objects which "taken as a whole, are of outstanding historic, artistic or scientific interest."

A museum entering into an arrangement with the National Heritage Memorial Fund trustees will need to be ready to discuss:

(a) Conditions about public access to, or display of, the property in question.

(b) Its repair, maintenance, safekeeping and insurance.

(c) Its lending or disposal.

(d) The conditions governing repayment of the grant or loan if the conditions are broken.[26]

---

[21] Public Libraries and Museums Act 1964, s.15, Sched. 2, which governs the financial arrangements.

[22] *Ibid.* s.19. The full discussion in this work is in Chap. 4.

[23] These can deal with all aspects of behaviour by the public on museum premises, *e.g.* creating a disturbance, holding an unauthorised meeting, eating and drinking, creating a nuisance by deposits of foul matter, or stink bombs or fireworks. The police can assist in enforcing the by-laws, if the museum staff cannot deal with breaches on their own.

[24] Public Libraries and Museums Act 1964, s.20.

[25] See National Heritage Act 1983, s.3.

[26] *Ibid.* s.3.

(7) *Other Public Museums*

3.49   There are, in addition to local authority municipal museums, many individual museums available to the public. These are frequently specialised in character, varying from industrial museums or those devoted to the possessions and property of a famous person or family, to the arts and crafts museums and folk museums which have been created in recent years. Many of the national museums have some enabling Act of Parliament in their history and it must suffice here to list the main national museums and indicate those Acts, to assist those who wish to study the subject in greater detail.

Museums	*Enabling Act*
1. British Museum	British Museum Act 1963
2. British Museum Natural History Museum	British Museum Act 1963
3. Museum of London	Museum of London Act 1965
4. Guildhall Museum	Museum of London Act 1965
5. National Maritime Museum	National Maritime Museum Acts 1934 and 1989
6. The Wellington Museum	Wellington Museum Act 1947
7. Imperial War Museum	Imperial War Museum Acts of 1920 and 1955
8. Imperial Institute	Commonwealth Institute Act 1958
9. Horniman Museum	London Government Act 1963, s. 7 and London County Council (General Powers) Act 1901, s. 46
10. Sir John Sloane Museum	London County Council (G.P.) Act 1952, s. 20
11. Geffrye Museum	London County Council (G.P.) Act 1959, s. 29
12. Victoria and Albert Museum	National Heritage Act 1983

(The above Act of 1983, in addition to setting up the National Heritage Memorial Fund, constituted a Board of Trustees for this famous museum in South Kensington, London. The Act distinguishes between those objects which are to be transferred to the new Board and those which remain with some Minister of the Crown.[27] The Victoria and Albert Museum also illustrates the complexity of museum management at certain levels, for that museum also manages the Wellington Museum and the Theatre Museum, as well as including the National Art Library.)[28]

The power to make admission charges for the first two of these national

---

[27] The Victoria and Albert Museum (Excepted Objects) Order 1984 (S.I. 1984 No. 226).

[28] The Tower of London is a national museum in its own right, with its safe-keeping of the Crown Jewels and other famous national items. Regimental museums, sometimes managed on an agency basis by the local authority, are to be found in many of the towns with close army links.

museums was contained in the Museums and Galleries Admission Charges Act 1972.

3. **Fieldwork**

(1) *Treasure Trove*

Gold or silver, in the form of coin, plate or bullion, which is found, having **3.50** been hidden, in the earth or other secret place, is Treasure Trove and thereby belongs to the Crown, under Royal prerogative. If the owner should be found, then it belongs to him.

The times when this part of our law was laid down seem ancient; the activity in our time, whether excavation for buildings, highways or general redevelopment of land, has yielded a crop of cases which have tested and to some extent modified the principle stated above.

The main legal elements illuminated by the cases are:
(a) Was it hidden?
(b) Was it gold or silver?
(c) Has the onus been fulfilled?

(a) **Was it hidden?**

In the most recent case, *Att.-Gen.* v. *G. E. Overton (Farms) Ltd.*[29] Dillon J. **3.51** at first instance, and the Court of Appeal, on appeal, dealt with a claim by the Crown for 7,811 third-century Roman coins. Found in a field on a Lincolnshire farm, they were below the level at which a plough-share would catch them. A broken Roman earthenware urn was close to the coins. Both courts readily accepted the inference from these circumstances that the coins had been "hidden."

Old English authorities have described this requirement. Sir Edward Coke[30] used the words "of an ancient time hidden" and Chitty "concealed . . . in a house or in the earth, or other private place."[31]

In an important Irish case, a gold bowl, a necklace, torques and a collar and chain were found in a ploughed field. The circumstances were accepted by Farwell J. as showing that this treasure had been "hidden." The circumstances included not only the location but the history of the site, which had suffered a great Norse invasion in the ninth century.[32]

---

[29] [1982] 2 W.L.R. 397.
[30] Coke, 3rd Inst. p. 132 (1628–1644).
[31] *Prerogatives of the Crown*, Joseph Chitty, 1820 p. 152.
[32] *Att.-Gen.* v. *Trustees of the British Museum* [1903] 2 Ch. 598. The court found the above conclusion easier to reach since it had been presented with an alternative, more romantic, theory for the location of the treasure. This relied on the site having formerly been sea-bed. The treasure, it was said, must have been votive offerings to a sea god: this must have happened between 300 B.C. and A.D. 700, and it must have been the custom for the kings or chiefs to make such votive offerings. The court found the evidence offered on these limbs of the museum's argument "of the vaguest description" (at p. 610).
Other examples of treasure "hidden" are given in an interesting article by C. S. Emden, "The Law of Treasure Trove—Past and Present" (1926) L.Q.R. 368. This was quoted by Denning M.R. in the *Overton Farms* case.

(b) **Was it gold or silver?**

3.52   This was the main issue in the *Overton Farms* case.[33] Samples were ana-
lysed from the large number of coins found. These sample coins were said
to have silver contents as low as 1.6 per cent. but some reached 18 per
cent. After a good deal of expert evidence had been given the Court of
Appeal reviewed earlier authorities and held that in order to be treasure
trove, the metal must be gold or silver. Furthermore, the proportion of
gold or silver in the treasure claimed must be "substantial." Lord Denning, indeed, said that he would treat that word as connoting more than
50 per cent. before it could be described as a gold or silver object.[34]

(c) **Has the onus been fulfilled?**

3.53   Normally the finder of property on the land he owns can claim it; thus
treasure trove forms an exception to the general law.[35] One of the
elements in treasure trove law is that the original owner is unknown. This
is invariably the position simply due to the time which has elapsed since
the hiding of the treasure.[36] Nowadays it is the practice of the Crown to
reward, with the full market value, the finder of the treasure when it has
been determined by the coroner's inquest to be treasure trove in law.
Alternatively, if the objects, for one reason or another, are not retained by
the Crown or a museum, then they will be returned to the finder.

     The correct practice, therefore, when a finding of potential treasure
trove occurs, is to report it to the police, who alert the coroner. He holds
an inquest, takes evidence and obtains a verdict on whether the articles in
question are treasure trove.

(2) Wrecks and Whales

Wrecks

3.54   The work of the public museums service of this country is not confined
to buildings. It extends to fieldwork, such as that described in the last sub-

---

[33] See *supra*, n. 29.
[34] *Ibid.* at p. 530(e) The case of *R.* v. *Thomas and Willett* (1863) 169 E.R. 1409 has some interesting details. Rings discovered in a ploughed field in Sussex had to be gold, not brass, it
was determined, if treasure trove law was to be satisfied. Twentieth century documen-
tation on this subject includes two Home Office circulars (12/6/31 and 68/1955) which
restrict the duties of coroners in connection with treasure trove to gold and silver.
[35] *Armorie* v. *Delamirie* (1722) 1 Stra. 505. *Parker* v. *British Airways Board* [1982] 2 W.L.R. 503,
contains a recent examination by the Court of Appeal of finder's rights in relation to those
of occupiers. The occupier has the prior title, said the court, when the object is in the soil,
as, for instance, embedded in the mud; he also enjoys the prior title when he has shown an
intention to exercise control over anything which might be on the premises and his intention is manifest.
[36] Thus if a member of the museum staff made a discovery of treasure trove, this belongs to
the Crown if it is silver or gold, it was hidden and the owner is not known. If the Crown
has to be eliminated from the title, then the owner of the soil has a claim, as indicated in n.
35, *supra*.

section, and also the exploration and exhibition of Viking and Roman artifacts, as at York, Bath, London and elsewhere. From time to time, it is further extended to take in wrecks.

Basic principle

A wreck is, in law, a ship or her cargo cast ashore after shipwreck and which thus has ceased to float.[37] By virtue of the prerogative, a wreck belongs to the Crown, in Cornwall to the Duke of Cornwall and in Wales to the Lords Marchers.[38] The Merchant Shipping Act 1894 now embodies this ancient legal custom in statutory form.[39] As a result of this principle, it is within the power of the Crown to grant a right to wreck, as it is called, and this right can be accompanied by the soil or not, as the case may be.

Legal practice

The Secretary of State for the Environment is entitled to be notified **3.55** whenever a wreck is found and to require the wreck to be handed into the custody of the receiver of wrecks when the finder is not the owner.[40] The receiver holds the wreck for 12 months before disposing of it and accounting for the net proceeds, in accordance with the above Act and Regulations made under it.

Protection of Wrecks Act 1973

Under the Protection of Wrecks Act 1973, the Secretary of State is **3.56** empowered to designate, by Order, wreck sites for two purposes. First, sites which are regarded as of historic, archaeological or artistic importance. These wrecks can be thus protected against unauthorised interfer-

---

[37] It can include a hovercraft if sunk, stranded or abandoned on a navigable river or the foreshore. (See Hovercraft (Application of Enactments) Order 1972 (S.I. 1972 No. 971)). A quaint Irish case of 1875, *Stacpole* v. *The Queen* I.R. 9 E. 619, concerned two logs from a wrecked ship, which floated on to the Clare beach. Though marked by a finder with his "A," one log floated away with another tide. The Lord Chancellor, before whose court the case came, first quoted Lord Coke and Lord Hale and said:

   "Had it been floating between high and low water mark, it would have been a droit in Admiralty. If taken and carried away when the beach is dry, it is clearly a wreck. . . . Goods vary in their character according to the circumstances . . . wrecks while the tide is out, and they lie on the beach, but when the tide is in and they are again floated, droits in Admiralty" (at p. 622).

[38] See *Halsbury* (4th ed.), Vol. 8, paras. 1505 *et seq.* where it seems there could be a possible claim by a subject in Cornwall. Flotsam, jetsam and lagan go to the first finder. The case of the wreck of the Lusitania (*Pierce* v. *Bemis* [1986] Q.B. 384) confirmed that the right of the Crown did not extend to extra-territorial waters (in that case a point 12 miles west of Eire).

[39] s.523.

[40] Merchant Shipping Act 1894, ss.72, 566. The law contains a number of subtleties about presumed grants and grants by prescription, which are outside the scope of this work. The York-Antwerp Rules of 1974 are also essential reading for anyone wishing to pursue this topic in detail. (*Halsbury* (4th ed.), Vol. 25, para. 923).

ence. Secondly, sites which are considered to be potentially dangerous to life or property can be safeguarded by one of these Orders.[41]

The Orders designate an area about the wreck which does not exceed the high-water mark of the ordinary spring tides.

Once made, the Orders allow entry to the area to take place only with the consent of the Secretary of State. For his part, he grants such consent only to persons who are considered competent and who have a legitimate reason for the activity in question. Fines, both at the level of summary jurisdiction and on indictment, are the sanction in the Act for offences of damaging the wreck or objects formerly contained, or for various other acts which imperil the wreck. There is also an offence for simply entering the area.[42]

Whales

3.57   A note on whales may be of interest to curators. A dead whale is indeed sometimes cast up on the beach, like a wreck, and to that extent the topics are allied. Whales are, in law, an interesting and special case.

(1) A whale, like the sturgeon, is a royal fish:

> "Also the King, shall have throughout the realm, whales (and sturgeons) taken in the sea or elsewhere within the realm, except in certain places privileged by the King."[43]

The seas are "within the realm" if in territorial waters.[44]

3.58   (2) Whales are, legally, in a group of things found derelict on the sea, as flotsam and jetsam, and which are called droits in Admiralty.[45] The Admiralty jurisdiction of the High Court deals with claims on behalf of the Crown to determine the rightful ownership of such things.

(3) Payment akin to salvage is payable to captors of royal whales. The procedure for recovery of such payments is that of an Admiralty action for salvage.

3.59   (4) A vivid account in the law reports relates to a whale found three miles from the shore and towed on to Whitstable beach by the masters and crews of seven oyster smacks in 1829.[46] They claimed and were granted salvage from the proceeds. The report also records the conclusion of the court that in the jurisdiction of the Lord Warden of the Cinque

---

[41] Protection of Wrecks Act 1973, s.1. At the present time, Orders protecting wrecks have been made under the Act of 1973 for over 34 sites including the Erme Estuary and, *e.g.* the *Mary Rose*, the *Grace Dieu*, the *Amsterdam*, the *Mary*, *HMS Assurance* and *HMS Dartmouth*. Four of the sites are on the south coast, one in Anglesey and one in the Sound of Mull.

[42] De Prerogativa Regis (of the King's prerogative), 17 Ed. II, time uncertain. Words which included wrecks at sea in this section about the Royal Prerogative were repealed when the Merchant Shipping Act 1894 incorporated a modern procedure for wrecks, as described above: s.184, Sched. 22.

[43] An interesting list of 31 types of whale is to be found in the Schedule to the Whaling Industry (Regulation) Act 1934.

[44] See Chapter 7, para. 7.61 about the Seaside and Crown rights on the foreshore.

[45] Administration of Justice Act 1956, s.1(1)(*s*), s.3(2).

[46] *Lord Warden and Admiral of the Cinque Ports* v. *H.M. in his Office of Admiralty* (1831) 166 E.R. 304; 2 Hagg. 438.

Ports, on the south coast, the Lord Warden had been granted the right to royal fish by the sovereign and, therefore, enjoyed the title to the whale in question.

(5) The present law has succeeded centuries in which the position was **3.60** more confused. Lords of the Manor, in towns possessing Admiralty jurisdiction, enjoyed these droits. Then the creation of the Court of Admiralty ended this diffusion of rights, for some of the Admiral's patents included droits, both fish and flotsam and jetsam, where these had not been granted to other persons. The sovereign resumed the right to the royal fish in the nineteenth century and the present position is as summarised above.[47]

(3) *Metal Detectors*

The leading case of the *Overton Farms* treasure trove[48] took its place in the **3.61** law reports after a man had used his metal detector on a Lincolnshire farm. Metal detectors have indeed been for some time an element in the fieldwork interests of museum authorities in this country.

Legally the subject can be considered conveniently in relation to the timing, the method and control exercised over the practice by the museum authorities. There is also a special provision on this subject in the Ancient Monuments and Archaeological Areas Act 1979, section 42.[49]

Timing

The occasion for metal detectors to be used in an area may be prompted **3.62** by impending development or it may simply be due to inspired curiosity by the practitioners of this pastime. It is likely that the town planning department at local authority level will be the first to learn of the wish of a metal detector club to survey a site, when that survey is linked to projected development. Thus liaison of the museums and planning departments at all times becomes important. The consent to enter land, and avoid a charge of trespass, will not normally concern the local authority when privately owned land is involved. (However, if the site is "ancient" it may be that the Ancient Monuments and Archaeological Areas Act 1979 will impinge, and this is discussed below.)

Control

When the local authority wish to permit entry by a club, as envisaged **3.63** above, then the normal conditions would cover matters such as:
(a) Limits upon the time allowed for the survey.
(b) An indemnity against damage or nuisance to third parties or the

---

[47] See Holdsworth A. *History of English Law*, Vol. 1, pp. 559–561. Both the Civil List Act 1831, s.2 and the Civil List Act 1837, s.2 contain the phrase "the produce of the hereditary casual revenues arising from any droits of Admiralty or droits of the Crown." These moneys were to go into the Consolidated Fund "for the support of H.M. Household and the Honour and Dignity of the Crown."

[48] See [1982] 2 W.L.R. 397.

[49] See paras. 3.78–3.81, below.

landowner and against claims for injury by club members, if the site has hazards.

(c) Possible financial consideration for the concession.

(d) A stipulation that artifacts or objects of any sort discovered and recovered from the site are the property of the landowner.

Since metal detector clubs have come into being, they have come to expect such arrangements.

Method

3.64 A complex site to be surveyed in advance of town centre development may well require detailed specification about the parts of the surface to be disturbed and phasing may be introduced at this point. Limitation to Sundays or special holidays would be another consideration before final consent was given to entry by a club.

3.65 The Ancient Monuments and Archaeological Areas Act 1979 deals with the use of metal detectors in a "protected place" and this covers three sorts of property:

(a) A monument scheduled under the Act.

(b) A monument under the ownership or guardianship of the Secretary of State or a local authority by virtue of that Act of 1979.

(c) Areas of archaeological importance.[50]

The Schedule is maintained and published from time to time by the Secretary of State.[51] The guardianship of ancient monuments is a practice embodied in the above Act of 1979, whereby privately owned monuments, after a guardianship agreement has been executed, pass into the guardianship of the Secretary of State or the relevant local authority.[52] With a view to controlling carefully the investigation of areas of archaeological importance, the local authority and Secretary of State are given powers to designate such areas. There are sanctions, in the form of offences created for investigating those areas without prior notice to the authority in question, obtaining due consent and complying with other statutory requirements.[53]

The Act of 1979 makes it an offence: (1) to use a metal detector in one of the protected places; (2) to remove an artifact ("object of archaeological or historical interest") which the user has found in a protected place by the use of a metal detector; and (3) to break a condition imposed in a consent to enter into a protected place. To the above three offences, the Act provides two particular defences: (a) When charged with "using" the instrument, that it was being used for a purpose other than to locate or detect objects of historical or archaeological interest; and (b) in relation to the second and third offences above, that he had made reasonable inquiries to ascertain if the location was a protected place and in good faith did

[50] Ancient Monuments and Archaeological Areas Act 1979, s.42.
[51] *Ibid.* Pt. I.
[52] *Ibid.* ss.12–18.
[53] *Ibid.* Pt. II.

not believe that it was such a place.[54] The definition of metal detectors is important: "any device designed or adapted for detecting or locating any metal or mineral in the ground." The expression "or adapted" covers the situation discussed in connection with the adaptation of a motor van in the case of *Popperwell* v. *Cockerton*.[55]

(4) *Wildlife Protection*

Legislation

This is a further area of fieldwork for a modern museums authority.   **3.66**
In this book, consideration of the specific legislation on the subject is to be found in Chapter 8, at paragraphs 8–10 to 8–14.

Preservation of secrecy

A museums curator is occasionally in possession of important secrets   **3.67**
and it may be useful to summarise the law in the light of the recent Contempt of Court Act 1981. The curator's secrets may be about the nest of a golden eagle or the location of some treasure trove or other items. There may have been a campaign to secure disclosure, which he can resist. It is only in the face of court proceedings that the pressure to reveal reaches its legal ultimate. It is that situation which, among other important matters, is dealt with in the above Act of 1981.

(1) It has always been a common law contempt of court to refuse to answer a question of the court, relevant to the proceedings, without lawful excuse. Fine and imprisonment are the sanctions to enforce compliance in that situation.[56]

(2) The Act of 1981, enacted after a special committee had studied the   **3.68**
problem,[57] defined certain actions as subject to a "strict liability rule." This meant that the action was regarded as contempt of court, though no intent to commit the offence was proved.[58] (Intent is a normal ingredient in a criminal offence.) This rule is limited to publications to the public which create a "substantial risk that the course of justice, in the proceedings in question, will be seriously impeded or prejudiced."[59]

(3) A condition is that the proceedings are "active," an expression which is carefully defined in terms of judicial process, *e.g.* the summons has been served, the accused has been arrested and likewise for other situations.[60] It is a defence that the defendant did not know that the proceedings were "active," though he had taken reasonable steps to find out.

(4) "A publication made as, or as part of, a discussion in good faith of public affairs or other matters of general public interest, is not to be

---

[54] Ancient Monuments and Archaeological Areas Act 1979, s.42.
[55] [1968] 1 W.L.R. 438.
[56] *Att.-Gen.* v. *Foster* [1963] 2 Q.B. 477; in the county court, the County Courts Act 1959, s.84; in the magistrates' court, the Magistrates' Court Act 1980, s.97.
[57] Report of the Phillimore Committee, Cmnd. 5794 (1974).
[58] Contempt of Court Act 1981, s.1.
[59] *Ibid.* s.2.
[60] *Ibid.* Sched. 1.

treated as a contempt of court, under the strict liability rule, if the risk of impediment or prejudice to particular legal proceedings, is merely incidental to the discussion."[61]

3.69   (5) The effect of the provisions referred to so far is that the museum curator, in our imaginary situation, would be moving towards a position of peril in relation to the law, only if:

(i) His statement was in relation to court proceedings.

(ii) Those proceedings were "active."

(iii) He published his statement to the public.

(iv) He is not within the protection of section 5, above.

(v) His remarks went beyond normal comment and reflected on the court.

The perilous statement would therefore be of the nature of: "he did not trust the court: he would not help the court: he would never yield up the secret about the nest or whatever it might be."

(6) At that point, the curator's attention must be drawn to section 10 in the Act of 1981, headed "Disclosure" and reading as follows:

> "No court may require a person to disclose, nor is any person guilty of contempt, for refusing to disclose, the source of information contained in a publication for which he is responsible, unless it is established to the satisfaction of the court that disclosure is necessary in the interests of justice or national security or for the prevention of disorder or crime."

Conclusion

3.70   It is evident to a reader of this statute that the publication in a newspaper or other organs of the media by a journalist or reporter and secondly the recalcitrant journalist in the witness box, are the orthodox problem situations to which this Act of 1981 is directed. But other persons and other situations could lead to the Act being invoked. It might be that bizarre circumstances could demand a revelation from a museum curator and then, being at the centre of a controversy, he would have to determine his attitude to the court in the light of the above Act of Parliament.

4. Collections

3.71   The acceptance, display, and transmission of collections of ethnographic, artistic or cultural material is the lifeblood of many museums. We turn now to the legal framework wthin which this activity takes place.

(1) *Contract*

3.72   Contracts may be made between the transmitting and receiving authorities when a collection is "on loan" at a museum. It may be that those terms will be adequate to cover any problems that may arise from the transaction. Basic contract law has been discussed in Chapter 1. Perhaps

---

[61] Contempt of Court Act 1981, s.5 and *Att.-Gen.* v. *The Times Newspapers Ltd.* [1974] A.C. 273.

formal contracts have not been used, but there has been an exchange of letters, which will serve as the starting point in assembling the terms of the implied contract, if that should, at some controversial stage, be necessary. Whilst in the possession of the museum, the collection is bailed with that museum and the law of bailment cannot be ignored when one inquires about the rights and responsibilities of the museum authority in relation to the sometimes extremely valuable collection.[62]

(2) *Duties of a Bailee*

The prime duty of a bailee of goods is to take "proper care" of them[63]:   **3.73**
   (1) The bailee must protect the goods against theft.[64]
   (2) If the goods are lost, the burden of proof is upon the bailee to satisfy a court that either he took appropriate care of the goods or that his failure to do so did not contribute to their loss.[65] This onus is an important one: it is different from the claim in negligence as described in Chapter 1, where the burden of proof lies upon the plaintiff, he who brings the action at law. (In the circumstances envisaged, the museum's curator would be the defendant in an action brought by the aggrieved owner of the goods.)
   (3) Proper care of the goods by the bailee may be adjudged by the degree of benefit or reward that the bailee is deriving from possession of the goods. In the case of a museum collection, this would involve holding a keeper responsible, on behalf of his employer, for slight neglect.[66]
   (4) Sometimes there can be a clause in the agreement between the bailee and the person to whom be passes the collection, *i.e.* the sub-bailee, designed to end further liability for the collection when possession passes into the hands of the sub-bailee. Cases show that such an exclusion clause, as it is called, may be effective as against the original bailor, despite the lack of any agreement by him about such an arrangement.[67]
   (5) A bailor can sue for the full value of goods lost or destroyed by the bailee's negligence. Normally, in tort, a claim for loss following negligence would be limited to the extent of the plaintiff's personal loss. Bailment is, here again, different.
   (6) The bailment comes to an end with the redelivery of the goods to the bailor or to another person to whom he has agreed to deliver them.
   (7) Finally, reference should be made to two important principles: **3.74**
      (i) The bailee, here the museum authority, is in possession. If the

---

[62] "It represents a conveyance of personal property, created by contract and enforceable in tort" N. E. Palmer, *Bailment* (1979), p. 1.

[63] *Morris* v. *C. W. Martin & Sons Ltd.* [1966] 1 Q.B. 716, *per* Salmon L.J. at p. 738. Also Diplock L.J. at pp. 731–732.

[64] *Lee Cooper Ltd.* v. *C. H. Jeakins and Sons Ltd.* [1967] 2 Q.B.1.

[65] See, *e.g. Bristish Road Services Ltd.* v. *Arthur Crutchley Ltd.* [1968] 1 All E.R. 811, *per* Sachs L.J.at p. 822

[66] See *Taylor* v. *Caldwell* (1863) 3 B. & S. 826, *per* Blackburn J. at p. 839; see also *Hedley Byrne* v. *Heller and Partners* [1964] A.C. 465, where gratuitous advice carried the onus of a duty of reasonable care.

[67] *Scruttons Ltd.* v. *Midland Silicones Ltd.* (1962) A.C. 446, 489–490, *per* Lord Denning M.R. and *Morris* v. *C. W. Martin and Sons Ltd.*, *supra* at pp. 729–730.

collection is stolen or damaged, he may sue the wrongdoer in trespass or for the full value of the chattel taken or the full cost of its
damage. "As against a wrongdoer, possession is title."[68]

(ii) If the bailee departs from the terms on which he received the goods
into his possession, he loses the benefit of terms in the contract of
bailment. This might be an exclusion clause or something else of
great importance.

Sometimes called "the four corners rule," this principle was authorita-
tively stated by Scrutton L.J. in a leading case, *Gibaud* v. *G.E. Railway
Co.*[69]:

"The principle is well known and perhaps *Lilley* v. *Doubleday*[70] is the
best example, that if you undertake to do a certain thing in a certain
way, or to keep a thing in a certain place, with certain conditions protecting it; and have afterwards broken the contract by not doing the
thing contracted for or not keeping the thing in the place in which
you have contracted to keep it, you cannot rely on the conditions,
which were only intended to protect you if you carried out the contract in the way in which you had contracted to do it."

Though there are no cases on museum collections in the reports, there
have been and will continue to be legal problems resulting from the loan,
display and transport of collections of exhibits. "Permanent loan" or some
similar method for the display of a collection is one more setting in which
the rights and liabilities of the law of bailment can be brought into full
play.

(3) *The Professional Duty*

3.75 Though the law of bailment, as set out above, touches on most problems
raised by the reception, display, care and transmission of a collection by a
museum, it is impossible to ignore one final question: what was the
proper, professional care required in the circumstances of that case?

An anti-Gainsborough maniac in the town may have broadcast evil
intentions in the week before the collection reached the museum for display; the lock system universally used in Scrimpshire for display cases
may have been found faulty by a neighbouring museum a day or two
before the collection arrived; the senior keeper may have shown signs of
mental instability at a bridge club contest the week before, as bruited in
the local paper; the technique of mounting paintings without the use of the
recently advertised thief-proof clasps may be suspect; an article in the
Museums Journal about the theft of a Van Gogh in Melbourne Art Gallery
two months previously may have disclosed a new technique by international art crooks, a combination of vapourising and neo-reductionism.

[68] *The Winkfield* (1902) P. 42, 60, *per* Collins M.R.
[69] [1921] 2 K.B. 426 at p. 435.
[70] [1881] 7 Q.B. 510.

These are purely imaginary examples of local circumstances and professional knowledge which might bear upon the appraisal of a museum curator's professional standards when some crisis casts a spotlight upon his competence. How do the courts approach that question? There being, happily, no evident museum case to draw upon, we will touch on the general principles and then apply them to this situation.

General principles

The standard of reasonable care expected of a professional man or **3.76** woman has been discussed in Chapter 1. It stems from *Donoghue* v. *Stevenson*[71] and is the duty to take reasonable steps to avoid reasonable harm to his neighbours. The "neighbours" are those he can foresee as likely to be affected by his acts. The foreseeable harm is the "conceivable" harm.[72] He is not an insurer against all risks. The question is judged by the standards of knowledge in his profession at the time. In *Roe* v. *Minister of Health*[73] the court considered the precautions to be observed in a hospital in relation to the use by the anaesthetist of ampoules of nupercaine. Knowledge changed between 1947, when the accident happened, and 1954, when the case was in court. "We must not look at a 1947 accident with 1954 spectacles," said Lord Denning.

The standard is objective. It does not vary with the competence or experience of the professional person. If he is inexperienced, he should seek advice. He cannot say: "I was doing my best and I could not help it."[74] He is judged by the standard of skill and care knowledgeable members of his profession bring to their professional duties.[75]

---

[71] [1932] A.C. 562.

[72] See, *e.g.* A. M. Dugdale & K. M. Stanton, *Professional Negligence* (Butterworths, 1982), para. 23.06. This area may be looked on as one application of the general principles described in relation to Negligence in Chapter 1. It could apply equally to many of the professionals involved in the public leisure services.

[73] [1954] 2 Q.B. 66.

[74] *Nettleship* v. *Weston* [1971] 2 Q.B. 691, 699.

[75] Some words of McNair J. in *Bolam* v. *Friern Hospital Management Committee* [1957] 1 W.L.R. 582 have become the accepted principle, having been approved in the House of Lords (*Whitehouse* v. *Jordan* [1981] 1 W.L.R. 246) and embodied in the Congenital Disabilities (Civil Liability) Act 1976, s.1(5). McNair J. said:

"Where you get a situation which involves some special skill or competence, then the test . . . is the standard of the ordinary skilled man exercising and professing to have that special skill. . . . There may be one or more perfectly proper standards . . . if a medical man conforms with one of those proper standards, then he is not negligent. . . . That does not mean that a [medical] man can obstinately and pig-headedly carry on with some old technique, if it has been proved to be contrary to what is really substantially the whole of informed (medical) opinion. . . ."

Our museum curator would no doubt enjoy reading the Court of Appeal judgment in *Luxmoore-May* v. *Messenger May Baverstock* [1990] 1 All E.R. 1067. This relates to the professional level of competence looked for in a provincial auctioneer who was asked to look at two paintings of foxhounds. He said their value was £30 to £50 the pair. Later they were sold in a London auction for £88,000 as the work of George Stubbs. Sued for the difference, based on his alleged negligence, these tests were applied and the plaintiff lost her claim. The auctioneer had acted reasonably.

Competence and the curator

3.77   To apply these standards to the museum director is to seek to turn principles into practical tests; these questions are simply indicative and not exhaustive:

(a) Was it a task where a consultant would normally be brought in?

(b) Were the premises secure, ventilated, safe for the objects in the collection, safe for visitors?

(c) Were there enough staff? Were they competent, briefed on special features of the exhibition? Had his delegation been reasonable? What had he kept as his own role?

(d) Ultimately, how far was he abreast of the shared knowledge of his profession, nationally and, nowadays, internationally?

(e) Was the mishap, the catastrophe, due to an error of judgment or was it due to negligence?

(f) Is his insurance cover in force and adequate?

5. Ancient Monuments and Archaeological Areas

(1) *Ancient Monuments*

3.78   The law relating to ancient monuments was consolidated and changed in the Ancient Monuments and Archaeological Areas Act 1979 (the Act of 1979). As a major Act of 65 sections and 5 Schedules, a full study is outside the scope of this work but the main legal provisions that will be of concern to museum authorities are set out below[76]:

The Secretary of State now keeps a statutory list of all scheduled monuments. These are the monuments which he considers to be of national importance.[77] (A dwelling-house not occupied by the caretaker of the adjacent monument and his family cannot be included in the list.[78])

The above group of *Scheduled* monuments are all, by the Act of 1979, deemed to be *ancient* monuments. So also are other monuments which the Secretary of State considers to be of historical, architectural, traditional, artistic or archaeological interest. The width of this definition may be gauged if we mention that it includes not only Hadrian's Wall and the Tower of London but also bridges, deserted villages, castles, crosses, inscribed stones, Roman remains and camps and settlements.

A guardianship system is retained whereby an ancient monument can be placed in voluntary guardianship with the Secretary of State or the relevant local authority.[79]

---

[76] For a full, helpful and specialist treatment of the Act of 1979, see *e.g.* R. W. Suddards, *Listed Buildings: The Law and Practice of Historic Buildings, Ancient Monuments and Conservation Areas* (1988, Sweet and Maxwell).

[77] Ancient Monuments and Archaeological Areas Act 1979, s.1. The list is published and local portions can be inspected at the offices of town planning authorities.

[78] *Ibid.* s.1(4). The definition of monument is now any building, structure or work, or the site thereof, a cave or excavation or any site comprising the remains of a vehicle, vessel or aircraft. It does not include a wreck protected by scheduling in the Protection of Wrecks Act 1973.

[79] Ancient Monuments and Archaeological Areas Act 1979, s.18.

A *protected* monument can now be defined as one which is either sched-   **3.79**
uled, as described above, or is under guardianship.[80]

Having established these groups of monuments, the Act proceeds to
buttress them by laying down a number of offences:

(a) To execute or cause or permit the execution of works damaging a
scheduled monument, unless authorised by the consent of the Secretary of State.[81]

(b) Destroying or damaging a protected monument.[82]

(c) Failing to give information about interests in land.[83]

There is a whole range of associated statutory powers which can be   **3.80**
used by the Secretary of State or local authorities to support the above
basic framework:

(a) Compulsory acquisition of the monument, adjacent land or supporting easements by the Secretary of State or use of ordinary
transfer.[84]

(b) Entry in the Local Land Charges Register of scheduled monuments.[85]

(c) Entry upon the site of a monument by the Secretary of State to
carry out urgent works for its preservation.

(d) Extensive powers of entry for the Secretary of State to ascertain by
inspection works needed to a scheduled monument.[86]

(e) Agreements by the Secretary of State with the owners of ancient
monuments to maintain them.[87]

(f) Transfer of monuments between local authorities and the Secretary of State.[88]

The Secretary of State may be obliged to pay compensation where consent for works to be carried out to an ancient monument is refused or,
again, where there is damage to a monument within a guardianship
order.[89]

At all times the Secretary of State can provide advice on works to monuments for the benefit of local authorities and can provide supervision for
those works.[90]

(2) *Areas of Archaeological Importance*

Part II of the Act of 1979 contains a code for protecting these areas. Legal
action begins when the area is designated in an Order[91] made by the Sec-

---

[80] Ancient Monuments and Archaeological Areas Act 1979, s.28.
[81] *Ibid.* s.2.
[82] *Ibid.* s.28. This provision of two offences—s.2 and s.28 one for scheduled and one for protected monuments—exemplifies the importance of the two categories under the Act.
[83] *Ibid.* s.57.
[84] *Ibid.* s.10.
[85] *Ibid.* s.5.
[86] *Ibid.* s.6.
[87] *Ibid.* s.17.
[88] *Ibid.* s.21.
[89] *Ibid.* ss.7–9.
[90] *Ibid.* s. 25.
[91] *Ibid.* s.33.

retary of State or by a local authority, subject to his confirmation.[92] The immediate consequence is that it becomes an offence to carry out any works which disturb the ground or cause flooding or tipping in that area unless an operations notice has first been served[93] upon the district or the London borough council.

3.81   The aim of the procedure is not to "freeze" the site for all time. Rather it is to delay development until adequate archaeological investigation has taken place. An initial four-week period for the investigating authority to give notice that it will be excavating the site can be extended to 18 weeks. A little detail will usefully fill out this picture:

(a) The person to carry out the archaeological investigation must be duly appointed.[94]

(b) A local authority can use the procedure of an injunction to combat operations in contravention of section 35 (the operations notice) in urgent cases.

(c) There is power for the Secretary of State to relax section 35 in certain cases.[95]

(d) There is also power for the investigating authority to move faster, and pay compensation for damage caused, where a site has been acquired compulsorily.[96]

(e) Use of metal detectors in an archaeological area without consent is an offence.[97]

(f) There are certain statutory defences to the offence created by section 35, *i.e.:*

(i) That all reasonable precautions were taken and due diligence exercised.

(ii) The defendant did not know and had no reason to believe that he was in an archaeological area.

(iii) The operation was urgently necessary in the interests of health or safety and that due notice was given.

---

[92] Ancient Monuments and Archaeological Areas Act 1979, Sched. 2, para. 13.
[93] *Ibid.* s.35.
[94] *Ibid.* s.64.
[95] *Ibid.* s.37.
[96] *Ibid.* s.39.
[97] *Ibid.* s.42 and see above, paras. 3.61–3.65.

CHAPTER 4

PARKS AND RECREATION GROUNDS

"The role of the judiciary is essentially that of a referee . . . The referee is only involved when it appears that some player has acted in breach of the rules . . . "

Lord Donaldson M.R. in *R.* v. *Secretary of State for the Environment, ex p. Hammersmith and Fulham London Borough Council* [1990] 1 A.C. 521, 561

INTRODUCTION

The law relating to parks and recreation grounds has not yet been consoli- **4.01** dated. The Law Commission regularly recommends parts of the law of this country which would benefit from consolidation but so far the Commission has not reached this branch.

Thus the main legal authority for the provision of public parks and recreation grounds is to be found in a statute of 1875.[1] That was the time when urban authorities were creating these leisure outlets in all our towns and cities; like the statute itself, many parks then brought into being still serve their communities.

This branch of the law well reflects changing trends. The related Public Health Acts, which, with the Act of 1875, contain the legal framework for modern parks management, were passed by Parliament at intervals, 1890, 1907, 1925, 1961 and 1976, to reflect the call from town halls for powers to provide an ever wider range of these facilities.[2]

In this chapter, the main legal provisions affecting parks management will be described in section A.[3] Historically those provisions have been glossed by a series of rating cases, which will be discussed later in this

---

[1] Public Health Act 1875. The expression there is "public walks and pleasure grounds."

[2] The Local Government (Miscellaneous Provisions) Act 1976, whilst replacing the Physical Training and Recreation Act 1937, also exemplifies the major enlargement of powers to meet this area of need.

[3] The full titles of the series of Acts referred to in this chapter are as follows:

Act of 1875	Public Health Act 1875
Act of 1890	Public Health Acts (Amendment) Act 1890
Act of 1906	Open Spaces Act 1906
Act of 1907	Public Health Acts (Amendment) Act 1907
Act of 1925	Public Health Act 1925
Act of 1961	Public Health Act 1961
Act of 1976	Local Government (Miscellaneous Provisions) Act 1976

Chapter.[4] By-laws play their part in the management of parks and these will be dealt with in section C.[5] The fourth section gathers up several otherwise unrelated items of law affecting parks, including animals, zoos and safaris, insurance against bad weather, elm disease and fire blight and, as a related facility to recreation grounds, street playgrounds.

A. THE CREATION, MANAGEMENT AND DISPOSAL OF PUBLIC PARKS

1. Acquisition

4.02   Local authorities[6] may acquire land by purchase or lease and lay it out for use as parks by the public.[7] They may do this, directly, themselves, or, indirectly, by other persons and contribute to that provision. The necessary ancillary power to maintain and improve those parks is also available to local authorities.[8]

   The expression "public walks and pleasure grounds" in the parent Act of 1875 has now been in operation for over a century. Though it does not include the words "parks" or "public parks," those amenities are recognised as coming within the statutory expression. The variety of lands laid out for public walks and pleasure grounds is immense, both in size and in treatment and it is remarkable that the somewhat vague statutory phrase has stood the test of time so well.

The Victorian Acts

4.03   The power to provide parks in the Act of 1875 was the culmination of a series of Victorian statutes, each of which dealt with a small aspect of the total subject. First the Public Health Act 1848, section 74, was in virtually the same terms as section 164 of the Public Health Act 1875, which replaced it. An Act of 1859, the Recreation Grounds Act, extended the powers of public authorities to grounds which the National Playing Fields Association has inherited.[9] The Town Gardens Protection Act 1863 was concerned with special public walking areas in towns, such as gardens and lawns in squares and crescents. A Public Improvements Act 1860, adop-

---

[4] See paras. 4.33–4.40 *et seq., post.*

[5] This account is referred to in other parts of this book, when by-law-making powers of other bodies, *e.g.* the Forestry Commission, come under consideration.

[6] Local authorities include county and district councils, London boroughs, parish councils and the Common Council of the City of London.

[7] Acquisition can be made by use of compulsory powers, under the Local Government Act 1972, s.121. The general power is in the Act of 1875, s.164, supplemented by the Act of 1890, s.45. This later Act added lands outside the authority's area to those described in the Act of 1875, provided that the lands outside the authority's district can be "conveniently used" by the inhabitants of the district engaging these powers.

[8] Public Health Act 1875, s.164.

[9] Charities Act 1960, s.39 repealed the Recreation Grounds Act 1859 as "no longer required." Trusts set up by the 1859 Act may, however, still be met, as they were preserved.

tive in nature, had taken the provision further; ratepayers in townships with 500 or more inhabitants could spend money to provide parks, exercise or playgrounds.[10]

Other open space

Public parks are a form of public open space. Chapter 2 deals with the **4.04** operation of the Open Spaces Act 1906 and also with commons, an important additional open space. Village greens are themselves a type of common. If it appears to a local authority that a public park can suitably be used as a "country park," then, from the date of the authority's decision, it must be so treated. Country parks are described in Chapter 8. Open spaces associated with the sea or inland waters will be found in Chapter 7 as an aspect of sport.

2. Management

The initial power in 1875 extended to "laying out, planting, improving **4.05** and maintaining" the parks. Soon, the precise meaning of those six words was tested, as local authorities sought sanction from government departments to borrow money for amenities considered reasonable in their parks. Under a sympathetic administration in Whitehall, sanctions were granted for greenhouses, reading rooms, bandstands, bowling greens, shelters, cycle tracks and gymnastic appliances. Nevertheless, the desire to extend these amenities, to charge for some of them and to place some in the temporary care of clubs and societies, led to the need for clarifying legislation over a period of 100 years (see paragraph 4.01). The resulting portfolio of powers available in parks to local authorities is as follows.[11]

(1) *Sport*

Boating lakes

Pleasure boats can be provided, let for hire or licensed to some person **4.06** or persons for letting for hire.[12] The provision of the pools and associated buildings and equipment is also authorised.[13]

---

[10] Repealed by the Parish Councils Act 1957.

[11] Local authorities in 1875 meant urban authorities. This was extended in 1906 (Act of 1906, s.14) to county councils and to rural authorities generally in 1931 (Rural District Councils (Urban Powers) Order 1931 (S.R. & O. 1931 No. 580)). Finally, by the Local Government Act 1972, Pt. II, Sched. 14, para. 27, all current local authorities were given the power of managing public parks. The Act of 1875 was kept in being when functions were defined but not codified.

[12] See, *e.g.* Public Health Acts (Amendment) Act 1890, s.44(2).

[13] Public Health Act 1961, s.54. Where the existence of a boating pool is likely to interfere with any water flowing directly or indirectly out of or into any watercourse vested in or controlled by a River Board or other public water authority, the local authority is required to confer with that body before providing the new pool, (Act of 1961, s.54(4)).

Ice skating

A power exists to enclose not more than one-quarter of the area of ice for skating and then to charge for admission to that area.[14]

Cricket, football and other games

Sports pitches involve some exclusion of the public and this has been authorised since 1907.[15] Power to charge the persons granted the use of those pitches is also authorised.[16] Nevertheless, the local authority must ensure that exclusive use, as above, does not extend to more than one-third of any one park or pleasure ground. Nor must they allow more than one-quarter of the total area of their parks to be the subject of exclusive use. Parliament has also laid down that the local authority must satisfy themselves that they have not unfairly restricted the space available to the public for games and recreations.[17] An obvious instance of such unfairness might be the exclusive letting of sports pitches, up to the legal maximum at the weekend, when experience had shown that public demand at that time was so great that it could not be met by the three-quarters of the total area which would, at those weekends, be available.[18]

The statutory principle set out above affects public rights and is thus the sort which is suitable for enforcement by an aggrieved ratepayer by judicial review in the High Court.[19]

The case of *Wheeler* v. *Leicester City Council*[20] shows the courts intervening against a misused discretion in the letting of a public park to a rugby club. A 12-month withdrawal of that facility, due to differences of opinion about the way to show opposition to apartheid in South Africa, was found to be an unlawful application of the council's duty under the Race Relations Act 1976, section 71 to consider the interests of good race relations, when carrying out "their various functions."

(2) *Seats, Games, Apparatus, Pavilions, Reading Rooms and Refreshment Rooms*

4.07 These are five amenities found in parks, different in nature but related in law. All were listed in the Act of 1907[21] as amenities which local authorities were in future authorised to provide. A power to charge for the use of such amenities was added, in the case of the apparatus, the reading rooms and the pavilions. That power, in the case of these two buildings, is

---

[14] Public Health Acts (Amendment) Act 1907, s.76.
[15] *Ibid.* The exclusion is, of course, only for the period of play and cannot be carried through to tenancies or leases. If the land is really surplus, it could now be appropriated and then let.
[16] Public Health Act 1925, s.56.
[17] Public Health Act 1961, s.52(3). These general powers can be varied by Local Acts.
[18] *Ibid.* s.52(3).
[19] But see the qualifications on this procedure under R.S.C., Order 53, as to the standing of the applicants or otherwise, in *I.R.C.* v. *Federation of Self Employed* [1981] 2 All E.R. 93 (H.L.).
[20] [1985] A.C. 1054.
[21] s.76.

not to be used on more than 12 days in one year, nor on more than four consecutive days.[22]

The Act of 1907 specifically safeguards terms imposed by a donor or lessor of a public park. The powers described above are not to be exercised so that they would contravene any condition or covenant imposed by such persons, unless consent has been obtained from the persons currently able to enforce them.[23]

(3) *Legal Claims for Negligence and Nuisance*

Those responsible for the management of public parks have particular hazards in the field of potential litigation in relation to the torts of negligence and nuisance and also the legal perils associated with the liability for the collapse or repair of walls. **4.08**

Equipment negligence claims

In so far as claims stem from the injuries which children in particular may suffer, from use or misuse of play equipment in a recreation ground, adventure playground or trim trail, the legal principles have been discussed in the first chapter, in connection with the duties of occupiers to visitors. (see paragraphs. 1.004 to 1.013). The situation in law is that the local authority has invited the public to use, for its pleasure and recreation, the sort of equipment mentioned. In those circumstances, the common duty of care rests upon the authority, with all the qualifications which are discussed in that chapter.

Nuisance

The second considerable area of concern to parks managers, at member and officer level, is more specialised. It is the potential liability for nuisance—with a difference.[24] The overriding legal principle which emerges is that a local authority, as owner of land acquired and held for the purposes of section 164 of the Public Health Act 1875, *i.e.* "public walks and pleasure grounds," is not, thereby, in beneficial occupation of that land. "They are incapable by law of using it for any profitable purpose; they must allow the public the free and unrestricted use of it," said Lord Halsbury, Lord Chancellor, in the *Lambeth Overseers* case.[25] **4.09**

Following that principle, the local authority in *Hall* v. *Beckenham Corporation*[26] were exonerated from liability for nuisance to a householder who lived near to the public park. The nuisance originated from the flying of **4.10**

---

[22] s.76.
[23] Public Health Acts (Amendment) Act 1907, s.76(4).
[24] See Section B for full discussion.
[25] *The Churchwardens and Overseers of Lambeth Parish* v. *The London County Council* [1897] A.C. 625, 631. Also *infra* at para. 4.37.
[26] [1949] 1 K.B. 716.

model aeroplanes powered by internal combustion engines inside the park. The court accepted the argument that the Corporation could not be liable in nuisance, since they were not, in law, occupiers of the park.

4.11   In the *Beckenham* case, two arguments were advanced by the plaintiff to distinguish the *Lambeth Overseers* case. First, it was argued that the Corporation could put the recreation ground to a profitable use by appropriating it to another use, *e.g.* a car park, by virtue of their powers under the Local Government and Town and Country Planning Acts. This argument did not prevail with Finnemore J. He relied on the view taken in the intervening case of *North Riding County Valuation Committee* v. *Redcar Corporation*.[27] There, a distinction was drawn between certain facilities in a park, such as a boating lake, a car park, a pavilion, which were used to yield income and of which the Corporation were held to be in occupation, and other non-profitable parts of the park. These comprised the expanse of grass, woodland and open space and were held to be within the *Lambeth Overseers* case principle. In other words, appropriation was irrelevant; the power to obtain income was available to the authority as a parks authority.

4.12   The second argument was that the control exercised by the local authority over the park in closing it at night and on certain days throughout the year, legally affected the role and status of the Corporation. However, the court held that these control measures were merely incidental to the role of the Corporation under section 164 of the Public Health Act 1875. They could not have a critical effect on the legal status of the local authority.

4.13   This brought the court to the position that the Corporation could be liable to the plaintiff in nuisance as an occupier, despite the Lambeth principle, but only if they had powers sufficiently extensive by way of management control, that they could prevent the nuisance:

> "They have the right to make by-laws for (the park's) proper conduct and they have express power, if they make by-laws which are confirmed, to eject from the ground those who infringe them. They have no general power to turn people out because they do not like them or because they are doing something of which a particular park keeper may not approve. They can only act against people in the park who offend against their by-laws or who commit some offence or crime for which criminal action can be taken.
>
> It seems plain that if they go beyond those powers, their officer and therefore they themselves will be liable for an action, for example, for assault or false imprisonment, if they lay hands on someone and forcibly put him outside the park."[28]

It was by this process of reasoning that the *Beckenham* leading case laid down that, not being legally the occupiers, the local authority were not liable in nuisance to the aggrieved neighbouring householder.

4.14   By making comprehensive by-laws, a local authority may, therefore,

---

[27] [1943] K.B. 114.
[28] [1949] 1 K.B. 716, 727.

bring themselves into the position of occupiers of the whole park and subject to actions in nuisance.

Nuisance: the general principle

It is worth restating here the principle that liability to a neighbouring property owner for a nuisance on one's own land arises in law if the nuisance has been adopted or continued on your own land. This is illustrated in the classic case of *Sedley-Denfield* v. *Callaghan*,[29] where flooding of the neighbour's land occurred due to an inadequate culvert on the defendant's land. The burden of the case was to ascertain that the defendant must have known of the nuisance and thus, in law "adopted or continued" it. The defendants were found liable because, in the words of Lord Porter, "with knowledge that a state of things existed which might at any time give rise to a nuisance, they took no steps to remedy that state of affairs."[30]

So if, in the circumstances discussed above, there is in the park a tree **4.15** dangerous to the neighbour because it is overhanging, or due to its spreading roots, or there is a tottering wall, or a group of stone-throwing boys,[31] and the park warden and his department do nothing, the authority are liable in nuisance. It is emphasised that it is not the creation of the potential nuisance that is critical—it was a trespasser who did it in the *Sedley-Denfield* case—it is the ability to stop it, after knowing of it. The other test, the test of reasonableness, comes into play once the nuisance is made out as above and the court considers what was done to prevent the nuisance. "The standard ought to be to require of the occupier what is reasonable to expect of him in his individual circumstances," Lord Wilberforce said in the case of *Goldman* v. *Hargrave*.[32]

(4) *Walls and Fences*

Walls and fences are a frequent problem for those managing public parks. **4.16** This is partly due to the sheer expense of repair, so that liability is worth detailed attention and often keen discussion. It is also because it is often desirable to maintain walls and fences, despite the growth of the school of thought which favours open parks. A practical approach, stemming from the legal principles involved, could be on the following lines:

(a) If someone is responsible for damaging the wall or fence, hold him responsible.

(b) If it is age or some non-human agency which has caused the damage or collapse;

    (i) The title deeds are the first guide to responsibility. Their clauses about repair and any "T" marks on the deed plan are the necessary starting point in determining legal liability. Of

---

[29] [1940] A.C. 880.
[30] *Ibid.* at p. 920.
[31] *Att.-Gen.* v. *Corke* [1933] Ch. 89.
[32] [1967] 1 A.C. 645, 663 E.

course, it can be frustrating to find from the deeds that Mr. Wiseacre built the wall but left the document silent on the question of maintenance.

    (ii) Trace the history of repairs. Was it last done on the basis of accepted liability or was it "without prejudice"?

    (iii) What does an inspection of the wall reveal?

        (1) By its construction, smooth outside and rough within, is it clear that it was a park boundary wall, that it was fencing *in* the park?

        or

        (2) Is it a fence wall, built on land at the same level on both sides? Is it thus what perhaps 75 per cent. of boundary walls are, namely, party walls, where each landowner owns an unsevered half, has a right of support from the other person's half and maintenance costs are shared equally?

        or

        (3) Is it, on the other hand, partly a retaining wall, with earth against a greater number of courses on one side than the other? This might be a highway embankment or the end of a house garden, where that structure needed the retaining wall for its own stability. Again, does history help? If not,

        A. If the adjoining property is a highway, that authority should accept the retaining portion of the wall as part of the highway and then they will discuss responsibility for the surmounting fence wall as a separate item.[33]

        B. Otherwise, the owner who is higher needs the retaining wall for his own support whilst his neighbour needs the wall to keep out the adjacent soil. The interest in having that sort of wall in that position might be agreed as one to be shared equally. These problems tend to go into court infrequently but there are several such cases which assist in establishing some of the above three points.[34]

4.17   (c) Finally, there are three statutory provisions which are sometimes relevant to this question of liability for walls and fences.

    (i) The Highways Act 1980 gives power to the highway authority to serve notice upon a property owner adjoining a street and at his own expense he must then fence adequately any part of his property which is a source of danger to persons using the street.[35] The authority have default powers should the owner take no action.

---

[33] See *Att.-Gen.* v. *Todmorden B.C.* (1937) 4 All E.R. 588 for a useful case showing (*inter alia*) that the highway authority need only keep the retaining wall in a state of repair sufficient to support the highway. Any better standard must be met by agreement with the adjacent landowner.

[34] See a useful article in (1909) 73 J.P.R. 285 about retaining walls.

[35] s.165.

(ii) Under the Burial Act 1900,[36] an obligation rests on the owner of a cemetery to keep the fences in good order and condition. Since disused burial grounds occasionally are transferred to the local authority, this initial obligation of a Parochial Church Council could become one in which the parks department of a local authority is obliged to take a close interest.[37]

(iii) By virtue of the Limitation Act 1980, a party taking legal action based on the terms of a deed, must do so within 12 years of his cause of action arising.[38] If the deed contained a covenant to erect a fence, then the 12 years would run from the date of the deed.

(5) *Metal Detectors*

These, also, are of interest to those responsible for parks and open spaces **4.18** and will be found discussed in Chapter III in relation to museums. This follows the development of relations by metal detector clubs with museum directors, due to mutual interest in treasure below the ground. (A museums department is invariably consulted when Treasure Trove is found.)

(6) *Trespass*

This is now the subject of the Occupiers' Liability Act 1984 and will be **4.19** found discussed in Chapter I, with other general legal principles.

(7) *Closure of Parks*

Shows

When a local authority grants permission for the holding of an agricul- **4.20** tural, horticultural or other show, to be held in one of their parks, or grants the use of a park to a charity or other institution, then the authority will wish to be able to close that park for normal public use. They may also wish to allow the temporary occupiers to make charges for admission to the show. The law allows such closure on a maximum of 12 days in a year, provided that not more than six of such days are consecutive.[39] Closure is not permitted on Sundays. Finally, whilst closure can now take place on public holidays, this power is qualified. On any bank holiday,[40] Christmas Day, Good Friday, or a day appointed for national thanksgiving or mourning, the power of closure can only be used if three-quarters of the total area of the parks of that authority is still open to the public.

The local authority has discretion to permit charges for admission to

---

[36] s.10.
[37] Local Government Act 1972, s.215 deals with closed churchyards.
[38] s.8.
[39] Public Health Acts (Amendment) Act 1890, s.44, and Public Health Act 1961, s.53.
[40] See Bank Holidays Act 1871 and Holidays Extension Act 1875.

the event in question, to be made whilst the park is closed to the public as a park.[41]

Public entertainment

4.21   An extension to this power of closure is now contained in the Local Government Act 1972, section 145(2). This allows a local authority to close a park when they wish to provide entertainment of any nature, or facilities for dancing. For this purpose they can enclose or set apart any part of a park or pleasure ground under their control.

A similar power of closure is available when a person is to provide entertainment in a theatre, concert hall, dance hall or other premises for entertainment, dance, or arts and crafts, under agreement with the parks authority; that authority can add part of their park to that letting.

In each instance, the authority must take care not to breach a condition or covenant entered into with the donor of the park or indeed, any other person who is entitled to enforce such terms.

(8) *Car Parks*

4.22   The pressing need for car parks near certain popular public parks drives local authorities to consider occasionally whether part of the park itself cannot sensibly be set aside for use as a car park.

In law, there is now the specific statutory authority to do this.[42] Even so, a local authority can still meet the kind of problems encountered in, *e.g. Attorney-General* v. *Southampton Corporation*.[43] When the local authority wished to set aside two areas of a common as car parks, objection was successfully taken to the move. The grounds advanced by the objectors were that the car parks would not be ancillary to the public park, *i.e.* Southampton Common, but rather would afford desirable car parking for an adjacent public house and an adjacent zoo. The case was complicated by the law relating to commons, when government consents became obligatory, and also Local Acts and open space considerations. Nevertheless, the judgment of Foster J. gave as a basis for his decision the view that the local authority held the common "under the Act of 1875 for the purpose of being used as public walks and pleasure grounds and under the Act of 1906 to allow enjoyment of it by the public as an open space. (It) can only exercise the powers given to it by those Acts, if such exercise is consistent with or ancillary to those purposes."[44] The judge was not satisfied that the car parks were reasonably necessary to enable the public to enjoy the common as an open space or to be used as public walks or pleasure grounds. Thus the Corporation were held to be in breach of their duties if they proceeded with their proposals.

---

[41] Public Health Acts (Amendment) Act 1907, s.44, and Public Health Act 1961, s.53.

[42] Local Government (Miscellaneous Provisions) Act 1976, s.19(1)(*f*).

[43] (1978) 21 P. & C.R. 281.

[44] *Ibid.* at p. 290. A curious anomaly relating to car parks is the generous power of providing car parks from this source available to rural parishes (s.46 of Road Traffic Regulation Act 1967) but not to cities or the Greater London Council.

Though the Act of 1976 has clarified the power to provide car parks, which is now available to a local authority, there is but a minor change in the test accepted by the court in the *Southampton* case. Would the car parking be a facility, says the modern court, "in connection with other recreational facilities?" *i.e.* that the authority was providing.[45] Thus the link between the proposed car park and enhanced use of the public park or pleasure ground, sought but not found by the court in the *Southampton* case, is still the cardinal test today.

(9) *Local Acts or Deeds of Transfer*

Public parks have frequently passed into local authority ownership as gifts **4.23** or as friendly transfers from local property owners of substance. In those circumstances it is not uncommon to find Local Act provisions touching on these properties. A century ago, such Acts were used more frequently to achieve land acquisition or schemes of improvement than is necessary now, when a wider range of public general Acts is available.

A sample list from Local Acts selected at random illustrates the recognition given to the donor's rights, in relation to adjoining land or otherwise. This element can often affect park maintenance and must be taken into account.[46]

Examples of third-party restrictions on public parks or open spaces

(1) Waltham Holy Cross Urban District Council Act 1958 **4.24**
    Marshes were created as public parks under section 164 of the Act of 1875, with ample powers to provide recreational facilities. Yet these were not to prevent the digging for or taking of stone sand or gravel from Hall Marsh, Waltham Marsh or Cheshunt Marsh (section 14).

(2) Bournemouth Corporation Act 1960
    Power was conferred upon the Corporation to provide in their parks a zoo, botanical gardens, a boating lake and facilities for games. But all these were subject to there being no contravention of private trusts which affected the land in question (section 44).

(3) Durham County Council Act 1968
    This authorised the provision of golf courses on lands of the local authority but included a similar proviso about private trusts as in the Bournemouth Act (*supra*) (section 58).

(4) Hertfordshire County Council Act 1960
    This Act contains a section (section 7) stemming from the requirement of the law of property that the person seeking to enforce a restrictive covenant should own adjacent land which benefits from that covenant. In order, therefore, to give efficacy to

---

[45] Local Government (Miscellaneous Provisions) Act 1976, s.19(1)(*f*).

[46] One park in Halifax, West Yorkshire has a Protector, to be consulted as of legal right on changes affecting the character of the park. He is this generation's descendant of the Protector appointed over a century ago. The arrangement has been working harmoniously in recent years.

such a covenant in an earlier statute (being one affecting public parks or open space), this provision acknowledged in this authoritative form that there was adjacent land of the Council which would benefit from such a covenant.

(10) *Park Wardens*

4.25   Management need wardens in their parks. Earlier statutes referred to them as officers, though an ancient power to have them sworn in and granted warrants to act as constables is out of harmony with present police practice.[47]

These wardens are usually needed to enforce park by-laws, which are regularly used to control conduct in parks. The wardens can be particularly useful to spot or discourage mischievous or dangerous conduct in recreation grounds. The legal liabilities of local authorities to children or other visitors to parks are dealt with elsewhere; clearly, evidence from alert wardens about the state of machinery in the play equipment, the frequency of its inspection, the location of any warning notices and any special features in the parks which later assumed legal significance—all these are areas of their work where good wardens can be invaluable to an authority.

3. **Disposal or Changed Use of Parks**

Background

4.26   The assembly by local authorities of lands for their public parks represents an historical phase. Urbanisation proceeded apace in the Victorian era and later, and the parks were a healthy outlet for the townsfolk. Recreation in every form was necessary and the parks met one part of that need.

The legal framework within which such land was owned by local authorities stemmed from that period. Parliament intended the land to be stamped with the trusts and obligations which were appropriate to its character. Thus in 1972 the land variously acquired by local authorities as public walks and pleasure grounds or as public open space[48] was designated as "public trust land"[49] and restraints placed upon its use for purposes other than those for which it was acquired. Local government reorganisation was the occasion for this reclassification and, ironically, it may be that the attention thus given to these lands later led to the significant relaxing of controls over them.

---

[47] Public Health Acts (Amendment) Act 1907, s.77, and Public Health Act 1961, s.52. There are exceptions, *e.g.* at Brighton with 2,500 acres of open space to oversee, where it has been found that the "Parks Police" and "Parks Constables" have a role worth maintaining. The staff in question have been sworn in as constables pursuant to Local Act powers which will lapse before long. Recourse to the more limited powers under the Act of 1907, s.77 then becomes necessary.

[48] Public Health Act 1875, s.164, and Open Spaces Act 1906.

[49] Local Government Act 1972, s.122 (6).

Certainly a new historical phase is now in being, when local authorities, as a matter of dire financial and legal necessity, review their land holdings.[50] They are under pressure to release land not needed beneficially. Thus parks, as well as schools, blocks of flats, and of course derelict sites, can from time to time come into that group. The movements of central area population can also be a social reason for wishing to abandon a park. The legal restraints upon this sort of action have, in recent years, been eased considerably but, in the absence of codification, it is necessary to set these out piecemeal.

(1) *Restrictive Covenants*

Sometimes the free use of park land is hindered by a restrictive covenant: **4.27** no games on Sundays: no drinks in the pavilion: no building nearer than 100 yards to the southern boundary. History has moved along, the circumstances giving rise to these provisions have altered, and it is now, happily, possible in law to challenge these covenants. The procedure, under the Law of Property Act 1925,[51] is worth consideration by anyone responsible for managing parks and restrained by this type of covenant.
    The basic submission to be made to a court by a landowner is:
  (a) by reason of changes in the character of the property or the neighbourhood, the restrictive covenant has become obsolete; or
  (b) it is obstructive in that it impedes the reasonable use of the land for public or private purposes; or
  (c) it is contrary to the public interest and the modification or discharge can be adequately compensated in money; or
  (d) the persons entitled to the benefit of the covenant have agreed to the modification or discharge and the court—it is currently the Lands Tribunal which exercises this jurisdiction—is satisfied that no injury will be thereby caused to those persons.[52]

(2) *Local Acts*

Reference has been made above to the types of restraint upon public parks **4.28** found in Local Acts.[53] A local authority is in a good position to judge whether one of these restraints has become otiose and should be removed. It may then be that an opportunity can be found to use a Local Act to

---

[50] See Local Government Planning and Land Act 1980, Pt. X, when reviews of land banks by local authorities are obligatory at the behest of the Secretary of State for the Environment.

[51] s.84, modified by Lands Tribunal Act 1949, Administration of Justice Act 1932, Landlord and Tenant Act 1954, and Law of Property Act 1969. A Law Commission report No. 11 of 1967, achieved, via the Law of Property Act 1969, a considerable widening of powers in this area. *Re 6, 8, 10 & 12 Elm Avenue, New Milton* [1984] 1 W.L.R. 1398 equates voluntary acquisition with compulsory acquisition in certain circumstances, when a s.84 application is made.

[52] The recent Court of Appeal case of *Gilbert* v. *Spoor* [1983] Ch. 27, is a useful corrective to any view that release of a restrictive covenant is simple, once planning permission has been given for the use which depends on that release.

[53] Paras. 4.23 *et seq.*

insert an amending provision. Such a procedure would involve discussion with the government department, usually the Department of the Environment, whose general support to the proposed change would in any event, with the procedure of a Local Act, be necessary in order to achieve success.[54]

(3) *Appropriation or Disposal*

4.29   There are several statutes which specifically exclude open spaces from those lands which can be acquired compulsorily to be used for the purposes of those Acts, *e.g.* housing, allotments, drainage works or agricultural purposes.

Having said that, appropriation is, in local government, the normal way in which to authorise resources to be placed behind a new use for land in the ownership of the local authority. An initial form which appropriation might take is to planning purposes, by virtue of the Town and Country Planning Act 1962, section 83. This deals with the development of such land, despite former restrictions placed upon it. Such a course would open up internal discussion about the zoning and permitted uses available for such land and the advice of town planning staff would be vital.

4.30   The Local Government Planning and Land Act 1980 marked a revolution in general powers for public parks to be disposed of or put to other public uses. The important provisions may be summarised as follows[55]:

    (a) The land in question—specifically held under section 164 of the Act of 1875 or section 10 of the Open Spaces Act 1906—must be "no longer required for the purposes for which it is held."[56]

    (b) Then a principal council[57] may appropriate such land to a purpose for which they are authorised to hold land.

    (c) The land will then be released "from any trust arising solely by virtue of its being land held in trust for enjoyment by the public in accordance with the said section 164 or, as the case may be, the said section 10."

    (d) Nonetheless, the land will still be subject to the rights of other persons in, over or in respect of, the land concerned.[58]

4.31   As appropriations are governed by the principles set out above, so dis-

---

[54] The beguilingly wide power in the Act of 1961, s.82, for the Secretary of State to repeal, by Order, certain Local Act provisions, is limited, in relation to the subject of this section at least, to the subject-matter of the three sections relating to parks in the Act of 1961; ss.52, 53 and 54.

[55] s.122 Local Government Act 1972 as amended by Local Government and Planning & Land Act 1980, s.118.

[56] It has been held that the question whether this is so is wholly for the local authority to decide, acting in good faith, and not for the court: *Att.-Gen.* v. *Manchester Corporation* [1931] 1 Ch. 254 and *Dowty Boulton Paul Ltd.* v. *Wolverhampton Corporation No. 2.* [1976] Ch. 13.

[57] Principal local authorities are the metropolitan districts and the non-metropolitan ("shire") counties and districts.

[58] Local Government Act 1972, s.131. Commons are the subject of separate restrictions.

posals, as a more radical step in relation to the land, are covered by the following[59]:

(a) Consent is required from the Secretary of State.

(b) This consent is not necessary if disposal is effected for the best consideration[60] that can be obtained.

(c) Public notice and consideration of objections resulting therefrom must take place in the case of "open space" land.[61]

(d) On disposal, the land is freed from any trust in the same way and to the extent stated at paragraph 4.30 above.

(e) Capital receipts from such a disposal are subject to directions under the Charities Act 1960.

(f) The Secretary of State's consent is not necessary for a disposal taking the form of a short tenancy, *i.e.* less than seven years, or an assignment with less than seven years to run.

Since the land in question was succinctly called "public trust land," local authorities are looked upon as accountable in various ways, as trustees are. The new facilities for appropriation and disposal do not relieve them of that responsibility: they are still accountable to the courts by way of judicial review or, financially, to the Audit Commission or otherwise, if they depart from the new legal framework.[62] **4.32**

B. Parks and Rates

1. The Statutes

Public parks have generated a steady flow of law cases during the last century on the question of their rateability. At first, the matter in dispute was their status as parks; then it was the effect upon liability to rating of various buildings erected in the parks, or specific uses to which parts of the parks were put. Whilst the radical revision of rating law in 1988 may have limited the scope for argument there is no reason to expect that disputes will no longer arise.[63] **4.33**

---

[59] See s.123 of the Local Government Act 1972 as amended.

[60] See *Buttle* v. *Sanders* (1952) 2 All E.R. 193; also *Caldwell* v. *Sumpters* (1971) 3 All E.R. 892. For an interesting early case on this principle, see *Oliver* v. *Court* (1820) 146 E.R. 1152. (The *Encyclopedia of Local Government Law* (Sweet and Maxwell) also quotes *R.* v. *Essex County Council, ex p. Clearbrook Contractors Ltd.* (1981, unrep.) about the best consideration in these circumstances. Vol. I, para. 2–283).

[61] See the interesting Court of Appeal case of *R.* v. *Doncaster Metropolitan Borough Council, ex p. Braim* (1987) 85 L.G.R. 233. The council wished to allow part of the St. Leger area of open space to be used for a new clubhouse by a golf club but fell foul of this requirement.

[62] The Local Government Planning and Land Act 1980, s.123A, is very important. It eases disposals of park land which has become unwanted. It modifies the principle of inalienability of that land, as laid down in some of the cases under discussion. But it does not fly in the face of para. 15 in §4.34; it takes its place as an enabling provision for conveyancers, whilst the new para. 15 is about the qualifying conditions for exemption from rates.

[63] The case of *Bowes Museum Park Trustees* v. *Cutts (V.O.)* (1950) 43 R. & I.T. 881, is notable as distinguishing between those who own property by virtue of statute and those whose ownership is by virtue of charter or private conveyance. The trustees in that case were found to be in beneficial occupation and rateable.

4.34 In the Local Government Finance Act 1988, the provision about the rating of parks embodies legal principles laid down in the stream of these court cases. This is the item in question:

para.15—

(1) A hereditament is exempt to the extent that it consists of a park which

  (a) has been provided or is under the management of a relevant authority or two or more relevant authorities acting in combination, and

  (b) is available for free and unrestricted use by members of the public.

(2) The reference to a park includes a reference to a recreation or pleasure ground, a public walk, an open space within the meaning of the Open Spaces Act 1906 and a playing field provided under the Physical Training & Recreation Act 1937.

(3) Each of the following is a relevant authority

  (a) a county council

  (b) a district council

  (c) a London borough council

  (d) the Common Council

  (e) the Council of the Isles of Scilly

  (f) a parish or community council and

  (g) the chairman of a parish meeting.

(4) In construing subparagraph 1(b) above any temporary closure (at night or otherwise) shall be ignored.[64]

2. The Cases

4.35 We will take two parts of paragraph 15 for fuller consideration:

(1) The extended definition in (2)

(2) "free and unrestricted use" in (1)(*b*)

(1) *The Extended Definition*

4.36 The recognition of five different expressions as connoted by "park" in paragraph 15 is a useful acknowledgment of the verbal confusion that can afflict this branch of our subject. "Public parks" is the expression currently in use for these bounded, walking out and recreation areas, yet history has bequeathed to us five other expressions, on each of which hangs the relevant law. Until consolidation comes, composite sections such as paragraph 15 are therefore necessary and indeed welcome.

(2) *"Free and Unrestricted Use"*

4.37 Liability to rates follows occupation of property. Thus the courts, faced with attempts to rate parks, had to ask if those parks could be said to have

---

[64] Local Government Finance Act 1988, s.51 and Sched.5.

an occupier. On it being demonstrated that the parks were open to the public, the argument moved to the question whether it was the public rather than the local authority which was the occupier in law. Lord Evershed said in one case[65]:

> "Are the premises occupied and if so, by whom?. . . . In the case of (a park or open space), the sensible answer to my mind would be . . . that the park or open space is not 'occupied' by anyone; the public have, when the gates are open, free and unrestricted access to the whole of it, save only such buildings as are reserved for the use of the park keepers or custodians."

Lord Evershed then had recourse, as, evidently, does every court deliberating upon this question, to the *Lambeth Overseers* case.[66] The House of Lords had there to adjudicate on an attempt to impose rates on Brockwell Park in London. The park contained buildings, such as residences for its departmental staff, shelters, a tool shed and a public gymnasium. But in the House of Lords, Lord Halsbury (L.C.) said:

> "I do not think there is here rateable occupation by anybody. 'The Public' is not a rateable occupier and I think that one sentence disposes of the case. . . . The fact that the park is vested in the county council does not make them the occupiers. . . . It would be absurd to contend that wherever the legal estate is, there is occupation. A road is vested in someone but . . . there is no occupation of it, any more than of a milestone or a direction post."

Lord Herschell, following, described the council as "merely custodians or trustees, to hold it and manage it for the use of the public."[67]

Thus Lord Evershed, in the *Kingston-upon-Hull* case above, followed these principles and looked in the case before him for evidence of the extent of public rights in the property. There was a staff of eight, normal hours of closing, and, because it was an art gallery, an exclusion of the public as visitors from a significant physical area of the premises. The court concluded that the local authority were in occupation of the property in that case and were, moreover, in rateable occupation.[68]

The inquiry for the actual occupiers of parks led the courts to consider   **4.38** the significance of occupation by the local authority of small buildings, such as pavilions, kiosks, shelters and conveniences. The principle evolved is that where these are ancillary to the management of the public park, as a public park, then they do not justify the court in derogating from the general principle in the *Lambeth Overseers* case. In other words, the local authority is not rateable because it is not in occupation but is a custodian or trustee for the public.

---

[65] *Clayton* v. *Kingston-upon-Hull Corporation*, [1961] 1 Q.B. 345, 355. This Court of Appeal decision was confirmed by the House of Lords at [1963] A.C. 28.
[66] *Lambeth Overseers* v. *L.C.C.* [1897] A.C. 625.
[67] *Ibid.* at pp. 629 and 631.
[68] The court rejected a plea that the art gallery should be exempt from rating.

An example is a case from Sheffield.[69] A pavilion in the park was let on a yearly tenancy to an ice-cream vendor. He was obliged to be open for business whilst the park was open, save for half an hour; his customers were all people frequenting the park. The agreement clearly gave the tenant exclusive occupation of the pavilion at £225 rent per annum and this feature was argued as adequate to isolate the pavilion from the park and leave it open to separate rating. The court did not accede to this argument. Lord Evershed, four years before the *Hull* case, was clear that as the pavilion "was being so used, not because it was surplus to the requirements of the park, but as part of the park," then the Valuation Officer's case to have the pavilion rated, failed. The tenant's activity, said Lord Evershed, "was nothing more than an ancillary activity of the conduct of the park itself." In the same judgment, the court accepted the corollary of the view here described, *i.e.* that where, as with the Thameside Restaurant on the bank of the Thames for the Festival of Britain, a building had been "severed" from the park as a park, and given "independent status" as a restaurant, then that building must be rated separately.[70]

4.39   Cases had accumulated under the earlier statutory provision on this topic, *i.e.* section 44 of the General Rate Act 1967 and its predecessors, on a third legal point. Those statutes used a technical term to describe the status in law of the property as distinct from the identity of the occupier. This was "dedicated in perpetuity." The 1988 Local Government Finance Act bypasses this problem, by referring to the land as a hereditament "provided or under management by" the relevant authority and there follow the six possible descriptions of the land under a series of statutes. Allowing for the traditional ingenuity of lawyers serving rating and parks authorities, there is no reason to think that cases will not arise on the new wording. Was it provided as "a park" for example in a New Town or new housing development? We have had no recorded cases to date, but the question is sure to arise whether a particular property was set aside as a temporary measure as a "park" or had the character that was described by one judge as being so provided "for the foreseeable future."[71]

3. Conclusion

4.40   The most recent relevant reported case is *Smith* (*V.O.*) v. *City of St. Albans.*[72] The question before the Lands Tribunal was whether an indoor heated swimming pool, standing within, or near to, a public park at Verulamium, St. Albans, was rateable. It was a recreational amenity, with no physical boundaries separating it from the park area. The Tribunal

[69] *Sheffield Corporation* v. *Tranter* [1957] 1 W.L.R. 843.
[70] *London County Council* v. *Robinson* [1955] J.P.L. 607. Another important case where rateability was found made out for a foreshore is *N. Riding of Yorkshire County Valuation Committee* v. *Redcar Corporation etc. Committee* [1943] 1 K.B. 114.
[71] *Burnell* v. *Downham Market Urban District Council* [1952] 2 Q.B. 55, Evershed M.R. at p. 64. The judge could not conceive that Lord Halsbury had meant to lay it down that the characteristic of permanence "as an obligation for all eternity" was essential to the conclusion that the L.C.C. was not rateable for a park.
[72] [1978] R.A. 147.

reviewed the cases from *Brockwell Park* onwards and observed that, since
the General Rate Act 1967, it was unnecessary to establish dedication to
the public, since section 44 says that this element shall be deemed to exist
when free and unrestricted use by the public is demonstrated. The Tribunal reached the point that exemption from rating was possible for the
pool, only if the pool was ancillary to the park. "Ancillary buildings," said
the Tribunal "seem to me to be those which subserve the enjoyment of the
park qua park."[73] The baths, being "a separate and distinct amenity,"
were not within the exemption afforded to parks. The Valuation Officer's
appeal to the Tribunal was thus successful.[74]

C. By-Laws

By-laws are regulations normally limited to one aspect of the legal powers **4.41**
exercised by the local authority, or other body so authorised. They operate
only within its own area or part of that area. They are a normal and recognised form of control of public parks by the management. The legal framework within which by-laws are used is a combination of statute and case law.

1. The Statutes

Individual statutes regularly empower local authorities and other legally **4.42**
constituted bodies to make by-laws. The Forestry Commission and the
Water Authority are examples outside local government. The schedule
below indicates, within the scope of this book, the wide range of subjects
that by-laws cover:

Subject	Statute	Confirming body
Allotments	Small Holdings and Allotments Act 1908, s.28	Dept. of the Environment
Ancient Monuments	Ancient Monuments Consolidation and Amendment Act 1913, s.13 Ancient Monument Act 1931, s.7	" "
Street Playgrounds	Road Traffic Regulation Act 1967, s.27	"
Libraries & Museums	Public Libraries and Museums Act 1964, s.19	Dept of Education and Science
Recreation in Public Parks	Public Health Act 1875, s.164	Dept. of the Environment
Open Spaces	Open Spaces Act 1906, s.15	"
Nature Reserves	National Parks and Access to the Countryside Act 1949, s.90	Home Secretary

[73] *Ibid.* at p. 30.
[74] Curiously, only the side heading of s.44 uses the word "exemption."

Subject	Statute	Confirming body
The seashore	Public Health Acts Amendment Act 1907, s.82	,,
Pleasure Fairs	Public Health Act 1961, s.75	,,
Pleasure boats in Parks	Public Health Acts Amendment Act 1890, s.44	,,
Seaside Pleasure Boats	Public Health Act 1961, s.76	,,
Country Parks	Countryside Act 1968, ss.4 and 8	Dept of the Environment
Commons	Commons Act 1899, s.1	Home Secretary
Promenades	Public Health Acts Amendment Act 1907, s.83	,,
Swimming Baths	Public Health Act 1936, s.223	Dept. of the Environment
Inland Waterways	Transport Act 1968, s.113	,,

Good rule and government

4.43   In addition, there is a class of by-laws known as good rule and government, which certain local authorities are authorised to make.[75] The authorising statute also uses the expression "the prevention and supression of nuisances," as an additional description of the subject-matter. A qualification is placed upon what may seem to be a wide power; such by-laws are not to be made "if provision for that purpose, as respects that area, is made by, or may be made under, any other enactment."[76] This good rule and government group is in the nature of a residual category for by-laws, after the powers for specific subjects have been exhausted. The broadening sweep of modern legislation, applying to all aspects of urban life, has made the use of good rule and government by-laws less important for a well-managed local authority.

Statutory safeguards

4.44   The grant of by-law-making powers to a local authority is hedged about with safeguards. The by-laws themselves, before coming into operation, must be confirmed by the appropriate government department. Furthermore, after they have become operative, they are open to challenge in the courts as being invalid.

   The power to make by-laws includes a power to amend or repeal those by-laws. Such a step is often taken in practice when making new by-laws; these then contain a by-law which amends or repeals the earlier ones.[77]

---

[75] Local Government Act 1972, s.235(1). District councils and London borough councils have this power.

[76] *Ibid.* s.235 (3).

[77] The Interpretation Act 1978, s.14, confers power to revoke or amend without necessarily replacing.

2. **The Cases**

This branch of law illustrates well the law-making powers of the courts.   **4.45**
The tests of the validity of a by-law are most important and these are illus-
trated, to a remarkably large extent, in the judgments of the Divisional
Court in the case of *Kruse* v. *Johnson*.[78]

As a body to whom law-making powers have been given, a local authority must act within those powers. If it should stray, wilfully or carelessly, outside those powers, it is at risk of challenge by means of judicial
review, or some other sanction, because it will be said to have acted *ultra
vires, i.e.* beyond its powers. In considering challenges made to local authorities over the years on this point, the courts evolved various tests: the
case of *Kruse* v. *Johnson* brought them usefully together and developed
them. This case is invariably consulted when a problem on the validity of
by-laws is met.

In the *Kruse* case, Kent County Council had made a by-law which forbade persons from singing or playing music within 50 yards of a dwelling-
house, after being requested to desist. A person duly convicted of an
offence appealed on the ground that the by-law was bad, because it was
unreasonable. The court held the by-law valid and in their judgments laid
down guidelines for similar cases. Lord Russell C.J. said that by-laws
should be certain, they should be reasonable, they should not be repug-
nant to other laws and they should be *intra vires* the local authority in question.

The court emphasised that a benevolent attitude should be taken by the
courts to local authorities, as public representative bodies. But if they
failed to conform to these tests, then the by-laws must be held invalid.

Against that background, some examples of each of these four tests are
now given.

(1) *Certainty*

In a recent leisure services case, a by-law failed to pass this requirement.[79]   **4.46**
In prohibiting hang-gliders from being flown in pleasure grounds, it failed
to stipulate a minimum height below which a glider must not be flown. A
person would not, in those circumstances, know when he was contravening the law. The by-law was, therefore, uncertain, invalid and unenforceable.

The classic example of a by-law held invalid for lack of certainty was in
the terms: "No person shall wilfully annoy passengers in the street."[80]

---

[78] [1898] 2 Q.B. 91.
[79] *Staden* v. *Tarjany* (1980) 78 L.G.R. 614 (Q.B.D.). There were several complicating legal
provisions about air traffic regulations but the *ratio decidendi* was as above. The local authority was Adur D.C. and the pleasure ground at Shoreham-by-Sea.
[80] *Nash* v. *Finlay* (1901) 85 L.T. 682.

(2) *Reasonableness*

4.47   The *locus classicus* is again a passage from the judgment of Lord Russell in *Kruse* v. *Johnson*:

> "If by-laws were found to be partial and unequal in their operation, as between classes, if they were manifestly unjust, if they disclosed bad faith, if they involved such oppressive or gratuitous interference with the rights of those subject to them, as could find no justification in the minds of reasonable men, the court might well say 'Parliament never intended to give authority to make such rules; they are unreasonable and ultra vires.' But, (continued Lord Russell) it is in this sense and in this sense only, that I conceive that the question of unreasonableness can properly be regarded. A by-law is not unreasonable merely because particular judges may think that it goes further than is prudent or necessary or convenient, or because it is not accompanied by a qualification or an exception which some judges think ought to be there."[81]

A good recent leisure services example is the case of *Burnley B.C.* v. *England*.[82] The local authority made by-laws under local acts for their parks and these were duly confirmed by the Home Secretary. In particular, these by-laws prohibited persons from causing dogs to enter or remain in certain specified "pleasure grounds." These amounted in total to some 141 acres in extent, out of 795 acres available for recreation in the borough.[83] The parks thus forbidden to dogs were carefully selected, as being ornamental gardens, children's playgrounds or play areas.

Substantial public protests followed the making of these by-laws. These included a walk through a prohibited park by some 200–300 people, some leading dogs. Similar protests were threatened. The local authority secured an interlocutory injunction to prevent such protest meetings or processions in the parks in question and the hearing for the final injunction followed some time later.

At that hearing, there was a challenge to the validity of the critical by-law, on the ground of reasonableness. It was argued strongly that the by-law should have been more limited in extent—more limited in relation to the people to whom it would cause hardship—and that it did not strike a fair balance between children and the elderly residents in the town.

The court indicated what sort of by-law about the entry of dogs into parks would have been viewed as unreasonable, found no such element in the by-law before the court and granted the final injunction sought by the council. The court based its approach upon the judgment of Lord Russell (*supra*) and said that it did not find the by-law in question "manifestly unjust or that it was an oppressive or gratuitous interference with the rights of others which a reasonable council would not countenance."[84]

---

[81] [1898] 2 Q.B. 91, 100.
[82] (1978) 77 L.G.R. 227.
[83] There was an exception for a guide dog with a blind person.
[84] (1978) 77 L.G.R. 227, p. 237.

There are numerous other cases in the reports[85]: one instance will suf- **4.48**
fice. In *Arlidge* v. *Islington Corporation*,[86] a by-law required landlords of
lodging houses to limewash them in April, May or June in each year. In so
far as some of these landlords had no contractual power to enter these
occupied houses, the by-law was held unreasonable and bad. A landlord
would have had to commit trespass or breach of contract in order to comply with it.

(3) *Consistency with other Laws*

In the 1955 case of *Galer* v. *Morrissey*,[87] the court had to consider a by-law **4.49**
which forbade the keeping of a noisy animal which was a serious nuisance
to nearby residents. The court was asked to say that the by-law was
invalid, because it covered the same subject-matter as the Public Health
Act 1936, section 92, about public nuisances, arising from the conditions
under which the animals were kept. Lord Goddard L.C.J. presided and
said: "No one doubts that if the statute deals with precisely the same
matter, the by-law would be *ultra vires*, because there would be no necessity for it."[88] But he drew distinctions between the subject-matter of the
two provisions and upheld the by-law.

In a different setting, a canal company in their by-law prohibited traffic **4.50**
on the canal on Sundays.[89] The court held the by-law void. There was
existing general legislation about Sunday observance and whilst the canal
company was entitled to make by-laws about the orderly use of the navigation, the by-law in question did not purport to achieve that end. "They
only say," said Rolfe B. about the canal company, "that it was decorous
that the canal should not be used on Sundays."[90] That was outside the
company's powers and thus the by-law was void.

(4) *Intra Vires*[91]

In the old case of *R.* v. *Wood*,[92] a by-law about the removal of several types **4.51**
of deposit about houses was held bad when, instead of staying within the
statutory limits relating to deposits of ashes, rubbish, soil and others, it
was sought to use the by-law to secure the removal of snow from footpaths. This was not within the by-law-making powers.

It is important to note that a by-law can be good in part even though **4.52**
bad in part. An instance comes from the common at Beverley in Yorkshire, where a by-law by the pasture masters imposed a penalty for pas-

[85] See, *e.g.* a useful summary in the *Encyclopedia of Local Government Law* (Sweet & Maxwell).
[86] [1909] 2 K.B. 127.
[87] [1955] 1 W.L.R. 110.
[88] *Ibid.* "A by-law cannot, in effect, dot the i's and cross the t's of a statute."
[89] *Calder & Hebble Navigation* v. *Pilling* (1845) 153 E.R. 396.
[90] *Ibid.* at p. 402.
[91] Within their powers.
[92] (1855) 5 E. & B. 49.

turing a vicious horse on their pastures.[93] The by-law stipulated that the "person so offending and the owner of the said horse shall respectively forfeit" the sum of five pounds. The owner, an attorney's clerk, let a pony on to the pasture, the animal being known as vicious. The pasture masters imposed the £5 penalty on him, as provided by the by-law, and when this was unpaid the matter was taken to the justices, who convicted the owner under the by-law. On appeal, quarter sessions confirmed that conviction.

The owner then took an appeal to the Court of Queen's Bench to have the conviction quashed on the ground that the by-law was bad. He argued that it made it possible to convict two persons of the one offence and moreover the owner might be unaware of the action of the herdsman in letting the horse on to the common. In so far as the owner in this case was himself culpable, this argument was academic, but it drew from the court an important statement. Cockburn C.J. said, maintaining the conviction, "Where a by-law is good in part and bad in part, the objectionable portion may be rejected and the remainder retained and acted upon."

3. The Practice

Making by-laws

4.53   The procedure to obtain a lawful by-law is laid down for local authorities in the Local Government Act 1972[94] and for other bodies in the parent statutes. It is at all times important and must be followed to the letter. It involves due public notice and the sealing of the by-law, after a period for public inspection and making formal objections. The by-law is then submitted to the confirming authority.

Model by-laws

4.54   That authority may well have a published model by-law and departure from that model will oblige the applicant local authority to make out a local need to depart from the standard by-law. The use of a model is justified by the desirability of consistency and by the reliability in practice of a by-law which is used extensively. Thus the scope for by-laws to be a field for local experiment is in practice severely limited.

Enforcement

4.55   The enforcement of by-laws is in practice left to the authority which made them, though in theory an individual can take steps to do so.[95] The

---

[93] *R.* v. *Lundie* (1862) 8 Jur.N.S. 640. The recent important House of Lords decision, *D.P.P.* v. *Hutchinson* (1991) 89 L.G.R.1, found *ultra vires* a by-law for Greenham Common. That by-law prohibited access without authority to all the R.A.F. airfield, though some of the land was a common. There was no power under the relevant statute to make such a by-law for a common and the court declined to sever the by-law and hold part good and part bad. They looked at principles developed in Australian and American courts which emphasised that severance should be agreed only if textual as well as substantial severance was reasonable. Since for example Lord Bridge (p. 15) found severed by-laws would be "of a totally different character," the court declined to sever.

[94] s.236.

[95] Though not under the Public Health Act 1936, s.298, which is only for the local authority.

Burnley Park case, above, is an interesting modern case of successful recourse by a local authority to the procedure of a High Court injunction to enforce a by-law. The unusual circumstances, with mass protests threatened and expected, were held by the courts at interlocutory and final injunction stages to justify that somewhat rare course of action.[96]

(d) **No relaxation**

The production of a printed copy of a by-law, duly certified by the   **4.56**
proper officer of the local authority, allows it to be used in court proceedings.[97]

There are no powers to waive or relax the provisions of a by-law. It has become, after confirmation, part of the law of the land for that area in which the relevant public authority operates.[98]

D. Miscellaneous Amenities

1. **Street Playgrounds**

Recreation grounds have for many years been set apart in public parks; in   **4.57**
the same spirit, street playgrounds have been developed as urban recreation areas. They are now the subject of a compact code of law contained in the Road Traffic Acts.[99] This may be summarised as follows:

  (a) Highway authorities are empowered to make Orders which will require streets to be kept clear of vehicles, so that they may be used as playgrounds for children.[1]
  (b) The Orders require the approval of the Secretary of State for Transport (or in Wales the Secretary of State for Wales).
  (c) The Orders, which are called Traffic Regulation Orders, specify the streets, or parts of streets, the days or hours of the week and the vehicles affected by the Orders.[2] These elements may be expected to vary from location to location, according to local circumstances.
  (d) The Orders must preserve access to premises in the affected streets.[3]

---

[96] The courts followed *Elkenford Ltd.* v. *Stafford Borough Council* (1976) 75 L.G.R. 337, a Court of Appeal decision, where Denning M.R. said:

  "Where there is a plain breach of the statute, I do not think that the local authorities concerned need wait for finality. It is open to the court to grant an injunction when the law is plain and there appears an intention to continue with the breach." (p. 341)

  That case concerned a Sunday market.

[97] Local Government Act 1972, s.238. For proper officer, see s.270.

[98] The legal merits of making or not making by-laws are discussed in Chap. 1, in relation to Nuisance, as well as in the shorter discussion at paras. 4.09–4.14 of this chapter. Once by-laws are made, the local authority is seen to have taken control of that area of activity in its park and its legal liability therefor as "occupier" is extended. See *Hall* v. *Beckenham Corporation* [1949] 1 K.B. 716.

[99] Road Traffic Regulations Act 1984, s.29 and Sched. 9.

[1] *Ibid.* Highway authorities for these Orders are county councils and metropolitan district councils outside London, and inside the London boroughs and the City of London Common Council. The pioneer Act was the Street Playgrounds Act 1938, now repealed.

[2] *Ibid.*

[3] *Ibid.*

(e) Offences carry fines.[4]
(f) By-laws may be made by the local authorities for the areas in question, relating to the safety of children, the access to the playgrounds and the safety of those playgrounds.[5]
(g) Traffic signs designating the street playgrounds are specified.[6]
(h) A procedure is set out for the making and confirmation of these Orders.[7]
(i) For the general liability in tort of those who manage street playgrounds, reference should be made to Chapter 1, which deals with general legal principles.[8]

2. Diseases

(1) Dutch Elm Disease

4.58   The affliction of elm trees by an insidious disease in recent years, has been on such a scale that the Government has harnessed the resources of local authorities as part of a national campaign to resist the scourge. Action taken has led to the felling of hundreds of trees and replacement planting. This skilled task has fallen on the Amenities Departments of local authorities, being those with responsibilities for parklands and their forest trees.

The legal framework within which the campaign has been waged stems primarily from the Forestry Act of 1967 and a series of statutory instruments made under that Act and two later Forestry Acts of 1979 and 1981. Authority has, however, also been drawn from the Plant Health Act 1967,[9] the European Communities Act 1972[10] and the Agriculture (Miscellaneous Provisions) Act 1972.[11]

There have been two main thrusts, from the purely legal point of view, in this campaign. First, powers were conferred on local authorities and others to deal with the diseased trees where they stand. Secondly, a general restriction was placed upon the movement of those trees from listed areas, until the timber had been rendered safe.

Diseased trees

4.59   The attack on the diseased trees as they grow required two legal weapons:
(a) The inclusion in the Forestry Act 1967 of a new exception to the general provision in that Act that felling of trees could take place

---

[4] See the Road Traffic Offenders Act 1988.
[5] Road Traffic Regulation Act 1984, s.31.
[6] *Ibid.* s.68.
[7] *Ibid.* Sched. 9.
[8] Background reading on this subject may be found in two reports of the Department of the Environment: *Recreation and Deprivation in Inner Urban Areas*, (1977 HMSO), and *Leisure Provision and People's Needs* (1981 HMSO).
[9] s.3 and 5.
[10] s.4.
[11] s.20.

only with a licence from the Forestry Commission. The new exception is in these terms:

"Felling an elm tree which is so affected by Dutch Elm Disease that the greater part of the crown of the tree is dead."[12]

(b) The conferring of powers on named local authorities to deal vigorously with diseased trees.[13] Those councils should appoint officers to:

(i) Enter land to inspect trees and examine the bark.

(ii) Arrange for the service upon the relevant landowner of notices which required him to cut down and then destroy or treat the felled timber. The appointed officer would act in default of compliance, in the period specified in the notice, by the landowner.

Movement of trees

Turning, secondly, to the movement restriction, an Order placed an   **4.60** embargo upon the movement of Dutch elm. No branches or felled trees of diseased elm were to be moved across highways or by rail or water, unless the bark had been removed. This embargo was supported legally by powers for Forestry Commission inspectors to inspect books of account and other relevant documents. Persons suspected of transporting diseased elms could have notice served upon them by the Commission inspectors to remove the bark from the diseased timber. That Order put the embargo on 64 districts.[14]

This outline indicates briefly the legal activity generated by one serious disease in one genus of tree. It is of interest to local authorities not only because of the duties imposed on them, but also because of their own role as major landowners with large numbers of trees on their own lands.

(2) Fire Blight Disease

Another scourge that has called for legal aid in combating it is Fire Blight.   **4.61** This is a bacterial disease that affects fruit trees but also ornamental plants. It has been the subject of a series of statutory instruments.

The current one is the Fire Blight Disease (Amendment) Order (S.I. 1966 No. 162). It obliges persons who discover or suspect the presence of the blight to notify the Ministry of Agriculture Fisheries and Food, so that appropriate action can be taken.[15]

---

[12] Forestry (Exception from Restriction of Felling) Regulations 1979 (S.I. 1979 No. 792) reg. 4, affects s.9 of the Act of 1967.

[13] Various groups of authorities were listed in successive Orders under the Acts mentioned in the text. See now Dutch Elm Disease (Local Authorities) Order 1984 (S.I. 1984 No. 687).

[14] Dutch Elm Disease (Restriction on Movement of Elms) Order 1984 (S.I. 1984 No. 686) is the current Order.

[15] The initial statutory instrument was the Fire Blight Disease Order 1958 (S.I. 1958 No. 1814), which lists the powers and the offences. The Orders are made under the Destructive Insects and Pests Acts of 1877, 1907 and 1927.

3. **Wild Animals in Parks**

Licensing under the Zoo Licensing Act 1981

4.62   A local authority desiring to establish a zoo now comes within the controls set up by the Zoo Licensing Act 1981. This Act, whilst requiring local authorities to licence the zoos of other persons, allows them to grant licences for their own zoos. They must then supply a copy of that licence to the Department of the Environment, together with a copy of any inspector's report upon the zoo in question. The Secretary of State then has, in relation to the local authority's zoo, the same powers that the local authority exercise over private zoos within their area.[16] This means that he has power to revoke that licence if:

    (a) A reasonable requirement to the zoo management, in consequence of some item in the inspector's report, is not met in the time specified.[17]

    (b) The zoo has been conducted in a disorderly manner, or so as to be a nuisance or in breach of the conditions in the licence.[18]

    (c) One of the persons responsible for the running of the zoo is convicted of an offence under the Act of 1981 or of a listed offence relating to the ill-treatment of animals.[19]

The licensing procedure to be followed by local authorities under the Act of 1981 requires the authority to consider the views invited from six named bodies, ranging from the police and fire services to any national body active in the area of operating zoos and also persons living in the locality of the proposed zoo. A licence once granted has to be exhibited at public entrances to the zoo. The whole code embodied in this Act is clearly intended to be both comprehensive and also to ensure that the best standards are applied to modern zoos.[20]

Keeping wild animals

4.63   Whilst a zoo is by definition in the above Act a place where the public have access to wild animals—as defined—on seven or more days in a year, in our society persons other than the local authority sometimes keep wild animals.[21] That can only be done lawfully under licence from the local authority, under the Dangerous Wild Animals Act 1976. That Act and the

---

[16] Zoo Licensing Act 1981, s.13.

[17] *Ibid.* s.17(1)(*a*). In the second reading debate on this Private Member's Bill, said to be the result of five years' research, the mover described its main purpose as "to lift the standard of the zoo industry." 22 zoos were said then to be directly affected by the Bill, though 60 were said to be under inspection by the Health and Safety Executive. *Hansard* (16.3.81) Vol. 1000, p. 525.

[18] *Ibid.* s.17(1)(*b*).

[19] See s.4(5) for a list of 10 Acts or groups of Acts.

[20] There is power for the Secretary of State to give a dispensation to a zoo too small to be brought within the machinery of the Act. A very important provision is the group of sections about special and periodical inspections, ss.10, 11 and 12.

[21] The Dangerous Wild Animals Act 1976 does not apply to a pet shop, a zoological garden, a circus or a place registered for experiments under the Cruelty to Animals Act 1976. A deer park is excluded from the definition of a zoological garden under s.7.

Zoo Licensing Act 1981 are mutually exclusive, in that the Act of 1976 does not apply to persons holding a licence under the Act of 1981.

4. Insurance and Bad Weather

The parks managements of local authorities from time to time need to take **4.64** advice about their insurance cover. Third-party claims for injury in recreation grounds are certainly one such area of risk.

Another is bad weather. All who organise public events in summer can insure against the risk of loss resulting from bad weather, other things being equal. A show, a procession, a carnival—all can be intended for large crowds and the budgeted break-even point can depend upon the sun.

This category in insurance law is pecuniary loss insurance[22] and cases reaching the courts are few and far between.[23] One case of interest, because of the principle involved, is *London County Cycling and Athletic Club Ltd.* v. *Beck*.[24] A cycling meeting was insured with Lloyd's in the sum of £250, provided that "the expenses attached to the meeting" were not less than the sum of £250.

When the meeting was held, and resulted in a loss, the Club wished to recover the £250 as covered by the policy. To demonstrate to Lloyd's that the expenses incurred were not less than £250, the Club sought to include as expenses the use of £21 4s. 0d., being the premium for the policy. This would bring the expenses to £267 12s. 9d. Lloyd's rejected the principle involved but after a court hearing the Club succeeded. "Meeting," said the judge," must mean not merely the actual meeting while in progress but the whole adventure."

The scope of this type of insurance has developed enormously but the principle is not out of date.

[22] The Insurance Companies Act 1974, s.83(6) defines the expression.
[23] The subject was mentioned in comments about a cricket match, almost in passing, by Scrutton L.J. in *Leon* v. *Casey* [1932] 2 K.B. 576, 581.
[24] [1897] 3 *Commercial Cases* 49.

CHAPTER 5

NATIONAL LEISURE SERVICE PROVIDERS

"Though the language of the decision does not achieve matchless clarity . . . "
Waite J. in *Cawley* v. *South Wales Electricity Board* [1985] I.R.L.R. 89,
E.A.T.

A. THE NATIONAL TRUST

1. Introduction

5.01   The National Trust is a unique national institution. It owns 565,000 acres of land, 517 miles of this country's coastline and attracted over 10 million visitors to its properties in a recent year.[1] Devotion to the purposes initially set out in its founding Act of 1907 and later enlarged has enabled the National Trust to reach its present position affording to many people the pleasures of a major leisure service.

2. Purposes

5.02   Its purposes were first legally embodied in the National Trust Act 1907, as follows:

> "Promoting the permanent preservation, for the benefit of the nation, of lands and tenements (including buildings) of beauty or historic interest and as regards lands, for the preservation (so far as practicable) of their natural aspect, features and animal and plant life."[2]

5.03   These were later significantly extended by the National Trust Act 1937, section 3 in three ways:

> "The promotion of
> (a)   the preservation of buildings of national interest or architectural, historic or artistic interest and places of natural interest or beauty and the protection and augmentation of the amenities of such buildings and places and their surroundings;

---

[1] Figures taken from the 1990 Annual Report.
[2] s.4. There was a short period of incorporation under the Companies Acts preceding the National Trust Act 1907. There have been five subsequent Acts: the National Trust Charity Scheme Confirmation Act 1919, the National Trust Act 1937, the National Trust Act 1939, the National Trust Act 1953, and the National Trust Act 1971.

(b) the preservation of furniture and pictures and chattels of any description, having national or historic or artistic interest;

(c) the access to and enjoyment of such buildings, places and chattels by the public.''

This enlargement of the legal purposes clearly reflected experience and contains a fuller definition in relation to buildings and places, the first reference to furniture, pictures and chattels and the first reference to "access to and enjoyment of" those features.

The purposes set out in that Act of 1907 were brought before the Chancery Division of the High Court by the National Trust itself in 1916, and held to be charitable in law, in the case of *Re Verrall. National Trust* v. *Attorney-General.*[3] It was necessary to satisfy the court that the purposes came within the legal expression, "other purposes beneficial to the community" and Astbury J. said that they were "plainly public purposes, expressly stated to be for the benefit of the nation."[4]

3. **Powers**

The National Trust has extensive statutory powers and these may be summarised as follows: **5.04**

(1) *General*

(a) Acquire land, buildings and rights and interests therein.[5]

(b) Maintain and manage;
(i) lands as open spaces or places of public resort;
(ii) buildings, for public recreation, resort or instruction.

(c) Accept property in trust for public purposes.

(d) Act in any trusts for any property devoted to public purposes.

(e) Do all acts and take all proceedings as deemed desirable in furtherance of the objects of the National Trust

(f) Do anything in relation to their property that may be "beneficial for the property or desirable for the comfort or convenience of persons resorting to or using such property."

(2) *Commons*

In connection with trust land which is common or commonable land: **5.05**

(a) Keep it at all times open for the recreation of the public.

(b) For the purposes in (i), plant, drain, level and improve the land and make temporary enclosures, in the interests of good estate management.

(c) Make and maintain paths, ponds and waters.

---

[3] [1916] 1 Ch. 100.

[4] There are three specific legal classes of charity in English law: relief of poverty, promotion of religion, support of education. This last, fourth, general class is occasionally chary of accommodating all applicants for the shelter it affords.

[5] National Trust Act 1907, s.4(2).

(d) Erect and maintain tool sheds.
(e) Resist and abate all encroachments.
(f) Set apart parts of the property for games, meetings or sport gatherings.[6]
(g) The restriction on the power of highway authorities to search for, dig and carry away, gravel, sand and other materials from commons in the Commons Act 1876, section 20, is applied to commons vested in the National Trust Act of 1907, section 36.

(3) Charges

To make "reasonable charges" for admission to National Trust property or for its use by the public. (This does not apply to commons.)[7]

(4) Local Authorities

In order to give effect to its objects, the National Trust is empowered to "act in concert with and make any arrangements and agreements with any local authority" or, indeed, any committee of residents in the neighbourhood of their property.[8]

(5) By-Laws

Buildings

5.06   The powers for which by-laws might be made in relation to its buildings were modelled on those which had been recently granted by Parliament for public libraries.[9] Hence the powers include:
(a) Regulating its use.
(b) Protecting its contents.
(c) Taking guarantees from users against loss or injury to the contents.
(d) Imposing fines.
(e) Enabling staff to remove persons who offend against the by-laws or against certain standards of behaviour. Being again imported from the Public Libraries Act 1892, these offences covered staying beyond permitted hours on the property, gaming, eating and drinking in places not set apart for those purposes, and general unsociable behaviour.[10]

---

[6] National Trust Act 1907, s.29.
[7] *Ibid.* s.30.
[8] *Ibid.* s.31.
[9] *Ibid.* s.33.
[10] The Public Libraries Act 1901, s.3 was repealed by the Public Libraries and Museums Act 1964, s.26 and s.19 of that Act of 1964 now contains comparable by-law-making power for regulating the use of facilities provided and the conduct of persons in the premises. The Interpretation Act 1978, s.17(2)(*a*) allows the use of the powers in s.33 of the Act of 1907 by reference to the Public Libraries and Museums Act 1964.

Lands and property

The powers for these extensive subjects were revised in the latest Act obtained by the National Trust, the Act of 1971.[11] Generally, the powers granted are to make by-laws to regulate and protect the property, to prevent and suppress nuisances; to preserve order and regulate the conduct and secure the safety of visitors.

Specifically, the Act of 1971 then lists 19 subjects which may be dealt with in the by-laws. These range from turves, sods and gravel, to trees, shrubs and plants; they include fires, missiles and deposits of offensive matter, defacements, notices, snares for birds and game, caravans, cycles and other vehicles, roundabouts and swings, games and horses, boats, bathing and fishing. They are comprehensive.

4. Special Properties

The Act of 1907 listed 29 properties which were declared to be held for the benefit of the nation; they should not be chargeable with any debts or liabilities; and they should be inalienable.[12]   **5.07**

The properties varied from 75 acres at Aira Force and Gowbarrow Deer Park, Cumbria, to a cliff at Barmouth and included the Ruskin monument at Friars Crag Keswick and the Vice-Admiral Hardy monument in Dorset.

In order to vary the provisions of that Act of 1907, it was necessary to include in the Act of 1971 a section authorising the possible disposal of one of those properties, namely Kanturk Castle in County Cork, Eire.[13]

The Wey Navigation and the Godalming Navigation were the subject of special provisions in the Act of 1971, since the assumption of their management by the National Trust departed from provisions in Acts of Parliament in 1670 and 1760.[14] The Act of 1971 allowed the two undertakings to be managed as one.

5. General Properties

There is a general provision in the Act of 1907 which enables a resolution of the Council of the National Trust to confer the same status of inalienability on newly acquired "properties or parts thereof." The resolution must declare that "such properties are proper to be held for the benefit of the nation."[15]   **5.08**

The Act of 1939 allowed the National Trust to accept a mansion house and amenity lands from a tenant for life under a settlement. These properties, also, were given the status of inalienability.[16]

---

[11] s.24.
[12] Sched. 1.
[13] National Trust Act 1971, s.28.
[14] Pt. IV.
[15] s.21(2).
[16] National Trust Act 1939, s.8.

By the National Trust Charity Scheme Confirmation Act 1919, a Scheme of the Charity Commissioners for the management of property was confirmed.[17] This was primarily to enable the Trust to grant leases (with the sanction of the Charity Commissioners) of land otherwise inalienable due to the above provisions in the Act of 1907. The grant of easements and rights over National Trust property made inalienable is valid and effectual as described above, without the sanction of the Charity Commissioners.[18]

Compulsory Purchase and National Trust Property

5.09   Various general Acts of Parliament have included provisions to take account of this special category of property held by the National Trust. It is inevitable that, with such a large landholding, from time to time a local authority or government department or other body with compulsory powers wishes to acquire some portion of National Trust land. Some of these Acts are of interest.

The general enabling Act for compulsory purchase is the Acquisition of Land Act 1981. That Act contains a section providing that a compulsory order which includes inalienable land of the National Trust, in respect of which the Trust has submitted and maintained an objection, shall be subject to Special Parliamentary Procedure.[19]

This is an elaborate procedure applied by the Statutory Orders (Special Procedure) Act 1945. Briefly, it involves:

(a) Notice in the *London Gazette* and a local paper.
(b) Laying the Order before Parliament.
(c) Submission of objections by petition to either House.
(d) Consideration of those petitions by the Chairman of Ways and Means and the Chairman of Committees. They deal with the petitions as either general objections to the Order or as seeking amendments to it, and report thereon to their respective Houses.
(e) Either House may then resolve that the Order be annulled and that ends that particular Order. On the other hand, the Order, petitions and Chairmen's reports may be sent to a joint committee of the two Houses, where detailed consideration ensues.
(f) In due course, the Order may be confirmed by the appropriate Minister or taken to be confirmed in a Bill, or if the joint committee so reports, it may not be confirmed until it is confirmed in an Act of Parliament.

5.10   Apart from the above general restrictions, there are express restraints on taking National Trust lands by compulsory purchase for:

(a) Allotments, under the Land Settlement (Facilities) Act 1919, section 28, and the Allotments Act 1922, section 10.
(b) National Parks, under the National Parks and Access to the Coun-

---

[17] National Trust Act 1939, s.12.
[18] *Ibid.*
[19] s.18.

tryside Act 1949, Parts V and VI, though not under Parts II and III of that Act of 1949, in relation to nature conservation.

(c) War damaged sites, under the War Damaged Sites Act 1949, section 1.

National Trust inalienable land may, however, be the subject of compulsory purchase for forestry purposes under the Forestry Act 1967, section 40(4) and section 49(1).

Finally, National Trust inalienable land is excluded from that to which rights of enfranchisement were conferred on leaseholds by the Leasehold Reform Act 1967, section 32.

6. **Restrictive Covenants**

There is one last legal incident of National Trust landholding that is of interest. In the National Trust Act 1937, there was a provision whereby a person entitled to land might agree with the National Trust to restrictions on his use of the property.[20] This might be described as a future use in a manner the Trust thinks fit or as subjecting the property to conditions in order to restrict the planning development. This agreement was to be legally effective and enforceable, although the National Trust was not the owner of adjacent land. (That condition is the normal requirement for legal enforcement of a covenant which restricts the use of real property in this country.)[21]   **5.11**

A second related provision is to be found in the Act of 1971. This states that when there are restrictions on National Trust[22] inalienable land which are designed to preserve it, protect or augment its amenities or secure access to or enjoyment of such property for the public, then in each of those instances the normal legal provision for modification of restrictive covenants shall not apply to those restrictions.[23]

That procedure is used to give effect to changes in the character of a neighbourhood, by relieving property of outdated restrictions. It is thus a mark of the importance attached to National Trust Property that it should be thus exempt.[24]

7. **Constitution**

The above short account of the purposes, powers and property provisions embodied in the six National Trust Acts of Parliament has dealt with those items thought to be most relevant to this work. It should be noted that the Acts provide in detail for the constitution of the Trust, its accounts and their auditing and other matters appropriate to a large national organisation, indeed "Britain's premier charity."   **5.12**

[20] s.8.

[21] See, *e.g. Marquess of Zetland* v. *Driver* [1939] Ch. 1.

[22] National Trust Act 1971, s.27.

[23] See also, for the position before this provision was secured, *Gee* v. *National Trust* [1966] 1 W.L.R. 170.

[24] See for fuller discussion, Chap. 4, para. 4.27.

B. THE FORESTRY COMMISSION

1. Introduction

5.13 It is in the last 50 years that the Forestry Commission has used legal powers to provide recreation facilities for the public. Since the creation of the Commission by the Forestry Act 1919, to stimulate the replenishment of the nation's timber reserves after depletion in the First World War, the Commission has extended its land-holding throughout the country, until two million acres were owned by the mid-nineteen-fifties. These were inevitably used by the public, initially for walking over permitted footpaths. Slowly, other outdoor activities developed.

2. The Countryside Act 1968

5.14 It was the Countryside Act 1968 which crystallised the position and the potential.

> "The Commissioners may, on any land placed at their disposal by the Minister of Agriculture, Fisheries and Food or the Secretary of State for Wales, provide or arrange for or assist in the provision of, tourist, recreational or sporting facilities and any equipment, facilities or works ancillary thereto."[25]

Some of the interesting facilities authorised in this way were:
   (a) Accommodation for visitors.
   (b) Camping sites and caravan sites.
   (c) Places for meals and refreshments.
   (d) Picnic places, places for enjoying views, parking places, routes for nature study and footpaths.
   (e) Information and display centres.
   (f) Shops in relation to any of the above facilities.
   (g) Public conveniences.
The clear assertion of the purpose of the facilities and the extensive list was a welcome development. This provision in the Countryside Act 1968 was supplemented legally by a power to make by-laws.

3. By-Laws

5.15 The Commission was authorised to make by-laws in relation to any of the above seven activities.[26] It had acquired, in the Forestry Act 1967, wide powers of by-law making. These were to prohibit and regulate "anything tending to injury or disfigurement of the land or its amenities"; and also "for regulating the reasonable use of land by the public for the purposes of exercise and recreation."[27]

The subjects have been extended as the Commission has had to meet

[25] Countryside Act 1968, s.23(2).
[26] *Ibid.* s.23(4).
[27] Forestry Act 1967, s.46.

the enlarged interests and increased ingenuity of its visitors. Thus, new items in the last issue of the Commission's by-laws were for operating a hot-air balloon, setting up beehives, using a metal detector, taking birds' eggs and evading tolls for car parks or forest roads.[28]

The by-laws are made by statutory instrument, having been laid before Parliament in draft. Though extensive, the Commission's by-laws are not to affect any "estate, interest, right of common, or other right of a profitable or beneficial nature in, over or affecting any land, except with the consent of the person entitled thereto."[29] In addition, such by-laws are forbidden to relate to a common which is the subject of a Scheme under the Commons Act 1899, or otherwise. Chapter 2 deals more fully with such Schemes.[30]

In the current by-laws, some relate to the New Forest by reference to an increased speed for vehicles and some to the Forest of Dean, *e.g.* where sheep are to have the owner's registration mark if the sheep are turned on to unenclosed areas. These two forests have their own regulating body, the Verderers, and so the by-laws recite, as obliged by the parent statute,[31] that the Verderers were consulted before the by-laws were made.

There are also, in the current by-laws, some with special reference to the Bedgebury Pinetum in Kent, and some referring to the Westonbirt Arboretum in Gloucestershire, banning, *e.g.* kite flying.

Offences against these by-laws are liable to give rise to fines, as provided, not in the by-laws but in the parent Act.[32] Offenders may also, after due warning, be removed from the Commission's lands. (Prosecution for by-law offences is, after all, the last stage in maintaining visitors' standards on the Commission's land. The Commission has issued a Forest Code based on the by-laws to encourage adherence to those standards and thus limit prosecutions.)

4. Tree Planting for Amenity

The Countryside Act 1968 also gave a new power to the Forestry Commission in relation to tree planting. This was the authority to plant, care for and manage trees "in the interests of amenity."[33] The Minister was at the same time authorised to acquire land needed to support this policy. Such acquisitions might be partly for afforestation and partly for the cause of amenity.

This is now supplemented by the Wildlife and Countryside (Amendment) Act 1985. This requires the Commissioners to try to achieve a balance between the development of afforestation, managing forests and

5.16

---

[28] The Forestry Commission By-Laws 1982 (S.I. 1982 No. 648).

[29] Forestry Act 1967, s.46(3)(*a*).

[30] *Ibid.* s.46(3)(*b*).

[31] *Ibid.* s.47. The Verderers are also empowered, as if magistrates' courts, to enforce the Commission's by-laws in their forests.

[32] *Ibid.* s.46(5). Fines are now determined by level 2 of the standard scale. See Criminal Justice Act 1982, s.39, and Sched. 3.

[33] Countryside Act 1968, s.24. This policy is also added, as a drafting amendment, to s.3 in the Forestry Act 1967, by way of an addition to the Commission's purposes.

supplying timber on the one hand, and on the other, "the conservation and enhancement of natural beauty and the conservation of flora, fauna and geological and physiological features of special interest" (section 4).

5. **General and Historical**

5.17   This short section has sought simply to give some understanding of the role available to the Forestry Commission, in the light of its legal powers, to provide recreation facilities for the public. It only remains to itemise the statutes which provide the Forestry Commission with its general powers by way of completing the picture, rather than adding significantly to the account of leisure service legal powers.

The Forestry Act 1967 is the consolidating statute for the Forestry Commission's powers and duties. It effectively repealed and replaced the Forestry Acts of 1919,[34] 1945, 1947 and 1951. Those Acts had contained provisions about the constitution of the Forestry Commission, the control of tree felling, the policy of afforestation and the balance to be sought in the various policies to be pursued by the Commission.

The Act of 1967 restates the duty of the Commission to take directions from the three Ministers with governmental responsibility for the Commission, *i.e.* the Secretaries of State for Scotland and Wales and the Minister of Agriculture, Fisheries and Food.[35] In this instance, the Secretary of State for Scotland acts as the senior Minister.

Since 1967, Parliament has passed eight Acts relating to aspects of forestry, though none alters the main thrust of the policies and powers described in the body of this section. They are:

    (a) The Trees Act 1970 which modifies the restriction on the power to attach conditions to a felling licence.

    (b) The Wild Creatures and Forest Laws Act 1971 which repealed many ancient laws about royal rights in forests and restricted royal rights for free game.

    (c) The Forestry Act 1979, dealing with grants and loans for forestry and also metrication.

    (d) The Forestry Act 1981, giving powers to dispose of land, authorising the appointment of another Commissioner, and giving Ministers a general duty to have regard to the national interest in maintaining and expanding forestry.

    (e) The Wildlife and Countryside (Amendment) Act 1985 which amended the Forestry Act 1967 to require the Commissioners, in the discharge of any of their functions under the Forestry Acts 1967 to 1979, to endeavour to achieve a reasonable balance between the needs of forestry and those of the environment.

    (f) The Forestry Act 1986 which gave powers to the Commission to require the restocking of land with trees after unauthorised felling.

---

[34] Although an Order-making power was retained in relation to the Destructive Pests Acts 1877–1927 (now the Plant Health Act 1967). This has been used by the Agriculture Ministers, *e.g.* for Fire Blight disease, as mentioned in Chap. 4.

[35] Forestry Act 1967, s.1(4).

(g) The Forestry Act 1991 about the size of the Regional Advisory Committees.

(h) The Agriculture and Forestry (Financial Provisions) Act 1991 which empowers the Commission to give grants to the New Forest Verderers.

6. Conclusion

The recreational facilities provided by the Forestry Commission are not **5.18** geographically comprehensive, as forests are not located in all parts of the country and not all forests, for tenure and other reasons, can be made available for recreation. Yet they are considered to be far more extensive than those of any other organisation, being widespread throughout Great Britain.

And since the opening of the first National Forest Park in 1935, the Commission has allowed public access for the quiet enjoyment of its forests, wherever it is able to do so. Its policy now is to satisfy as wide a range of the community as possible by providing appropriate recreational facilities of a high standard of design. In recent years, greater emphasis has been placed on the development of such facilities in woodlands near towns.

CHAPTER 6

PUBLIC ENTERTAINMENT

"In this melody of decisions . . . a discordant note was struck by the Court of Appeal"

Lord Templeman in *Smoker* v. *London Fire and Civil Defence Authority* [1991]
2 All. E.R.

A. THEATRES

6.01   This traditional form of public entertainment has been the subject of various legal controls in the last two centuries. At present the Theatres Act 1968 governs the licensing position, in convenient summary form. The same Act is also the point of reference for the legal limits to the contents of stage performances. In addition to these two matters, those engaged in managing theatres need to take account of the law relating to the safety of buildings where the public gather, the law of contract as it relates to the engagement of artists, legal safeguards imposed for the protection of young persons appearing on the stage, certain items concerning animals and also legal aspects of the provision of refreshments and intoxicating liquor.

1. Licensing of Premises

6.02   Licences, normally renewable annually, are issued by district councils, or, for the London area, by the relevant London borough council or the Common Council.[1] A fee will be payable, unless the licensing authority are satisfied that for specific occasions the performance will be of educational or other like character or is to be given for charitable "or other like purpose."[2] The same Act, the Theatres Act 1968, contains the law about the provisional grant, renewal and transfer of licences, as well as their transmission on death.

A licence will normally contain terms about the safety and good management of the theatre; if deemed oppressive or otherwise inappropriate, the licensee has a right to go back to the issuing authority to seek some

---

[1] Local Government Act 1972, s.204(6). and Local Government Act 1985, Sched 8, para. 3. Such a licence also ensures exemption from night café licensing procedure—London Local Authorities Act 1990, s.4.

[2] Theatres Act 1968, s.13 and Sched. 1.

variation in those terms.[3] This simple licensing code is fortified by the creation of offences for performing a play at unlicensed premises or for contravening the terms of a licence.[4] The persons liable to be prosecuted include those who let the premises or allow them to be used for the unlawful performance.

Appeals against a refusal of the licensing authority to grant a licence go to the magistrates' courts, in accordance with the time limit and other procedures contained in the 1968 Act.[5]

2. The Nature of the Performance

For over 200 years, censorship of plays was in this country exercised by the Lord Chamberlain. The Theatres Act 1968 abolished that practice and in its place laid down standards to which plays and other presentations coming within its definition of "play" should conform in order to remain within the law.[6] The main provisions are as follows: **6.03**

Obscene performances

(1) A person who, whether for gain or not, directs or presents an obscene performance of a play in public or in private, is liable to prosecution before the magistrates or on indictment.[7] There is a two-year time limit on prosecutions on indictment for this offence.[8]

(2) A performance of a play is obscene, for this purpose, if its effect, taken as a whole, is such as to tend to deprave and corrupt persons likely to attend, having regard to all the circumstances.[9]

(3) This statutory offence is designed to replace any other common law offence in relation to the character of a play.[10] Wilful exposure of an indecent exhibition—to use the old wording in the Vagrancy Act 1824—is also replaced by the new offence.

The new defence—the public good

(4) A most important section in the Act is that containing a new statutory defence to a prosecution. For this defence to succeed, it has to be shown that the performance was for the public good, as being in the interests of art or ballet or opera or any other art or of literature or learning.[11] This is a wide protection, and judicial construction of the terms it embodies is taking place slowly in the courts. However, as the wording is similar to that applied to obscene publications by the Obscene Publi-

---

[3] Theatres Act 1968, s.12 and Sched. 1, para. 7.
[4] For a recent case testing the terms on the grant of a licence, see *Fischer's Restaurant* v. *Greater London Council* (1980) 18 L.G.R. 672.
[5] Theatres Act 1968, s.14.
[6] *Ibid.* s.18.
[7] *Ibid.* s.2(2).
[8] *Ibid.* s.2(3).
[9] *Ibid.* s.2(1).
[10] *Ibid.* s.2(4).
[11] *Ibid.* s.3.

cations Act 1959, the view of the court in a case under that Act has relevance when construing the Theatres Act defence. The book *Last Exit to Brooklyn* came before the Court of Appeal in the case of *R. v. Calder & Boyars*.[12] Attention centred upon the correct legal direction to be given to the jury when they had to consider the defence in question. The court held that the jury should be told to consider the number of readers they believed might be depraved or corrupted, the strength of the tendency to deprave or corrupt and the nature of the depravity or corruption. On the other hand, the jury ought to consider the merits the book had, literary, sociological and ethical. These factors were to be balanced and the jury had then to decide whether the publication was for the public good.

Allowing for the changed subject-matter, similar criteria can be applied to a stage performance.

(5) The onus resting upon the defendant under the Theatres Act is to establish the statutory defence on the balance of probabilities; that on the prosecution when seeking a conviction is heavier, *i.e.* to establish guilt beyond reasonable doubt.[13]

6.04   (6) An offence is created in the Theatres Act concerning a performance which is likely to stir up hatred against a section of the public distinguished by colour, race, ethnic or national origins. It is committed by the person who directs or presents the performance and he must be shown to have intended to stir up hatred against that section of the public.[14]

(7) Another offence, couched in similar phraseology, is created for provoking a breach of the peace through the stage performance.[15]

6.05   (8) Certain exceptions are allowed from the overall operation of the provisions concerning these new offences. These are:

(i) A rehearsal.

(ii) A recording or filming or broadcast, provided that the performance was not attended by persons other than those involved in the activity listed above.[16]

(9) A limited exemption from a threatened prosecution for the basic section 2 offence is also given for a play given on a domestic occasion in a private dwelling.

(10) The Attorney-General's consent is necessary to initiate proceedings for the three offences described in paragraphs (i), (vi) and (vii) above.[17]

This is clearly a most important Act, for local authorities who manage civic theatres in particular, as well as their employees. Though local auth-

---

[12] [1969] 1 Q.B.157. In a more recent case, *R. v. Michael Bogdanov* (unreported), the play "The Romans in Britain" was under scrutiny in a prosecution under this Act in London in 1982. The play had been produced at the National Theatre. After a defence submission that there was no case to answer, the judge gave a ruling and stopped the case.

[13] See *Public Prosecutor* v. *Yuvaraj* [1970] A.C. 913 about this "historic distinction."

[14] Theatres Act 1968, s.5.

[15] *Ibid.* s.6.

[16] See *Ibid.* s.7, for the detailed qualifications on these exceptions, which also include cable transmission.

[17] *Ibid.* s.8.

orities are corporate bodies, that status does not relieve them, if managing a theatre, of the various offences in the Act.[18]

3. **Professional Contracts**

Theatrical usage will be taken into account when construing contracts for **6.06** the hire of artists. Making this allowance, those contracts must be clear in their terms, avoid illegality, and conform to the normal requirements of the law of this country relating to contracts.[19] One or two of the most common legal problems arising in practice may usefully be discussed.

(1) *Restraint*

A contract to engage an artist to perform at a theatre would be expected to **6.07** contain management provisions imposing restraint upon the artist from performing within a stipulated distance and time from the engagement at the theatre in question. The courts provide a point of reference should difference of opinion arise about the reasonableness of such restraints.

The case in 1914 of *London Theatre of Varieties Ltd.* v. *Evans*[20] concerned a contract for a music hall performer. The contract provided that there should be "no colourable imitation, representation, or version" of his performance within a prescribed radius or time of that dealt with in the contract. When such a version was discovered in a "picture palace" close enough in time and location to constitute a contravention of the contract, the case was taken to the High Court. It was there decided that the performer was not liable for the breach since any performance at the picture palace took place without his permission.

Again, "the only concert by this artist in the month of May in Yorkshire" might be an unreasonable term, having regard to the large population, area and length of time. On the other hand, "the only concert in May in Wiltshire," could be reasonable, in the light of the lesser area and population.

(2) *Non-Performance*

The law has frequently been invoked to resolve differences arising from **6.08** non-performance by an artist under contract. Weather, illness, the death of a member of a troupe, the absence of a management provision—say of props or supporting staff or performers—are all the sort of factors which have led to legal disputes. The practice of the courts, is, first, to construe the terms of the contract and then to look for a reasonable interpretation in the light of the intentions of the parties and earlier decisions of the courts in relevant circumstances.

---

[18] Theatres Act 1968, s.16.
[19] The manager in an argument with the agents about the small print of artistes' contracts may benefit from a compendium like L. E. Colkrell, *Performance* (2nd ed., 1985.)
[20] (1914) 31 T.L.R. 75.

Death or illness

In *Harvey* v. *Tivoli Manchester Ltd.*[21] the death of one of a troupe of three intimate performers was held to be a good reason for the other two artists avoiding the contract. On the other hand, a contract was held not to be frustrated by the illness of a principal in a larger company. (See *Terry* v. *Variety Theatres Controlling Co.*[22] The contract permitted Terry to provide a substitute in such circumstances and this is what he had done.)

Loss of enhanced reputation

Fielding v. *Moisevitch*[23] was a Court of Appeal case which contains legal appraisal of several practical factors which must arise in theatrical management on failure of an artist to fulfil his contract. It is therefore of general interest.

M., a celebrated pianist, was under contract to the plaintiff, a concert impresario, to perform at the Theatre Royal, Nottingham in 1943 and did not do so. He suffered illness and so informed F. on the day before the concert was to take place. A substitute pianist played at the concert, a loss in box office takings occurred and the plaintiff brought the matter to court, primarily to let the public know that it was not his fault that they had been disappointed. First, the court held that a breach of contract had occurred. In so doing they rejected a contention of the defendant that there was a general custom in the theatre that an artist was released from his contract if he felt unable to perform to his usual standard and without fault on his part. Secondly, the plaintiff was awarded damages based on the extra expenses of engaging a substitute pianist and also taking into account a loss in box office takings. He was not, however, allowed recompense for alleged lower returns at a later promotion nor for loss of publicity. This last was an important point for theatrical management, since it distinguished an impresario such as Mr. Harold Fielding, the plaintiff, from an actor, who does have that right.

Contract cancelled

6.09   The actor's right had emerged in the case of *Withers* v. *The General Theatre Corporation Ltd.*,[24] again in the Court of Appeal. There, an American artist under contract to perform at the London Palladium was given notice by that theatre management to cancel his contract, less than a week before he was to perform. Management did so on seeing what they considered an inadequately rehearsed show during the trial run at Portsmouth in the week before the opening, for a three-week run, at the Palladium. The plaintiff succeeded in his claim for damages, for loss of that enhanced reputation he would have gained at the Palladium and not for injury to that reputation which he already possessed. What may seem

---

[21] (1907) 23 T.L.R. 592.
[22] (1928) 44 T.L.R. 451.
[23] (1946) 175 L.T. 265.
[24] [1933] 2 K.B. 536.

an over-subtle distinction was made by the court in the light of earlier House of Lords decisions and allied cases from the field of employment law.

(3) *Management Discretion*

Thirdly, a cause célèbre relating to a ticket for a seat on the first night of a   **6.10** new production, illustrates another area of management where awareness of legal principles is needed. *Said* v. *Butt*[25] concerned the situation created when the management of the Palace Theatre, London, had the plaintiff removed from the theatre, even though he had a valid ticket, on the occasion of the first night of a new play, "The Whirligig." Naturally there was a background. The plaintiff had worked with the defendant on a previous production and serious differences between the two had resulted. Indeed the plaintiff knew that he would not be sold a first night ticket if he went to the Palace box office in person. Thus he arranged for a friend, a Mr. Pollock, to purchase the ticket for him. After the débacle, the plaintiff brought an action for damages for breach of contract. He was met by the defence that, in the circumstances, the person with whom the contract was made was important: that there was a fundamental mistake about that person and thus no legal contract was in existence to be broken. The court was told of the special regard for his audience which a manager has in connection with a first night; he feels entitled to choose the people to whom seats are given for that occasion. It is "a special event with special characteristics," said a witness. The defence succeeded. McCardie J. held that non-disclosure by the friend that the ticket he purchased was intended for the plaintiff was a material fact. A legal contract had not been concluded and could not, therefore, be broken.

4. The Premises

(1) *Safety under the Health and Safety at Work Act 1974*

The subject of the safety of the theatre will be dealt with in the licence   **6.11** obtained under the Theatres Act. There are provisions in other statutes which are also relevant to this subject. The Health and Safety at Work Act 1974 affects theatres as places where people at work are entitled to safety and health in their working conditions. The gantry and other potentially dangerous areas behind the front curtain will call for scrutiny, in the light of the extensive duties laid upon the occupiers of premises where people work.

It is important to note that this Act of 1974 has avoided creating rights of legal action in the courts concerning the rights and duties it so clearly defines. Thus, on the one hand, the Act states that it is the duty of every employer, so far as is reasonably practicable, to provide for the health, welfare and safety at work of all his employees.[26] In particular, this duty

---

[25] [1920] 3 K.B. 497.
[26] Health and Safety at Work etc. Act 1974, s.2.

extends to the provision and maintenance of plant and systems of work that are, so far as reasonably practicable, safe and without risks to health.[27] But, on the other hand, in a section about civil liberty, the Act states that nothing in the Act shall be construed as conferring a right of action in any civil proceeding in respect of any failure to comply with (*inter alia*) the duties described above.[28] By contrast, an associated subsection says that breach of a provision under Health and Safety Regulations, as distinct from the Act, is, so far as it causes damage, actionable.[29]

Since this creation by legislation of rights and duties, coupled with the removal of statutory rights of enforcement through the courts, is unusual, there is another subsection designed to remove any doubts that this is indeed what Parliament intended. This says that the earlier provisions in this important section 47 are "without prejudice to any right of action which exists apart from the provisions of this Act."[30] There are not at present any Health and Safety Regulations specifically about theatres.

(2) *Safety under the Public Health Acts*

Exits and entrances

6.12   There are important provisions in the Building Regulations made under the Public Health Acts, which affect the exits and entrances of a theatre. What those regulations require are:

> "means of escape consisting of exits and escape routes, of such number, size, layout, design and construction as may reasonably be required in the circumstances of the case to enable the occupants to reach a place of safety in the event of fire; and other works to ensure that such means of escape can be safely and effectively used."[31]

This puts the provision of exits and entrances in the context of danger from fire, perhaps the ultimate hazard for a theatre. The requirements have behind them the sanctions common to all the Building Regulations.[32]

(3) *Safety at Common Law*

6.13   Section 47 of the Health and Safety at Work Act 1974 clearly leaves the common law operative in respect of health and safety at work of theatrical employees. The main obligations resting upon an employer from that part of our law are to provide a proper system of working, to provide compe-

---

[27] Health and Safety at Work etc. Act 1974, s.2(2)(*a*).
[28] *Ibid.* s.47(1)(*a*).
[29] *Ibid.* s.47(2).
[30] *Ibid.* s.47(4).
[31] Reg. E 22, the Building Regulations 1976 (S.I. 1976 No. 1676) as slightly amended by S.I. 1981 No. 1338, reg. 21. The requirement to raise and lower the safety curtain in the sight of the audience is an associated provision.
[32] Public Health Act 1961, s.4(6). A specific provision about exits and entrances in theatres in the Public Health Act 1936, s.59, is superseded by the above Building Regulation. See Fire Precautions Act 1971, s.30.

tent managers and supervisors for the employees and to provide suitable equipment for their use.

A case showing how this obligation operates in the complexity of a theatre is *Fanton* v. *Denville*.[33] For a production of "Maria Martin or Murder in the Red Barn," the classic melodrama, a drop scene was necessary when the villain was to be executed by hanging. Though the stage manager successfully demonstrated the required fall on to a mattress, the plaintiff, the principal when the show appeared at Gateshead, unfortunately broke his ankle at rehearsal when trying the drop himself. He proceeded to sue his employer for failing to provide fit and safe plant and machinery and properties and for failing to take reasonable precautions to prevent danger to the plaintiff. In particular, he alleged, a sufficient mattress should have been provided.

The case reached the Court of Appeal, which, in its judgment, touched upon other matters but emphasised that the employer's common law duty described above is not an absolute warranty of fitness of buildings and plant. It is rather an obligation to use reasonable care to see that they are fit and this obligation is associated with the duty to appoint competent servants. In the circumstances, there was no personal negligence proved against the defendant.

(4) *Coats of Arms*

A unique incident in theatrical history deserves a brief note. The case of **6.14** *Manchester Corporation* v. *Manchester Palace of Varieties*[34] describes how the Court of Chivalry was assembled and ruled that the famous Manchester theatre was not entitled to exhibit the coat of arms of Manchester Corporation on a pelmet above its main front of stage curtains without the consent of the Corporation, the grantee of the coat of arms in question. Though the sitting of the court was special, the question raised is not, since coats of arms of the local authority are often found in civic theatres. It is true that the gravamen of the Corporation's complaint was the further use of its seal by the theatrical company but the judgment of Lord Goddard dealt with the pelmet display of the coat of arms and this is of general interest to those involved with theatres.

5. **Young Persons Taking Part in Performance**

Some basic restrictions on this subject need to be borne in mind by theatre **6.15** managers and their advisers.

(1) No person under 16 years of age is to take part in a performance in which his life or limbs are endangered. "Performance" is defined in the Children and Young Persons Act 1933, section 23, in wide terms.

(2) An under-12-year-old is banned from being trained to take part in

---

[33] [1932] 2 K.B. 309.
[34] [1955] 1 All E.R. 387.

performances of a dangerous nature. An under-16-year-old can do so only under licence from the local authority.[35]

(3) An under-16-year-old is only to take part in public performances, for which a charge is made, if duly licensed by the local authority.[36]

(4) A licence under (iii) above is qualified further in the case of a child under the age of 13. Such a licence is not to be granted unless:

    (a) The licence is for acting and a declaration is made to the licensing authority that only a child of his age can act the part in question; or

    (b) The licence is for dancing in a ballet, being part of an entertainment which is wholly ballet or opera and a like declaration as in (i) above is made about the part the child is to dance; or

    (c) The child's part in the performance is wholly or mainly musical. In addition, the nature of the performance must be wholly or mainly musical or consist only of opera and ballet.[37]

(5) When conditions in licences granted for performances described in (iii) and (iv) above are not observed, the licensing authority may vary or revoke the licence. They have to give the licence holder a chance to be heard before taking such action.[38] The Act also sets out the procedure to be followed when a child licensed by one local authority is to take part in a performance in the area of another local authority.

(6) Sanctions for breaches of these licensing requirements are contained in the Act. They include both fines and imprisonment and the courts are given power to revoke the licences. There is also an offence for knowingly making false statements in the licence application.[39]

(7) An associated legal provision states that when a performance is for an audience of children, in total or as a majority, and the number of children is more than 100, then duties are laid upon managers about the instruction and stationing of their attendants, in order to cope with such an audience.[40]

6. **Animals**

6.16   The Performing Animals (Regulation) Act 1925 contains important provisions about the exhibition and training of performing animals. Exhibitors and trainers have to be duly registered with local authorities. In particular, exhibitions or performances accompanied by cruelty to animals give rise to punishable offences. In a later Act,[41] untrained bulls and

---

[35] Children and Young Persons Act 1963, s.37.

[36] *Ibid.* s.37, where details can be studied of the conditions under which no licence is needed. Broadly, these are that the performance is non-commercial, under the aegis of school or local authority and it is an exceptional activity for the performers. For details of the conditions relating to child performances mentioned in this paragraph, see the Children (Performances) Regulations 1968 (S.I. 1968 No. 1728). The 43 regulations cover very important details.

[37] *Ibid.* s.38.

[38] *Ibid* s.39.

[39] *Ibid* s.40.

[40] *Ibid* s.12.

[41] Protection of Animals Act 1934.

unbroken horses are given special legal protection against being used in so-called rodeo performances.

7. **Refreshments**

Ice-cream

Under the Food Safety Act 1990, theatres, music halls and concert halls   **6.17**
are expected to lose their exemption from requirements that premises
where ice-cream is sold shall be registered.[42]

Intoxicating liquor

The Theatres Act licence has to be produced to the licensing justices
when application is made to retail intoxicating liquor in pursuance of the
normal excise licence.[43] Section F (paras. 6.61 *et seq., post*) deals fully with
that subject.

Young persons as sales staff

The Shops Act 1950 controls night employment of young persons, normally under-18-year-olds, to discourage exploitation. A work-free interval
of eight hours from 10 pm to 6 am is prescribed in this Act, for this group
of people. However, the special needs of theatres are recognised in a provision that the eight hour period shall not start, for their staff, until the
evening performance ends.[44]

8. **Sunday Observance**

The Sunday Theatres Act 1972 introduced an exemption for theatres from   **6.18**
the general ban under the Sunday Observance Acts on entertainment for
payment on Sundays. In a duly licensed theatre, the presentation of a play
is lawful, provided that, outside London, it is not performed between 2 am
and 2 pm.[45]

B. Cinemas

Historical

Cinemas as a form of public entertainment are now legally regulated in   **6.19**
a consolidating Act, the Cinemas Act 1985. This contains a welcome and
long-awaited codification of the law earlier scattered in Acts of 1909, 1952
and 1982. The essential law was not significantly changed in 1985 but it
was brought up to date.

Throughout the legislation of the last 80 years, there have been four
main themes. These are the licensing of the premises, the safety of these

---

[42] Food Safety Act 1990, s.19.
[43] Licensing Act 1964, s.199(*c*).
[44] Shops Act 1950, s.3.
[45] The London times are 3 am to 2 pm.

premises, the best safeguards for children and young persons and, lastly, the control to be exercised over the films themselves. These are the matters dealt with in this section.

1. Licensing of Premises

6.20   District councils are the licensing authorities for cinemas, since the local government reorganisation in 1974.[46] They may grant licences to such persons as they think fit, to use the premises for the purposes of film exhibitions. The licence can contain terms imposed by the district council, subject to any restrictions that the Secretary of State may issue, in the form of regulations.[47] Twenty-eight days' notice of an application for a licence is required.[48] The Local Government (Miscellaneous Provisions) Act 1982 contains a provision that if a cinema is licensed under the Cinematograph Acts, the music played with or forming part of the cinematograph exhibitions shall not attract the need for an Entertainment Licence under that Act, in respect of the cinema premises.[49]

The Home Secretary has made regulations, under the power referred to above. These relate mainly to safety and are dealt with in the next subsection.

Terms of cinema licensing

The nature of the terms imposed in cinema licences by the present local authorities and their predecessors cannot be dealt with as briefly. There have been numerous interesting cases in the courts, as variations in the conditions imposed throughout the country have been tested. The main principles which have emerged are as follows:

(1) The licensing authority has a wide discretion and the courts, acting in a judicial and not an appellate capacity, will be slow to alter or quash what they have decided.

(2) However, the district councils must not deal with applications under a blanket policy. Each application must be dealt with on its merits.[50]

6.21   (3) The district councils must not themselves flout the law. This may seem obvious but in *R.* v. *London County Council, ex p. the Entertainment Protection Association*[51] the Court of Appeal condemned a practice of stating that no action would be taken for Sunday opening accompanied by payments

---

[46] Local Government Act 1972, s.204(5).
[47] Cinemas Act 1985, s.4. The House of Lords in *British Amusement Catering Trades Association* v. *Westminster City Council* [1988] 2 W.L.R. 485, decided that the definition of film exhibition, namely "moving pictures," did not include a video game. The reasoning, stemming from common sense, called by lawyers first impressions, was distinctly heartening.
[48] Cinematograph (Amendment) Act 1982, s.3.
[49] Local Government (Miscellaneous Provisions) Act 1982, Sched. 1, para. 21(*b*).
[50] See, for instance, *Ellis* v. *Dubowski* [1921] 3 K.B. 621, and *R.* v. *Flintshire C.C. County Licensing Committee* [1957] 1 Q.B. 350 and *R.* v. *Windsor Licensing Justices, ex p. Hodes* [1983] 1 W.L.R. 685.
[51] [1931] 2 K.B. 215.

to charities by the cinema managers in the area of that local authority. An Order was issued by the court to stop the practice. "Has the Theatres Committee ever heard of the Bill of Rights?" asked Lord Justice Scrutton, giving the leading judgment of the court.

(4) The terms must not be so unreasonable that no reasonable body could have reached them. In the leading case of *Associated Provincial Picture Houses Ltd.* v. *Wednesbury Corporation*,[52] the Court of Appeal declined to intervene where the term challenged was that "No children under the age of 15 years shall be admitted to any entertainment, whether accompanied by an adult or not." (The actual grant of licence was under the Sunday Entertainment Act 1932, but the principle was the same.) Lord Green said:

> "Nobody, at this time of day, can say that the well-being and the physical and moral health of children are not matters which a local authority, in exercising its powers, can properly have in mind when those questions are germane to what it has to consider."[53]

The Master of the Rolls continued that it would require "overwhelming proof" to say that a decision of a local authority was so unreasonable that no reasonable authority could ever have come to it. The facts in that case, he said, "do not come anywhere near such a thing."

(5) The local authority must not take into account extraneous matters but only those germane to their decision.[54] This was a point emphasised by Lord Greene, in his strong judgment in the *Wednesbury* case.

(6) In the interests of completeness, it is worth mentioning that in earlier cases in particular, the courts have stressed that the conditions must be in the public interest.[55] This term was interpreted widely to cover the health, including the spiritual health, and welfare of the public. Local authorities have a vestigial power of film censorship, rarely exercised in these days. It stems from a general term in the licence which usually follows the Home Office model. This refers to public taste or decency, being likely to encourage crime, or disorder, or being offensive to public feeling. Action is initiated by notice from the local authority to the licensee.

A fee is payable for the licence.[56] A penalty may be incurred for contravention of the licence.[57] An appeal system exists to the Crown Court against refusal of a licence or against the terms in the licence actually granted.[58]

---

[52] [1948] 1 K.B. 223.
[53] *Ibid.* p. 683.
[54] See also *Harman* v. *Butt* [1944] K.B. 491, approved in the *Wednesbury* case. Also *Lidster* v. *Owen* [1983] 1 W.L.R. 516, where the degree of public disorder when they were leaving premises was held to be germane to consideration of the grant of an entertainment licence.
[55] See, *e.g. Theatre de Luxe (Halifax) Ltd.* v. *Gledhill* [1915] 2 K.B. 49, where the dissenting judgment of Atkinson J. is notable, as it was preferred in the *Wednesbury* case.
[56] Cinemas Act 1985. s.3.
[57] *Ibid.* s.10.
[58] *Ibid.* s.16.

2. **Enforcement**

6.22 The police, the fire authorities and the district councils are invested with varying powers of enforcement and control.[59]

The police have powers of entry to cover not only regular cinemas but also cinema clubs and sex cinemas in occasional or movable buildings or structures. A search warrant requires the authority of a justice of the peace.[60]

The fire service are to give 24 hours' notice of inspection and then may enter to see if the precautions are adequate and if terms laid down are being complied with. The punishment for an unlicensed exhibition has increased to a fine not exceeding £20,000.[61]

3. **Exempted Exhibitions**

6.23 Premises used on not more than six days in the year and only occasionally and exceptionally for cinematograph exhibitions, do not require a licence, provided that seven days' notice of an exhibition is given to a local authority and to the police and the exhibitor complies with the conditions subsequently imposed. If the exhibition is to be in a building of a movable nature, then two days' like notice is required, and due compliance with conditions imposed. A private dwelling-house is not within the Acts, provided that no charge is involved, and the show is not for private gain. The major exception provision is for non-profit-making bodies such as film societies, or indeed, any non-commercial committee, society, institution or other organisation. A certificate from the Home Office is needed and then an exhibition by an "exempted organisation" is not in peril as an unlicensed exhibition, notwithstanding a charge for entrance. (This can, however, only be made on three days out of a period of seven days.)

4. **The Safety of the Premises**

6.24 The power of the Secretary of State to make regulations is defined in relation to the subject of safety as follows:

> " . . . safety, in connection with the giving of cinematograph exhibitions (including the keeping and handling, in premises where other entertainments are being given or meetings held, of cinematograph film used or to be used for the purposes of cinematograph exhibitions or other articles or equipment so used or to be used")[62]

The relevant regulations,[63] in force since 1955, contain 51 provisions and in the main deal with exits, staff, fire precautions, the structure of pro-

---

[59] Cinemas Act 1985, s.11 (penalties), s.12 (revocations).
[60] *Ibid.* s.13.
[61] *Ibid.* s.11.
[62] *Ibid.* s.4.
[63] See the Cinematograph (Safety) Regulations 1955 (S.I. 1955 No. 1129). There have been amending regulations of a minor character since 1955.

jection and rewinding rooms, the design of film projectors, as well as lighting and electrical installations and equipment.

5. **The Safety of Children and Young Persons**

The Secretary of State has also used his power, mentioned above, to make **6.25**
regulations about children. The 1985 Cinemas Act defines the ambit of
this subject as: "the health and welfare of children in relation to attend-
ance at film exhibitions."[64] The Regulations were issued in 1955[65] and
state that they do not derogate from the terms of licences issued by local
authorities. What they do is to:

(a) Prohibit the admission of a child apparently under five years of
    age, unless accompanied by a person over 16 years old;
(b) Prohibit the admission of an under-12-year-old after 7 pm unless,
    first, they are accompanied by a person over 16 years old, and
    secondly, the film in question has not been shown on that day
    before 7 pm.
(c) Require the provision of attendants, when a show is for children, in
    the proportion of at least one per 1,000 children in respect of the
    lower floor of the cinema, and one per 50 children for the higher
    floor, and, in total, to see that there are at least as many attendants
    as there are exits to the cinema.

For its part, the licensing authority is placed under a statutory duty to:

"impose conditions or restrictions, prohibiting the admission of children to film exhibitions, involving the showing of works designated
by the licensing authority or such other body as may be designated in
the licence as works unsuitable for children."[66]

The licensing authority, in addition to the above *duty* is also charged to
consider:

"what (if any) conditions or restrictions should be imposed as to the
admission of children to other film exhibitions involving the showing
of works designated by the authority or such other body as specified
in the licence as works of such other description as may be specified
(in the licence)."[67]

This "other body" is the British Board of Film Classification, which has
currently six categories of films available for public exhibition. These are
Universal, or suitable for all, Parental Guidance, when some scenes may
be unsuitable for small children and three groups: 12, 15 and 18 being
passed only for persons of those respective ages or over. The sixth category
is R18, for Restricted Distribution Only and this means via specially

---

[64] Cinemas Act 1985, s.4.
[65] See the Cinematograph (Children) (No. 2) Regulations 1955 (S.I. 1955 No. 1909), *i.e.* under
    earlier Acts of 1909 and 1952 (now repealed) but still in force as Regulations until revised.
[66] Cinemas Act 1985, s.1(3).
[67] *Ibid.* s.1(3).

licensed cinemas or sex shops to which no one under the age of 18 is admitted.

Where a special film show for children takes place, then there is reserved, to both the Home Secretary and the licensing authority, power to impose special conditions or restrictions on the necessary consent for such shows. Whilst films shown for children in a private dwelling-house or shown as part of the activities of an educational or religious institution will be exempted exhibitions, these are special cases.

6. **Regulation of Film Renting and Exhibition**

6.26 The Films Act 1985 is the current statute about the degree of government involvement in production of commercial films. The quota system, the Cinematograph Films Council and the National Film Finance Corporation have all gone and this is not the place for a flashback.

The Government are now empowered to give financial help for the production of British films. Almost 100 films have been thus supported up to the present time. In the case of companies these have to be planned on a "commercially successful" basis: with individuals that condition does not apply. But for both recipients, the definition of "British film" in the first schedule is as complex as the plot of a John le Carré mystery novel!

C. LOCAL AUTHORITIES AND PUBLIC ENTERTAINMENT

6.27 It is essential for all engaged in public entertainment to know about the extent of the legal powers and duties of local authorities in that field. There are over 450 such authorities now in possession of the powers in question and the use made of them is a vital part of the provision of public entertainment in this country.[68]

After various national statutes and local Acts granting powers to local authorities in this field, the Local Government Act 1948 conferred wider powers than any previously granted. The national stimulus given to public entertainment during the war was part of the background to this step.

1. **The Local Government Act 1972**

6.28 Now the Local Government Act 1972 has included in the functions of local authorities section 145, which embodies all that was in the 1948 Act and at the same time extends it and removes a number of restraints earlier imposed. Section 145 is the effective comprehensive statutory power available for nearly all the activities of local authorities in the public entertainment field:

---

[68] It is not always realised that local authorities operate 260 theatres, 100 concert halls and 50 arts centres (Audit Commission report, *Local Authorities Entertainment & the Arts 1990*). This whole report, on how local authorities achieve value for money in this field, is instructive.

"**Provision of entertainments**

145.—(1) A local authority may do, or arrange for the doing of, or contribute towards the expenses of the doing of, anything (whether inside or outside their area) necessary or expedient for any of the following purposes, that is to say—

(*a*) the provision of an entertainment of any nature or of facilities for dancing;

(*b*) the provision of a theatre, concert hall, dance hall or other premises suitable for the giving of entertainments or the holding of dances;

(*c*) the maintenance of a band or orchestra;

(*d*) the development and improvement of the knowledge, understanding and practice of the arts and crafts which serve the arts;

(*e*) any purpose incidental to the matters aforesaid, including the provision of refreshments or programmes and the advertising of any entertainment given or dance or exhibition of arts or crafts held by them.

(2) Without prejudice to the generality of the provisions of subsection (1) above, a local authority—

(*a*) may for the purposes therein specified enclose or set apart any part of a park or pleasure ground belonging to the authority or under their control;

(*b*) may permit any theatre, concert hall, dance hall or other premises provided by them for the purposes of subsection (1) above and any part of a park or pleasure ground enclosed or set apart as aforesaid to be used by any other person, on such terms as to payment or otherwise as the authority think fit, and may authorise that other person to make charges for admission thereto;

(*c*) may themselves make charges for admission to any entertainment given or dance or exhibition of arts or crafts held by them and for any refreshment or programmes supplied thereat.

(3) Subsection (2) above shall not authorise any authority to contravene any covenant or condition subject to which a gift or lease of a public park or pleasure ground has been accepted or made without the consent of the donor, grantor, lessor or other person entitled in law to the benefit of the covenant or condition.

(4) Nothing in this section shall affect the provisions of any enactment by virtue of which a licence is required for the public performance of a stage play or the public exhibition of films, or for boxing or wrestling entertainments or for public music or dancing, or for the sale of intoxicating liquor.

(5) In this section the expression "local authority" includes the Common Council."

2. **Removal of Limitations**

Section 145 is in extremely wide terms. An understanding of the real **6.29** extent of these powers is assisted by noting the seven areas in which this section releases local authorities from pre-1972 restrictions.

(1) The powers now specifically include the arts and crafts.

(2) They apply to all local authorities and in particular to county councils and parish and community councils.[69] County councils are those authorities best able to look at art and entertainment provision which straddles the boundaries of district councils, such as the national orchestras or opera companies.

(3) A local authority can now exercise these powers outside its own area. It is no longer necessary to be able to prove benefit to its own inhabitants. An example of the steps needed to overcome this former legal hurdle is the special Eisteddfod Act 1959, which was passed to allow local authorities in Wales, including Monmouthshire, to contribute to the costs of the famous musical event. A comparable Act was passed in 1967 in connection with the Llangollen International Musical Eisteddfod.

(4) In exercising these powers, a local authority no longer has to obtain the consent of the local authority for the area where the powers are exercised.[70]

(5) An earlier limit to an annually budgeted item is removed so that longer-term financial planning is possible.[71]

(6) Borrowing money for activities in this field is no longer subject to special procedures.

(7) There was formerly a limit upon the proportion of a public park which was to be devoted to public entertainment purposes, such as a concert, open air theatre or dancing. That limit also is now removed.

3. **Private Covenants**

6.30 Section 145(3) restrains a local authority from contravening "any covenant or condition subject to which a gift or lease of a public park or pleasure ground has been accepted or made without the consent of the donor, grantor, lessor or other person entitled in law to the benefit of the covenant or condition." Though this stipulation is necessary and, indeed, repeats an earlier provision in the Local Government Act 1948, its impact is not always appreciated. Hence one or two examples of the way it works may be useful.

(1) An important local Act in 1980 was the West Midlands County Council Act. This was taken through Parliament not only on behalf of the County Council but also for the City of Birmingham and the other strong metropolitan district councils lying within that county. One section in that Act related to the Cannon Hill Park in Birmingham and stated that whilst this could in future be used, free from a number of restraints laid down in the documents which had transferred it to the local authority, the

---

[69] Responsibility for certain important public halls, *e.g.* the Philharmonic at Liverpool, on the dissolution of metropolitan counties in 1986 is detailed in the Local Government Reorganisation (Property etc.) Order 1986 (S.I. 1986 No. 148) and the Local Government Reorganisation (Property etc.) (No. 2) Order 1986 (S.I. 1986 No. 413).

[70] This follows the repeal without replacement of s.132 of the Local Government Act 1948.

[71] But a separate account for publicity expenditure is required by Local Government Act 1986, s.5.

park was still subject to restraints, set out in those documents, which concerned among others the sale of intoxicating liquors, the use of boats and playing by bands, on Sundays.[72]

(2) Again, in a comparable local Act, the West Yorkshire Act 1980, a section relating to the People's Park in Halifax states that it shall be "used as a promenade only and no games or sports, swimming or dancing shall be permitted therein."[73] Even so, musical performances in the park are in order if "the Protector" appointed at the time of transfer to the local authority so consents. Again, an entertainment for a charitable object is in order, subject again to the Protector's consent. This is an interesting example, since the section quoted represents the residual legal constraint upon the district council's entertainment provision, after a substantial pruning and redrafting of the legacy of conditions and covenants from the Victorian age had taken place.

(3) Another Halifax park, subject to restraints upon its use when conveyed to the local authority many years ago, had those restraints modernised in the Act mentioned above. Even so, the condition laid down at the time of transfer still prevails, *i.e.* that any building must be first approved by the President of the County Archaeological Society.[74]

(4) A somewhat quaint survival in a Cheshire County Council Act is of interest.[75] The Act takes up section 145 with its saving subsection (3) for local Acts and says this is not to apply to the Grosvenor Park, Chester. This means that old conditions are not to be saved. The local Act then says that this repeal shall not extend to an indenture of 1867 so far as it precludes "the erection of buildings or structures, the holding of fairs, the sale of intoxicating liquor or dancing, other than country dancing." Perhaps those last four words exemplify the nice battles joined whenever the opposed forces of retention and repeal try to revise this type of legislation.

4. **Allied Provisions**

Section 145 of the Local Government Act 1972 is available to the local **6.31** authority in its general capacity. There are three other comparatively minor legal provisions which have a bearing on this topic:

Education authorities

Significant changes in public education both in the sphere of powers and duties as well as finance, throw much of the initiative locally, if a contribution to local public entertainment is to be found. School orchestras, higher education brass bands and such ventures may be harder to discover under the current regime.[76]

---

[72] West Midlands County Act 1980, s.85.
[73] West Yorkshire Act 1980, s.71.
[74] *Ibid.* s.70(5).
[75] Cheshire County Council Act 1980, s.16(1).
[76] The former 1944 Education Act duty is now a discretionary power in relation to higher education (s.41 and Education Reform Act 1988, s.120).

Swimming pools

Under the Public Health Act 1936, a swimming pool can be closed in order to assist in the provision of entertainment.[77]

Children

The Children and Young Persons Act 1933[78] has to be borne in mind as imposing restrictions on the numbers of attendants when there is an entertainment for children.

5. Conclusion

6.32 In view of their very wide powers, local councillors and their advisers are more likely to ask: What may we not do? than otherwise. The areas of prohibition, comparatively small though they may seem, can be vital in practice.

Yet the final word in this section must be with the Royal Commission on Local Government when considering their duty to plan for the future of these functions.

> "Local authorities will increasingly be the main and, for the more elaborate facilities, the only providers, and their responsibilities, whether for the larger scale regional sport and recreation centres or for the smaller and more local projects, seem bound to increase."[79]

In their first reference, entertainment was not mentioned with the other two topics but in the subsequent chapter containing the Commission's view of the future, it was so mentioned. That is how the law rests at present and we still await testing in the courts of some of the key expressions in which it is set out.

D. PUBLIC HALLS

6.33 As managers of public halls in the towns within the enlarged local authorities, district councils find themselves involved in legal provisions governing a variety of forms of entertainment performed in those buildings. The halls are naturally important to local societies and are consequently expected to be available for differing purposes. They often become "multi-purpose halls." Managers have to be tightrope performers themselves on occasion. Disappointment to the promoters of the dog show can perhaps be the sad result of giving pleasure to the baby show committee. Some of the principal forms of entertainment likely to be provided in these halls are now considered, in the light of current legal requirements for their performance.

---

[77] s.226.
[78] s.12. And see para. 6.25.
[79] Cmnd. 4040, June 1969, para. 67.

1. **Entertainment Licences**

Music, singing and dancing form a significant part of the usage made of **6.34** many of our public halls. The law relating to these new licences is therefore vital to all who have to do with their ownership, management, hiring and use. A complete code of law governing the licence is contained in the Local Government (Miscellaneous Provisions) Act 1982,[80] and is summarised below. It effectively supersedes all previous somewhat intermittent legislation about music, singing and dancing licences; it puts the licensing of boxing and wrestling on a uniform basis and it introduces for the first time specific powers appropriate to pop and rock festivals.

(1) *Scope of the Licence*

The licence is needed for "public dancing or music or any other public entertainment of the like kind." As such the normal Entertainment Licence does not apply to an open-air entertainment, nor to an entertainment at a pleasure fair, nor to music in a place of public religious worship, nor music performed as an incident of a religious meeting or service.[81]

(2) *Pop Festivals*

In connection with open-air pop and rock festivals, the new licence is **6.35** called a Special Entertainment Licence and the only conditions for its use are that the event is wholly or mainly in the open air, it is on private land and it is "a public musical entertainment."[82] Without using the words pop and rock festivals, the purport of this provision is made clear by eliminating one or two other events. These are a garden fete, a bazaar, a sale of work, a sporting or athletic event, exhibition, display or other function or event of a similar character, or a religious meeting or service, merely because music is incidental to it. Finally, it is made clear that the legislation is not directed at a pleasure fair.

The Special Licence may have terms relating to the following and no other matters:
  (a) The safety of the performers and their patrons.
  (b) Access for fire, ambulance and police to deal with all emergencies.
  (c) Sanitary provision.
  (d) Noise nuisance to the people in the neighbourhood.

[80] s.1 and Sched. 1.
[81] The Private Places of Entertainment Act 1967 remains on the Statute Book. It is adoptive, of limited use and works side by side with the large new legal machinery for public entertainment. The definition in the Act of 1982 raises questions for the licensing authority in relation to music played as incidental background music at, *e.g.* a café on a juke box, or at a hairdressers. Is the music merely incidental to the dominant object? Is it public entertainment which does not require a licence? See *Quaglieni* v. *Matthews* [1865] 6 B. & S. 474; *Hall* v. *Green* [1853] 9 Exch. 247. Music for ice skating would seem to be more obviously an essential part of the public entertainment.
[82] The procedure in the Act of 1982 requires a special resolution and two public notices. A council was held to have exceeded its powers in trying to ban any political activity at such an event—*R.* v. *Barnet London Borough Council, ex p. Johnson*, (1991) 3 Admin. L.R. 149, C.A.

(3) *The General Entertainment Licence*

6.36   Let us turn to the normal and general Entertainment Licence.

(1) The licence is annual, or shorter if stated, and is granted by district councils.

(2) A licence can be for one or more specified occasions or it can be for a longer period, *i.e.* as in (1) above.

(3) Transfer of licences rests with the licensing authority.

(4) The police and fire authorities have to be given notice of an application for a licence, so that their views can be before the licensing authority when considering the application.[83]

(5) A reasonable fee is to be determined by the licensing authority. (No fee can be levied for events at religious buildings or village or county halls. Again the fee can be remitted if the licensing authority consider that the event is of an educational or like character or the performance or event is given for charitable or other like purpose.)

(6) There is provision for cancellation or transmission on death of the licence holder.

(7) The licensing authority can make regulations prescribing standard terms and conditions, to be applied to all entertainment licences.

6.37   (8) Offences are created for unlicensed entertainments and breach of the terms of a licence.[84] A licence can be revoked by a licensing authority after conviction for an offence. A defence is set out in the schedule to the offences described. This is that the person charged proves that he took all reasonable precautions and exercised all due diligence to avoid commission of the offence.

(9) A special order of exemption for the premises, under the Licensing Act 1964,[85] is a good answer to an alleged offence for breach of the terms of an Entertainment Licence, in so far as the latter may have placed a limit on hours of opening and the exemption order can authorise extended hours.

6.38   (10) Police and fire officers have rights of entry for their respective functions.

(11) The licensing authority is given the useful power to grant a provisional licence when a building for which it is required is at the plan stage. Once the building is complete in accordance with the plans, the full licence must be granted. Similar powers exist for extensions and alterations. The authority have, in each case, to be satisfied that the licence is held by a fit and proper person.

(12) The terms of a licence can be varied by the authority.

(13) Appeals lie first to the magistrates and secondly to the Crown

---

[83] When dealing with applications for an Entertainment Licence, a local authority is obliged to inform the applicant of the substance of any objection it has from, *e.g.* the police, fire services or members of the public. See Glidewell J. in *R.* v. *Huntingdon District Council, ex p. Cowan* (1984) 1 All E.R. 58.

[84] The maximum penalty for these offences was raised to £20,000 or six months' imprisonment or both by the Entertainments (Increased Penalties) Act 1990.

[85] s.74(4).

Court, against (a) refusals by the licensing authority to grant, renew, transfer or vary a licence or (b) against a term in the licence or (c) against a proposed revocation of the licence.[86]

(14) An ice rink dealt with in an Entertainment Licence does not also have to comply with Public Health Act by-laws whilst the licence endures.[87]

(4) *Relation to Other Statutes*

In view of the comprehensive character of this legislation, it is important **6.39** to record, finally, as Schedule 1 does, that the introduction of these Entertainment Licences does not affect:
  (a) Theatre licences under the Theatres Act 1968.
  (b) Cinema licences under the Cinemas Act 1985.
  (c) Musical entertainment licences under the Sunday Entertainments Act 1932.
  (d) Fire Certificates under the Fire Precautions Act 1971.
  (e) Licences for premises under the Licensing Act 1964.
  (f) Premises of the armed forces, authorised by the Secretary of State for public entertainment or amusement.

(5) *Boxing and Wrestling*

The Entertainment Licence is now available for public displays of boxing **6.40** and wrestling, as discussed below (paragraph 6.44).

2. Hypnotism

As a form of public entertainment, hypnotism is seen comparatively rarely **6.41** in this country. It was considered desirable to have a simple form of legal control some 30 years ago and the Hypnotism Act 1952 was enacted. Apart from a technical amendment to adapt it to the new Entertainment Licence system, in the Local Government (Miscellaneous Provisions) Act 1982, the Act of 1952 stands as passed by Parliament and does not, indeed, appear to have been tested in the courts. The legal framework now in force is as follows:

(1) It is the premises, not the performer, that are to be licensed. The licence can be either the Entertainment Licence or a specific authorisation from the district council. In either event, special conditions can be imposed.

---

[86] See *R.* v. *Birmingham City Council, ex p. Sheptonhurst Ltd.* [1990] 1 All E.R. 1026, C.A. for an interesting discussion on a local authority which refused to renew a licence, despite no change in circumstances, but where they gave rational grounds for their decision. The case came before the Court of Appeal on judicial review and is a very full judgment on the issues properly taken into account by four local authorities on renewing applications. All had been refused; and three refusals were upheld in the Court of Appeal.
[87] Local Government (Miscellaneous Provisions) Act 1982, Sched. 1, para. 18, and Public Health Act 1961, s.75.

(2) Offences are created to prevent a performance in unlicensed premises, or a performance upon a person under the age of 18 years.

(3) A police constable has a legal right of entry to see that the law is being complied with. He should have reasonable cause to believe that an act is being or may be done in contravention of the Hypnotism Act.

(4) The essential activity which gives rise to the need for authorisation of the premises is an exhibition, demonstration or performance of hypnotism.

6.42   Hypnotism is defined in the Act to include:

"Hypnotism mesmerism or any similar act or process which produces or is intended to produce in any person any form of induced sleep or trance in which the susceptibility of the mind of that person to suggestion or direction is increased or intended to be increased."[88]

(5) The definition and the offence are not to include:

   (i) Hypnotism, mesmerism or any similar act or process which is self-induced.
   (ii) An exhibition, demonstration or performance, otherwise than at an entertainment, which is for scientific or research purposes, or for the treatment of mental or physical disease.
   (iii) An exhibition of hypnotism in a performance of a play, as defined in the Theatres Act 1968.

3. **Billiards Licensing**

6.43   Public billiards tables are normally regulated by reference in the justices' licences for licensed premises under the Licensing Act 1964 and associated statutes. Billiards tables, with which the law has traditionally associated "bagatelle boards or instruments used in any game of the like kind," are normally found in inns, public houses or licensed hotels or restaurants. Where, however, a saloon for public billiards is independent of such premises, then a Billiards Licence was formerly necessary. However, Parliament in spring-cleaning mood abolished this little historical pocket game by the Billiards (Abolition of Restrictions) Act 1987.

4. **Boxing and Wrestling**

6.44   Legal control over these forms of public entertainment had been local rather than national, until the Local Government (Miscellaneous Provisions) Act 1982 introduced a national code. The London area and local councils which acquired Local Act powers were the only ones with regulating powers. Croydon, Rochdale and Ipswich are examples of the latter.

The Act of 1982, mentioned above, which brings into existence a comprehensive code of licensing public entertainment, specifically applies that code to:

"any entertainment which consists of or includes any public contest

---

[88] Hypnotism Act 1952, s.6.

exhibition or display of boxing, wrestling, judo, karate or any similar sport."

This applies to amateur as well as to professional participants.

The procedure for obtaining an Entertainment Licence from the local authority is now of general application to these sports.

5. **Breach of Copyright**

Persons managing theatres or halls where copyright music is played, or **6.45** other artistic performances, such as drama, take place, in which copyright may be present, should be aware of the extent of their potential liability under the Copyright, Designs and Patents Act 1988. Not only can they be a party to an infringement of copyright if they authorise a breach but they may find that they commit a direct offence themselves. Under section 107 of the above Act, a person who causes a "literary dramatic or musical work to be performed in public," when "he knew or had reason to believe that copyright would be infringed" is himself guilty of an offence.

The normal and prudent step to take as a protection against this risk is to take out a licence from the copyright holder, often the Performing Right Society Ltd., or to ensure that the performer holds such a licence.[89]

6. **Video Recordings Act 1984**

The manager of a public hall which is used occasionally for public cine- **6.46** matograph displays will now have to take account of the Cinemas Act 1985, in so far as it defines the exemptions from general licensing for such displays. As it will become commonplace to display video recordings at society and other meetings, note must also be taken of the Video Recordings Act 1984, which introduces classification certificates for video recordings.

Under this Act of 1984, the video works themselves will normally be exempt works, under section 2 of that Act, if they are designed to inform, educate, or instruct, or are concerned with sport, religion or music. It is

---

[89] See the discussion of the possible infringement of copyright a hall manager can commit by "authorising" the performance. (Chap. 3, paras. 3.15–3.19 & 3.37.) Interested readers are also referred to the following cases: (1) *Performing Right Society Ltd.* v.*Bradford Corporation* (1921) Macgillivray's Copyright Cases 21 (Vol. 1917–1923), where Roche J. held the Corporation liable for a breach because they published the programmes of their concerts in their Baths Hall. Disclaimer notices on the premises did not avail them. (2) *Monaghan* v.*Taylor* (1885) 2 T.L.R. 685, where the manager was responsible, since he "took the chance of the songs sung (at a Blackpool music hall) being such as could be lawfully or unlawfully sung" (Bowen L.J.). (3) The Performing Right Society also won in *Performing Right Society* v.*Mitchell and Booker (Palais de Danse)* [1924] 1 Q.B. 762, where McCardie J. called the dance band "a migratory thing" and acknowledged the prudence of the case being brought against the manager of the Hammersmith Palais de Danse. The definition of a "place of entertainment" in the above new Copyright Act of 1988 should be noted. It would bring in many multi-purpose halls. See also Part II of the above Act of 1988 which contains the law formerly in the Performers Protection Acts. Performers are still well protected against unauthorised performances in public.

indeed only when such recordings are to be "supplied" that the Act may come into play. However, that word is defined to cover exchange and loan, as well as hire and sale. In certain circumstances, therefore, an unlawful activity could occur and the manager might wish to impose a condition of letting that the hiring society comply with the relevant legislation relating to video recordings and indemnify the management in respect of any breach of it.

E. OUTDOOR ENTERTAINMENT

1. **Horseracing**

6.47 The "sport of kings" retains its popularity, and nearly 60 racecourses are currently in operation. The Jockey Club, at one time the national manager for the whole industry, now shares the task of administration with three other bodies but is still the major force in the running of what is undoubtedly a complex enterprise.

The numerous groups of participants are to be licensed, the grounds brought to the right standard at the right time, relations with the Home Office and other major government departments maintained, the technical services involved in dope testing, photo-finishes and other matters kept abreast of the latest technology, and, at certain critical points, an inquiry arranged that will satisfy participants and the courts that standards of "natural justice" have been met.

The four legal institutions mentioned are the Jockey Club, the Horserace Betting Levy Board, the Horserace Totalisator Board and the Bookmakers Committee.

(1) *The Jockey Club*

6.48 Incorporated by Royal Charter, the Club exercises day-to-day control over horseracing. A racecourse needs an annual licence from the Jockey Club before it can open. This licence is subject to the "Rules of Racing," which maintain the role of the Jockey Club. The other major legal functions of the Jockey Club are:

(1) Licensing of personnel, *i.e.* owners, trainers, flat race jockeys, apprentice jockeys, steeplechase and hurdle race jockeys and the registration of stable employees.

(2) Through Racecourse Security Services, to keep abreast of technical aids needed for the running of horseraces.

(3) Control over race meetings. In one year, this involved pre-race horse identification and vaccination checks on 10,000 horses.[90]

(4) Arranging occasional inquiries into disciplinary decisions that have given rise to formal appeals. The courts have from time to time given rul-

---

[90] The 1982 report of the Jockey Club.

ings on aspects of such hearings and the extent to which the rules of natural justice must be followed.[91]

(2) *The Horserace Betting Levy Board*

The Levy Board assesses and collects annually money to be devoted to the **6.49** improvement of horseracing. In the year 1982/83, this was £21 million and the main heads of the allocation were grants for prize money, assistance to racecourses, maintaining the integrity of horseracing, assistance for veterinary science and education and, finally, assistance for breeding.[92]

Another important role of this Levy Board, under the Betting Gaming and Lotteries Act 1963, is the grant of certificates for betting areas at racecourses.[93] These certificates are not annual but are renewed when there are changes made in the areas in question. This Board also approves the facilities for the Totalisator Board at racecourses.

(3) *The Horserace Totalisator Board*

The Horserace Totalisator Board has the power and the exclusive right to **6.50** engage in, or authorise others to engage in, pool betting, as amplified in the Betting Gaming and Lotteries Act 1963.[94] The Board has powers to acquire land, borrow money and manage its affairs. Its accounts are open to public inspection.[95]

(4) *The Bookmakers Committee*

The Bookmakers Committee is constituted under the Betting Levy (Book- **6.51** makers Committee) Regulations 1961.[96] These were made by the Secretary of State for Home Affairs under the Act of 1963 and provide a representative body to negotiate with the Levy Board about the categories used to settle the annual levy, as described in (2) above. Under the Regulations, bookmakers are granted a right of appeal to the Betting Levy

---

[91] See, for instance, *Nagle* v. *Feilden* [1966] 2 Q.B. 633. Also as to judicial review being not available to question the Club's decisions—*R.* v. *Jockey Club, ex p. RAM Racecourses* [1990] C.O.D. 346; and *R.* v. *Disciplinary Committee of the Jockey Club, ex p. Massingberd-Mundy* [1990] C.O.D. 260. It is this evident lack of accountability, among other things, which has led to detailed discussions, as we go to press, to replace the Jockey Club by a more representative body, the British Horseracing Board.

[92] Annual report of Horserace Betting Levy Board 1982–83, App. 4.

[93] Horserace Totalisator and Betting Levy Boards Act 1972, s.5, and Betting, Gaming and Lotteries Act 1963, s.13. The charge to bookmakers and their assistants for the enclosure is not to be more than five times the maximum charge to the public for admission: s.13 of the Act of 1963. The general restriction on the use of premises for betting does not apply to a racecourse on a day when horseracing is taking place: s.1 of the Act of 1963.

[94] s.14.

[95] *Ibid.* s.31.

[96] The Betting Levy (Bookmakers' Committee) Regulations 1961 (S.I. 1961 No. 1546).

Appeal Tribunal against the proposed levy categories.[97] This is a further body in connection with which the rules of natural justice fall to be observed in its deliberations.

6.52 These four bodies each operate under the appropriate legal authority. There are two final points in connection with the organisation of this sport.

(1) Racecourse Association Ltd. is the representative body for all the racecourse managers in this country. It provides a useful forum for the Jockey Club and others who wish to enter into negotiations about the many aspects of horseracing.

(2) Racecourse ownership is not on a uniform pattern; some are privately owned, some on lease and some, like Pontefract and Doncaster, are on municipally owned land.[98] There are two large owner groups, nevertheless, which contain the majority of the racecourses currently in use.

2. Greyhound Racing

6.53 A greyhound racing stadium is in law but one of several possible types of premises called "tracks" in the Betting Gaming and Lotteries Act 1963.[99] The legal features associated with its management are as follows:

(1) It requires a licence from the local authority. This is the district council, outside London.[1]

(2) Former restrictions on the number of betting days at dog racecourses were abolished in 1985. The only days on which such betting is currently prohibited are Sundays, Good Friday and Christmas Day.[2]

(3) A totalisator can be installed to carry on pool betting business on a dog track.

(4) The track occupier must provide convenient facilities for bookmakers. The case of *Cutler* v. *Wandsworth Stadium Ltd.*[3] reached the House of Lords and is an authority on this point. The decision went against an aggrieved bookmaker on the ground that, although *ubi jus ibi remedium*,[4] the remedy for the right was with the public and not the bookmaker. It was, said the court, for the benefit of the public that the duty was imposed. An offence of non-compliance by the occupier existed, for which prosecution was available and the occupier should not, under the Betting and Lotteries Act 1934, have to face civil liability as well.

---

[97] The Betting Levy Appeal Tribunal (England and Wales) Rules 1963 (S.I. 1963 No. 748).
[98] For Pontefract see the West Yorkshire Act 1980 and for Doncaster, the South Yorkshire Act 1980.
[99] s.5(1)(*b*).
[1] Betting Gaming and Lotteries Act 1963, Sched. 2, para. 1(*a*) and Local Government Act 1972, ss.251 and 273.
[2] Betting Gaming and Lotteries (Amendment) Act 1985, s.1.
[3] [1949] A.C. 398. Followed in *Pole Stadium* v. *Squires* [1982] 1 All E.R. 404. (The maxim in the text means: Where there is a legal right, there will be a legal means to enforce it.)
[4] *Pett* v. *Greyhound Racing Association* [1969] 1 Q.B. 125. A trainer was summoned before the stewards of the Association on a doping charge. He was denied a legal representative and only permitted a kennelman. The High Court said this was wrong and a legal representative must be allowed; the man's livelihood was at stake, said the court.

(5) The occupier has the same rights in relation to pool betting as the Horserace Totalisator Board has on a horserace track. (See above paragraph 6.50.)[5]

(6) The law has some strict and detailed requirements about the operation of the totalisator on a greyhound track. It must be mechanically or electrically operated to comply with prescribed conditions and in good working order. Rigorous controls on its publicity and on its supervision also exist. An accountant and mechanic appointed by the local authority are to be present when the totalisator is in operation.[6]

3. **Athletic and Sporting Tracks**

This section relates to tracks for events "at which races of any description, athletic sports or other sporting events take place."[7] **6.54**

(1) These, like greyhound tracks, require a track betting licence from the district council, if betting is to take place on such events.

(2) There are limited restrictions upon betting on these tracks, imposed under the Betting Gaming and Lotteries Act 1963 and associated statutes.

(3) The police have powers of entry.[8]

(4) The operation of bookmakers is subject to detailed restrictions affecting their licences.

(5) The grant of a track betting licence is legally elaborate. The licence can be refused on several grounds:

    (i) It would be injurious to the health and comfort of the residents.

    (ii) It would be detrimental to schoolchildren in the neighbourhood.

    (iii) It would seriously impair the amenities of the neighbourhood.

    (iv) It would result in undue traffic congestion.

    (v) It would seriously prejudice the preservation of law and order.[9]

Finally, as a legal hurdle, a licence can be withheld from an applicant with a previous conviction.

(6) The track betting licence normally lasts for seven years.

(7) It can be revoked if the track is conducted irregularly.[10] From such a decision an appeal lies to the Crown Court.

(8) The charges which an occupier can make to a bookmaker for his facilities are controlled as for horseracing, *i.e.* they must not exceed five times the highest admission charge to the public.

---

[5] Betting Gaming and Lotteries Act 1963, s.17.

[6] See Dog Racecourse (Totalisator) Regulations 1967 (S.I. 1967 No. 10). The above amending Act of 1985, which slackened the belt on betting days, also eased betting facilities. It allows the carry forward of pool bets made with the totalisator.

[7] Betting Gaming and Lotteries Act 1963, s.55.

[8] *Ibid.* s.23.

[9] *Ibid.* s.6 and Sched. 3, para.7.

[10] *Ibid.* Sched. 3, para. 13.

4. **Safety of Sports Grounds**

6.55   The main points of the governing Act, the Safety of Sports Grounds Act 1975, can be usefully summarised as we did in our first edition. But the Taylor Report,[11] after the disaster at the Hillsborough football stadium, had to take account also of the Fire Safety and Safety of Places of Sports Act 1987. Full of detail which we do not set out here, one of its basic steps was to extend the designation procedure below to stands at undesignated grounds where there is uncovered accommodation for 500 or more spectators. No less than 170 Designations have been made since 1975.

   The summary of the 1975 Act is a follows:

(1) The Act is aimed at the sports ground which will hold more than 10,000 spectators. The provisions in the Act are set in motion when the Secretary of State designates such a ground as needing a Safety Certificate.

(2) The local authority is empowered to issue a Safety Certificate on receipt of an application from the ground proprietor. The certificate will be either for a limited number of occasions or it can be indefinite. It must give a maximum number of permitted spectators and also details of exits, entrances, means of access, crush barriers and means of escape in case of fire. As an option, the certificate may specify different numbers of spectators for different parts of the premises.

(3) This short Act contains procedures to tbe followed for the consideration of the application, amendments to a certificate, appeals against refusals to grant a certificate, alterations and extensions at the premises, entry by the police and by the building authority.

(4) The Secretary of State has power to make various regulations.

(5) Offences are created for contravening a Safety Certificate and in particular for exceeding the permitted number of spectators. A defence is available, namely to satisfy the court that the holder of the certificate took all reasonable precautions and exercised all due diligence to comply with the certificate.

(6) The Act is not to be treated as creating new civil liabilities.

(7) Whilst a Safety Certificate is in force,[12] certain other statutory requirements are not to apply, *i.e.* (a) the Public Health Act 1936, section 59, where it relates to entrances, exits and passageways; (b) the Public Health Acts Amendment Act 1890, about public platforms (section 37); (c) the Fire Precautions Act 1971, about fire certificates; and (d) any relevant Local Acts. These are not to apply in so far as they would be duplicating matters dealt with in the Safety Certificate.

(8) A special emergency procedure exists, if a risk to spectators is considered to be so great that an Order should be made at once. The magis-

[11] Cm. 962. (1990).
[12] Safety of Sports Ground Act 1975, s.9. The certification of football grounds under this Act was accelerated in August 1985, following the Bradford football stadium fire tragedy. The Sporting Events (Control of Alcohol, etc.) Act 1985 and its Designation Order for Football Association clubs was a parallel measure.

trates' court has power to make this Order and it can prohibit or restrict spectators until steps are taken to reduce the risks in question.

There has undoubtedly been a spate of legislation on this subject recently. It is, from the point of view of this book, in danger of becoming a large specialist topic, and thus for the reader we are only providing signposts. The sequence was the fire disaster at Bradford football ground (May 11, 1985); then the two Popplewell Reports.[13] These also reacted to the Belgian Heysel Stadium disaster (May 29, 1985); then the Fire Safety and Safety of Places of Sport Act 1987—to enact many of the Popplewell recommendations. Then the Hillsborough disaster (April 15, 1989) and the two Taylor Reports. One of the striking features for the lawyer of the final stages of this somewhat bobsleigh sequence was the provision when the Football Spectators Act of 1989 was passed in the summer of 1989, that Parliament would hold its hand on implementing the National Membership Scheme until the final Taylor report was complete.[14] This came out in January 1990; it commented adversely on that Scheme and the Scheme has not subsequently been implemented. What is in force is a Part of the Act of 1989 which gives power by statutory instrument to designate matches outside England and Wales and confer powers on police and others to control spectators travelling to them. A schedule to this Act lists some 12 offences related to violence and alcohol abuse. The Sporting Events (Control of Alchol) Act 1985 is one of the several Acts which is used in the compilation of this formidable list.

5. **Pleasure Fairs**

(1) Local Authorities have powers to regulate pleasure fairs under the   **6.56** Public Health Act 1961 and the Local Government (Miscellaneous Provisions) Act 1976.[15] Under the Act of 1961, they were authorised to make by-laws about ingress, egress, prevention of nuisances, preservation of safety, order, cleanliness and sanitary conditions. The Act of 1976 extended these powers to cover measures to prevent outbreaks of fire, both to the fair stalls and also to the caravans or other sleeping quarters of the fair holders.

(2) The definition of a fair in the Act of 1961 is interesting. "Pleasure Fair" is the statutory term and there are two components. First, it is the place where one of the following entertainments is provided and an admission charge is made.

Secondly, there is then a long list containing a wide range of outdoor entertainments:

    (i) Circuses.

    (ii) Exhibitions of human beings or performing animals.

---

[13] Cm. 9588 (1985) and Cm. 9710 (1985).

[14] Not to express my views, said Taylor L.J. on "the terms of an Act expressing the . . . will of Parliament" in these circumstances "would be thought surprising if not pusillanimous." Cm. 962, para. 17.

[15] Public Health Act 1961, s.75, and Local Government (Miscellaneous Provisions) Act 1976, s.22.

   (iii) Merry-go-rounds, roundabouts, swings, swtichback railways.
   (iv) Coconut shies, hoop-las, shooting galleries, bowling alleys.
   (v) Dodgem cars and like machines.
   (vi) "Automatic or other machines intended for entertainment or amusement."

This concludes with the somewhat enigmatic:

   (vii) "Anything similar to the foregoing":

The by-law powers are not to apply to a fair held under royal charter or like ancient authority, nor to custom. The statutes impose upon the by-law-making councils a duty to consult interested bodies and, particularly, the fire authority. As by-laws, these requirements of course fall to be confirmed by the Secretary of State and he is enjoined by the statutes to be satisfied that the consultations have been adequate.

6. Local Authorities

6.57   The earlier section about indoor entertainment has dealt in detail with the powers placed upon local authorities by section 145 of the Local Government Act 1972. An important set of related powers for local authorities is found in section 19 of the Local Government (Miscellaneous Powers) Act 1976. That section is headed "Places of Entertainment" and is concerned wholly with recreational facilities. For the purposes of this book, whilst both recreation and entertainment are regarded as within "leisure services," entertainment has been treated as the right category for sporting, athletic and allied events when taking place primarily for the benefit of spectators. When such events are, on the other hand, primarily for participation by people who want exercise or recreation, then they have been discussed in the Sport or Open Air Exercise chapters. Clearly such a distinction cannot be universally clear-cut. However, sports centres, ice rinks, swimming pools and riding schools have been treated as sport and recreation, rather than entertainment.

7. Local Government (Miscellaneous Provisions) Act 1976

6.58   There is one small but useful power conferred on local authorities which those concerned with outdoor entertainment should know about. It is power to serve notice requiring sanitary provision at a place where there is to be an entertainment or exhibition. The county court can deal with appeals against these notices.[16]

8. Ancient Custom

6.59   A brief reference is due to two cases where courts allowed outdoor entertainment and pastimes to continue as established customs.

   (1) *Hall* v. *Nottingham* involved a custom, claimed and upheld for parishioners in Ashford Carbonell, Shropshire, to go on a field, called Maypole Piece, in the parish, set up a maypole and dance round it "and

---

[16] Local Government (Miscellaneous Provisions) Act 1976, s.20.

otherwise enjoy on the land any lawful and innocent recreation at any times in the year."

Since the legal tests for such a claimed custom are that it should be both reasonable and certain, this custom was challenged on the ground that it was not certain. Evidence being that the custom was enjoyed over many years at the holiday seasons, the court upheld the custom, holding that the expression should be interpreted as meaning "at all seasonable times."[17]

(2) *Fitch* v. *Rawlings*[18] was the second case based on a claim of custom. A right was claimed and upheld by the court to play cricket at Steeple Bumstead in Essex. As in the *Salop* case, the decision was arrived at after the court had received convincing evidence that there were limits upon the right claimed. In this case, those limits were, first, as to the duration—namely only at all seasonable times and, secondly, as to the persons benefiting—namely, only the inhabitants of the parish.

9. **Animals**

The Protection of Animals Act 1911 is a general point of reference for legal **6.60** restrictions upon those seeking to offer a dubious form of entertainment by subjecting animals to cruelty.[19] The Act makes it an offence to bait an animal or arrange fights between animals for paying spectators. Likewise, it is an offence to keep a house, pit or other place in which animals might fight.

Cockfighting has an Act to itself, the Cockfighting Act 1952. In addition to the prohibition of the fighting, there is also an offence of possessing spurs for cocks *viz* "instruments or appliances."

F. SUNDAY OBSERVANCE, LICENSING AND CATERING

1. **Introduction**

The five previous sections have dealt with the present law for some of the **6.61** most substantial forms of public entertainment. Theatres and cinemas are large groups of business, each of which has been shown to have a significant legal framework within which it works. Apart from their involvement with theatres and cinemas, local authorities are now in the entertainment business and the legal powers available to them are vital, not only for themselves but also for their associates, whether performers, contractors, agents and sometimes too, for their customers. The nine areas of public entertainment grouped in the last two sections as public halls or outdoor entertainment have collectively covered a large part of the British public entertainment scene. They too have been found to have varying legal structures within which to operate.

In this section we turn to three areas of law which can affect most if not

---

[17] (1875) L.R. 1 Ex. D. 1.

[18] (1795) 2 Hy.Bl. 393.

[19] The recent Protection of Animals (Penalties) Act 1987 greatly increased penalties for offences under the Act of 1911, thus embodying current public hostility to these barbaric practices.

all of the other specific entertainments. Sunday observance, the licensing law and catering, otherwise unrelated, have this in common: they impinge upon the individual forms which public entertainment takes in this country. The law controlling the sale of intoxicating liquor is, for historical and social reasons, more bulky and complex than the other two; all three are important for the country's leisure services.

2. Sunday Observance

6.62   This is a tangled subject, primarily because the law is not yet codified.

The Sunday Observance Act 1780 is still on the Statute Book and provides that:

> "Any house, room or other public place which shall be opened or used for public entertainment or amusement on any part of the Lord's day called Sunday and to which persons shall be admitted by the payment of money, or by tickets sold for money, shall be deemed a disorderly house or place."

A potential fine of £200 upon the keeper of the "house" and £50 upon doorkeepers or servants collecting admission money, is contained in this statute.[20]

Exemptions

6.63   However, the situation is materially affected by three other Acts of Parliament:

    (a) Cinemas are now exempt, by virtue of the Sunday Cinema Act 1972, and subject to licensing authority concurrence.

    (b) Theatres are also exempt, under the Sunday Theatres Act 1972, apart from the time restriction from 2 am to 2 pm outside London and 3 am to 2 pm in London.

    (c) Licensed premises are exempt, under the Licensing Act 1964.[21]

In the result, the other legal problems that remain are as follows:

    (1) A limited exception to the Act of 1780 was made by the Sunday Entertainment Act 1932, which provided that the authority granting music, singing and dancing licences could grant such a licence in respect of "a musical entertainment on Sundays" and attach appropriate conditions.[22]

    (2) There is, however, no power to authorise public dancing on a Sunday, where such dancing would contravene this provision.[23]

    (3) For the two main types of public entertainment for which the Sun-

---

[20] *Houghton le Touzel* v. *Mecca* [1950] 2 K.B. 612, shows that a company can be liable as a "keeper."

[21] s.88.

[22] The introduction of the new Entertainment Licence to supersede music singing and dancing licences, in the Local Government (Miscellaneous Provisions) Act 1982, specifically leaves this section 3 position untouched. (See para. 6.39). A "musical entertainment" is there defined as a "concert or similar entertainment, consisting of the performance of music, with or without singing or recitation."

[23] See *R.* v. *Britton, ex p. Newton* (1940) 4 All E.R. 479; Sunday Entertainment Act 1932, s.4.

day Entertainment Act 1932 was passed, *i.e.* musical and cinematographic performances, a liberal interpretation was incorporated about the persons thereby exempted from the peril of conviction under the Act of 1780. The conductor and the persons managing or assisting or otherwise taking part in or attending or advertising those two activities were all exempted.[24]

(4) Exemption is now given, in the Act of 1932, for other public attractions to open on Sundays. These are museums, picture galleries, zoological gardens, botanical gardens and an aquarium.[25] The views of the courts were once tested about a wedding reception coming within the statutory exemptions; it was held that such a gathering was private in nature. An application by a hotel licensee for an extension of the entertainments licence was thus inappropriate. *A fortiori*, the Sunday Observance Acts had no application since they relate to "public" activities. If the Private Places of Entertainment (Licensing) Act 1967 were adopted, that might be a different matter.[26]

One can only conclude that a consolidating Act would be welcome for this slightly confused area of law.

3. The Public Leisure Services and the Sale of Intoxicating Liquor

Introduction

A useful approach to this complex branch of the law may be made with **6.64** a recognition of the main service points for the sale of intoxicating liquor. These are public houses, clubs, off-licence shops and other premises, restaurants and hotels. The law has followed community practice and its provisions relate to these various buildings. So the classes of licence available under the law include on- and off- licences, new licences, removals, provisionals, transfers and table licences.

Though the subject is wide, an effort has been made to restrict what is dealt with below to that which is relevant to the provision of public leisure services. A manager of a civic theatre or a civic sports centre will no doubt wish to provide licensed bars in those premises. The limited knowledge of licensing law needed by such persons and their advisers forms the content of this subsection. Certainly for the full law on the Licensing Acts, reference should be made to the standard professional books on the subject.[27]

(1) *Classes of Premises and Licences*

The current law relating to the sale of intoxicating liquor is found in the **6.65** Licensing Acts 1964 to 1990. The licensing districts for the purpose of the

---

[24] Sunday Entertainment Act 1932, s.4.
[25] *Terry* v. *Brighton Aquarium Co.* (1875) L.R. 10 Q.B. 306.
[26] *Roe* v. *Harrogate Justices* (1966) L.G.R. 465. The current tangled legal scene on Sunday trading is sufficiently on the fringe of leisure services for it to be left there, at least until it is clarified.
[27] See, *e.g.* Paterson's *Licensing Acts* and Anthony and Berryman's *Guide to Licensing Law*. Also D. Field and M. Pink, *Liquor Licensing Law* (1983, Sweet and Maxwell).

Acts are the petty session areas, as defined by the Magistrates' Courts Act 1980. The basic function rests with the licensing justices, composed of justices who sit in those areas.[28]

Sale

6.66   The sale by retail of intoxicating liquor is regulated by a system of justices' on-licences and justices' off-licences. (The Licensing (Low Alcohol Drinks) Act 1990 amends the classic definition of intoxicating liquor to take account of changing fashions. Drinks with a strength of 0.5 per cent. alcohol or less when sold are not within the definition. This operates from January 1, 1994, if not brought into force before then.) The former authorises the sale for consumption either on or off the licensed premises. The off-licence, on the other hand, only authorises sales for consumption off the licensed premises. Whilst an on-licence may authorise the sale of intoxicating liquor of all descriptions, it can, alternatively, be limited to beer, cider and wine only, or beer and cider only, or indeed wine only. There are only two alternatives with the off-licence. It must be for intoxicating liquor of all descriptions or for beer, cider and wine only.[29]

Licences

6.67   Licences may be granted as new licences or by way of renewal, transfer or removal of existing licences. New licences are normally granted subject to conditions about tenure and the justices being satisfied about the suitability of the premises.[30] When it is proposed to construct, alter or extend premises for which it is intended to apply for a licence, it is possible to obtain a Provisional Licence.[31] This allows the applicant to ascertain if a licence will be granted when the works have been completed. A Protection Order is the name of the justices' order sought when a person seeking the transfer of a licence wants authority to sell intoxicating liquor pending the outcome of the application for the transfer.[32]

A restaurant licence is one granted for premises structurally adapted and bona fide used to provide habitually a customary main meal at midday or in the evening or both for patrons, and where the liquor is sold or supplied to persons taking meals, as an ancillary accompaniment.[33]

A residential licence is granted for premises used to provide habitually for reward board and lodging, including breakfast, and one other customary main meal. In this case, the liquor must be sold or supplied only to residents or their bona fide friends. A combined residential and restaurant licence can be granted.

---

[28] Licensing Act 1964, s.2.
[29] *Ibid.* s.1.
[30] *Ibid.* s.4. Transfer is to another person on the same premises: removal is to different premises.
[31] *Ibid.* s.6.
[32] *Ibid.* ss.10 and 11.
[33] Pt. IV.

Duration

A licence now runs from the time it is granted for three years. If granted in the last three months of a licensing year, then it runs to the end of the next licensing year. A licence granted by way of renewal, transfer or removal supersedes any existing licence.[34]

Occasional licences

The holder of an on-licence may apply to the justices for the granting to himself of an occasional licence.[35] This is to allow him to sell any liquor covered by his existing licence at other premises. This licence can cover three weeks at a time and be subject to its own conditions. Occasional licences are also subject to certain special provisions:

(a) 24 hours' notice of the application has normally to be given to the police.

(b) Liquor cannot be sold under such a licence on Christmas Day, Good Friday nor any day appointed for a public fast or thanksgiving.

(c) Unless an electors' poll is held and produces a majority in favour, then this type of licence does not apply to Wales or Monmouthshire.

(d) A public hearing can be avoided by giving one month's previous notice of the application to the clerk to the justices.

(e) Finally, the name of the licence-holder must normally be displayed over the entrance of the premises where the dinner, dance or other function takes place.

An addition to this procedure was effected by the Licensing (Occasional **6.68** Permissions) Act 1983. This enables the application to the licensing justices to be made by "an officer of an eligible organisation," or of a branch of such an organisation. The "occasional permission" can be granted to that applicant, provided that the function in question is in connection with the organisation's activities, that the applicant is a fit and proper person, that the place will be a suitable place and that the sale of intoxicating liquor is not likely to result in a disturbance or annoyance to the residents in the neighbourhood of that place or in any disorderly conduct.

The other elements in this new legislation are:

(1) There are to be no more than four such permissions in any 12-month period granted to that organisation in respect of the same place.

(2) This new procedure does not affect or authorise sales of intoxicating liquor in Wales or Monmouthshire, where the Welsh Sunday Polls procedure must still apply.

(3) The organisations which can use this procedure must not be conducted for private gain.

(4) The full procedure relating to notices and timetable must be referred to, in section 2 of the new Act of 1983.

---

[34] Licensing Act 1964, s.26 and Licensing Act 1988.
[35] *Ibid.* s.180.

(5) Significantly, the simple reference to the situation dealt with in this Act of the sanctions contained in the Licensing Act 1964, so far as appropriate, results in 14 such offences being listed in the schedule to the Act of 1983. They should be studied.

(6) In perhaps the first case to reach the law reports under the new Act, *R.* v. *Bromley Licensing Justices, ex p. Bromley Licensed Victuallers Association,*[36] the licensing justices were corrected on two points in a decision. First, for four functions on four nights, albeit by the same organisation, there must be four separate "permissions," since each one is limited to a 24-hour period. Secondly, an objection from persons other than the police is valid and must be heard.

(2) *Obtaining a Licence*

6.69 The licensing justices have discretion to grant to a fit and proper person the licence sought.[37] The licensee will normally be the person who will be selling the liquor. In the case of a local authority or other corporate body, a nominated director or manager can be the licence holder. There has to be a named and accountable individual.

There are certain disqualifying features affecting applicants, such as previous criminal convictions.[38] There are also rights of appeal against decisions of the justices and these now go before the Crown Court.[39] Likewise for clubs aggrieved by refusals of applications for registration, there are rights of appeal to the Crown Court.[40]

(3) *Special Hours and Extensions*

6.70 Permitted Hours form a general legal restraint upon holders of both justices' licences and club registration certificates. A person may consume or take away liquor on those two classes of premises only during permitted hours.[41] These are, for licensed premises, normally on weekdays other than Christmas Day or Good Friday, 11 am to 11 pm. On Sunday, Christmas Day[42] and Good Friday, the permitted hours are 12 noon to 10.30 pm with a break of four hours beginning at 3 pm. Licensing justices, if satisfied that the interests of their district make it desirable, can modify those general hours though not to start before 10 am.

Clubs

6.71 Club rules fix permitted hours for the club. The rule to be followed is that the hours fixed shall not on any day be longer, nor begin earlier, nor

---

[36] [1984] 1 W.L.R. 585 (Q.B.D.).
[37] Licensing Act 1964, s.3.
[38] *Ibid.* s.9.
[39] *Ibid.* s.21.
[40] *Ibid.* s.50.
[41] *Ibid.* s.59.
[42] *Ibid.* s.60 and Licensing Act 1988, ss.1 and 19.

end later, than the general licensing hours. This can take account of any licensing justices' modifications for the district, as above. The club rules must also ensure that there is a break of not less than two hours in the afternoon. Finally, on Sundays, Christmas Day and Good Friday, the break shall include the hours from 3 to 5 pm and there shall not be more than three and a half hours after 5 pm.[43]

Legal relaxation

There are two traditional, and legal, mini-extensions to these permitted **6.72** hours. Twenty minutes' drinking-up time is in order for consuming liquor served on the premises and for taking away from the premises liquor not supplied nor taken in an open vessel.[44] Also, half an hour is allowed for the consumption of the accompanying liquor by persons taking meals. A resident at the licensed premises, and his bona fide private friends, are not subject to those restraints.

The licensing justices have power to vary the above standard permitted hours for the provision of either refreshment or entertainment or both. Those extensions can have conditions attached.

Special Hours certificates are also obtainable for both licensed premises and clubs where Entertainment Licences for those premises have been granted by the local authority under the Local Government (Miscellaneous Provisions) Act 1982.[45]

(4) *Inspection and Alterations*

The Acts contain provisions for inspection of premises before their first **6.73** registration or licensing. The local authority, the police and the fire authority have rights of inspection; from the point of view of applicants, the clerk to the licensing justices is the main initial point of contact.[46]

Important provisions in the Licensing Acts require consent to be sought from the justices by licensees for alterations to the licensed premises. This duty arises when:

  (a) The effect of the works would be to afford increased drinking facilities in the public or common parts of the premises.

  (b) Their effect would be to conceal from observation a public or common part of the premises used for drinking.

  (c) The proposed works affect the communication between the parts of

---

[43] Licensing Act 1964, s.62. The afternoon break was abolished by the Licensing (Restaurant Meals) Act 1987 for the parts of club premises to which restaurant certificates apply.

[44] *Ibid.* s.63(1)(*b*) and Licensing Act 1988.

[45] Licensing Act 1964, s.79. The close relation of the Entertainment Licence and the Special Hours Certificate is exemplified in the provision in the Act of 1982, Sched. 1, para. 13, whereby the daily hours of operation of an Entertainment Licence are effectively extended until the end of the exemption order, granted by the Licensing Justices under s.174(4) of the Licensing Act 1964.

[46] *Ibid.* Sched. 1.

the premises where intoxicating liquor is sold and the remaining parts of the premises or any streets or any public way.[47]

Furthermore, justices have the power to require certain alterations to be made to premises, in the interests of the proper conduct of the business, when they are dealing with a renewal of a licence.[48]

(5) *Young Persons*

6.74 The holder of a justices' licence must not allow any persons under 14 years to be in the bar of the licensed premises during permitted hours.[49] A bar for this purpose includes any place wholly or mainly used for the sale and consumption of liquor.

The licence holder and his staff must not sell liquor to any person under 18 years or allow a person under 18 years to consume liquor in a bar.[50]

However, a person who is 16 years of age may buy beer, porter, cider or perry for consumption with a meal in a part of the premises set apart for the service of meals and which is not a bar.[51]

The licence holder will be liable to a fine if any person under 18 years is employed in a bar of licensed premises at any time when the bar is open for the sale and consumption of liquor. (A bar set apart solely to supply table meal customers is outside this restriction.)[52]

(6) *Offences*

6.75 In an Act such as the Licensing Act 1964 with 200 sections and 15 Schedules, and designed to restrain the sale and consumption of liquor in its various forms, there are offences created which are too numerous to tabulate here. Some have been identified above; some can give rise to loss of a licence or club registration, apart from the fines or other punishments which provide the normal sanction for offences in Acts of this sort. Basically, all arise in respect of the breach of requirements laid down in the Licensing Acts.

4. Catering

6.76 Catering is a normal accompaniment to most forms of public entertainment. For local authorities, the main section relied upon is section 145 of the Local Government Act 1972. This empowers local authorities to "provide refreshments," in connection with the very wide range of entertainments listed and quoted in section C (paragraphs 6.27 *et seq.*) of this chapter.

---

[47] Licensing Act 1964, s.20. Consent may not be given retrospectively by licensing justices to alterations—*R.* v. *Croydon Crown Court, ex p. Bromley Licensing Justices* (1988) 152 J.P. 245.
[48] *Ibid.* s.19.
[49] *Ibid.* s.168.
[50] *Ibid.* s.169.
[51] *Ibid.* s.169(4).
[52] *Ibid.* s.170.

The Civic Restaurants Act 1947 is the other statutory source for local authorities' powers in this field. Though somewhat curtailed by the Local Government Act 1972, this Act of 1947 empowers councils to "establish and carry on restaurants and otherwise provide for the supply to the public of meals and refreshments . . . and carry on such activities as are reasonably incidental or ancillary,"[53] thereto. The main remaining section in that Act of 1947 lays down guidelines for financial responsibility in respect of those activities.[54]

In providing a catering service, public authorities have to take account of employment law so far as staff are concerned and also the laws of tort and contract in connection with relations with their customers and claims resulting from the condition of premises used or provisions supplied. These areas of law are outlined in Chapters 1 and 2.

The other detailed area of law affecting catering is that associated with the Food and Food Safety Acts and the highly detailed Regulations, both via the European Economic Community and nationally, about standards for food and drinks of all sorts. For these, interested readers are referred to the specialist text books.[55]

G. GAMBLING

1. Introduction

"The English working man is less interested in the equality of men than in the inequality of horses." G. K. Chesterton's aphorism comes to mind as one turns to the succession of statutes handed down by Parliament on gambling. A major consolidation Act was passed in 1963, the Betting, Gaming and Lotteries Act. It repealed in whole or part seven earlier Acts. But in the period since 1963, at least 12 further Acts have appeared on the Statute Book, including another two consolidating Acts. The subject is clearly of abiding interest to the British.   **6.77**

The forms in which gambling is legally regulated in this country may be conveniently summarised as Betting, Gaming, Lotteries, Prize Competitions and Amusements with Prizes. (Horse and greyhound racing are treated as complex forms of Betting in this simplification.) Each of these involves some public body to carry out duties mentioned in the Acts referred to above and it may help the reader to scan the total scene initially, by tabulating those bodies and their various spheres of activity:

1. County Councils   Registration of Pool   1963 Act, s.4 &
                         Promoters (*eg*. foot-   Sched.2
                         ball pools)

---

[53] Civic Restaurants Act 1947, s.1.

[54] *Ibid.* s.3. "Best endeavours," it says, are to be used to match income and expenditure.

[55] See Butterworth's *Law of Food and Drugs*, now in six volumes, as the most comprehensive publication. Over 100 individual foods and drinks are now dealt with in the Regulations, which have proliferated in the last two decades, as the law has sought to keep pace with scientific and dietetic advances. Purely as caterers, it behoves the public services to engage management who are familiar with this formidable background.

2. Licensing Justices	Betting Office Licences *i.e.* the premises	*Ibid.* s.9 & Sched.1
3. *Ibid.*	Betting Agency Permits *i.e.* the betting office managers	*Ibid.*
4. *Ibid.*	Gaming Act licences *i.e.* Clubs	1968 Act, s.11 & Sched.2
5. *Ibid.*	Bingo Club licences *i.e.* the premises	*Ibid.* ss.2 & 20, Sched.2, para.25
6. *Ibid.*	Gaming machine registration *i.e.* for clubs and miners welfare institutes	*Ibid.* s.30 & Sched.7
7. District Councils, London Boroughs & City of London	Registration of societies for small lotteries	1976 Act, s.5 & Sched.1
8. *Ibid.*	Grant of permits for amusements with prizes	*Ibid.* s.16 & Sched.3
9. *Ibid.*	Permits for amusement machines	1968 Act, s.34 & Sched.9
10. Gaming Board	Issue of certificates of approval to persons assisting in gaming	1968 Act, s.19 & Sched.5
11. *Ibid.*	Certificates for gaming by machines	1968 Act, Pt.III with 1976 Act, Sched.4 and 1990 Acts
12. Home Secretary	Regulations to regulate licensed club premises	1968 Act, ss.21, 22
13. *Ibid.*	Regulations about the sale & supply of machines for gaming	*Ibid.* s.28
14. *Ibid.*	Regulations about gaming machines at non-commercial entertainments	*Ibid.* s.68
15. *Ibid.*	Regulations about records and accounts for gaming machines	*Ibid.* s.35
16. *Ibid.*	Regulations to vary limits on certain fees, prizes and other monies	1980 Acts

(1963 Act—Betting, Gaming and Lotteries Act; 1968 Act—Gaming
Act; 1976 Act—Lotteries and Amusements Act; 1980 Acts—Gaming
(Amendment) Act 1980 and Betting, Gaming and Lotteries (Amend-
ment) Act 1980; 1990 Act—Gaming (Amendment) Act 1990).

2. **General Principles**

Before describing and commenting upon the law in each of the five areas   **6.78**
identified above, it is important to note certain broad principles:

   (a) Local authorities are precluded by law from maintaining or contri-
       buting to the maintenance of premises for which a Gaming Act
       licence is in force.[56]

   (b) A code regulating the limited nature of advertisements for gaming
       is contained in section 42 of the Act of 1963. Broadly speaking, this
       contains a general prohibition on such advertising and then this is
       modified by exceptions for machines, charities, entertainments and
       fairs. These exceptions are in each instance carefully qualified and
       merit close study.

   (c) A system of inspection is set up, with both the police and Gaming
       Act inspectors authorised to inspect premises to see that the pro-
       visions of the Act are being honoured. Fire authority representa-
       tives have the same right in relation to the inspection of requisite
       fire precautions. There are sanctions by imprisonment and fine for
       failure to provide information sought by the inspectors or, gener-
       ally, to co-operate with them.[57]

The classes of gambling regulated by law are as follows:

3. **Betting**

(1) *Betting Offices*

Under the Act of 1963, a code of law for Betting Offices was established.[58]   **6.79**
The manager of the Betting Office must obtain a licence from the licensing
justices' committee, after giving due notice to that committee, to the police
and to the local authority.[59] This is to allow references to be taken and the
proposed premises to be inspected. The licence holder has either to be the
holder of a bookmaker's permit himself or be accredited by a bookmaker
as an agent and be the holder of a betting agency permit from the licensing
justices.

---

[56] Gaming Act 1968, s.44.
[57] *Ibid.* s.43.
[58] Betting Gaming & Lotteries Act 1963, s.10 and Sched. 4.
[59] s.9 and Sched. 1. Local authorities for this purpose are county districts, London boroughs
and the Common Council of the City of London. A premature application can be lawfully
adjourned by the Licensing Committee until relevant issues can be clearer—*R.* v. *North
Westminster Betting Licensing Committee, ex p. Ladbroke's Racing Ltd., The Times,* January 2,
1989, D.C.

The Act, with modifications made by the Betting Gaming and Lotteries (Amendment) Act 1984, contains strict rules for the conduct of Betting Offices. It prohibits the employment of or bets with persons under 18 years of age,[60] regulates radio and television broadcasts received within the Office,[61] the serving of refreshments or the provision of entertainment on the premises[62]; and indeed forbids the licence holder and his staff to "encourage" anyone on the premises to bet.[63] In a Divisional Court case upon this code, it was said by the court that documents in these offices would have to be kept "in a somewhat austere form and lose a certain amount of glamour . . . That appears to be exactly what the legislation intended." The case showed that a licence holder would not be convicted of "encouraging" a visitor to bet, unless it was shown that he had "incited" him, in the sense that the encouragement "reached the mind" of the visitor.[64] Finally the Act prescribes the notices that may be exhibited and also requires the office to be separated from other premises.[65]

(2) *Sporting Events*

Betting at an approved horse racecourse, greyhound track or other licensed track is dealt with in section E of this chapter, paragraphs 6.47 *et seq.*, above.

(3) *General*

Betting is prohibited in streets or other public places[66] and, as indicated above, there is strict control over the form of betting at certain places to which the public "resort." That word is deemed by the courts to connote close physical proximity but a clearer definition of that key word still awaits a suitable court case.[67]

4. Gaming

6.80   Gaming is "the playing of a game of chance for winnings in money or money's worth, whether any person playing the game is at risk of losing any money or money's worth or not."[68] The law is codified in the Gaming

---

[60] Sched. 4, para. 2. Whilst not repealed or amended by the Act of 1984 cited in the text, the facilities for radio, TV, refreshments, entertainment and also advertisements, are all to be "more civilised and less spartan," said the mover of this successful Private Bill.
[61] *Ibid.* para. 5.
[62] *Ibid.*
[63] *Ibid.* para. 4.
[64] *Wilson* v. *Danny Quastel (Rotherhithe) Ltd.* [1965] 2 All E.R. 541. Sachs J. at p. 544. But see now the Act of 1984 (n. 60 *supra*.)
[65] s.10 and Sched. 4 (*supra*), para. 6. See also *re* notices under this code *Windsors (Sporting Investments)* v. *Oldfield* [1981] 1 W.L.R. 1176.
[66] Betting, Gaming and Lotteries Act 1963, s.8.
[67] See, *e.g. R.* v. *Brown* [1895] 1 Q.B. 195.
[68] Gaming Act 1968, s.52(1).

Act 1968 as amended, in which Parliament has tried to grapple with the current forms taken by this leisure service. Commercialised gaming is regulated primarily by the Gaming Board and is made subject to gaming licence duties. Commercial clubs are brought within a system of licensing, whilst members clubs come into a registration system. Gaming with machines now warrants a Part of the 1968 Act to itself and is subject to a new system of control.

This section concentrates upon those aspects of the law which fall to be administered by local licensing justices, namely, members clubs, bingo clubs and gaming with machines.

(1) *Members Clubs*

(1) When gaming takes place in club premises, that club must be regis- **6.81**
tered with the local licensing justices.[69] The application can be made at any time and notice that it is being made must also be given to the police and the Customs and Excise authority.[70]

(2) There are numerous grounds for refusing an application if the club has a bad record; or if gaming appears to be the main purpose of the club (with an exception to cover bridge and whist playing); or if it has less than 25 members, appears to be temporary in character or not to be a bona fide members club.[71]

(3) This procedure with its application and the service of notice, and the criteria applied to an application is also the one followed when a miners' welfare institute seeks registration.[72]

(4) Registration of either club or institute premises can include a condition limiting the gaming to part or parts of the premises.[73]

(5) The Crown Court is the designated forum for hearing appeals by applicants against refusals of their applications or the nature of conditions attached to registration.[74]

(6) The code of procedure includes a further right of appeal to a court,

---

[69] Gaming Act 1968, s.11 and Sched. 3.
[70] *Ibid.* s.1 and Sched. 1. Also the Gaming (Amendment) Act 1982, in relaxing the time at which these applications are made.
[71] *Ibid.* Sched. 3, paras. 7–9.
[72] *Ibid.* ss.1 and 11 and Sched. 3.
[73] *Ibid.* Sched. 3, para. 11. Those provisions of the Gaming Act 1968 which affect the registration of members clubs and miners' welfare institutes were brought into force on May 1, 1969 by the Gaming Act 1968 (Commencement No. 3) Order 1969 (S.I. 1969 No. 549). *Lock* v. *Rank Leisure Ltd.* (1984) 148 J.P. 340: a club cannot lawfully carry on gaming, in respect of which money, apart from the stake hazarded, was charged, on premises not licensed under Pt. II of the Gaming Act 1968, "unless they were its own premises." A regional competition final of the Top Rank Club took place at the Wembley Conference Centre, which was not licensed or registered under Pt. II of the above Act of 1968. Prizes to the value of £25,000 were given out: there was nothing to pay at Wembley because all the payments by the entrants had been made at their "home" clubs. The court held that section 40, as amended by the Gaming (Amendment) Act 1973, was meant only for bridge and whist clubs and not for this situation. S.3 of the 1968 Act had been contravened and there should be a conviction.
[74] *Ibid.* para. 12.

whereby any person can, at any time, apply to the clerk to the licensing justices for the club licence to be cancelled. This gives rise to a formal hearing, the views of both police and Customs and Excise being sought by the court. The schedule incorporates 11 reasons for cancelling the registration and these cover all aspects of mismanagement in the running of the club.[75]

(7) Registration certificates normally run for one year, with discretion to extend that period up to 10 years. Renewal of the registration and payment of prescribed fees is built into the system.[76]

(2) *Bingo Clubs*

6.82 Where gaming at a club is limited to bingo, it is subject to certain special conditions:

(a) The aggregate winnings paid in a week shall not exceed the aggregate stakes by more than £250.[77]

(b) Persons under 18 years of age may be present, if not playing.

Linked bingo

(a) Games played simultaneously in several premises are regarded as one game, provided that:
  (i) Winnings in aggregate do not exceed the stakes in aggregate; and
  (ii) A limit fixed by the Secretary of State is not exceeded as the total money paid in winnings for the whole week's bingo at those premises.

(b) If the conditions in (a) apply, then the normal member and guest conditions for registered clubs apply too, but the 48-hour entrance condition is relaxed to a period of 24 hours.[78]

(3) *Gaming with Machines*

6.83 Part III of the Gaming Act 1968 now embodies a legal code about gaming with machines. In outline, it provides:

(1) Gaming by machines, outside the terms of the Gaming Act, is unlawful and constitutes an offence. Selling, supplying and maintaining the machines are also offences.[79]

---

[75] Gaming Act 1968, para. 14.

[76] *Ibid.* para. 20.

[77] *Ibid.* s.20. For Bingo Duty, see Customs and Excise Act 1952, Betting and Gaming Duties Act 1972 and Finance Act 1980, s.8. The Gaming (Amendment) Act 1980 introduced the power for the Home Secretary to vary monetary limits. The maximum for prizes for linked games played on several premises in one week is currently £4,000.

[78] See now too the Gaming (Bingo) Act 1985 and regulations made thereunder, on multiple bingo.

[79] Gaming Act 1968, s.38.

(2) However, gaming by machines is exempted from this prohibition if certificates and permits granted by the Gaming Board are in force for the persons and premises involved and the machines are used on a pleasure pier or a travelling showman's pleasure fair, or on a pleasure fair devoted wholly or mainly to amusements, or are for use on premises to be used wholly or mainly for amusements by means of these machines.[80]

(3) Again there is exemption, where the premises are registered under Part II or Part III of the Gaming Act. This will usually be a members club or miners' welfare institute. Stringent conditions apply to the use of the machines.[81]

(4) Two more exemptions are available: first, where machines are incidental to non-commercial entertainment and secondly, where these machines are used primarily for amusement and the value of the prizes is limited.[82]

(5) The number of machines is normally limited to two but this can be increased in certain circumstances.[83]

(6) Only authorised persons may remove money from the machines.[84]

(7) Records, accounts and verification can be required of the gaming machine user both by the Gaming Board and by the police for the area.[85]

(8) Offences carry fines of £400 maximum or two years' imprisonment or both.[86]

5. **Lotteries**

The classic definition of a lottery is the distribution of prizes by chance. **6.84** For the main provisions on this subject, one turns to the Lotteries and Amusements Act 1976, where it is laid down that all lotteries which do not constitute gaming are unlawful "subject to the provisions of this Act."[87] Exemptions from this prohibition are then defined and in practice four of these are important.

(1) *Small Lotteries* incidental to entertainments. This expression is defined to cover bazaars and dances, as well as sporting, athletic and other events. Special rules apply to the expenses, the prizes, the limits on

[80] Gaming Act 1968, s.27.
[81] *Ibid.* s.31. These, for instance, limit the machines to two, limit the prize, also the charge for playing, the minimum percentage of the total charges which must be paid out as prizes, and the need for displaying on the machines a statement of the above amounts. The machines are not to be in use when the public has access to the premises.
[82] *Ibid.* s.33 and Sched. 4 to the Lotteries and Amusements Act 1976.
[83] *Ibid.* s.32 and *R. v. Herrod, ex p. Leeds City Council* [1974] 3 All E.R. 362.
[84] *Ibid.* s.36.
[85] *Ibid.* s.37.
[86] *Ibid.* s.39.
[87] Lotteries and Amusements Act 1976, s.1, and see also the Lotteries Regulations 1977 (S.I. 1977 No. 256) for the terms which must go into the schemes prepared by societies or local authorities for the promotion of a lottery. The Lotteries (Amendment) Regulations 1981 (S.I. 1981 No. 109) vary the 1977 Regulations. The various offences in section 2 of the Act of 1976, in relation to unlawful lotteries, have been slightly reduced by the Lotteries (Amendment) Act 1984, which abolished some offences relating to foreign lotteries.

sale of the tickets and the meaning given to the word "incidental" in the above phrase.[88]

(2) *Private Lotteries* are those limited to members of a society or people who work together or reside together. Again, there are severe conditions to be met in order to ensure that such a lottery is lawful.[89]

(3) *Societies' Lotteries* are the third class. These are small lotteries promoted on behalf of a society established for purposes which are not commercial nor for private gain. Those purposes must be charitable and to do with athletic sports or games or cultural activities, or more than one of those purposes. The society has to be registered with the local authority and its scheme registered also with the Gaming Board,[90] if the total value of the tickets is to exceed the prescribed limit.

(4) *Local Lotteries* are those promoted by local authorities and they must comply with these points:

   (i) A scheme regulating the lottery must be approved by the local authority.
   (ii) The scheme must be registered with the Gaming Board.
   (iii) The normal powers of delegation available for local authorities under the Local Government Act 1972, section 101, do not apply to approval of these schemes.
   (iv) The object for which the Local Lottery is promoted must be one within the powers of the local authority. The object can include section 137 of the Local Government Act 1972, *i.e.* benefit of the inhabitants of the area. Devotion of the proceeds of the lottery to a purpose other than the declared object of the lottery can be made only with the consent of the Secretary of State.
   (v) A lottery fund must be set up to take the net proceeds of Local Lotteries and the interest on invested money in this fund.
   (vi) There are not to be more than 52 lotteries in 12 months.

There are prescribed offences for breaches of these conditions. The local authorities who are to oversee these lotteries, and who are charged with the difficult task of deciding when some of the conditions have been breached, are district councils, London boroughs and the Common Council of the City of London.[91]

---

[88] Lotteries and Amusements Act 1976, s.3. The lottery is not to be the only, or the only substantial, inducement, to attend (s.3(*d*)).

[89] *Ibid.* s.4. This forbids sending lottery tickets through the post, limits deductible expenses to printing and stationery and requires the balance to be used as prizes or for the purpose of the society. Further, there must be no advert, save on the appropriate premises of the society and on the tickets; the price of all tickets must be the same and stated on the ticket; the ticket must contain the name and address of the promoters, the persons who may take part in the lottery, that the prize can only be given to the holder of the winning ticket, that no ticket must be sold except for the full price and that in no circumstances must any ticket money be returned. Lastly, each branch of a society is, for the purposes of a lottery, "a separate and distinct society," and so a single lottery promoted for members of the main society is unlawful. (*Keehan* v. *Walters* [1948] 1 K.B. 19).

[90] *Ibid.* ss.5 and 11. Total ticket value limit is now £5,000. These conditions include making a return to the local authority of a lottery, with details of proceeds, expenses, prizes and money devoted to the purposes for which the lottery was run.

[91] *Ibid.* s.6 and Pt. II.

6. **Prize Competitions**

It should also be noted that prize competitions also are unlawful. The   **6.85**
definition in the Act of 1963 incorporates these points:

  (a) The offence involves conducting the competition in a newspaper or
      in conjunction with a trade or business or the sale of an article to
      the public.
  (b) The prizes are for forecasts of a future event or even a past event
      the result of which is not yet ascertained or generally known.
  (c) It is a condition of a competition being unlawful that success does
      not depend on skill "to a substantial degree."[92]
  (d) A proviso exempts sponsored pool betting and also a bookkeepers'
      pool betting operations.
  (e) If it transpired that the competition were a lottery, then there
      would be a second offence and a risk of prosecution for that also.[93]

7. **Amusements with Prizes and Gaming Machines**

(1) Amusements with prizes has become a technical term in Acts relat-   **6.86**
ing to betting, gaming and lotteries. It connotes a lottery, or gaming, or
both, but not gaming as, *e.g.* roulette, to which Part II of the Gaming Act
1968 applies.

(2) Amusements with prizes are lawful at bazaars, sales of work, fetes,
dinners, dances, sporting or athletic events and other entertainments of a
similar nature, whether limited to one day or extending over two or more
days.[94]

(3) There are two conditions to be complied with in order to secure this
exemption from normal legal strictures against lotteries.

     (i) The whole of the proceeds are devoted to purposes other than
         private gain. It is permitted to deduct expenses, including the
         cost of prizes, in ascertaining "proceeds."
    (ii) The opportunity to win prizes at the event is not the only or
         only substantial inducement to people to attend the event.[95]

---

[92] Lotteries and Amusements Act 1976, s.14 and see *Ladbrokes (Football)* v. *Perrett* [1971] 1
W.L.R. 110, for a spot-the-ball competition in a newspaper held to be unlawful.
[93] *Ibid.* s.14. In *Coles* v. *Odhams Press Ltd.* [1936] 1 K.B. 416, a crossword competition in a
newspaper was held to be a lottery. This was because there were alternative appropriate
answers to the clues and the solution was determined beforehand. Lord Hewart said it
was the opportunity "of blind shots at a hidden target." For a case illustrating the borderline between a lottery and a prize competition, see also *Imperial Tobacco* v. *Att.-Gen.* [1979]
2 W.L.R. 805. A "spot cash" scheme of cards in packets of cigarettes was held to be
neither an unlawful lottery nor an unlawful prize competition, in the Court of Appeal. The
reasons were the absence of any charge for the cards as such and the lack of any "purpose-
ful striving" by the entrants. The House of Lords, however, in a comprehensive review of
cases throughout this country, held the scheme to be an unlawful lottery, though not an
unlawful competition ([1981] A.C. 718). This scheme contravened section 14 of the Lotteries and Amusements Act 1976.
[94] *Ibid.* ss.3 and 15.
[95] *Ibid.* s.15.

(4) The promoter of the event must obtain a permit from the local authority.[96]

(5) Pleasure fairs are granted statutory exemption from this procedure, on not more than 27 days in one year, on one site.[97]

(6) The Lotteries and Amusements Act 1976 contains monetary restraints on the price of a chance, the total money proceeds, the amount for prizes and a prohibition on one prize becoming the grant of an opportunity to take part in a further amusement with prizes or gaming or a lottery.[98]

(7) Enlarged powers for local authorities in these matters under the Gaming Act 1968 cover refusals, imposition of conditions and dealing with appeals against refusals.[99]

In relation to amusements with gaming machines, the same two conditions relating to the bazaars and other events described in (ii) above apply as set out in (iii) above. "The whole of the proceeds are devoted to purposes other than private gain" is a key condition in this field.[1] As such, it has been before the courts more than once. The House of Lords had to consider it in the case of *Avias* v. *Hartford Shankhouse & District Workingmen's Social Club and Institute*.[2] The court concentrated attention on the time when, and the extent and manner in which, "takings" were reduced to "proceeds," and when and to what purpose the "proceeds" were applied. The case should be studied by any affected by this point.

8. Competition for Prizes

6.87   This is yet one more refinement in this branch of the law. The expression is defined in the Pool Competitions Act 1971. It involves an allocation of prizes dependent upon the result of sporting events; each competitor having the right to forecast the outcome of those events; and prizes being allocated whether those rights are exercised or not. A scheme of this nature was held to be an unlawful lottery in *Singette* v. *Martin*,[3] and not, as the promoters contended, lawful pool betting. The above Act of 1971 was meant as temporary relief for clubs dependent upon income from schemes of this kind.

The Act lays down a procedure for certificates and licences from the Gaming Board to regulate this area of gambling. Fees, excise duties and the sanction of certain offences are included in the provisions of this important Act.[4]

---

[96] Lotteries and Amusements Act 1976, ss.16, 17, 18 and 24.

[97] *Ibid.* s.16(1)(*c*).

[98] *Ibid.* ss.18(1) and 24(2). For current amounts see Amusements with Prizes (Variation of Monetary Limits) Order 1984 (S.I. 1984 No. 245).

[99] *Ibid.* s.16 and Sched. 3.

[1] Gaming Act 1968, s.33(2).

[2] [1969] 1 All E.R. 130.

[3] The full title is *Singette Ltd.* v. *Martin* (1970) All E.R. 570 and 3 All E.R. 938.

[4] Initially in force for five years, this Act has now been renewed annually by statutory instrument, and is still in force.

H. SEX ESTABLISHMENTS

The powers of legal control over the two forms of sex establishments, sex **6.88**
shops and sex cinemas, are adoptive for local authorities and are contained in the Local Government (Miscellaneous Provisions) Act 1982.
Due public notice by the local authority in question, of a resolution to
adopt these powers, is needed as part of the procedure to bring into operation in its area Part III of this Act.[5] The local authorities for this purpose
are district councils, London boroughs and the Common Council of the
City of London.

1. Statutory Code

The legal framework provided by the Act is the same for both sex shops **6.89**
and sex cinemas and is as follows:

(1) A licence is needed when premises are to be used as a sex establishment. The licence will remain in force for one year, or less if so prescribed.[6]

(2) The licensing authority can grant, transfer and renew licences. The
procedure includes due public notice of the making of the application, an
opportunity for objection by the police and others, and an opportunity to
appear before the appropriate committee of the council at the hearing of
the application.[7]

(3) A decision by the licensing authority to refuse one of the above three
forms of application must be embodied in a statement giving reasons for
the decision and supplied on request to the applicant.[8]

(4) Licences are not to be granted to:
    (i) Persons under 18 years of age.
    (ii) Persons legally disqualified. (A person is disqualified for 12
    months for this purpose if his licence has been revoked.)
    (iii) A body corporate not incorporated in the United Kingdom.
    (iv) A person who, as an applicant, has had his application for
    grant or renewal refused within 12 months of the new appli-
    cation.

(5) Grounds for declining to grant these applications laid down in the
Act are as follows[9]:

---

[5] Expressions in this new Act are being tested in the courts. An early case in the Court of
Appeal was *R.* v. *Chester City Council, ex p. Quietlynn* (1985) 83 L.G.R. 308, C.A. The local
authority lost on one point of procedure, having wrongly, said the court, taken the hearing
of objections before a sub-committee, rather than the full committee which was to take the
effective decision on behalf of the Council. The case should be studied for observations on
notices under the Act and the need for an actual hearing of objections.
[6] Sched. 3, paras. 6 and 9.
[7] Local Government (Miscellaneous Provisions) Act 1982, Sched. 3 paras. 8 and 10.
[8] *Ibid.* para. 10.
[9] *Ibid.* para. 12. Developing law cases show support by the courts for local authorities
reviewing a locality and its need for sex shops in the light of changed circumstances, and
to refuse an existing shop's renewal on that ground—*R.* v. *Birmingham City Council, ex p.
Sheptonhurst Ltd.* [1990] 1 All E.R. 1026.

   (i) The applicant is unsuitable.

  (ii) The person who derives the benefit of the business is not the applicant but a person whose application would be declined if he applied in person.

 (iii) The number of sex establishments in the locality is sufficient.[10]

 (iv) The character of the locality or the use of premises in the vicinity of the proposed premises or the layout, character or condition of the premises[11] for which the application is made.

(6) The local authority may make standard conditions, embodied in Regulations, in relation to sex establishments, distinguishing not only sex shops from sex cinemas, but also different types of both businesses. The subject-matter of such Regulations is set out in the Act.[12]

(7) A licence holder may apply at any time for a variation in the conditions attached to his licence.

(8) Offences are created for using sex establishments whilst unlicensed or disqualified or in contravention of the terms in a licence. There is another offence for making a false statement in connection with an application under this Act to the licensing authority. An additional offence arises where a person under 18 years is employed in one of these establishments or is permitted to enter one of them. A paragraph in the Schedule adapts the wording to the case of corporate bodies so that they also can be prosecuted. These offences are punishable with fines not exceeding £10,000.[13]

(9) Powers of entry to the sex establishments to enforce the law are conferred upon police constables and also authorised officers of local authorities. A warrant from a justice of the peace is required before such powers can be exercised.[14]

(10) An appeal procedure to the magistrates' courts and, subsequently, to the Crown Court is afforded to applicants who are refused new licences,

---

[10] In a debate on the Bill in Parliament, a government spokesman said that a local authority could decide that the appropriate number of sex establishments for Art. 12(3)(c) might be nil! (*Hansard*, July 2, 1982, col. 1141).

[11] Sched. 3, para. 12(3).

[12] *Ibid*. para. 13. Inclusion in conditions for a sex shop licence of a condition that the holder will comply with relevant legislation would seem sufficient, unless new guidance is given by the courts, to take initial account of the Video Recordings Act 1984, s.12. This deals with video recordings bearing a classification certificate under the Act, to the effect that no video recording, containing that work, is to be supplied other than in a licensed sex shop. The section sets out both offences and defences arising from that provision. A licensee of a sex shop who intends to supply video recordings will thus be obliged to ensure that classification certificates have been given for the video recordings he may intend to supply through that shop.

[13] Local Government (Miscellaneous Provisions) Act 1982, Sched. 3, paras. 20, 21, 22, 23 and 26. *Quietlynn Ltd.* v. *Southend Borough Council* [1991] 2 W.L.R. 611 shows the European Court of Justice at work on this law. Though an appeal that the Local Government (Miscellaneous Provisions) Act of 1982 contravened Art. 30 of the Rome Treaty was dismissed, the 14-page judgment is calculated to provide a fertile quarry for further litigation.

[14] *Ibid*. para. 25.

transfers, variations or are otherwise aggrieved by local authority decisions in these matters.[15]

(11) The terms sex shop and sex cinema are fully defined in the Act. The shop has to be used for purveying sex articles and the cinema definition is based on an exhibition of moving pictures. A dwelling-house to which the public is not admitted is specifically excluded from the sex cinema definition. Films, sound recordings and reading matter devoted to the stimulation of sexual activity are fully defined and brought within the scope of this Act.[16]

2. **Relation to Existing Law**

Finally, it is important to note the relation of this new law to existing legislation. In the first place, there is in the 1982 Act no reference by way of repeal, amendment or otherwise to the Indecent Display (Control) Act 1981. That Act had dealt with indecent displays which were visible from a public place and had repealed an earlier law on that subject, the Indecent Advertisements (Amendment) Act 1970. Some overlap between that Act of 1981 and the code for Sex Establishments in Schedule III to the Act of 1982 is now evident. In debate, the government spokesman indeed made it clear that the same premises were subject not only to these Acts of 1981 and 1982 but also to the Obscene Publications Act 1959. **6.90**

Furthermore, it is laid down, in the Local Government (Miscellaneous Provisions) Act 1982, that the powers under three recited provisions are not to be superseded. These three Acts, relating to indecency or obscenity are:

(a) The Obscene Publications Act 1959, section 3.
(b) The Protection of Children Act 1978, section 5.
(c) The Customs and Excise Management Act 1979, Schedule 3.

There is, strangely, no reference to the Cinematograph (Amendment) Act 1982,[17] which, by removing a 30-year-old exemption, allows licensing of sex cinemas. An overlap by the two Acts is avoided, in logic at least, by a provision that premises licensed or exempt from licensing under the Cinematograph Acts are not to be registered as sex cinemas within the Local Government Act. This does not, however, resolve all issues created by having two statutes dealing with the licensing of the same premises as cinemas.

[15] Video Recordings Act 1984, para. 27.
[16] *Ibid.* para. 4. *Lambeth London Borough Council* v. *Grewal* (1985) 150 J. P. 138 is an important case on the definition of a sex shop.
[17] Local Government (Miscellaneous Provisions) Act 1982, Sched. 3, para. 3(2).

CHAPTER 7

SPORT

The practice of sport is subject to Community Law only in so far as it constitutes an economic activity.

Walrave v. *Association Union Cycliste Internationale* [1974] E.C.R. 1405.

A. MANAGING SWIMMING POOLS

1. **Introduction**

7.01   The original legal code for the provision of swimming pools by local authorities is Part VIII of the Public Health Act 1936. This is now supplemented by the Education Act 1944 in relation to swimming pools for schools and further education.[1] It is also placed in the wider context of public leisure and recreation by the Local Government (Miscellaneous Provisions) Act 1976, where the formal power of provision is now contained.[2]

The legal framework for the provision of public swimming pools is completed by consideration of the by-laws, the areas of management legal risks and comments on two aspects of financial management of swimming pools.

2. **Provision**

7.02   The power to provide swimming pools is now contained in the Local Government (Miscellaneous Provisions) Act 1976.[3] This replaces the formal power in the Public Health Act 1936 but is still supplemented by the additional sections in Part VIII of the Act of 1936. The items of interest in Part VIII are:

(1) When a swimming bath is under the management of a local auth-

---

[1] s.53.
[2] s.19.
[3] Local authorities for that function were revised and are now contained in s.44 of the above Act of 1976 (see Local Government Act 1985, s.84). They are county councils, district councils, London borough councils, the Common Council, the Council of the Isles of Scilly, and a parish council and a community council. The duty formerly given to the Inner London Education Authority, is now placed with the appropriate inner London borough council, which is the local education authority for that part of inner London—Education Reform Act 1988, s.163.

ority, it is deemed to be a public and open place for the purposes of the laws against indecency.[4]

(2) Public swimming baths may be closed temporarily to facilitate the organisation of aquatic sports, contests or similar entertainments either by the local authority or by schools, clubs or other persons.[5]

(3) Swimming baths may be closed between the beginning of October and the end of April in the following year and used for other purposes.[6]

(4) The trustees of a public swimming bath are empowered to sell it to the local authority.[7]

(5) Statutory undertakers are empowered to supply gas, electricity or water on favourable terms.[8]

Under the Education Act 1944, swimming baths may be provided by **7.03** local education authorities.[9] The Act provides this power, as one of a number of ways of fulfilling a duty to secure adequate facilities for recreation, and social and physical training; these again form part of the primary, secondary and further education for the area of the authority. The Education Act 1944 requires local education authorities, when providing such facilities, to "have regard to the expediency of co-operating with any voluntary societies or bodies," who might be engaged in similar schemes.[10]

The Local Government (Miscellaneous Provisions) Act 1976 empowers **7.04** local authorities to provide a wide variety of recreational facilities. These include swimming pools.[11] The pools may be inside or outside the area of the authority; the power extends to "buildings, equipment, supplies and assistance of any kind"[12]; and the initiating local authority may achieve the provision by contributing to the expenses of another local authority who provide the particular facility or by a grant or a loan to a voluntary organisation which is to provide it.

3. By-Laws

Power to make by-laws for their swimming baths is conferred on local **7.05** authorities by the Public Health Act 1936.[13] The general power is described as being for the management of baths, and the regulation of per-

---

[4] Public Health Act 1936, s.224. Thus indecent exposure could be a public nuisance in such premises. Serious unsociable behaviour is however best dealt with in the by-laws.
[5] *Ibid.* s.225.
[6] *Ibid.* s.226. This is to facilitate the practice in some places of covering the pool and using the building as a public hall. Licences for those other activities must of course, be obtained.
[7] *Ibid.* s.228.
[8] *Ibid.* s.229.
[9] Education Act 1944, s.53(1).
[10] *Ibid.* s.53(2). In practice, education authorities fulfil this obligation by a combination of their own school swimming pools and hired used of the public pools, rather than those of voluntary societies contemplated some years ago.
[11] Local Government (Miscellaneous Provisions) Act 1976, s.19(1)(a).
[12] *Ibid.* s.19(2).
[13] Public Health Act 1936, s.223.

sons using them and this can cover the exclusion of undesirable persons.[14] The by-laws may include penalties for breach and also power for swimming pool staff to exclude persons who contravene the by-laws. A copy of the by-laws must be exhibited at the relevant premises.[15]

In practice, by-laws assist in regulating day-to-day matters in the running of a swimming pool and only if controversial do they attract publicity. One would expect the by-laws to deal with serious unsociable conduct in the pool or its surrounds, obedience to the directions of the attendants and due hygiene by swimmers.

4. Areas of Management Risk

7.06 The managers of a swimming pool owe to their employees, by the employment law outlined in Chapter 1, the various obligations there set out and to the visitors to the pool, whether patrons, caterers, workmen or the public generally, the common duty of care also discussed in Chapter 1.

The complex range of activities at a swimming pool encourages an analysis of other areas of legal risk. Some have been highlighted by past cases in the courts; to draw attention to others may help to minimise similar cases in the future.

(1) *The Water*

7.07 The temperature is regulated to accommodate persons with normal susceptibilities; to other persons, the management incur legal liability for mishap only when they are negligent. This arises where the duty of reasonable care to swimmers is breached by some action or inaction which reasonable foresight should have avoided. From time to time, an inexperienced swimmer no doubt ventures into a pool and alert management will try to prevent a mishap. The eggshell skull principle obliges a defendant in an action for breach of duty in tort to compensate his successful plaintiff for whatever injury is suffered, though greater than expected. "Take the plaintiff as you find him," is the summary. But in the absence of negligence, management do not enter into this area of risk.[16] Apart from the temperature of the water, the chemicals added in order to purify the water are a matter in the control of management and again afford scope for negligence and consequent legal risk.

(2) *Tickets*

All patrons of the swimming pool may expect to receive a ticket as receipt for payment on admission to the premises. The impact of the Unfair Contract Terms Act 1977 on such a situation was considered in Chapter 1.

---

[14] Public Health Act 1936, s.223(1).

[15] Public Health Act 1936, s.223(2). For the general law about by-laws see Chap. 4. The by-laws may deal with the use of the hall during any closed period of the pool.

[16] See, *e.g. Smith* v. *Leech Brain & Co. Ltd.* [1962] 2 Q.B. 405 and *Dulieu* v. *White and Sons Ltd.* [1901] 2 K.B. 669, where the unusually weak heart was added to the eggshell skull class and is perhaps a little more relevant to swimming pool accidents.

Briefly, liability as a result of negligence cannot be excluded by such a ticket, if it is in respect of death or personal injury.[17] In other cases, perhaps damage to a swimmer's personal rings or other property, the test of reasonableness by both parties, the plaintiff and the defendant, is imported by the above Act of 1977.[18]

(3) The Surround

In law, the surround to the swimming pool is simply part of the premises **7.08** which patrons are invited to use. The common duty of care and its qualifications, as discussed in Chapter 1, are relevant. Thus the notices or by-laws about running or horseplay are also relevant; so is any contributory negligence by the swimmer. Any hazard due to negligent cleaning, before the pool was opened to the public, would of course give rise to legal risk if an accident ensued.

(4) The Pool

The two areas of legal risk to which the swimming pool itself gives rise are **7.09** any unusual features in its construction below water level and also dangerous objects on the bottom. When the level of the bottom of the pool varies, as with the diving area, the management discharge their legal duty of care by informing swimmers of this feature in the notices about the varying depths of water. This is normal and reasonable.

No swimmer expects to find broken glass or other hazards on the bottom of the pool; still less, sharp projections round its edge. Management are expected to be reasonable and to have some system of inspection which tries efficiently to guard against hazards like broken glass.[19] Other hazards like a jagged tile at the side of the pool ought to be seen on inspection but if present when swimming takes place, can hardly fail to give rise to legal liability for any ensuing injury.

(5) The Diving Boards

These are mentioned separately from the pool since, by their nature, they **7.10** involve greater risk for those using them and hence call for greater care than ordinary swimming. The defence *volenti non fit injuria*—there is no legal liability to the person who has willingly accepted the risks—was discussed in Chapter 1 as one of the available defences in tort. The diver is a "volunteer" within that maxim: he decides to climb and dive. He accepts a risk but he does not expect to find a trap, nor any hazard which is not

---

[17] Unfair Contract Terms Act 1977, s.2.
[18] *Ibid.* s.2(2).
[19] For the paddling pool equivalent, see *Ellis* v. *Fulham Borough Council* [1938] 1 K.B. 212. No reported cases on swimming pools have been found; the relevance of a system of inspection to the hazards in each local situation has been considered by the courts in relation to slipping on spilt yoghurt in a supermarket and tripping over an uneven paving stone in a busy highway (*Griffiths* v. *Liverpool Corporation* [1967] 1 Q.B. 374 and *Whiting* v. *Hillingdon L.B.C.* (1970) 68 L.G.R. 437).

obvious on inspection.[20] Any unusual feature of any sort must, therefore, be the subject of warning notices.

(6) *Children*

It should also be borne in mind that children call for greater warning. "An occupier must be prepared for children to be less careful than adults," says the Occupiers' Liability Act 1957,[21] in language that the brothers Fowler could approve. This is the legal background for the frequent practice of restricting the use of the high diving boards to persons over a certain age.

(7) *The Supervisors*

7.11 Staff trained in life saving, with effective equipment available, will be on duty when the public use a swimming pool. They are the ears and eyes of management and their negligence becomes the negligence of management. The staff who supervise swimming control the number of swimmers allowed in the pool at one time; they are also expected to be alert for any signs of group danger or individual danger. The test of reasonable foresight is relevant to a situation, where the alleged negligence of a supervisor has given rise to a situation leading to a legal claim for damages.

(8) *The Spectators*

7.12 Statute has not yet provided specific guidance for swimming pool managers on their duties to spectators. The Safety of Sports Grounds Act 1975 has been passed by Parliament to impose a safety inspection system on many sports grounds with large numbers of the public congregating on or near stands. Swimming pools are not normally of a size to attract such numbers and the legal duties of management fall to be framed from the common law and due compliance with such requirements as result from inspection under the Fire Service Acts. Thus the managers again have an ordinary occupier's duty of common care, under the Occupiers' Liability Act 1957, to spectators or other visitors. That duty is to "take such care as in all the circumstances of the case is reasonable to see that the visitor will be reasonably safe in using the premises for the purposes for which he is invited or permitted by the occupier to be there."[22]

A quotation from Diplock L.J. in *Wooldridge* v. *Summer*, the horse trials case, is helpful:

> "A person attending a game or competition takes the risk of any damage caused to him by any act of a participant done in the course

---

[20] Occupiers' Liability Act 1957, s.2(3)(*a*). The same Act places in statutory form the maxim *volenti non fit injuria* as a defence for occupiers to their visitors, who accept risks of which they are aware. The section below on participatory sports discusses this aspect in some detail.

[21] *Ibid.* s.2(2).

[22] *Ibid.*

of and for the purpose of the game or competition, notwithstanding that such act may involve an error of judgment or a lapse of skill, unless the participant's conduct is such as to evince a reckless disregard of the spectator's safety."[23]

The common duty of care is always present for the safety of the premises, the staircases, the seats, the ceiling, the floor and the lighting. At a swimming competition, the risk of injury from participants may be slight and thus no reported law case has been traced. The risk remains with the distance of the spectator seating from the participants being the initial critical element.

The legal consequences of personal injury suffered by a spectator are not invalidated by any disclaimer on the ticket of admission.

(9) *Saunas*

Sauna baths are often found at modern swimming pools and carry an **7.13** added legal liability for management; the risks are different due to the specialist equipment upon which they depend. Management may reasonably expect their equipment suppliers and service arrangements to protect them from the more obvious hazards to users of the sauna. Even so, managers cannot avoid certain duties resulting from the common duty of care; they are expected also to have competent staff and a reasonable system of inspection of the equipment.

Users should be clearly warned of any dangers they might incur by staying for an excessive time in the different parts of the sauna.

(10) *Sales*

Sales of food and drink as part of a cafeteria at a swimming pool, or from **7.14** vending machines, are subject to the general laws about the sale of goods (see Chapter 1) and the standards to be found in the Food Safety Acts.

(11) *Loans of Swimming Equipment*

The supply to users of a swimming pool of costumes, towels or other **7.15** equipment for use on the premises and return, is a separate activity in respect of which legal risks may attach to management. The loan transaction is essentially a separate contract, governed by the law of contract.

This basic contractual relationship of swimmer and manager does not oust the duty in tort. That is the duty of care for the legal neighbour, as defined in *Donoghue* v. *Stevenson*.[24] Clothing sold featured in an early case applying the principle in Donoghue, *i.e. Grant* v. *Australian Knitting Mills*.[25] The duty is akin to that attaching to clothes hire firms, namely to see that the clothes are safe and suitable for their purpose.

---

[23] [1962] 2 All E.R. 978 at p. 989. It was a horseriding competition where the cameraman was injured by a horse.
[24] [1932] A.C. 562.
[25] [1936] A.C. 85.

(12) *Lockers*

7.16 When a swimmer's own clothing is placed in the management's locker or other receptacle, the clothing passes for a time into the care of that management. The notice to place valuables in a place of separate protection is normal and reasonable; it does not ensure that all swimmers will do so; nor does it avoid a normal bailee's legal duty to look after the goods in his custody (See Chapter 3.)

Management will be liable to the swimmer if they are careless in their duty; they lessen this risk if they have good staff and an efficient system. Even so, from time to time something will go wrong and they must expect to recompense the patron, who suffers through no fault of his own.

(13) *Car Parks*

7.17 The management of a swimming pool will nowadays normally also be in charge of an associated car park. (If it is a public car park, it falls to be managed by the highway authority or district council under the Road Traffic Acts and that is outside the scope of this work.)

The legal problems resulting from that responsibility usually centre upon the sanctions available to remove the cars belonging either to persons who do not use the pool or the cars of those who overstay or otherwise misuse the parking facility.

In these respects, the management are in no different position from the management of any other private car park. This means that normal commercial prudence is the main resource. It can take the form, *e.g.* of a charging system which is heavily weighted in favour of the swimming pool user; again, it could be an attendant controlled system.

(14) *Private Swimming Instructors*

7.18 Occasionally, management permit private swimming instructors to use the pool for private lessons. Such an arrangement calls for a simple but comprehensive contract which will cover (1) payment, (2) duration, (3) acceptance of liability for all accidents by the instructor, (4) submission of proof of adequate insurance to cover that risk by the instructor, (5) advertising, permitted on terms set out or prohibited.

5. **Finance**

7.19 The financial aspect of management of a swimming pool calls for comment in two respects only. These are the subjects of admission charges and the extent of sales.

(1) *Admission Charges*

The Local Government (Miscellaneous Provisions) Act 1976, section 19, empowers local authorities to provide swimming pool facilities "for use by such persons as the Authority thinks fit, either without charge or on payment" of such sums as the authority thinks fit.[26]

In so far as this confers discretion, that discretion is to be exercised on the principles laid down in *Associated Picture Houses Ltd.* v. *Wednesbury Corporation*.[27] In other words, the discretion is to be used reasonably and not to take into account extraneous factors.

When management is prompted to admit groups of patrons without charge or at a nominal charge, the case of *Prescott* v. *Birmingham Corporation*[28] has some relevance. The municipality in that city wished to grant free travel on its transport undertaking to some 70,000 old age pensioners. The Court of Appeal upheld Vaisey J. at first instance and held such a scheme to be *ultra vires*. The principle applied, as stated by Jenkins L.J. is as follows:

> "They (*i.e.* the local authority) are not entitled, merely on the strength of a general power to charge different fares to different passengers or classes of passengers, to make a gift to a particular class of persons of rights of free travel on their vehicles, simply because the local authority concerned are of opinion that the favoured class of persons ought, on benevolent or philanthropic grounds, to be accorded that benefit."[29]

The court cited in support the leading case of *Roberts* v. *Hopwood*.[30] The specific power to admit without charge is of course a feature in the above Act of 1976, which distinguishes it from *Prescott's* case; the duty to discharge a discretion responsibly is one that never departs, when a public body like a local authority is concerned.

(2) *Sales*

The Act of 1976 now empowers specifically the sales of food and drink as   **7.20**
part of the facilities at swimming pools. For other sales, a local authority relies on the powers in the Local Government Act 1972, section 111, to do that which is incidental to their authorised duties. In those circumstances, whilst the sale of items related to the use of the swimming pool is clearly

---

[26] s.222. The Public Health Act 1936 is also relevant.
[27] [1948] 1 K.B. 223.
[28] [1955] Ch. 210.
[29] p. 235.
[30] [1925] A.C. 578. The House of Lords disallowed special payments to a class of municipal employees, to mitigate their economic difficulties at the time. The text deals only with the general ongoing legal situation. The grant of free or special facilities for the unemployed is currently common in our society and may well be a practice that would not be challenged. What ultimate limit the courts may place upon the statutory discretion in s.19 of the Act of 1976 is yet to be seen. The line of cases stemming from *Liversidge* v. *Anderson* [1942] A.C. 206 under the Defence Regulations, on the test to be applied to the words "as he thinks fit," is a cautionary reminder that absolute, unfettered discretion, akin to that of even a benevolent despot, is rarely to be found in our law when Parliament is granting powers to local authorities, who are always trustees for their ratepayers.

within their powers, it is possible that any wider range of sales would be outside those powers and thus unlawful.[31]

B. MANAGING SPORTS CENTRES

7.21 Sports centres are now to be found in nearly every town. Statutory recognition of their place in the public leisure services scene was given in the Local Government (Miscellaneous Provisions) Act 1976. They form today the active sportsman's equivalent of the "compendium of games," which housed draughts, ludo, halma and the like in close proximity. The sports centre can now often provide space for archery, indoor cricket, badminton, swimming and a host of other sports under one roof.

Nevertheless, the legal problems associated with sports centres are not essentially different from those discussed in some detail in relation to swimming pools. Here, two legal aspects are noted; then the Gateshead thumb-nail sketch is a vivid summary of this key leisure activity.

1. **Provision**

7.22 The statutory provision is the same as that for swimming pools, *i.e.* the Local Government (Miscellaneous Provisions) Act 1976.[32] The section also details the powers to provide staff, and supporting facilities in the following terms:

"(*e*) staff, including instructors, in connection with any such facilities or premises as are mentioned in the preceding paragraphs and in connection with any other recreational facilities provided by the authority;

(*f*) such facilities in connection with any other recreational facilities as the authority considers it appropriate to provide including, without prejudice to the generality of the preceding provisions of this paragraph, facilities by way of parking spaces and places at which food, drink and tobacco may be bought from the authority or another person;

and it is hereby declared that the powers conferred by this subsection to provide facilities include powers to provide buildings, equipment, supplies and assistance of any kind."[33]

As the same statute enables a local authority to provide the premises for the use of clubs having athletic, social or recreational objects, it would be possible to combine such premises with a sports centre building, if it were locally expedient to have that sort of collaboration.

---

[31] The full text, in the Local Government Act 1972, is the power to do anything "which is calculated to facilitate or is conducive or incidental to, the discharge of a local authority's functions."

[32] s.19(1). This lists some of the main sports as follows: "pitches for team games, athletic grounds, swimming pools, tennis courts, cycle tracks, golf courses, bowling greens, riding schools, camp sites and facilities for gliding."

[33] s.19(1)(*e*) and (*f*).

Since there is no specific power to make by-laws for sports centres, managers can have by-laws made for their pools, as described in the last subsection, and domestic regulations for the remainder of the centre. The power of charging for admission implies a power of control over admission.

2. **Running the Sports Centre**

The legal responsibilities for unsafe premises and equipment have been **7.23** considered in Chapter 1, in relation to the Occupiers' Liabilities Acts 1957 and 1984 and also in relation to swimming pools (above at paragraphs 7.08–7.10). Those principles apply also to sports centres and their patrons.

The principles of contract, too, apply to sports centres. The existence of a contract does not eliminate liability also in tort for, *e.g.* negligence by managers and their staff.

Bars and cafeteria are subject to the same considerations mentioned in relation to swimming pools. Licensing law is to be found in Chapter 6.

Hire of equipment is extensive in sports centres; the legal principles were considered in the last subsection.

Hire of rooms to clubs is likely to feature in management of a sports centre. The legal elements in the agreement have been touched on in Chapter 1 in relation to property as well as contract.

For a series booking by a club or an individual room booking, a well-drawn hire agreement will cover:

(a) Hiring fee and times for payment;
(b) Dates, times and duration of the occupancy. (Perhaps closed on certain public holidays);
(c) Permitted use;
(d) No nuisance or damage;
(e) Hirer responsible for order in the hired premises;
(f) Cancellation of booking, financial consequences, retention of deposit or otherwise;
(g) In a series booking for, *e.g.* martial arts, insurance by the club against claims by its members would be prudent and the sports centre management would be entitled to know, by the production of premium receipts or otherwise, that such an arrangement was in operation and was effective.

It is common to have a special provision at sports centres for use by the unemployed. Useful guidance on this aspect is to be found in the Sports Council's publication "Sport for the Unemployed."[34]

The management of sports centres is one of the first group of local authority functions to be made subject to compulsory competitive tendering by the Local Government Act 1988 Part I. The description is "managing

---

[34] A research working paper by S. Glyptis and A.C. Riddington, available from the Sports Council at 16, Upper Woburn Place, London WC1H OQP.

sports and leisure facilities" (section 2(2)(*f*)). It is still too early to see whether this massive exercise results in any significant shift of the function away from local authorities.

3. **Cameo of a Sports Centre**

7.24   Gateshead International Stadium enjoys well merited support from the public. It embodies many of the features and thus encounters the legal problems touched on above in relation to sports centres. It also exemplifies the pattern of recent years for certain centres to stage national and international sporting events and thus become hosts to very large numbers of spectators. The older fame of Crystal Palace has by this development been shared by Billingham, Hastings, Reading, Sheffield, Preston and Gateshead and doubtless other provincial centres which have, one by one, won acclaim as hosts of specialist sports and leisure pursuits.

     Gateshead's provision covers ladies' recreation, coaching at all levels, childrens' play activities, local community events, weight training, as well as the sports of tennis, boxing, fencing, gymnastics, volleyball, badminton, football, basketball, disabled sports, table tennis, cricket, judo, netball, hockey and, of course, athletics. An imaginative cross-country course outside the Stadium is a major asset and was the venue for the 1983 World Cross Country Championships. A five-a-side football area outside has proved very popular and the newly installed full size floodlit synthetic pitch and warm-up strip is proving equally attractive.

     The Stadium also houses a Centre of Excellence, supported by the local authority, the Governing Body and the Sports Council, to cover middle distance running, hammer, discus, long jump, pentathlon and high-jump training.

     This summary is to illustrate a significant trend among provincial centres. Since 1985 the Stadium has hosted the Europa Cup Athletics Final and European U23 Championships. Rugby League and American Football feature in the sports provision. Pop concerts to a 33,000 capacity are now possible. These significant developments, no doubt paralleled in other places, are happily recorded to show posterity by one shining example how large a place in community recreation sports centres now provide.

C. P<small>ARTICIPATORY</small> S<small>PORTS</small>

7.25   A recent annual report of the Sports Council listed over fifty sports in which that body took some interest. All would be styled participatory. Some of the legal areas of interest and risk to providers of swimming pools and sports centres have already been considered. These are both clearly attractions for those seeking participatory sports. In the discussion of the law of nuisance in Chapter 1, it was convenient to introduce that consideration in the context of cricket grounds.

     The great participatory sports of our country, golf, football (both kinds), tennis, cricket and athletics, have from time to time given rise to cases in the courts and we shall now attempt to gather together the legal principles which govern them. There is no sign that the Law Commission or any other body is proposing to present parliament with a draft code of law on this subject; it is a day to day matter for many people and the law to be applied is the common law.[35] There would seem to be at least seven areas of legal interest:

1. The parties:
   (a) The players and the organisers.
   (b) The spectators.
2. The place for the maxim *volenti non fit injuria*.
3. The premises.
4. Nuisance.
5. Comparative Commonwealth cases.
6. The Safety of Sports Grounds Act 1975.
7. Private clubs.

1. **The Parties**

(1) *The Players and the Organisers*

The players willingly accept the risks associated with their particular   **7.26**
sport, within the rules. Those risks may be regarded as twofold. In a case about rugby football, the court described that acceptance in terms of "risks which are by no means small, because it is a game involving great physical effort by one side or the other." A footballer also "willingly accepts all the risks of playing a game on such a field as complies with the by-laws laid down by the governing body of the game."[36]

In other words, the risks accepted are, first, those arising from engagement with other players and, secondly, those resulting from the nature of the ground, pitch, court, course or other physical arena used for his or her sport. What the player does not thus accept is the unreasonable danger, the extreme peril, the unjustified tackle or assault. In addition to some of the actions which can be described in these ways as contravening the laws of the sport, they may also contravene the laws of the land.

The organisers are considered with the players, since in the somewhat sporadic law cases in this country, they have been sued, together with the players, by aggrieved spectators.

We turn to some examples to illuminate from the sometimes colourful   **7.27**
instances of sport, the principles outlined so far.

---

[35] In *Participatory Sports and the Law* (Sunday Telegraph), Mr. E. Grayson has drawn together many instances of sports cases in the courts; the author is indebted to that work for illustrating the extent to which the law has reached into the details of sporting life. Mr. Grayson's main aim, he says, is to show "the manner in which the law of the land transcends and supplements the laws of the game." His book includes draft clauses for a Bill about participants and spectators.

[36] *Simms* v. *Leigh R.F.C.* [1969] 2 All E.R. 923 at p. 927 i.

Simms v. *Leigh Rugby Football Club*[37]

In a rugby football match, a player was tackled and fell; in the course of this accident, his leg was broken. In an action against the ground organiser, he alleged that his injury was due to his being struck by a concrete wall, which was too near the pitch. After a full hearing, the court was not satisfied that the wall was involved in the accident and the plaintiff failed. A broken leg was treated as an accepted risk in rugby football.

Harrison v. *Vincent*[38]

A motorcycle racing circuit near Scarborough was the scene of a motorcycle and sidecar combination race. In a six-lap race, the accident occurred in the fifth lap, when, at a hairpin bend, the plaintiff was the passenger in the sidecar and the defendant his driver. The defendant needed to brake down from 100 m.p.h. to about 30 m.p.h. for this bend and the brakes produced only reduced power for this emergency. Missing the change of gear, the defendant did not have the benefit of added braking power from his engine. He went off the track and struck a standing vehicle on a side road. The plaintiff was injured.

The case was brought against the motorcycle rider and his employers and also against the race organisers, based on the inadequate inspection of the brakes before the race and also the layout of the course. The case reached the Court of Appeal. That court had to consider whether the accident and injuries were reasonably foreseeable by the defendants. On that point, the court said that they preferred the way the test was framed in the *Wagon Mound* case[39] to the way it was put in *Simms'* case (above). The preferred phrasing was:

> "A person must be regarded as negligent, if he does not take steps to eliminate a risk which he knows or ought to know is a real risk and not a mere possibility which would never influence the mind of a reasonable man."

Also, the qualification in the *Wagon Mound* case:

> "It is justifiable not to take steps to eliminate a real risk if it is small and if the circumstances are such that a reasonable man, careful of the safety of his neighbour, would think it right to neglect it."

The court referred with approval to the Australian case of *Rootes* v. *Shelton*[40] and put their judgment in favour of the passenger in the following way:

> "The acceptance of risks by the passenger did not extend to the risk

---

[37] [1969] 2 All E.R. 923.
[38] [1982] 1 R.T.R. 8. See also *Condon* v. *Basi* (1985) 2 All E.R. 453 C.A. when £4,900 damages were awarded against a footballer for a late and dangerous tackle giving rise to a broken leg.
[39] *The Wagon Mound (No. 2)* [1967] 1 A.C. 617 at p. 642.
[40] *Rootes* v. *Shelton* (1967) 116 C.L.R. 383.

of injury in the avenue of escape, following an involuntary departure from the race track."

Latchford v. Spedeworth International Ltd.[41]

This recent case by a participant against the stadium owner related to **7.28** hot rod motor racing at Wimbledon Stadium in London. The plaintiff, a racing driver, familiar with the track, knew that two concrete flower beds, near to the inner edge of the track, were potentially dangerous to drivers. The defendant, the stadium owner, had for some months used small tyres on the ground as a form of boundary marking. These indicated the boundary near to the flower beds. In fact, small tyres were hazardous for this use and large tyres would have been safer, for demarcation purposes.

The case arose because of injuries suffered by the plaintiff in a race on this track. The preceding car struck some of the small tyres, propelling some onto the track and one jammed under the rear axle of the plaintiff's car. This catapulted the car sideways out of control and the plaintiff suffered a head-on collision with the concrete flower beds.

The interesting judgment of the court in favour of the plaintiff, was to the effect that though the plaintiff had an objective awareness of the flower beds and thus could be said to have accepted the risk thereby created, he did not, using the test of Watkins J. in *Harrison* v. *Vincent* (above), have a "full appreciation of the nature and extent of the risk, because of his ignorance of the peril created by the use of the small tyres." The defence of *volenti* failed and the plaintiff succeeded in his claim.

Brown v. Pelosi and St. Johnstone

The clearest instance of a player's legal rights is perhaps that of a foot- **7.29** ball player recovering damages for injuries resulting from a foul tackle.

Brown v. *Pelosi and St. Johnstone*[42] related to two Scottish football players and the case was settled out of court. The case is nonetheless of persuasive interest as the principle is that applied in the courts in this country. The essence of the claim was damages for injury due to a reckless assault over and beyond the inherent risks of the game. The defendant player had been sent off for his conduct and this provided strong supporting evidence for the plaintiff.

For a century there have also been convictions in the criminal courts of footballers for unlawful assaults, which gave rise to broken limbs in their opponents.[43]

Wider aspects of the law affecting participants were before the Court in *Van Oppen* v. *Clerk to the Trustees of the Bedford Charity*.[44] A 16 year old schoolboy was seriously injured in a house game of rugby football. No insurance policy had been taken out by the school to cover liability of, *e.g.*

---

[41] (1984) 134 New L.J. 36.

[42] The case was widely reported in the English press in December 1983, when £30,000 was said to be the amount of the claim.

[43] See E. Grayson, *supra*, pp. 32–33.

[44] [1990] 1 W.L.R. 235, C.A.

a coach to the boys. Whether this omission constituted a breach of a duty of care depended on various factors such as proximity, and foreseeability. The court also considered whether it was reasonable to impose such a liability and found it important in that context to decide, on evidence, that rugby football was not an inherently or specially dangerous game.

(2) *The Spectators*

7.30   Whilst it is helpful to identify the separate roles of players, organisers and spectators and then the differing legal rights and obligations of each of these parties, in the limited number of English law reports on these subjects, the three are often found together.

Hall v. *Brooklands Auto-Racing Club*[45]

A racing car broke through the barrier between track and spectators after a collision at high speed. Two spectators were killed and others injured. In 23 years, no accident had occurred. An action by an injured spectator against the drivers was dismissed, negligence not being proved. An action against the ground organiser was successful at first instance but in the Court of Appeal, the court said that the findings of the jury could not be supported. The ground occupiers had done all that reasonable care and skill could do to make the course free from danger. They were not insurers against dangers which were inherent in the sport, which any reasonable spectator could foresee and of which he took the risk.

Murray v. *Harringey Arena Ltd.*[46]

A boy spectator was injured by a puck flying from the pitch during an ice hockey game at Haringey Stadium. He failed in an action for damages based on the negligence of the stadium organisers. The barriers and other protection they had provided were not regarded by the Court of Appeal as betraying any negligence. Further, the flying puck was one of the dangers inherent in the game.

Wooldridge v. *Sumner*

A photographer was injured whilst a spectator at the National Horse Show at the White City Stadium. An experienced horseman, taking part in a competition for heavy hunters, galloped at speed down a straight, with the result that his horse could not take the approaching corner without a wide sweep. This took the horse off the course down a line of shrubs, where the plaintiff photographer was watching. He tried to pull a lady out of the path of the horse and succeeded in doing so but was then himself struck and hurt by the horse.

His action for damages against the horseman was dismissed by the Court of Appeal. The court said that the horseman's actions both in rela-

---

[45] [1933] 1 K.B. 205.
[46] [1951] 2 Q.B. 529.

tion to speed and recovery of the horse to the course were not negligent but at most the speed was an error of judgment. (The action against the ground owner had been dismissed at the first hearing.) The judgment included the following passage about spectators and the law:

> "A person attending a game or competition takes the risk of any damage caused to him by any act of a participant done in and for the purposes of the game or competition, notwithstanding that such act may involve an error of judgment or a lapse of skill, unless the participant's conduct is such as to evince a reckless disregard of the spectator's safety." *per* Diplock L.J.[47]

Wilks v. *Cheltenham Car Club*[48]

The plaintiffs were spectators at a motorcycle scramble. They were **7.31** injured when a machine left the track and crossed two barrier ropes. There was no explanation for this conduct of the motorcycle: it suddenly veered to one side.

In legal proceedings, the ground organisers were exonerated. No negligence was found against them. The plaintiffs did succeed at first instance against the motorcycle rider but in the Court of Appeal the rider's appeal against that decision was upheld. The court considered both the *Wooldridge* case and comments upon it and laid down a modified standard expected of both competitors and players. It was in these terms:

> "The competitor's duty in relation to the spectators was not to cause injury by an error of judgment which a reasonable competitor, being a reasonable man of the sporting world, would not have made and which could not, in the stress of the circumstances, reasonably be regarded as excusable" *per* Edmund-Davies L.J.[49]

White v. *Blackmore*[50]

This case arose from an accident at a jalopy race in Gloucestershire. A field was laid out and the track roped round the boundary but all the stakes and ropes were linked to one master stake. During the race, a jalopy car got caught on a rope and as its rear wheel rotated, this acted as a winch, pulling up all the stakes with the rope rapidly. One man standing against the rope was catapulted into the air and later died of his injuries. His estate brought a successful action against the organisers of the race meeting.

The case had special points of interest, in that the deceased was at one time during the meeting a rider and thus a competitor and, at the time of the accident, he was a spectator, though not standing on the spectators' side of the barrier ropes. A further point was that the Court of Appeal rejected the ground on which the court of first instance had dismissed the

---

[47] [1963] 2 Q.B. 44 at p. 68.
[48] [1971] 1 W.L.R. 668.
[49] *Ibid.*
[50] [1972] 2 Q.B. 651.

claim of *volenti non fit injuria, i.e.* no legal liability to one who willingly accepts risks. The Court of Appeal held, that the deceased had not appreciated all the risks, due to the way in which the barrier ropes and stakes were fixed. He was not, therefore, *volenti.* This important qualification on the application of this maxim was elaborated in *Latchford's* case (above).

2. The Place of the Maxim: Volenti Non Fit Injuria

7.32 It will be apparent that the defence of *volenti non fit injuria* is raised regularly in these cases brought by spectators against players and organisers or by players against organisers. It is said, with some evident justification, "You cannot complain: there are always risks to these games or events, which you have willingly accepted, whether you come as a player or as a spectator."

Two Irish race cases, one concerning horses and the other cars, embody the typical use of the maxim. In *Callaghan* v. *Killarney Race Co. Ltd.*[51] a horse jumped over the wing of a race hurdle and injured the plaintiff spectator. The case was withdrawn from the jury: the occurence was simply a danger inherent in racing. There was no evidence of breach of duty by the organisers. Again, in *McComisky* v. *McDermott,*[52] plaintiff and defendant were respectively passenger and driver in a car in a motor rally. To avoid an unexpected obstruction in the road, the defendant drove his car into a ditch. It overturned and injured the plaintiff. On the dashboard of the car was a notice saying that passengers drove at their own risk. The Court of Appeal, upholding the exoneration of the defendant, discussed also the evidence about the extent to which the passenger, who was also the driver's navigator in the rally, had agreed to abandon his legal claims if injured by the driver's negligence. How far was he *volenti?* The court decided that the evidence on that point before them was tenuous.

On the other hand, in the case of the jalopy race, *White* v. *Blackmore,*[53] the circumstances ruled out the application of that maxim. The accident was due to the linkage of stakes and barrier ropes and this was something the deceased knew nothing about. All three judges agreed that in those circumstances the rule was not relevant. "It cannot be said that the deceased had full knowledge of the risk he was running" (Buckley L.J.)[54]; "Never willingly accepted the risk due to this default" (Denning M.R.)[55]; "the risk of which the deceased man was not and could not be aware" (Roskill L.J.).[56]

7.33   The use of the maxim is not as relevant where contributory negligence by the plaintiff exists, said Lord Reid in *I.C.I. Ltd.* v. *Shatwell.*[57] He instanced the case of a disobedient servant's act being the sole cause of his

[51] [1958] I.R. 366.
[52] [1974] I.R. 75.
[53] See n. 50, *supra.*
[54] *Ibid.* at p. 169(a).
[55] *Ibid.* at p. 164(d).
[56] *Ibid.* at p. 173(e).
[57] [1965] A.C. 656 at p. 672.

injury and said it did not matter whether the defence of *volenti* was raised or whether 100 per cent. contributory negligence was alleged. If substantiated, the result would be the same.

The maxim has limited use in any claim by a spectator against a player, since in the absence of negligence, the maxim does not apply.[58]

However, as the cases set out in this section show, there are still some where the maxim is useful and operative. Its fuller use was discussed in the section about defences to an action in tort, in Chapter 1, at paragraph 1.123.

3. The Premises

Management of sports grounds has, in our age, been subject to public nuisances, protests or other disturbances which raise legal questions. **7.34**

"Public place" is an expression used in the Public Order Act 1936, section 5, in defining an offence for causing a breach of the peace; "or other public place" is the collective expression used in the section after a number of particular locations have been listed. What is "a public place"?

In *Cooper* v. *Shield*,[59] Lord Parker C.J. and his court had to consider how far the railway station at West Kirby in Cheshire was a public place, in relation to the above Act of 1936. The arguments related to the entry by ticket only, the proportion of buildings, the platform and the general layout. In due course, the court held that buildings were excluded from the definition of "public place" in that Act. Further, that even though the platform was open, it was all part of the station, which was not a public place.

But at the end of the judgment, Lord Parker said:

> "The position may be very different when one is considering what ordinarily one would call open spaces and asks oneself the question whether they cease to be open spaces because incidental to their use, there happen to be buildings. One immediately thinks of a race course and stands, one thinks of a football ground with stands. It seems to me that in these circumstances, it is perfectly apt to describe the complex as an open space."[60]

So when in *Cozens* v. *Brutus*[61] a demonstration took place on a court at Wimbledon during Wimbledon fortnight, and the above section was used for prosecution, the persons prosecuted, even though employing every possible argument in three hearings (the last being in the House of Lords), conceded, as being beyond argument, that the tennis court was a public place.[62]

---

[58] See headnote to *Wooldridge*'s case, n. 47, *supra*, at p. 45.
[59] [1971] 2 Q.B. 334. "Open space" is considered, since "public place" in the Act is defined as any "highway, etc. . . . and includes any open space to which for the time being the public have or are permitted to have access, whether on payment or otherwise."
[60] *Ibid*. at p. 340.
[61] [1973] A.C. 854.
[62] *Ibid*. at p. 857.

In the case of *Cawley* v. *Frost*,[63] a breach of the peace at a football ground in Halifax between rival supporters gave rise to a prosecution under the above Act of 1936. The point taken by the defence was that the location of the fracas was a speedway track, which lay between the football stands and the pitch and that this was not a public place as far as the football spectators were concerned. The Crown Court had accepted this point and dismissed the case but on appeal the Divisional Court took a different view:

> "Where you have an establishment which is set up for the public, such as the Halifax Town Football Club or Wembley Stadium, one ought to approach it on the basis that it is a public place in its entirety," (Lord Widgery L.C.J.)

4. Nuisance

7.35   This is an important point for sports organisers and sports have been closed at some grounds on its account; there is a full discussion in Chapter 1 and a further consideration of this subject in Chapter 4, in relation to nuisance in public parks.

5. Comparative Commonwealth Cases

7.36   It has been remarked that there is an almost complete dearth of judicial authority about the duty of care owed by the actual participants in sports and pastimes to their spectators.[64] Speculating on this feature, Professor A.L. Goodhart inferred that the number of sports accidents involving spectators in this country was minimal, as major spectator sports are rarely dangerous to spectators.[65] In those circumstances, it is instructive and interesting to look briefly at the cases in the Commonwealth law reports. These deal with perhaps more robust sports, viewed from sometimes more rudimentary grandstands. The conclusions in these reports are of persuasive authority only in the precedence accorded to judicial decisions in this country. Yet recent reports in other branches of our own law show a readiness by our courts to turn to Commonwealth decisions, when legal authorities in the United Kingdom are difficult to find.[66]

Payne & Payne v. *Maple Leaf Gardens Ltd., Stewart and Marucci*[67]

During a professional hockey game, two players on opposing sides dropped their hockey sticks on the ice. Play proceeded away from them as they sought to pick up their sticks. One player, Stewart, thought the other player Marucci had his stick. Stewart thus got hold of the stick and was resisted by Marucci who knew that the stick was his own. This struggle

---

[63] (1976) 64 Cr.App.Rep. 20.
[64] Diplock L.J. in *Woodridge* v. *Sumner* [1962] 3 W.L.R. 616 at p. 631.
[65] A. L. Goodhart, "The Sportsman's Charter" (1962) 78 L.Q.R. 490.
[66] See, *e.g.* copyright decisions in Chapter 3 (paras. 3.17–3.18) of this book.
[67] [1949] 1 D.L.R. 369.

took the two men to the side of the ice, where boards four feet high separated the pitch from the front row of spectators, who were two feet away from the boards. When Marucci suddenly released the stick, it flew into the air, over the boards, and struck in the face a lady spectator in the front row of seats. The game was stopped and Stewart was penalised by the referee for violation of the rules.

An action for personal injury was brought by the spectator and her husband, season ticket holders, against the stadium owners for inadequate protection for the spectators and against the two players for assault or negligence arising from their illegal struggle during the game.

The Ontario Court of Appeal dismissed the case against both the stadium owners and against Marucci and held Stewart to be liable for negligence to the spectator and her husband for damages and for loss. The court's reasoning in relation to the owners is of particular interest:

"Such an occupier is under a duty only to see that reasonable skill and care have been used to make (the premises) safe. He is obliged to guard spectators, not against every possible danger, but only against those which may reasonably be assumed possible to happen"[68]

That court cited with approval *Hall* v. *Brooklands Auto Racing Club*.[69] There had been, said the court in the *Maple Leaf Gardens* case, evidence of pucks escaping among the spectators but no evidence of this kind of incident. "The misadventure was of so unusual and unexpected a kind that it could not reasonably have been expected."[70] With regard to the negligent player Stewart, the court said he showed "reckless disregard for the safety of the spectators."[71] He knew or ought to have known that the people in the front row were in danger of injury, if he continued his struggle with Marucci. It was also, said the court, "not without importance that at the time of the accident, Stewart was not engaged in the course of play."[72]

With regard to the spectators, the court said they were taken to have assumed the risk of injury from known accidents, when no player was at fault. But the case in question was not that sort of case.

Rootes v. *Shelton*[73]

The plaintiff and two others were being towed by the defendant in his boat for water skiing. The plaintiff and the other two skiers had tow ropes of different lengths, so they could do "cross-overs" with one another. On one of these operations, the plaintiff struck a boat in the river where this sport was taking place. He was injured and sued the boatman for negligence in failing to take due care of his speedboat and for failing to warn the plaintiff of the presence of the stationary boat. (The plaintiff said he

---

[68] Laidlaw J.A. *Ibid.* at p. 371.
[69] [1933] 1 K.B. 205. Para. 7.30 (*supra*).
[70] The *Maple Leaf Gardens* case (*supra*) at p. 371.
[71] *Ibid.* at p. 372.
[72] *Ibid.* at p. 373.
[73] (1967) 116 C.L.R. 383.

was temporarily blinded from being able to see the stationary boat by spray.)

The High Court in Australia, on appeal from the Supreme Court of New South Wales, upheld the plaintiff's claim. He had assumed risks by participating in the sport, said the court. But those risks were the ones inherent in the sport. By doing so, the duty of care by one participant to another was not eliminated.[74]

Reese v. *Coleman and 27 others*[75]

A snowmobile race was held in Saskatchewan, where such races are a frequent occurrence. The plaintiff was one of about 500 spectators who had paid for admission. The track was oval and had been scraped out of snow to allow the participating machines to make their circuits. Because the machines might come off the track at the curves at the ends of the oval, spectators were not allowed there. But at the sides, called "the straight-ways," spectators watched on foot or in cars. Here also was the pit where machines were adjusted or repaired for the races.

The injury occurred when a snowmobile went out of control, left the track, came through the pit area at about 30 m.p.h. and struck the plaintiff. He was thrown through the air. The plaintiff recovered damages against the snowmobile driver and the judgment of the court concentrated on the liability of the club, the organisers of the races. The court adopted the principles laid down in the English *Brooklands* case and the Canadian *Maple Leaf Gardens* case, above, and said that the promoter was not liable for "injuries to paying spectators resulting from such risks as by the nature of the spectacle, the spectator must have understood and be presumed to have assumed."[76] The club had made a rule that a racer should not go through the pits; the court held that this meant that the club had by implication promised the plaintiff that by standing in the pits, he was standing in a safe area. The club's failure to protect this area was a breach of its duty to the plaintiff.

Magee v. *Prairie Dusters Motor-cycle Club, Laurence & Dunn*[77]

A racing competition was held by the defendants in a hilly area on a course more than a mile long. Spectators along the route were not protected by barriers, nor were they prevented from entering the track area, nor motor cycles from leaving it.

The plaintiff sold refreshments to the spectators and was injured when struck by the defendant on a motor cycle which went out of control. The plaintiff was just inside the track area when struck. The plaintiff failed in

---

[74] Barwick C.J. *Ibid.* at p. 383. The court also made some useful observations on the relation of the rules of a sport to the rules of the relevant law. "Non-compliance with such rules is one consideration to be attended to upon the question of reasonableness; but it is only one and it may be of much or little or even no weight in the circumstances." (Killo J.) *Ibid.* at p. 389.

[75] [1976] 3 W.L.R. 739.

[76] MacPherson J. *Ibid.* at p. 742.

[77] [1975] W.W.D. 165 (Western Weekly Digests), Saskatoon, No. 579, 24/9/75.

an action against the club and against the driver of the motor cycle. The court said the club was not negligent in not providing barriers. The defendant was a skilled driver and no excessive speed or lack of care was alleged against him. The case of *Wilks* v. *Cheltenham Home Guard Motor Cycle and Light Car Club* was applied. (See paragraph 7.31, *supra*.)

Klyne v. *Bellegarde Lloyd and Indian Head*[78]

In a game of ice hockey, in an arena owned by the defendant, in the town of Indian Head, the plaintiff suffered injury to an eye from being struck with the hockey stick of one of the players. He was standing in an aisle next to the ice rink boards round the arena at the time. The aisle had to be used by spectators for exit and entrance and they were not required to use the seats available. There were no protective shields over the boundary boards.

The plaintiff sued the club for negligence and succeeded in his claim. The club, said the court, should have foreseen injury by a player with his stick to a spectator and put protective guards above the boards. However, as the spectator was also negligent in standing where he did, damages were reduced by two-thirds. The case of *Reese* v. *Coleman* (above) was applied. The court said that the owner's liability was "not to ensure safety but to use reasonable care." (Halvorson J.)[79] The court made an interesting point about technical development. At the time of *Payne*'s case, transparent guards, in plexiglass or a similar material, were not available or economically feasible. "The predicament of the arena owner was thus considered favourably."[80] But the changed situation allowed the court to say that he should have put up some protective guards. "Custom is lagging behind technical and engineering capacity."[81]

The risk of a flying puck at a game of ice hockey was one accepted by the spectators, said the court. This did not mean that the spectators accepted the risk of being hit over the head by a hockey stick.[82]

The regular reference in each of these cases, not only to earlier sporting accidents considered in their own Commonwealth countries but also to the leading English reports, has clearly contributed to the even development of this branch of the law, both in this country and in the Commonwealth countries concerned.

6. **The Safety of Sports Grounds Act 1975**

This Act is discussed generally in Chapter 4. Since 1975, a large number **7.37** of Designation Orders have been made. The Safety of Sports Grounds Regulations 1976 (S.I. 1976 No. 1263) contain full details of the procedure

---

[78] *Klyne*'s case [1978] 6 W.W.R. 743.
[79] Halvorson J. *Ibid.* at p. 746.
[80] *Ibid.* at p. 747.
[81] *Ibid.* at p. 747.
[82] *Ibid.* at p. 748.

to be followed in applying for a Safety Certificate. This includes the hearing of the application, the inspection of the ground, the notices to be served on interested parties and the rights of appeal to the Secretary of State, both for general and for special Safety Certificates.

7. **Private Sports Clubs**

7.38 There are no doubt thousands of sports clubs in this country which fall into the category, in law, of unincorporated associations. They handle business contracts of all kinds, for catering, sports supplies, or building; they host competitions where large sums of money are involved. Yet not being local authorities or limited companies, they are simply groups of individuals, banded together as sports clubs. They have their rules, they agree that the committee can act for the members. But when it comes to legal action in the courts, the club dissolves. "Such a fluid or anonymous aggregate is not a fit party to sue or be sued," said an Australian legal writer.[83] He was troubled by the gap between the law and the real world, where such clubs exist and discharge their day to day duties effectively. Four comments are offered on this situation, particularly since local authorities regularly act in close liaison with such clubs in providing the leisure facilities sought by the public.

(1) Such clubs can and do appoint trustees from their members to act in land transactions, as conveyances or leases. This arrangement is effective. Yet the trustees are still acting for the club, for the association and not for themselves. "As long as they act *intra vires* the trustees are purely nominal holders, with a full right to indemnity from the club fund."[84]

(2) When the committee itself is brought into the legal action, it is to enable the club to sue and be sued.[85]

(3) Such a members club can be a "voluntary association" with which a local authority can deal when making grants or loans, under the Local Government (Miscellaneous Provisions) Act 1976.[86]

(4) When the above Act of 1976 empowers a local authority also to make available the various sporting facilities for the use of clubs and societies, this by implication accepts licences or leases as the necessary and normal legal machinery for effecting such arrangements.[87]

---

[83] Prof. S. Stoljar, "Sporting Clubs and Corporate Theory," Melbourne Law Review (1982) Vol. 13, p. 491.

[84] *Ibid.* at p. 495.

[85] See *Carlisle and Silloth Golf Club* v. *Smith* [1913] 3 K.B. 75, where the club as a club was held liable for tax on gate and green fees. The case of *Miller* v. *Jackson* [1977] 3 W.L.R. 21, the cricket club case, was typical in that the chairman and secretary of the club were sued by the aggrieved neighbours "on their own behalf and on behalf of all the other members of the club." *Ibid.* at p. 22. (See Chap. 1.) R.S.C. Ord. 15, r. 12, provides the High Court machinery for such representative actions.

[86] s.19(3). This opinion treats such a club as "a person carrying on an undertaking otherwise than for profit," within the section.

[87] The limit on the length of such a lease, without Ministerial authorisation, is seven years: Local Government, Planning and Land Act 1980. s.123.

D. HORSE RIDING

The popular sport of horse riding, for many years a private leisure **7.39**
activity, becomes part of the public leisure services, partly because parliament has, in two Acts, put reins on the riding establishments in the Riding Establishment Acts of 1964 and 1970, the provisions of which may be summarised as follows:

(1) Local authorities are required to license riding establishments.[88] As part of that process, they are to obtain and consider a report of a veterinary surgeon on the establishment.

(2) The authority has to be satisfied on seven points, covering the stabling, its ventilation and drainage, fire risk, adequacy in relation to disease, pasture, and food as well as the applicant's experience in horse management.[89] This first list in the Act of 1964 was significantly extended in the later Act of 1970, to refer to care for the horses and the availability of the Fire Service telephone number.

(3) A provisional licence for three months was a device introduced in the later Act. This allowed fuller deliberation by the authority and more time for the applicant to install all necessary facilities.[90]

(4) The basic licence is for 12 months, renewed annually.[91]

(5) Against refusal there lies an appeal to the magistrates' court.[92]

(6) A riding establishment must never be left in the charge of a person under 16 years of age.[93]

(7) The licence holder must have an insurance policy to cover the risks undertaken by his riders.[94]

(8) He must also keep a register of his horses.[95]

(9) A series of offences is set out in the Acts. These cover concealing horses from inspectors, defective equipment, as well as unsatisfactory keeping of the horses. The Horses (Protective Headgear for Young Riders) Act 1990 adds a potential liability to managers of riding schools who take young riders onto "roads" as distinct from fields, footpaths and bridleways. Appropriate helmets are now a legal requirement.[96] The Act of 1970 also tightened the law about those horses which were not to be the subject of hiring.[97]

---

[88] Riding Establishment Act 1964, s.1. This means District Councils, the Common Council of the City of London and London Boroughs. There are four exemptions from the licensing requirements, *i.e.* Defence Department premises, police premises, premises of the Zoological Society of London or a university which provides an approved course for veterinary students.

[89] *Ibid.* s.1(4) and Riding Establishment Act 1970, s.2.

[90] Riding Establishment Act 1970, s.1.

[91] Riding Establishment Act 1964, s.1(7).

[92] *Ibid.* s.1(5).

[93] Riding Establishment Act 1970, s.2, becoming s.4A of the Act of 1964.

[94] *Ibid.*

[95] *Ibid.*

[96] s.1 of the Horses (Protective Headgear for Young Riders) Act 1990 makes it an offence to "permit" a contravention to take place. Regulations under the Act with details of exemptions, the types of headgear and the manner of using it, are still awaited as we go to press.

[97] *Ibid.* s.3, as amended by the 1964 Act, s.3, being seven offences in all.

The three classes are:
  (a) Any horse aged three years or under.
  (b) Any mare heavy with foal.
  (c) Any mare within three months of foaling.[98]

E. WATER RECREATION

1. **Boats**

(1) *Provision*

7.40 The public leisure services charter, that is to be found in the Local Government (Miscellaneous Provisions) Act 1976, section 19, includes boats.[99] This takes up and extends a power that was granted to local authorities a century ago, to provide boats in their lakes, in their parks or pleasure grounds.[1] This recent power is in relation to inland and coastal waters. In coastal waters, there are many privately managed boating facilities which fall within the scope of the Merchant Shipping Acts as the guide for management.

Boats for use in pleasure grounds are currently dealt with in the Public Health Act 1961.[2]

(2) *Licensing of Pleasure Boats and Boatmen*

7.41 The Public Health Acts Amendment Act 1907 grants to local authorities the power to grant licences, on such terms as they think fit, for the pleasure boats and also for the boatmen.[3]

The boats

The pleasure boats and pleasure vessels thus regulated, are those to be let for hire to the public or used for carrying passengers for hire. The licences incur annual fees to the licensing authority. The licences may be suspended or revoked by the licensing authority, when they deem such

---

[98] The basic definition relates to the carrying on of a business of keeping horses to let them out on hire for riding, or for use in providing instruction in riding for payment, or both.

[99] s.19(1)(c): "facilities for boating" is the expression, which is taken to include not only the boats but the waterway or lake, any jetty or landing stage needed for the public use. "Boats" are in law for use in inland waters, "ships" for the sea. "Hovercraft" becomes a ship when used at sea and a boat when used on inland waters or harbours—Hovercraft Act 1968, ss.3 and 4(3).

[1] Public Health Act 1875, s.172, now repealed; Local Government Planning and Land Act 1980, Sched. 34, Pt. XVI.

[2] Public Health Act 1961, s.54. The power covers associated buildings, and facilities as well as letting of the management of the boating lake.

[3] Public Health Acts Amendment Act 1907, s.94 as amended by the Local Government (Miscellaneous Provisions) Act 1976, s.18, and again by the Local Government Planning and Land Act 1980, s.186.

266

action to be necessary in the public interest. The existence of this power must be plainly stated in the licence. A right of appeal against this action is granted to the licence holder in the Act of 1907.[4]

It is an offence to let for hire a boat or pleasure vessel, when not duly licensed. Guidance is given in the Act of 1907 about some of the contents of a boat licence. For instance, the licensee has to paint his own name and the number of permitted passengers on a conspicuous part of the boat or vessel. Vessels licensed by the Board of Trade under the Merchant Shipping Acts are exempted from this licensing procedure. Again, no licence is required under the above Act of 1907 for pleasure boats or pleasure vessels on any canal owned or managed by the British Waterways Board.[5] The section of the Act of 1907 about the licensing of both boats and boatmen, operates only in those districts approved by Order of the Secretary of State.[6]

The absence of a definition of "pleasure boat" has given rise over the years to doubts about the application of these licensing provisions to specific situations. It seems evident that a boat can be a pleasure boat, for the purposes of section 94 of the above Act of 1907, when used for enjoyment and pleasure trips, even if at other times, the boat is used for commercial fishing work.

The boatmen

The licensing requirements of the Act of 1907 extend also to the boat- **7.42** men. These are defined as "the boatmen or persons in charge of or navigating such boats or vessels."[7] These licences also carry an annual fee. Powers of suspension or cancellation are available to the licensing authority for them, as for those licences relating to the boats. The wording of the offence committed by the person, who carries passengers for hire in an unlicensed pleasure boat, was revised in 1976 so that it now reads[8]:

"No person shall carry or permit to be carried passengers for hire in any pleasure boat or vessel unless:
  (a) the boat or vessel is so licensed and the licence is not suspended; and
  (b) the person in charge of the boat or vessel or any other person navigating it is so licensed and his licence is not suspended and the conditions of his licence are complied with."

When the boat or vessel is licensed by the Department of Trade and Industry, as above, it is not necessary to have a boatman's licence, under the Act of 1907.[9]

---

[4] Public Health Acts Amendment Act 1907, s.94(7).
[5] Local Government Planning and Land Act 1980, s.186.
[6] Public Health Acts Amendment Act 1907, s.3.
[7] *Ibid.* s.94.
[8] Local Government (Miscellaneous Provisons) Act 1976, s.18.
[9] *Ibid.*

(3) *By-laws*

7.43 The local authority which licenses boats and boatmen under the above Act of 1907 may also make by-laws for regulating the use of such boats.[10]

The by-laws may:

(a) Regulate the specification of the pleasure boats.

(b) Regulate their use, in order to prevent navigation in a dangerous manner or without due care and attention and without reasonable consideration for other persons.

(c) Require the use of effectual silencers, on pleasure boats propelled by internal combustion engines.

The Secretary of State is the confirming authority for such by-laws. These by-laws can be effective, not only within the area of a local authority, but also within a distance seawards, not more than 1,000 metres from the low water mark; they are of no effect, to the extent that they are in conflict with by-laws made by bodies manning the docks or piers in the district of the local authority in question.

Since the subject-matter of the by-laws is limited by the Act of 1961, the local authority wishing to impose additional requirements is left to include them in the licences. These might cover carrying capacity, the range of activity or the qualifications of the boatmen. In so far as the boats towing water skiers are also pleasure boats, by-laws framed to keep within section 76 of the Public Health Act 1961 above, could deal with their use too, though not their construction. By-laws for pleasure boats and their boatmen on inland waters as here defined, are now empowered by the Local Government Planning & Land Act 1980, section 185. Again these are carefully limited powers, dealing with subjects such as the naming and numbering of boats and their mooring places and the good conduct of boatmen.

(4) *Application*

7.44 An interesting case arose in the courts in 1979 when an injunction was obtained in the Court of Appeal against a motor boat racing club, on account of the noise it created. The case was *Kennaway* v. *Thompson*,[11] and the location was a man-made lake of some 38 acres in Gloucestershire. The injunction was obtained by the owner of an adjoining house. At the first hearing, nuisance was proved and the judge considered damages for the past nuisance and for the diminution in the value of the house (£1,000 and £15,000 respectively) to be a satisfactory award for the successful claimant. The householder, being aggrieved not to obtain an injunction, appealed and thus the main issues in the Court of Appeal were the merits and otherwise of damages and an injunction. In due course, the Court of Appeal decided that an injunction was appropriate. However, in view of the plaintiff's knowledge when her house was being built that some motor racing took place on the lake, the injunction was qualified. At the time of

[10] Public Health Act 1961, s.76.
[11] [1981] Q.B. 88.

the hearing, racing every weekend from March to November was proved and noise levels touching 100 decibels measured.

The limits in the court injunction were interesting and as follows:

(a) International events—one per season—duration three days.

(b) National events—two per season—duration two days. Spacing between these three major events—four weeks.

(c) Club events—duration one day, with three week spacings from the other events.

(d) Limits on the decibels.

(e) Limits to other club activities, including water skiing.

This order resulted from the court's approach, as Lawton L.J. said, "There must be a measure of give and take and live and let live."[12]

2. **Fishing**

Introduction

The sport of fishing is, in the context of this work, one where limits have **7.45** to be imposed. The subject, in legal terms, extends from Common Market policy to the niceties of the question of when a fish has been appropriated to the ownership of a fisherman, so that trespass and poaching may be defined and controlled.

Fishing in the sea and tidal waters has given rise to a considerable amount of legislation, of which the Sea Fisheries Regulation Act 1966, and the Sea Fisheries Act 1968 are recent examples. Fishing in inland waters is the subject of the Salmon and Freshwater Fisheries Act 1975, a recent consolidating measure, which greatly eases the task of those who wish to see a broad picture of legislation in that field.

Seals and whales have attracted legislation on their own account and lead the reader to ancient laws on the Royal Prerogative, in relation to whales and sturgeon.

Lastly, the land law of this country, is the basis for the law about fishing waters, since ownership of the soil carries with it ownership of the water and all within it, until parliament or the agreements of men lead to variants.

Against this background, a work attempting to select the law of the public leisure services must omit sea fishing, as being primarily commercial and also seals and whales, for the same reason, and will therefore concentrate on:

(1) The Salmon and Freshwater Fisheries Act 1975.

(2) Land law, so far as it bears upon fishing as a leisure pursuit.

(1) *The Salmon and Freshwater Fisheries Act 1975*

This is a consolidating Act of 43 sections and 5 Schedules. It repeals five **7.46** earlier Acts and it is convenient to consider its provisions in relation to

---

[12] [1981] Q.B. 88 at p. 94D.

unlawful practices, licensing, by-laws, National Rivers Authority duties and offences.

Unlawful practices and obstructions

Parts I and II of this Act of 1975 list the prohibited implements and methods of fishing, *i.e.* firearms, otter lath or jack, wire or snare, a cross-line or set line, a spear, gaff or stroke haul; a snatch or similar instrument, a light, stone throwing or use of other missiles to take or kill salmon, trout or other freshwater fish.

The Act proceeds to outline the prohibited techniques of fishing in relation to roe, spawning or unclean fish, namely nets, poisonous matter and polluting effluent, explosives, poisons, dams, and electrical devices. "Obstructions" is a general term used in the Act of 1975, when listing prohibited methods of fishing, *i.e.* fixed engines, fishing weirs, fishing mill-dams, new dams without fish passes, boxes and cribs in weirs and dams, taking salmon or trout above or below obstructions or mill races, except as permitted in the Act.[13] These prohibitions are supplemented by the creation of an offence for obstructing a legally authorised person who is engaged on work on fish passes or National Rivers Authority gratings. These safeguard water flow, as distinct from that "frequented by salmon or migratory trout."[14]

Licences

7.47   The licensing of fishing falls upon the National Rivers Authority set up by the Water Act 1989.[15] The fish in question are salmon, trout and (unless excused by the Ministry of Agriculture, Fisheries and Food) also all other freshwater fish and eels.[16] A licence defines the area, the duration and the name of the licensee. It is personal, except that the licensee's servant or agent can use the licence in defined circumstances.[17] The person or association entitled to an exclusive right to fish, may be granted a general fishing licence by the National Rivers Authority. This entitles any other person, duly authorised by the secretary of the association or the individual licence holder, also to enjoy the right of fishing in the inland waters in question.[18] Licence duties are regulated by Schedule 2 of the Act of 1975. The fishing licence does not authorise the erection of structures or the use of installations or instruments which would otherwise be illegal.

The number of fishing licences granted by the National Rivers Authority for the areas there defined can be limited by Order confirmed by the

---

[13] Salmon and Freshwater Fisheries Act 1975, s.17. An unattended net suspended in tidal waters to catch herring was a "fixed engine" said the Court in *Gray* v. *Blamey* [1991] 1 All E.R. 1.

[14] *Ibid.* s.15(1)(*a*).

[15] s.141 and Sched. 17.

[16] Salmon and Freshwater Fisheries Act 1975, s.41(2), (acting with the Secretary of State for Wales, as appropriate).

[17] *Ibid.* Sched. 2, paras. 9–14.

[18] *Ibid.* s.25(7).

Minister.[19] The limit will take the form of an annual maximum number and the arrangement is not to be made for more than ten years. The licences in question are those for salmon and trout (other than rainbow trout), with any instrument specified, other than rod and line. The Act contains a procedure for determining the number of licences thus limited; that procedure is designed to hold the balance between "the conservation of the fishery"[20] and those persons who have held a fishing licence previously and are "dependent on fishing for their livelihood."[21]

It is an offence to fish in regulated inland waters without a licence.[22] Part II of the Act of 1975 and Schedule 1 contain the various close seasons for salmon, trout, other freshwater fish and eels. Those parts of the same Act also set out restrictions on the export and the consignment of salmon and trout.[23]

By-laws

Under the Water Act of 1989 the making of by-laws is a function of the **7.48** National Rivers Authority.[24] Such by-laws require confirmation by the Minister (or Ministers, in the case of Wales).

The Act of 1975 sets out 18 purposes with which the by-laws may deal. They are all aspects of regulating fishing in the waters of the Authority.[25]

Duties of the Water Authorities

The Act of 1975, in section 28, sets out the duties now transferred to the **7.49** National Rivers Authority as being:
  (a) To maintain, improve and develop the salmon fisheries, the trout fisheries, the freshwater fisheries and the eel fisheries in its area.
  (b) To establish advisory committees of persons interested in the fisheries of that area and consult them on the various duties set out in (a) above.

There are regional rivers advisory committees set up under these powers in National Rivers Authority areas.

The Ministers may make Orders by way of Statutory Instrument to regulate the above groups of fisheries in particular areas.[26]

Offences

The offences created by the Act of 1975 are set out in Schedule 4 of the **7.50** Act, with corresponding fines or terms of imprisonment.

---

[19] Salmon and Freshwater Fisheries Act 1975, s.26. and Water Act 1989, Sched. 17, para. 6.
[20] *Ibid.* s.26(5).
[21] *Ibid.* s.26(4). A case on this phrase confirmed its latent scope for argument. "How dependent?" was the issue in *R. v. S.W. Water Authority, ex p. Cox, The Times,* January 2, 1982.
[22] *Ibid.* s.27.
[23] *Ibid.* ss.23 and 24.
[24] Water Act 1989, s.186 and Sched. 24.
[25] Salmon and Freshwater Fisheries Act 1975, s.28 and Sched. 3.
[26] *Ibid.* s.28(3) and (4). as amended in Sched. 17 of the above Act of 1989.

The National Rivers Authority is entitled to appoint water bailiffs to enforce the law and detect these manifold and often cunning offences, armed, as may be necessary, with search or other warrants for that purpose.[27]

(2) *Land Law and Fishing*

7.51 A right to fish goes in law with the ownership of the soil over which the water lies, be it stream, lake, pool, or river.

Because a fishery is a profit of the land, as distinct from an estate in the land, it can be sold or bequeathed or otherwise transferred separately from the land.

There are a number of technical terms which are used in land law:

(a) A *several fishery* is an exclusive right of fishing in a given place.

(b) A *common of fishery* is a right of fishing in another person's water, in common with other persons.

A fishery may be kept with the land to which it relates. When transferred separately, a lease or licence can be used, depending on the nature and duration of the right the owner wishes to give.

In an non-tidal river, the law presumes ownership of the fishery by a riparian owner to the middle of the water. This can be varied by the two riparian owners so that one may own the fishery over the whole water.

A right to use the river bank for fishing can be acquired by prescription, *i.e* twelve years' uninterrupted use for that purpose.

The Theft Act 1968[28] creates an offence for unlawfully taking or destroying any fish in water which is private property or in which there is a private right of fishing. The offence is absolute.

3. **Canals**

7.52 In 1947, 18 listed canals were taken into public ownership by the Transport Act 1947.[29] Initially the property of the Transport Commission, they came, in due course, under the authority of the British Waterways Board, which currently manages them. They are used for both commercial and leisure service purposes; this account is limited to the statutes and common law relating to the leisure service use. That use has been extended and the Board has been involved in opening for this use lengths of disused or blocked canals.

The British Waterways Board is placed under a duty by the Transport Act 1962 in wide terms:

"To provide, to such extent as they may think expedient, [. . .] ser-

---

[27] Salmon and Freshwater Fisheries Act 1975, ss.31–36. The Salmon Act 1986, s.32 defines in some detail a new offence of "receiving" stolen salmon, in the Act referred to as "handling."

[28] Sched. 1, para. 21.

[29] s.12 and Sched. 3. Others not nationalised were referred to as "independent inland waterway undertakings." Transport Act 1962, s.52.

vices and facilities on the inland waterways owned or managed by them."[30]

Part VII of the Transport Act 1968 provides the main group of statutory law about the canals of this country. It divides canals into commercial, cruising and the remainder. "Cruising" waterways are those "principally available for cruising, fishing or other recreational purposes."[31] These canals are separately listed in Schedule 12 of the above Act of 1968. They now number 28 and are described in detail. The description is qualified only by the words: "the main navigable channels of the following waterways." The duty of the Waterways Board in relation to the cruising canals is:

> "to maintain the cruising waterways in a suitable condition for use by cruising craft, that is to say, vessels constructed or adapted for the carriage of passengers and driven by mechanical power."[32]

A standard is included in the section, for the vessels for which the Board is to provide canals as above, *i.e.* those which customarily used that waterway during the nine months between April and December 1967.[33]

It is of interest that the guideline generally given to the Waterways Board about a commercially meritorious management policy, "in the most economic manner possible and to secure the best possible financial return," is not laid down in relation to the cruising canals.[34]

The Transport Act 1968 set up the Inland Waterways Amenity Advisory Council of persons with knowledge and interest in the use of inland waterways for amenity or recreational purposes including fishing. This Council advises the Board and the Minister on these aspects of their duties.[35] The Act of 1968 authorises local authorities to assist other persons to maintain or improve waterways in or accessible to their areas for amenity or recreational purposes, including fishing.[36] The Board is granted extensive powers to make by-laws.[37]

Towpaths

A towpath alongside a canal is often a public highway, though the soil   **7.53**
remains in the canal owners. The dedication for highway use may be specific or the result of prescription (*i.e.* 20 years uninterrupted user). It can even then be defined as a use which recognises the rights of the canal undertakers to use the same towpath for their own legitimate purpose, *e.g.*

---

[30] Transport Act 1962, s.10(1)(*a*).
[31] Transport Act 1968, s.104.
[32] *Ibid.* s.105.
[33] *Ibid.* s.105(2). The Minister is empowered by Order to vary that duty on the Board, if the development of design for cruising vessels makes it desirable to do so: *ibid.* s.105(3).
[34] Transport Act 1968, s.107.
[35] *Ibid.* s.110.
[36] *Ibid.* s.114.
[37] British Transport Commission Act 1954, s.16.

the horse and its rope.[38] The by-law making powers of the Board include the prohibition of passing along a towpath without the consent of the Board.[39]

4. Inland Waters

7.54 Boating and fishing are the main leisure service activities associated with the inland waters of this country. This subsection gathers together other legal provisions affecting inland water recreation; these can be conveniently grouped about those relating to the National and Country Parks, those about other inland waters and, thirdly, the bearing of the common law on these matters.

(1) *National and Country Parks*

7.55 As National and Country Parks comprise the main scenically attractive parts of the country, it is not surprising that among their statutory controls are a number about water recreation.

A local planning authority, whose area includes the whole or part of a National Park, may stimulate the enjoyment of bathing, boating, fishing, sailing and other forms of recreation in the waters on its boundary.[40] Similar powers are available for a local authority in relation to a Country Park in its area.[41]

The use of land for such activities may depend on negotiation with owners, unless an Access Order or Agreement, as discussed in Chapter 8, has facilitated that use.[42]

The local authority has powers to make by-laws about the matters described above.[43]

Lakes in National Parks are the subject of a separate section in the Countryside Act 1968. This authorises by-laws to prohibit or restrict traffic on those lakes.[44] The purposes of those by-laws are to be:

(a) To ensure the safety of the persons resorting to the lake.
(b) To regulate sports and in particular the use of boats and other vessels.[45]

---

[38] See, *e.g. Grand Junction Canal Co.* v. *Petty* [1888] 21 Q.B. 273. "The public must be taken to have accepted it as a limited dedication. . . . If the horse or the towrope and the foot passengers are in one another's way, the foot passenger must look out for himself and get out of the way." Though this may speak of another age, it underlines the dual use likely on towpaths.

[39] s.16, see n. 37, *supra.*

[40] National Parks and Access to the Countryside Act 1949, s.13, and Countryside Act 1968, s.12. Local authority action of the sort described is authorised only when such existing facilities are inadequate. Local authorities are encouraged to agree on joint public action. The Minister can require them to act if necessary: s.13 of the 1949 Act.

[41] Access orders and agreements are made under Pt. V of the above Act of 1949, s.74 of which says that access arrangements apply to waterways.

[42] *Ibid.* National Parks and Access to the Countryside Act 1949, s.12(5).

[43] Countryside Act 1968, s.8.

[44] *Ibid.* s.13.

[45] "Boat" includes hover vehicle or craft. *Ibid.* s.49.

(c) To conserve the natural beauty of the lake and its surrounding area.

(d) To prevent damage or nuisance, especially in relation to excessive noise.

The local planning authority must consult the Countryside Commission about such by-laws and act in the context of the two main guidelines for National Parks in sections 1 and 5 of the National Parks and Access to the Countryside Act 1949.[46]

Such by-laws cannot relate to the lakes of a statutory undertaking or a river authority. They cannot override private property rights. They may be jointly enforced by any other local authority with property from its area in that National Park.

The draftsmen of the National Parks and Access to the Countryside Act **7.56** 1949 had water recreation in mind when they defined land as including land covered with water, for the purposes of that Act.[47] "Waterway" was a generic term then introduced as meaning "any lake river canal or other waters," being (in any case) waters suitable, or which can be rendered suitable, for sailing, boating, bathing or fishing.[48] "Open country" was another expression carefully defined to give full scope to water, whether it were canal, river or some other expanse of water.[49] In making provision for access orders and agreements, which would enable the public to enjoy the open country, the Act of 1949, supplemented by the Countryside Act 1968, contained detail to ensure that, *e.g.* small boat users could have full and satisfactory access to a waterway. So if they had to carry a small boat "to circumvent obstacles or obstructions on the water by passing round on foot with their boats,"[50] this was a situation that local authorities and the Commission had to consider when framing their access documents. Another example is the case of "obtaining access from a highway to a convenient launching place for small boats."[51]

(2) *Other Inland Waters*

Reservoirs are frequently made available for water recreation. The statu- **7.57** tory provision on this point is the Countryside Act 1968, section 22, supplemented by the Water Act 1989, section 8. The relevant Water Authority is to "take steps to secure the use of water and land associated with water for "recreational purposes and is so made available in the best manner." The Authorities, following privatisation in the 1989 Act, have moreover a duty generally to "promote the use of such waters and land for recreational purposes."[52] The section is a strong and positive one. A Code

---

[46] See Chapter 8 on Open Air Activity.
[47] National Parks and Access to the Countryside Act 1949, s.114.
[48] *Ibid.* s.114(1).
[49] Countryside Act 1968, s.16.
[50] *Ibid.* s.16(4).
[51] *Ibid.*
[52] Water Act 1989, s.8(4).

of Practice has advanced this matter and the following extract is illuminating.[53]

6.2.4. Use of water and associated land for recreation

Certain general considerations should underlie the policies of the relevant bodies towards provision for recreation.

   (a) Recognition of the social importance of sport and recreation and the particular contributions which they are in a position to make in this field.
   (b) Contribution, as circumstances allow, to the wider provision of opportunities for sport and recreation and to secure the best use of suitable existing and new resources.
   (c) Consultation on a regular basis with the regional councils for sport and recreation and with appropriate representatives of users of their sporting and recreational facilities.
   (d) The need to cater fairly and equitably for as broad a range of interest groups as practicable.
   (e) The need to ensure that the recreational needs of the surrounding area are taken fully into account, and not unreasonably prejudiced by proposals designed to meet more specialised demands.

The relevant bodies are expected to ensure that the arrangements made by water authorities as to access are not disturbed, so far as is reasonable and practicable.

In the establishment and operation of specific facilities, the principal considerations which should be taken into account are the following:

   (a) Subject to suitable terms and conditions, public use of sporting and recreational facilities, once established, should be maintained by the grant or renewal of leases of licences.
   (b) Facilities which become available should be offered for recognised recreational pursuits on terms which take account of those applying to similar facilities elsewhere.
   (c) Existing users of sporting and recreational facilities on land or water belonging to the relevant bodies, together with appropriate conservation bodies, should be consulted prior to the introduction on those lands or waters of any new sporting or recreational activity.
   (d) In considering what steps to take in performance of their recreational duty, provision should be made, where possible, for the needs of chronically sick or disabled people.
   (e) Reasonable account should be taken of the need for public car parks, toilets and picnic sites; and facilities upon reasonable conditions for groups to study nature, geology or archaeology on otherwise restricted sites.

As with similar Codes, it is stated that breaches are not of themselves breaches of civil or criminal law but may be taken into account by Minis-

[53] Water & Sewerage (Conservation, Access and Recreation) (Code of Practice) Order 1989 (S.I. 1989 No. 1152).

ters when considering their general powers of enforcement under the Statute.[54] If a reservoir is a "large raised reservoir," being over 25,000 cubic metres capacity and above ground level, then whether called a dam or a reservoir, it comes within the regulatory provisions of the Reservoirs Act 1975, since this Act deals with artificial lakes not used for water supply purposes. A register of such undertakings is kept by the metropolitan districts and London borough councils and county councils; an engineer's certificate is needed every ten years about its safety and if it should be abandoned or the water level lowered, statutory safety precautions must be observed. If the Rule in *Rylands* v. *Fletcher*, discussed in Chapter 1, is the response of the Common Law to the evident danger in a large raised reservoir, then this is the current statutory complement, in terms of safety regulations.

(3) *The Common Law and Water Rights*

This may be a suitable point to take note of certain fundamental common law principles relating to rights concerning water.   **7.58**

Water flowing in defined or undefined channels is not, at common law, capable of ownership; it is when the water has been taken into possession, in reservoirs, pools, tanks or pits, for instance, that it can be "owned." The owner of the land on which the water stands is then also the owner of the water; if the pool stands on land with two owners, one on each side, then the water also is owned by those two landowners in proportion to their land holdings.

Whilst flowing water is not owned, it can be used. The Water Resources Act 1973 has considerately modified the common law on this point and under the Act of 1973, a licence is required from the National Rivers Authority for the abstraction of water, except where taken for domestic purposes or for agricultural purposes other than spray irrigation.[55]

Unless there is evidence to the contrary, the common law presumes that the owners of the banks or sides of non-tidal waters own the land forming the bed of the waters to the centre line of the water.[56] If one person owns land on both sides of, say, a river, he will be the presumed owner of all the river bed.[57]

In general, there is no public right of navigation in a non-tidal river or   **7.59** inland lake; these are under the control of the riparian owners.[58] However, a right of navigation can arise by grant from those riparian owners, by statute or by prescriptive use, similar to the creation of a highway over land.

---

[54] Water Act 1989, s.10.
[55] Water Resources Act 1973, s.24. and Water Act 1989.
[56] *Lamb* v. *Newbiggin* [1844] 1 Car. & King 549, also the recent interesting case of *Lovett* v. *Fairclough* (1990) 61 P. & C.R. 385 about fishing across the middle line of the Tweed which was also the boundary between England and Scotland.
[57] *Blount* v. *Layard* [1891] 2 Ch. 681.
[58] *Hargreaves* v. *Diddams* [1875] L.R. 10 Q.B. 582.

Where a right of navigation does exist, it does not extend to landing on the banks of the water, to towing along the bank, to mooring or to fishing: the consent of the owner is required for any of these purposes.

Statute is now involved in the regulation of rights in many non-tidal waters, particularly where public expense assisted in the formation of improved navigation. With docks and harbours, statute is usually the paramount legal governing factor.

5. The Seaside

(1) *Bathing*

7.60   A local authority may make by-laws to regulate public bathing at the seaside.[59] The power is now in the Public Health Act 1936.[60] The by-laws may deal with areas of bathing, the times for bathing, the location of bathing huts or tents, the provision of life-saving appliances and the navigation of pleasure boats in relation to bathing areas. The by-laws may also regulate "so far as decency requires," the costumes to be worn by bathers.[61]

We have in these days to take account of the classification "BW1" as applying to territorial, coastal or inland waters which meet the definition of bathing waters within EC Directive 76/160/EEC. Our United Kingdom Regulations applying the mandatory standards in the Directive are the Bathing Waters (Classification) Regulations 1991,[62] under the Water Act 1989 sections 104, 171 and 185(2). The Directive contains 19 parameters, described as "physical, chemical and micro-biological," a timetable for implementation and provisions to restrict derogation from the standards by member states where "a risk to public health is involved."[63]

(2) *The Foreshore*

7.61   The foreshore is that part of the seashore which lies between the high and low water marks of ordinary spring tides. Seabed, lying below low water mark of medium tides, is Crown Estate property and the Crown's proprietary jurisdiction extends to the limit of territorial waters. The foreshore itself, around the coasts of the United Kingdom, is also in great part in the Crown Estate. The important exceptions include the counties of Cornwall and Lancaster, where the respective Duchies own the foreshore. The other exceptions are lengths of coast where grants have been made to

---

[59] For an academic discussion of whether a right to bathe in the sea exists, see *Brinckman* v. *Matley* [1904] 2 Ch. 313.

[60] s.231. (The power extends to rivers and lakes.) The purpose, 150 years ago, was to segregate the sexes. The wording has altered with successive Acts to that in the Public Health Act 1936, which seems a little out of date now. The model by-laws keep abreast of social mores.

[61] *Ibid.* s.231(1)(*d*).

[62] S.I. 1991 No. 1597.

[63] Art. 8.

individuals or other bodies, such as the National Trust, especially in some of the major estuaries.[64]

The term "foreshore" is a legal technical term.[65] "Seashore" has been treated, judicially, as equivalent[66] but "beach" was looked on as vague. It became important to define this area of land and its ownership when reclamation of land from the sea was undertaken in the sixteenth century. A subsequent treatise on the law of the sea in the seventeenth century supplied our modern definition of the foreshore.[67]

Baxendale v. *Instow Parish Church*[68] raised a practical point about the definition of the foreshore in North Devon, under the Commons Registration Act 1965. The estate owners had a conveyance of 1855 which, in detailed wording and with the aid of a plan, identified a plot of land which "lay between high water mark and low water mark and is covered with water at ordinary tides." Since 1855, the sea had receded and left this plot standing above high water mark. Was the "high water mark" that which was inscribed on the 1855 conveyance or the mark to be seen on the ground by beachcombers in the 1960s?   **7.62**

The Devon County Council registered this strip of old foreshore as waste land of a manor under the Commons Registration Act 1965, *i.e.* as common land. Sir R. Megarry V.-C. ruled against the local authorities when this action was challenged in his Chancery court. The conveyance was so precise, he said, that it did not allow for the use of any rule about moveable freeholds. The land must be taken off the register, since the objection had been made and sustained by the successors of the 1855 conveyance.

Taking shingle

Laird v. *Briggs*[69] concerned an action by the tenant in possession of part   **7.63** of the foreshore at Margate to stop the defendant removing shingle from the shore. The defendant claimed 40 years prescription at first and he made the same claim for a right to place bathing huts on the beach. In the course of the case this claim was abandoned and the plaintiff won. The case is a simple illustration of the rights of a foreshore owner, here the Marquis of Conyngham, to charge for the rights enjoyed by others on the foreshore.

This case involved a personal plaintiff and a personal defendant. Some cases have related to the efforts of groups of persons to establish rights over the foreshore. The inhabitants of a village or of a parish are examples of these sorts of actions. As with other customary rights claimed in

---

[64] See The Crown Estate, HMSO 1980, annual report, para. 74. There are many examples of industrial development on the foreshore, given in this report.
[65] See *Tito* v. *Waddel* (*No. 2*) [1977] 2 W.L.R. 496 at p. 644, *per* Megarry V.-C.
[66] *Mellor* v. *Walmsley* [1905] 2 Ch. 164 at pp. 174, 175, 177 and 179.
[67] *De Jure Maris*: Sir Matthew Hale. The Local Government Act 1972 describes local government areas on the coast as stretching at least to "the low water mark" (s.72), whilst the Countryside Act 1968, s.8, refers to country parks "bounded by the sea."
[68] [1981] 2 W.L.R. 1055.
[69] [1880] Ch.D. 440.

Chapter 6, these foreshore claims have foundered if the class of persons making the claim has been fluctuating and thus undefinable.[70]

Taking mussels

7.64 *Loose* v. *Castleton*[71] related to a person who took mussels from a mussel scalp or bed on the coast of the Wash. Action in the courts was successful in bringing this practice to a stop. The plaintiff was the lessee of the alleged rights of shellfishery on that foreshore. The case turned on the historical merits of the plaintiff's claim. Though not precisely traceable to the time of Henry II, the title was, said the court, "in due course of law and must have been created before legal memory." There was evidence, said the court, of a lost grant of free fishery "almost if not completely without a break to the 11th century." (The Norfolk county archivist produced records of two manorial lordships for this purpose.)

7.65 *Brighton Corporation* v. *Packham*[72] was a case where the foreshore owner secured an injunction to restrain the defendants from holding religious meetings on the foreshore. There had been complaints by residents of nuisance and the Corporation took action accordingly. A defence that the practice had been followed from time immemorial was not made out. This was not a claim based on prescription, said Warrington J.; that would have to be by an individual. It was not based on custom: that would have to be a defined group of inhabitants. It was said to be a right of "the public" but the court said: "A right to hold public meetings on private property is not known to the law."

Llandudno Urban District Council v. *Woods*[73] is a useful case in defining rights on the foreshore. It is in line with all those above. The only rights of the public, said Cozens-Hardy J., were for navigation and fishing. Public meetings, similar to those in the Brighton case above, were therefore disallowed. The judge treated the matter as too trivial to justify the issue of an injunction: he simply granted a declaration. He also said: "The plaintiffs are entitled to treat every bather, every nursemaid with a perambulator, every boy riding a donkey and every preacher on the shore at Llandudno as a trespasser."

7.66 *Lord Fitzhardinge* v. *Purcell*[74] was in essence a successful claim by the owner of a foreshore to prevent the defendant from shooting and taking wild duck from that foreshore. It was memorable however for two reasons:
  (a) The foreshore was not on the seacoast but in the tidal waters of the River Severn. It demonstrated a common application of the common law to both classes of foreshore.

---

[70] *Beckett Ltd.* v. *Lyons* [1967] 1 Ch. 449, where a claim to recover sea coal in the name of "the inhabitants of the County Palatine of Durham" was held to be too vague.

[71] (1978) 22 S.J. 487, C.A.

[72] (1908) 723 P. 318.

[73] [1899] 2 Ch. 705.

[74] [1908] 2 Ch. 139. The location of this case was Slimbridge in Gloucestershire. The drama of the leisure services has moved on from this first Act eighty years ago to the second Act, in which this is part of the home of the Wildfowl Trust, and wild ducks may fly, without fear, to its welcoming lagoons.

  (b) The defendant set up four heads of claim to shoot and take the wild duck:
- (i) As a prescriptive right of his ancestors: this failed due to lack of supporting evidence.
- (ii) As a trust implied in the original grants of the manors in favour of the inhabitants: this too failed for lack of evidence.
- (iii) As a member of the public, as being a right for all the King's subjects over the foreshore of a tidal navigable river: the court held that the public have no rights in such a place, except rights of navigation and fishing and rights ancillary thereto.
- (iv) As an inhabitant of the manors, by custom: this failed since a *profit à prendre* cannot be claimed by custom.

The 30 page report is full of interest on the historical background of the law of the foreshore.

Conclusion

  The position at common law is not always the position to be found in **7.67** practice. The ownership or rights in the foreshore have from time to time been granted to local authorities to enable them to be used for the benefit of the public resorting to the foreshore. Attention has earlier been drawn to the rights of local authorities to make by-laws regulating conduct on the seashore and adjoining promenades and esplanades. What this survey of the common law shows, is that the purely legal rights of the public on the foreshore may be limited, but local authorities, on behalf of the public, have scope to take initiatives to afford access to part of the country's finest leisure territory.

(3) *Beach Activities*

By way of conclusion, note is taken of three common beach activities, in **7.68** the light of the body of law and history discussed above.

Deck chairs

  The local authority may be the owners of the foreshore, in addition to the promenade at the top of the sea wall, the cliff top greens, gardens and walks. It may be that the authority are troubled about the growing habit of visitors to bring their own deck chairs and avoid payments to the authority's own hire service. To regulate the practice under local authority control, as they may wish, the authority will have to make by-laws. They need this specific legal sanction, before they can deal with those who might be inclined to challenge some more general legal claim to make charges.

Donkeys

  When are donkeys on the beach part of a riding establishment? The **7.69** earlier account of the Riding Establishment Acts of 1964 and 1970, showed that "hiring" was the essential feature of the practice, if the law is to bring such a business under the licensing system. If a youngster on a beach donkey is never allowed to ride it himself, it would seem that the animal has never been put into his possession and thus not "hired." This is the situation when the "donkey-boy" holds the bridle for the whole beach walk. If, however, the pony is hired out and the rider goes along the beach himself, the legal situation is different and, subject to other tests, the law about riding establishments is relevant.

Lobster catching

7.70   The law is also catching up with lobster catchers. For instance, on England's eastern coast nowadays, this leisure pursuit can only be safely followed under the aegis of the local District Fishery Committee, operating under the Sea Fisheries Regulation Act 1966. The duty of the Committee is to conserve stocks of lobsters and it has to work within the EEC Common Fisheries Policy. Hence Acts and Orders have prescribed minimum sizes of lobster that are catchable and, to complement that stipulation, other regulations about the size of the mesh for the lobster net.

CHAPTER 8

OPEN AIR ACTIVITY

"Salisbury Plain is barren of criticism but Stonehenge will bear a discussion anti-quarian, picturesque and philosophical"

William Hazlitt

INTRODUCTION

This chapter deals with a group of open air leisure activities. The largest, **8.01** in legislative provision and in terrain, are the national and countryside parks. With them can conveniently be considered footpaths, caravans, and picnic sites, which have their own legislation.

The other subsections will deal with allotments, wildlife preservation, light railways, skiing and car races in towns.

A. ALLOTMENTS

There are some half million allotments in this country,[1] forming part of **8.02** what has been described as "recreational gardening." They are governed by a body of statute law, extending generally from 1908 to 1950, supported by very few cases in the law reports. Perhaps allotment gardeners have little time to spare for litigation!

The legal framework is easy to summarise, dealing as it does with the definition of allotments, their provision, the terms of letting, the basis for termination, compensation on yielding up allotments and the established legal bodies involved.

1. Historical

Allotments were originally small areas of land let by parish officers to the **8.03** poor of the parish for cultivation. Alternatively, they were plots "allotted and awarded," under the Inclosure Acts, for the benefit of the poor. Another group were called "fuel allotments," since the rent derived from

---

[1] House of Commons debate on Local Government, Planning and Land Bill in Committee D, February 12, 1980. Mr. T. King col. 46. About one quarter of these are privately owned (Departmental Committee of Enquiry into Allotments, Cmnd. 4166 (1969), para. 320).

their letting by the parish was applied for the purchase of fuel for poor parishioners.[2] In one form or another, allotments were incidental to the administration of the Poor Law. As time passed, they were considered to be better managed on their own; when they numbered twenty or more under a vestry or trustees, then separate managing trustees were required.[3] Eventually, in 1894, management passed to local authorities.[4] The Small Holdings and Allotments Act 1908 marks the start of the modern era in legal control over allotments; by that Act, earlier ones were repealed and a general code of management prescribed.

An allotment is, by reference to the definitions in the Allotments Acts of 1922 and 1925, "an allotment garden, not exceeding 40 poles in extent, which is wholly or mainly cultivated by the occupier for the production of vegetables or fruit crops, for consumption by himself or his family."[5] Not being used for trade or business, the allotment is not agricultural land.[6]

2. **The Statutes**

8.04 The Allotment Acts 1908 to 1950 comprise the Small Holdings and Allotment Act 1908 (so far as it relates to allotments), the Land Settlement (Facilities) Act 1919 (with the same qualification), the Allotments Acts respectively of 1922 and 1925, as much of the Agricultural Land (Utilisation) Act 1931 as relates to allotments and the Allotments Act 1950.[7]

By the Emergency Laws (Miscellaneous Provisions) Act 1953, section 5, local authorities are empowered to let to tenants or tenants' associations, for allotments, land initially occupied by local authorities[8] under Defence Regulation 62A of the Defence (General) Regulations 1939.

A duty to provide and let allotments is laid upon the local authorities, which since the Local Government Act 1972 are the allotments authorities. These are district councils and, where the parish decides to exercise the function, the parish councils.[9] This duty arises where the authority are of the opinion that "there is a demand for allotments."[10] It involves acquiring land and if this cannot be obtained by agreement, compulsory powers are available.[11]

There are certain lands which cannot be taken for this purpose. These are part of a public park, garden or pleasure ground; part of a home farm, occupied with a mansion house; property of the National Trust; woodland

---

[2] Allotments Act 1832, s.8.

[3] Poor Allotments Act 1873, ss.3–4.

[4] Local Government Act 1894, s.33.

[5] Allotment Act 1922, s.22; Allotment Act 1925, s.1.

[6] Agriculture Act 1947, s.109.

[7] Plainly this miscellany of statutes is in need of codification and the Government has indicated that such a measure is at the planning stage.

[8] *i.e.* City of London, metropolitan and other district councils and county councils.

[9] See DOE Circular 121/72, Local Government Act 1972 Sched. 29, Pt. II, and Allotment Act 1908, s.23. Where the population is more than 10,000, the Allotment Act 1950, s.9, limits the duty of provision to allotments not exceeding one eighth of an acre in extent.

[10] A representation by six or more registered electors for allotments in the locality is to be one recognised as calling for due consideration: Allotment Act 1908, s.23.

[11] The powers are in the Allotment Act 1908, s.25.

or land required for the amenity of a dwellinghouse.[12] Certain other limits are placed on taking farm land, which might displace workers or which, being less than 50 acres, would take away an occupier's principal means of livelihood.[13]

3. Terms of Letting

With some of the Poor Law lettings were requirements that the occupier **8.05** should "cultivate to preserve in a due state of fertility." A local authority managing allotments has power under the Allotments Acts to improve the land, with drainage, fencing, roads and suitable buildings.[14] The statutory provisions bearing upon lettings are as follows[15]:
  (a) Avoid undue preference in lettings.
  (b) Comply with the Allotments Rules (Model Rules are available).[16]
  (c) Sub-letting is forbidden without local authority consent, as landlords.[17]
  (d) Clauses in a tenancy agreement purporting to restrict the keeping of hens and rabbits are forbidden.[18]
  (e) It is permitted to let allotments to an association or to persons working on a co-operative basis, provided that the division of profits among members is forbidden or restricted.[19]
  (f) The rent charged must be "such as a tenant may reasonably be expected to pay for the land, taking into account the proposed terms."[20] Not more than one quarter of the rent can be made payable in advance, except where the rent is below a stipulated amount.

4. Offences

The Allotment Acts prescribe offences for damaging growing crops, fences or buildings. To support a prosecution, there must be a notice about these offences on display on the site.[21]

5. Termination

A notice to quit for 12 months or more, is required to terminate the letting **8.06** of an allotment. This must expire in the winter or close season, *i.e.* September 29 to April 6.[22]

[12] Allotment Act 1908, s.41, and Allotment Act 1919, ss.16 and 28.
[13] Act of 1908, s.41; Act of 1919, s.16.
[14] Act of 1908, s.26.
[15] *Ibid.* s.28.
[16] *Ibid.*
[17] *Ibid.* s.28(4).
[18] Allotment Act 1950, s.12.
[19] Allotment Act 1908, s.27(6).
[20] Allotment Act 1950, s.10.
[21] Allotment Act 1922, s.19.
[22] *Ibid.* s.1, and see *Wombwell U.D.C.* v. *Burke* [1966] 2 Q.B. 149, where the question of effectiveness of such a notice reached the Court of Appeal.

The above is the normal situation. An exception is permitted in that three months is legally sufficient if such is provided in the tenancy agreement for a reason which is realised. This is that the land is needed for building or mining or some industrial use or for roads or sewers.[23] A similar exception is available when it is a housing use that is stipulated and realised.[24]

The last exception of this nature is when some other non-agricultural use is stipulated in the tenancy agreement as a contingency which might result in the land being needed on short notice. Then at least three months notice is needed "except in emergency."[25]

There is also the traditional basis for terminating any tenancy, *i.e.* that the rent has fallen into arrear, or that there is a breach of covenant or that bankruptcy or, in the case of a company, liquidation, has taken place. Re-entry by the landlord is allowed.[26] These provisions are necessary in law for special situations: the reality is that many allotment tenancies last for life.

Reference should be made to the situation where the local authority is itself the tenant of land used for allotments. An indication of the protection parliament wished to give to allotments is seen in the provision, that if notice to quit is served upon the local authority, as tenant, the authority can serve counter notice and go to arbitration, if desired, on whether the termination has been put in hand in good faith.[27]

6. **Compensation**

8.07   On determination of an allotment tenancy, compensation is payable by the landlord in respect of:
   (a) Growing crops and fertilisers upon the land.[28] The basis is their value to an incoming tenant. This is on the footing that the tenancy has been duly terminated by re-entry or notice to quit.
   (b) In respect of the disturbance, a sum equal to one year's rent.[29]
The tenant may remove bushes, fruit trees, and associated huts or sheds he has been using.

For his part, the landlord is legally entitled to counter-claim from the tenant for deterioration, if he can make out a claim that the land has not been maintained in a good condition of cultivation and fertility.[30]

7. **Administration**

8.08   The Secretary of State for the Department of the Environment is the Minister with responsibility for allotment regulation.

---

[23] Allotment Act 1922, s.1(1)(*b*).
[24] *Ibid.* s.1(1)(*d*).
[25] *Ibid.* s.1(1)(*c*).
[26] *Ibid.* s.1(1)(*e*).
[27] *Ibid.* s.11.
[28] *Ibid.* s.2.
[29] Allotment Act 1950, s.3.
[30] *Ibid.* s.4.

Local authorities are encouraged to promote allotment societies and associations.[31] It is normal for them to run annual prize competitions for well kept allotments. Local authorities are empowered to make financial advances to allotment societies.[32]

Such societies have the right to the free use of school rooms to facilitate meetings on allotment problems.[33]

A local authority has power to make Rules about allotments.[34] They will be made and confirmed like by-laws.

Allotment management is a function which a parish council is empowered to undertake. If it does, then in its area, the district council does not do so.[35]

8. **The Present Day**

In the case of *Harwood* v. *Borough of Reigate and Banstead*,[36] an allotment tenant successfully challenged an increase of his annual rent of more than 300 per cent. The case was said to be the first in thirty years on the section in the Allotments Act 1950 which stipulates that the rent should be "such as the tenant may reasonably be expected to pay."[37]

8.09

The facts were simply that an increase in the plaintiff's annual rent for his allotment in 1976 to 1977 from 90p to £3, was followed in 1977 to 1978 by a proposed new rent of £10. In his case, the plaintiff drew attention to the provisions in the Act of 1950 and other Allotment Acts, which gave guidance on what parliament had implied by "reasonably" in the above section 10. The section provided that the local authority as landlord "can charge less if the circumstances of that person (*i.e.* the tenant) warrant it."[38]

Another section in the Act of 1950 indicated the latest step by parliament in the financing of allotments. In the Act of 1908, it was provided that allotments should not be a burden on the rates. In 1922, the Allotments Act was requiring income and expenditure to balance. By 1950, however, the Allotments Act was placing a maximum rate product on the monies to be spent in providing allotments.[39] From this, the court in *Harwood's* case accepted the argument of the plaintiff, that parliament expected allotments to be subsidised, like other recreational activities. This was the crucial item in the eventual decision of that court in the

---

[31] Allotment Act 1908, s.49. A proposal by the Government to amend s.8 of the Act of 1908 and abandon the role as final arbiter, on a proposal by a local authority to dispose of allotment land for other use, was withdrawn after combined opposition resistance. (See debate referred in n. 1, *supra*).

[32] *Ibid.* s.49.

[33] Education Act 1944, ss.9 and 120, and Act of 1908, s.35.

[34] Allotment Act 1908, s.28.

[35] Local Government Act 1972, s.251.

[36] (1980) 43 P. & C.R. 336.

[37] Allotment Act 1950, s.10.

[38] *Ibid.*

[39] *Ibid.* s.11, duly converted by the Decimal Currency Act 1960 to 0.8p in the pound. The same Act repealed s.11(1) of the 1950 Act as superfluous, leaving the effective control in the Act of 1922.

plaintiff's favour. A significant change in Government thinking was noted. The decision of the court was as follows:

(1) The rent sought under section 10 should be that appropriate from a notional rather than an actual tenant.

(2) All relevant circumstances should be taken into account, in a broad common-sense way, using the expression about settling a "reasonable rent" used by Lord Greene, M.R. in an earlier case.[40]

(3) The evidence was accepted that allotment gardening was a recreational activity, to be subsidised like other such activities.

(4) An increase in rent should be in line with the annual increase for other recreational activities. It was not for the court to determine the new rent. It had been asked for a declaration about the legal basis on which rent under section 10 should be assessed and that declaration was given, on the lines here set out.[41]

B. WILDLIFE PRESERVATION

8.10   This section considers the current legal protection available for birds, animals and plants in this country. The present Act is the Wildlife and Countryside Act 1981 and this consolidated certain Protection of Birds Acts, so that provisions of a similar nature might be brought together. Whilst there are points at which this protective legislation touches on aspects of the national conservation policies and laws, these are best considered separately.[42]

1. **Protection of Birds**

8.11   The Act of 1981 re-enacts the Protection of Birds Acts 1954 to 1967, so that it is an offence intentionally:

(a) To kill, injure or take away any wild bird.

(b) To take, damage or destroy its nest whilst in use.

(c) To take or destroy an egg of a wild bird.

(d) To disturb such a bird, whilst building its nest or in its nest, whilst containing eggs or young, or to disturb the dependent young of such a bird.[43]

Some seventy or more wild birds are listed in a Schedule to the Act of 1981. For the above offences committed in relation to such birds, a "special penalty" is enacted, *i.e.* a fine not exceeding £1,000, as compared with a normal maximum fine of £200.

---

[40] The sentence comes from *Cumming* v. *Danson* (1943) 112 L.J.K.B. 145, as quoted in *John Kay Ltd.* v. *Kay* [1952] 2 Q.B. 258 at p. 264.

[41] The case illustrates the changed social status and popularity of allotments.

[42] The Wildlife and Countryside (Amendment) Act 1991 created a further offence to allow prosecution of those who direct, or allow others to commit, these offences, *i.e.* employers. We have not attempted to summarise the large number of Acts from 1911 onwards entitled Protection of Animals Acts.

[43] *Ibid.* s.1(5).

Exceptions are made for actions outside the close season[44] (generally, February to September, inclusive), in relation to these birds and also for authorised persons,[45] who include the owners and occupiers of the land where the birds are, in relation to a second short list of thirteen common birds which are thought to do damage. These include crows, gulls, magpies and house-sparrows and their killing is not an offence when in the interests of public health, preventing the spread of disease, or preventing serious damage to livestock, crops or agricultural needs.

Certain *methods* of killing or taking wild birds are forbidden, as traps or electrical stunning devices and various specified guns or other weapons and equipment, the use of decoys and other devious methods and the use of vehicles for chasing wild birds. Again, there are exceptions for authorised persons and, in the case of wild ducks and game birds, for particular circumstances.

The sale or offer for sale or advertising in relation to these protected birds, or their eggs, is another offence. It is also an offence to enter them in competitions.

Certain captive birds can be registered and marked in circumstances prescribed in Regulations but associated offences relate to the conditions in which such birds may be kept. Poultry are excluded from this group of exceptions.

2. **Protection of Animals**

The Act re-enacts the Conservation of Wild Creatures and Wild Plants **8.12**
Act 1975. It also effects amendments to the Badgers Act 1973[46] and the Conservation of Seals Act 1970. Deer have been the subject of two recent Acts, in 1987 and 1991. The former recognises the growth of deer farms; the latter is a new consolidating Act on this topic.

Some 40 animals, ranging from the toad to the swallowtail butterfly and from otters to snails and grass snakes, are protected by a series of provisions similar to those summarised above in relation to birds. The intentional killing, injuring or taking of these animals are the basic offences and then associated offences are contained in the Act of 1981 in connection with the sale, offer for sale, advertisement with a view to disposal, and also the intentional spoliation of the dens, lairs or shelters of these animals. Again, there are exceptions on the same lines as for the birds described above and a list of forbidden methods and devices for killing and taking these animals.

---

[44] The Wildlife and Countryside (Amendment) Act 1991, s.2.
[45] *Ibid.* s.27. This includes the owner, the occupier, a person authorised by the local authority, the water authority or the Nature Conservancy Council. In these last three groups, however, the authorisation does not confer any legal right of entry to the land.
[46] The Badgers Act 1973 was strengthened by the Wildlife and Countryside (Amendment) Act 1985 to put an onus on persons prosecuted for attempting to kill, injure or take a badger, to show that the activity disclosed in evidence was not of that nature and for that purpose. The Badgers Act 1991 and the Badgers (Further Protection) Act 1991 also strengthened the law, the latter particularly in relation to predatory dogs.

3. **Protection of Plants**

8.13   The essential offences are the picking, uprooting or destroying of some sixty listed wild plants. There are also offences for selling or advertising for sale these plants when either dead or alive.

In any legal proceedings, a plant is deemed in law to have been a wild plant within the Act, until the contrary is proved.

4. **New Species**

The Act of 1981 creates an offence for introducing into the wild an animal which is not ordinary resident in, and not a regular visitor to, Great Britain, in a wild state. A list is then given of some forty illustrative animals, from the coypu and the gerbil to the porcupines and the zander, though this is not exhaustive.

There is a defence in the statute, in this instance, that all reasonable steps were taken and all due care exercised to avoid the commission of this offence.

5. **General**

8.14   There are exceptions in the Act of 1981 for various classes of scientific work, whether taking the form of photography, education, conservation or other ways. Licences to protect such operations are obtainable from the Secretary of State or other appropriate minister or from the Nature Conservancy Council.

There are offences in relation to false statements made in order to obtain such licences. The Secretary of State has the responsibility of establishing advisory bodies in the specialised fields described above. The Secretary of State is empowered to vary the schedules of birds, animals and plants, to take account of changing scientific information and advice. Police constables have powers of arrest for certain suspected offences listed above.

The Nature Conservancy Council is made responsible for advising the Secretary of State on the animals and plants considered suitable for inclusion in the Schedules to the Act of 1981. Background legal information about that Council is found in the Nature Conservancy Council Act 1973, where it is given a special responsibility for the maintenance and management of nature reserves in National Parks. The Council's statutory function is particularly in relation to the conservation of flora, fauna, geological or physiographical features. It has to produce annual reports about its work and is subject to directions from the Secretary of State. Once a nature reserve is brought into being, it becomes an offence to harm its features without prior consent from the Council.

Local authorities are to bring to the notice of the public and particularly schoolchildren the Part of this Act and Orders made under it which affect their own area. Local authorities also have power to take proceedings for the offences under this Act of 1981.

C. Light Railways

There are some fifty private railways in use in this country at the present **8.15** time, which use the standard gauge or the narrow gauge. These are not all used for leisure pursuits; some are in use industrially, in association with factories, quarries or docks. There was an instance in the Conway Mussel Fishery Light Railway Order in 1975. But many are for holiday-makers, in conjunction with railway enthusiasts. Examples are to be found in the attractive scenery of the North Yorkshire Moors railway in its National Park or the Worth Valley railway in West Yorkshire.

It is the Light Railways Act of 1896 and 1912, which form the legal framework for this comparatively small leisure service. Those Acts were passed to simplify the legislative requirements for authorising the construction of these railways, which were of a local nature. It was in the rural, sparsely populated areas that such railways were needed and the likely amount of traffic was not thought to justify full Parliamentary proceedures and their expenses.

The legal procedures then devised have, fortunately, been found suitable for the private light railways of our day; though in the leisure context, it is not necessary to raise all the commercial and land questions that the Ministry of Transport would investigate otherwise.[47]

When appraising a new application for an Order under the Light Rail- **8.16** ways Acts, to authorise a leisure service line, the Ministry, under the terms of these Acts, inquire about:
 (a) The safety of the public.
 (b) Objections to the application.
 (c) The attitude and location of nearby residents.
 (d) The financial prospects of the application.
Certainly, if there is some clearly foreseeable danger, the application will be declined.[48]

The legal framework, within which the application is studied, is contained in the Acts of 1896 and 1912 (as amended) and in the rules of procedure, laid down in 1927 and revised in 1962[49]:

(1) A light railway company includes any person or body of persons, who are authorised to construct, or who are the owners or lessees of, any light railway authorised by the Light Railways Act 1896, or who are working that railway under a working agreement.[50]

---

[47] "Light railway," no doubt prudently, is not defined in the Acts. This gave rise, at one point, to strenuous argument whether a tramway might not be a "light railway," at least for certain rating benefits. See *Wakefield Corporation* v. *Wakefield and District Light Railway Co.* [1908] A.C. 293 and especially in the Court of Appeal [1907] 2 K.B. 257.

[48] Railways Act 1921, s.68(1)(*b*): "take all such matters into consideration." And see *Rother Valley Rail Co. Ltd.* v. *Ministry of Transport* [1971] Ch. 515 C.A. Also Light Railways Act of 1896, s.9.

[49] Ministry of Transport (Light Railways Procedure) Rules 1927 (S.R.O. 1927 No. 196), and Ministry of Transport (Light Railways Procedure) (Amendment) Rules 1962 (S.I. 1962 No. 1806).

[50] Light Railways Act 1896, s.28.

(2) A promoter can be a local authority, a corporation, a company or an individual.[51]

(3) An application must go before the Ministry of Transport; a century ago it went to three Light Railway Commissioners. The pattern of the procedure has not altered significantly.[52] The Railway Acts apply as far as appropriate in relation to standards of operation and safety.[53] The Department of Trade and Industry has to concur in any approval; there must be available finance and amenity considerations must also be met.

(4) The successful application results in the making of a Light Railway Order by Statutory Instrument, under the Acts of 1896 and 1912.[54]

(5) As mentioned above, local authorities may be associated with an application and in fact, several such authorities have done this, in liaison with the promoters. Few have been active operators themselves.[55]

(6) The Acts contain an offence for operating a light railway in contravention of any of the conditions attached to a consent by the Minister of Transport.[56]

(7) The most recent Act of Parliament, with a short direct reference to this subject, is the Transport Act 1968.[57]

D. NATIONAL PARKS AND ACCESS TO THE COUNTRYSIDE

Historical background

8.17   As a social counterweight to the industrialisation of this country in the last century, amenity societies began to emerge. On the one hand, vast areas of hitherto open and pleasant land were gathered into the growing towns and coalescing urban areas, whilst on the other, groups of people created new associations, which sought the preservation and protection of the remaining countryside. The Commons Preservation Society, the Ramblers Association, the Council for the Preservation of Rural England and the National Trust became powerful lobbies for their various causes. They can take great credit for awakening fellow citizens and a series of Governments to the need for, and the value of, open space and open air recreation.

The first aims of successive governments in the face of the tremendous

---

[51] Light Railways Act 1896, s.2(*b*).

[52] *Ibid.* ss.2, 7 and 9.

[53] *Ibid.* s.12.

[54] It was the Railway Act 1921 which transferred the approving function from the Light Railway Commissioners to the then Ministry of Transport. The power is currently with the Department of the Environment, by virtue of the Secretary of State for the Environment Order 1970 (S.I. 1970 No. 1681).

[55] Light Railways Act 1896, s.3. There are six at the time of going to press, which include s.3 in their Orders, though a private company is the operator, under lease. These are, by reference to their Orders, the Midland Centre, the Shackerstone and Bosworth, the Isle of Wight (Havenstreet and Wooton), the Loughborough and Birstall and the British Railways Board (Minehead Branch) and Leicester North Station.

[56] Regulation of Railways Act 1868, s.28.

[57] s.121(4). The latest new railway is covered by the North Tyneside Steam Railway, Light Railway Order 1991.

growth in population and in urban life were high standards of public sanitation, control over diseases and building construction. Attention then turned to increasing the nation's housing stock and to town and country planning.[58] By the middle of the nineteenth century, central government was actively encouraging the concept of the countryside for air and exercise. The pendulum has now swung so far in this direction that a number of statutory duties are imposed on public bodies requiring them, in the performance of those functions, to take into account "the desirability of conserving the natural beauty and amenity of the countryside."

The Statutes

The Countryside Act 1968 imposes a duty on every Minister, govern-   **8.18** ment department and public body to have regard in the exercise of their functions to this objective.[59] The Act[60] also requires all Ministers, the Countryside Commission, the Nature Conservancy Councils and local authorities in the exercise of their functions under the National Parks and Access to the Countryside Act 1949 (the Act of 1949), to have due regard to the needs of agriculture and forestry and to the economic and social interests of rural areas.[61] The Wildlife and Countryside Act 1981, (the Act of 1981) imposes on the Minister of Agriculture, Fisheries and Food, the duty, when giving free advice under an earlier Act,[62] to include advice to persons carrying on agricultural businesses, about the conservation and enhancement of the natural beauty and amenity of the countryside, as well as the other benefits to the rural economy.[63]

A similar principle is enshrined in the procedure for a farm capital grant under the Agricultural Act 1970; if a grant is refused, because the local authority has objected to the proposal for which the grant was sought, on the grounds that it would have an adverse effect on the natural beauty or amenity of the countryside or its enjoyment by the public, then the local authority must offer to enter into a management agreement with the applicant.[64]

Water authorities, in the discharge of their functions, must have regard to the conservation and enhancement of natural beauty and the conservation of flora, fauna and geological or physiographical features of special interest which are dependent on an aquatic environment. They are also to have regard to the desirability of protecting buildings and other objects of archaeological, architectural or historic interest.[65]

---

[58] A useful account can be found in Sir Desmond Heap, *Outline of Planning Law*, 10th ed., 1991, Sweet and Maxwell).
[59] Countryside Act 1968, s.11.
[60] By the Environmental Protection Act 1990 the one was replaced by the three, *viz.* England, Scotland and Wales, but still a Joint Nature Conservation Committee as well— s.128.
[61] *Ibid.* s.37.
[62] Agriculture (Miscellaneous Provisions) Act 1944, s.1.
[63] Wildlife and Countryside Act 1981, s.41.
[64] Agriculture Act 1970, s.29, and see below, para. 8.42.
[65] Now the Water Act 1989, s.8.

1. **The Countryside Commission**

8.19 The main body of law on access to the countryside is now to be found in these Acts of 1949, 1968 and 1981, as amended by other major statutes such as the Water Act 1989 and the Environmental Protection Act 1990. The Act of 1949 established the National Parks Commission, whose title was changed by the Act of 1968 to the Countryside Commission.[66] The Commission is a corporate body not to be regarded as a Crown agent or holding property on behalf of the Crown.[67] The Chairman and members are appointed by the Secretary of State; a separate Committee of the Commission is appointed for Wales.[68] In its obligatory annual report, the Commission is to give a statement of action taken to promote the interests of disabled persons in the countryside.[69] Whilst the Commission may acquire land for their functions, land occupied by the Commission is to be regarded for rating purposes as land or property occupied by the Crown.[70]

8.20 The main general duties of the Commission under the above three Acts are:

    (a) the preservation and enhancement of natural beauty in England and Wales, particularly in designated National Parks and in areas of outstanding natural beauty,

    (b) encouraging the provision or improvement of facilities for persons resorting to National Parks, and

    (c) promoting the enjoyment of the Parks and of the opportunities for open air recreation and study of nature.[71]

The Minister may give directions to the Commission for the exercise of their functions.[72] Those functions were enlarged by the Act of 1968 to include wider responsibilities for the conservation and enhancement of the natural beauty and amenity of the countryside and for encouraging the provision and improvement of facilities for the enjoyment of the countryside and of open air recreation.[73]

The Commission may charge for its services. It may also accept gifts and contributions which assist its work. It is also empowered to do anything conducive or incidental to its functions.[74]

The Commission is required to hold a watching brief over all countryside matters and to advise and assist all persons who submit proposals to them. It must also confer with local planning authorities.[75]

Where special problems arise, the Commission may arrange for their own staff, or consultants engaged by them, to be available to the local

---

[66] Wildlife and Countryside Act 1981, s.47 and Sched. 13 now govern the constitution of the Countryside Commission.
[67] *Ibid.* Sched. 13, para. 2.
[68] *Ibid.* para. 5.
[69] *Ibid.* para. 13.
[70] *Ibid.* paras. 14 and 15.
[71] National Parks and Access to the Countryside Act 1949, ss.5 and 6.
[72] *Ibid.* s.3.
[73] Countryside Act 1968, s.1.
[74] *Ibid.* s.1.
[75] *Ibid.* s.2.

authorities or other persons who are submitting proposals. The Commission can provide publicity and other information services.[76] The Commission also have the power to engage in experimental schemes in the performance of their functions. In these, they are enjoined to consult with local or other interested authorities; they are given power to acquire land, erect buildings, carry out other works and, with the approval of the Minister, undertake the management of the project.[77]

2. National Parks

(1) *Designation*

One of the prime functions of the Countryside Commission is the designation of National Parks. These comprise extensive tracts of countryside in England and Wales where it appears desirable to the Commission that steps should be taken to promote their enjoyment by the public.[78] The factors to be taken into account by the Commission in designating such areas, are their natural beauty and the opportunities they afford for open air recreation by reason of their character and their situation, in relation to centres of population.   **8.21**

The procedure for the designation of a National Park is set out in the Acts of 1949 and 1981.[79] The local planning authorities in the area must be consulted; there are extensive requirements about publication of the proposal; should objections be received, then a resulting public inquiry must receive ample publicity, as must the confirmation of the Designation Order in due course, if that result should follow.

Well known National Parks include the Lake District, the Peak District, the Yorkshire Dales, Dartmoor, Snowdonia, Pembrokeshire and the Brecon Beacons.

(2) *Duties in a Park*

The more important duties of the Commission in a designated Park are as follows[80]:   **8.22**

(a) To make recommendations to the local authorities in the Park and the Minister of appropriate action to promote its enjoyment by the public.

(b) To keep the objectives in paragraph 8.20, above, under review.

(c) To advise the relevant planning authorities of ongoing arrangements for the management of the Park.

(d) To provide information about the Parks, their access, accommodation and facilities.[81]

---

[76] Countryside Act 1968, s.2(5).
[77] *Ibid.* s.4, as amended by the Act of 1981, s.40. The former need for the consent of the Secretary of State has been removed.
[78] National Parks and Access to the Countryside Act 1949, ss.5, 6 and 7.
[79] *Ibid.* s.7.
[80] *Ibid.* s.6.
[81] *Ibid.* s.86.

    (e) To provide facilities to enable people to learn about the history and natural features of the Park.

    (f) To publish recommended codes of conduct in the countryside.

    (g) To maintain regular liaison with local planning authorities and the Minister about planning applications affecting the Park.

(3) *Long Distance Routes*

8.23   A related function of the Commission is the creation of long distance routes, for the making of extensive journeys on foot, horseback or by bicycle (not motorised).[82] The Commission is required to submit reports to the Minister on the possible provision of such routes, and dealing with matters such as the maintenance or improvement of existing public paths and roads used as public paths, and the provision of new paths, ferries and facilities for accommodation, meals and refreshments. Suggestions may also be made for the restriction of traffic on existing routes. The estimated capital and revenue costs of the Commission's proposals are also to be included. The Commission must consult any affected Joint Planning Boards, and the county and district councils whose areas will be traversed by the route. The Ministers, after considering the report, may approve a proposal relating to a long distance route with or without modifications, or reject it and must inform the local authorities of his decision.[83]

Highway authorities

It becomes the duty of the highway authorities, through whose areas the route passes, to enforce the public's right to use the route. Penalties are provided for putting up any notice containing false information with a view to deterring the public from using the route. The highway authorities on either side of water crossed by the route may provide a ferry service or make arrangements for another person to provide one but the exercise of this power is not to prejudice any other ferry operator.

The local planning authorities along the route may provide, or make arrangements to provide, accommodation, meals and refreshments (including intoxicating liquor) but authorities may only provide these services themselves if the existing ones are not satisfactory or adequate.[84]

(4) *Local Planning Authorities*

8.24   As stated above, local planning authorities are to confer with the Countryside Commission in the preparation of development plans. Further, county planning authorities, whose areas include a National Park, are required to publish maps which show areas of moor and heath, which are

---

[82] National Parks and Access to the Countryside Act 1949, ss.51–57.

[83] *Ibid.* s.52.

[84] National Parks and Access to the Countryside Act 1949, s.54. Howard Hill *Freedom to Roam* (1980, Moorland Publishing) is a fascinating study of the history of the ramblers clubs as a force for the creation of some of these routes.

especially important to conserve.[85] In respect of such areas, the Department of the Environment for Wales and the same department in conjunction with the Ministry of Agriculture, Fisheries and Food, in respect of England, can make Orders:

   (a) To stop ploughing into agricultural land of such areas, if 20 years have passed since that land was last used for agricultural purposes.

   (b) On the other hand, to forbid any agricultural operation or forestry work which would be likely to change the character and appearance of the moor or heath.[86]

Landowners have certain legal rights of representation and objection during the procedure to be followed before such Orders are final.

(5) *Powers of the Minister*

In addition to the powers in relation to moor and heath, the Minister has power to acquire land in a Park. He is expected, however, to transfer it to other bodies or trusts.[87] The Minister additionally has power to acquire land to afford public access to a Park.[88] His important power to give directions to the Countryside Commission has already been noted above.

(6) *Administration of a National Park*

The administration of a National Park is the responsibility of a Special   **8.25** Planning Board, in the case of the Peak District and the Lake District. For the other National Parks, a National Park Committee is appointed, in accordance with procedure in the Local Government Act 1972. County and district councils are both involved in the appointment of members of the Committees.[89]

It falls to these committees, under the Local Government Act 1972 to produce and review every five years National Park plans, embodying their ongoing policy for managing the respective Parks and fulfilling their statutory objectives.[90]

Wardens may be appointed in respect of any land or waterway for   **8.26** which by-laws may be made and in respect of land within a National Park to which section 193 of the Law of Property Act 1925 applies.[91]

There is a wider power to appoint wardens in respect of land in a

---

[85] Wildlife and Countryside Act 1981, s.43. The Town and Country Planning Act 1990 consolidates earlier relevant Town and Country Planning Acts. Section 4 states the role of the planning authority for National Parks.

[86] Wildlife and Countryside Act 1981, s.42.

[87] National Parks and Access to the Countryside Act 1949, s.14.

[88] *Ibid.* s.77.

[89] Local Government Act 1972, Sched. 17 and Act of 1981, s.46. With these should be read DOE Circ. 63/73 on Local Government Act 1972 and the Administration of National Parks. This explains the areas for agency arrangements by National Park Committees with district councils and planning authorities. The earlier Circular 65/74 contained extensive guidance on the National Park Plans.

[90] National Parks and Access to the Countryside Act 1949, s.92 (amended by ss.41 and 42 of the Countryside Act 1968).

[91] *Ibid.*

National Park or in the countryside, to which the public are allowed access and where wardens may not be appointed under the provisions of the 1949 and 1968 Acts. In such cases the only function of the wardens is to advise and assist the public. Wardens may also be appointed for footpaths and bridleways.[92]

8.27 Local planning authorities may, at the request of and in accordance with terms prescribed by the Countryside Commission, make arrangements for securing the provision in their areas of study centres and other facilities for enabling the public to learn about the features of the National Park and its associated facilities.[93]

8.28 Where any part of a National Park is bounded by the sea or a waterway, the local planning authority is empowered to carry out such works and do other things for facilitating the use of the waters and it has additional powers to regulate the use of waters by by-laws.[94]

3. Areas of Outstanding Natural Beauty

8.29 Apart from these extensive duties in relation to National Parks, the Commission has a general duty to advise on natural beauty and to advise the Minister on matters which could prejudice the natural beauty of this country.[95] Orders designating areas of outstanding natural beauty may be made by the Commission and powers are available, similar to those for National Parks,[96] for their protection. These are normally smaller areas and examples of the many areas thus designated are the Malvern Hills, the Quantock Hills, the Forest of Bowland, Cannock Chase, Anglesey, the Solway coast and the Wye Valley.

By-laws, access agreements and plans for any development, in or affecting such areas, would normally follow the making of these Orders.

4. Country Parks

8.30 The Act of 1968 extended the access of the public to open land, by creating the concept of Country Parks. The underlying principle is the provision or improvement of opportunities for the enjoyment of the countryside by the public.[97] Local authorities[98] are to have regard to the location of the relevant area, in relation to an urban or built-up area and to the availability and adequacy of existing facilities for the enjoyment of the countryside by the public. These powers are available within and outside the area of the local authority exercising them.[99]

8.31 A local authority has power to provide a Country Park, defined as a

---

[92] Wildlife and Countryside Act 1981, s.62.
[93] Countryside Act 1968, s.12.
[94] *Ibid.* s.13. See also Chap. 7.
[95] National Parks and Access to the Countryside Act 1949, s.85.
[96] *Ibid.* ss.87 and 88.
[97] Countryside Act 1968, s.6.
[98] *i.e.* County and District councils, the relevant London Borough Council, the City of London Common Council and a National Park Joint Planning Board.
[99] Countryside Act 1968, s.6(3).

park or pleasure ground to be used as a country park, on any suitable site in the countryside.[1] The authority may manage and maintain the park in particular by erecting buildings, carrying out works, providing facilities for meals, refreshments, parking and sheltering and facilities and services for open air recreation (not including organised games). Accommodation, meals and refreshments can only be provided by the local authority if no other satisfactory facilities exist. Local authorities have extensive powers to acquire land for the purpose of creating a country park but their powers may be exercised in respect of land in the ownership of another person with his agreement. The power may also be exercised in respect of an existing park or pleasure ground already owned by the authority, subject to the terms of any trust affecting it.[2] Similarly, a Country Park can be designated for any land acquired under Part V of the 1949 Act for access to open land. A country park is not subject to any of the enactments which regulate public parks and pleasure grounds as described in Chapter 4, namely[3]:

Section	Act
164	Public Health Act 1875
44	Public Health Acts Amendment Act 1890
76 & 77	,, ,, ,, ,, ,, 1907
56	,, ,, Act 1925

Apart from the general powers given to provide facilities in country parks, local authorities are given specific powers in respect of waterways situated in country parks.[4] These powers are dealt with in Chapter 7. Reference has already been made in Chapter 2 to the powers of local authorities in respect of land taken out of the common land.[5]

5. Access Arrangements and Local Authorities

General administration

The 1949 Act created opportunities for public access to and enjoyment   **8.32**
of open land in private ownership by giving local planning authorities a range of powers to secure access to open country for open air recreation.[6]

For the purposes of Part V of the Act, "open country" means any area appearing to the authority with whom an access agreement is made, or to the authority by whom an access order is made or by whom the area is acquired, as the case may be, to consist wholly or predominantly of mountain, moor, heath, down, cliff, or foreshore, (including any bank, barrier,

---

[1] Countryside Act 1968, s.7.

[2] *Ibid.* s.7(5).

[3] *Ibid.* s.7(7).

[4] *Ibid.* s.8, as part of water recreation and the Water Act 1989, in relation to the privatised authorities.

[5] Countryside Act 1968, s.9.

[6] See National Parks and Access to the Countryside Act 1949, Pt. V, as amended by the Countryside Act of 1968 and Wildlife and Countryside Act 1981.

dune, beach, flat or other land adjacent to the foreshore).[7] To this definition was added by the 1968 Act, woodlands in the countryside. Rivers and canals in the countryside were also added by the 1968 Act, except in relation to reservoirs owned or managed by statutory undertakers or a river authority and canals owned or managed by the British Waterways Board. Where land outside a National Park is adjacent to a river or canal and the local authority proposes to make an access agreement or order in relation to it, the authority should consult with and obtain the agreement of the river authority and such other authorities as the Minister may direct. By section 74, these provisions of Part V of the 1949 Act apply to waterways in a National Park as they apply to open country.[8] The provisions relating to access do not apply to Epping Forest, Burnham Beeches or to National Trust land.[9]

(1) *Reviews*

8.33 Local planning authorities are under a duty to review their areas to ascertain whether any open country needs to be opened up to public access for their own inhabitants or for persons not living in their areas.[10] If a local authority, after a review, are of the opinion that there are no, or no appreciable, areas of open country or that no action needs to be taken to provide access, they have to inform the Minister of the fact and publish a notice in the London Gazette of their findings.[11] Otherwise, the authority must prepare a map showing such areas and a statement of their proposed action to afford public access.[12]

(2) *Access Orders and Agreements*

8.34 Access to open land in private ownership can be obtained with the agreement of the owners of the land or, alternatively, by means of an access order.

An access agreement may be irrevocable or subject to such conditions as may be agreed between the authority and the land owner.[13] These may provide for the payment of contributions for the facilities made available. The Countryside Commission must be consulted, if the access affects a National Park.[14]

---

[7] National Parks and Access to the Countryside Act 1949, s.59.
[8] *Ibid.* s.74.
[9] *Ibid.* ss.112 and 113.
[10] *Ibid.* s.61 as amended by the Environmental Protection Act 1990, s.130.
[11] National Parks and Access to the Countryside Act 1949, s.62.
[12] *Ibid.* s.63.
[13] *Ibid.* s.64 and the Environmental Protection Act 1990, s.130. The new Broads Authority (Norfolk and Suffolk Broads Act 1988) is involved in this area of law, in some as a National Park, s.111A of the 1949 Act.
[14] *Ibid.* s.65. The Commission may ask the local authority to make an Access Order, under s.65(5).

An access order can be made if the authority find that an access agreement or a series of access agreements proves impracticable. Both access agreements and orders may provide for new means of access as well as maintaining existing ones.[15] The access order cannot relate to land which is in an already concluded access agreement.[16]

A local authority can enforce these agreements for access, not only by default action in respect of works, but also by court proceedings, after failure by an owner to comply with a notice relating to the provision of an access or the removal of some physical obstruction to an access. This enforcement applies to access orders, as well as access agreements.[17]

(3) *Land for Access*

Where necessary to facilitate access to the open country, local planning **8.35** authorities may acquire land. This does not include excepted land as defined in (3)(a) below, but it can include adjoining land to that acquired for access.[18] The legal duty laid upon the acquiring authority is to manage the land in question with due regard to any dangers it may contain, as well as the public need for open air[19] recreation. The Minister also has similar powers of acquisition and he, like local planning authorities, has compulsory powers available as a last resort.[20]

A person who enters land covered by an access agreement or order, for the purpose of open air recreation, and without damaging any wall, fence, hedge or gate, is not to be treated as a trespasser or incur any other liability, by reason only of being on the land. (This right to be on the access land is, however, subject to any other legal provision or prohibition which may be applicable).[21]

Exclusions

Certain lands, called excepted lands, are not included in this right of **8.36** access. These are as follows:

(a) Agricultural land (other than rough grazing).
(b) Nature reserves as declared by the Nature Conservancy Council.
(c) Land covered by buildings, or the curtilage of such land.
(d) Land used as a park, garden or pleasure ground, at the time the access arrangement was made.
(e) Land used for surface mineral extraction.
(f) Railways, golfcourses, racecourses or aerodromes.
(g) Land covered by statutory undertaker's works.

---

[15] National Parks and Access to the Countryside Act 1949, s.51.
[16] *Ibid.* s.65(2).
[17] *Ibid.* s.69.
[18] *Ibid.* s.76.
[19] *Ibid.* s.77.
[20] *Ibid.* ss.76 and 77.
[21] *Ibid.* s.60.

(h) Land affected by the public's rights under the Law of Property Act 1925, section 193.[22]

Land does not become excepted land if planning permission is needed for its development and either consent has not been given or there is a breach in any condition attached to such consent. The Act of 1968 enables restrictions to be imposed in access agreements to prevent land becoming excepted land.[23]

Public duties in access areas

8.37   The second Schedule of the Act of 1949 contains a number of general restrictions to be observed by persons enjoying access to open country by virtue of Part V of that Act. By flouting these restrictions, a person loses the protection of section 60 of the Act of 1949 (whereby he was not to be treated as a trespasser). These restrictions are as follows:

GENERAL RESTRICTIONS TO BE OBSERVED BY PERSONS HAVING ACCESS TO OPEN COUNTRY OR WATERWAYS BY VIRTUE OF PART V OF THE ACT

1. Subsection (1) of section sixty of this Act shall not apply to a person who, in or upon the land in question,—
   (a) drives or rides any vehicle;
   (b) lights any fire or does any act which is likely to cause a fire;
   (c) takes, or allows to enter or remain, any dog not under proper control;
   (d) wilfully kills, takes, molests or disturbs any animal, bird or fish or takes or injures any eggs or nests;
   (e) bathes in any non-tidal water in contravention of a notice displayed near the water prohibiting bathing, being a notice displayed, and purporting to be displayed, with the approval of the local planning authority;
   (f) engages in any operations of or connected with hunting, shooting, fishing, snaring, taking or destroying of animals, birds or fish, or brings or has any engine, instrument or apparatus used for hunting, shooting, fishing, snaring, taking or destroying animals birds or fish;
   (g) wilfully damages the land or anything thereon or therein;
   (h) wilfully injures, removes or destroys any plant, shrub, tree or root or any part thereof;
   (i) obstructs the flow of any drain or watercourse, opens, shuts or otherwise interferes with any sluice-gate or other apparatus, breaks through any hedge, fence or wall, or neglects to shut any gate or to fasten it if any means of so doing is provided;
   (j) affixes or writes any advertisement, bill placard or notice;

[22] Excepted land is dealt with in the National Parks and Access to the Countryside Act 1949, s.60. The Law of Property Act provision is the one dealt with in Chap. 2 in relation to commons, which allow access by the public for air and exercise. The procedure of the 1949 Act is not to supercede that under the Law of Property Act 1925.
[23] Countryside Act 1968, s.18.

(*k*) deposits any rubbish or leaves any litter;

(*l*) engages in riotous, disorderly or indecent conduct;

(*m*) wantonly disturbs, annoys or obstructs any person engaged in any lawful occupation;

(*n*) holds any political meeting or delivers any political address; or

(*o*) hinders or obstructs any person interested in the land, or any person acting under his authority, in the exercise of any right or power vested in him.

2. In the application of the foregoing provisions of this Schedule to waterways,—

(*a*) for references to land there shall be substituted references to a waterway;

(*b*) Sub-paragraphs (*a*) and (*b*) of paragraph 1 of this Schedule shall not apply; and

(*c*) Sub-paragraph (*f*) of the said paragraph 1 shall have effect as if the words from "or brings" to the end of the sub-paragraph were omitted.

Rights and duties of landowners in access areas

Because of the acceptance or imposition of public rights over his land, **8.38** the legal rights of the landowner or other affected person need to be adjusted. This is done by the following provisions:

(1) No person interested in the land may carry out any works (apart from works to make the land into excepted land), whereby the rights of the public under an access agreement or order are substantially reduced.[24]

(2) The right of the public not to be treated as trespassers, under section 60 of the Act of 1949, does not increase the liability[25]—it does not absolve them completely—of those interested in the land under the general law, in respect either of the state of the land or of anything done or omitted to be done thereon.

(3) In relation to covenants affecting the land, any liability for breach of covenant may be the subject of compensation.[26]

(4) The possibility of a way created by an access agreement or order becoming a highway is countered by the provision that the period when the land is affected by such access is to be disregarded, so far, that is, as any prescription period is concerned.[27]

(5) If the Minister is satisfied, on the application of any person interested in the land, that by reason of exceptional weather conditions or the risk of fire, that the rights of access should not apply, he may suspend them.

(6) Compensation is payable where the value of the interest of any person in the land is depreciated in consequence of an access order.[28] The

[24] National Parks and Access to the Countryside Act 1949, s.66.
[25] See now the Occupiers Liability Act 1984 on duty to trespassers.
[26] National Parks and Access to the Countryside Act 1949, s.70.
[27] Under the Highways Act 1980, s.32, 20 years unchallenged use would otherwise form the legal basis for a presumption of a public highway.
[28] National Parks and Access to the Countryside Act 1949, s.70.

compensation, which is payable by the local planning authority, is claim-able five years after the order has come into operation. This is to allow a realistic appraisal of the effect of the order upon the land, in the light of experience gained in that period. The compensation is calculated to allow for this inbuilt delay.[29]

(4) *Maps*

8.39 Local planning authorities, whose areas are included in access arrange-ments, whether by order, agreement or land acquisition, are required to prepare and maintain maps.[30] These maps are to show land and also excepted land, as explained above, and also land from which the public are excluded (*e.g.* for reasons of danger).[31] Copies of the maps have to be available for public inspection and may be displayed where the public have access to the land. Boundary notices may also be displayed on land subject to public access.

6. Other General Local Authority Powers in Relation to the Countryside

8.40 The Acts of 1949, 1968 and 1981 give many powers to local authorities in National Parks and generally in respect of the countryside. Local planning authorities have power under the 1949 Act to "take all such action" as appears expedient and for the accomplishment of the purpose of preserv-ing and enhancing the natural beauty of any part of their areas within a National Park.[32] The conferment of specific powers elsewhere in the 1949 Act is not to affect the generality of this broad power. They may make arrangements for the provision by themselves or by other persons, of accommodation, meals and refreshments, camping sites and parking places. Accommodation, meals and refreshments may only be provided direct by the authority if there are no other satisfactory or adequate facili-ties. The facilities may also be provided on land in the neighbourhood of a National Park. Land required for these purposes may be acquired com-pulsorily.[33]

Section 13 gives power to local planning authorities to improve water-ways for the purposes of open air recreation.[34]

Nature reserves may be established by local authorities other than on land held by or managed in accordance with an agreement entered into with the appropriate Nature Conservancy Council.[35]

8.41 For the purpose of preserving or enhancing the natural beauty of any

---

[29] National Parks and Access to the Countryside Act 1949, ss.72 and 73.
[30] *Ibid.* s.78.
[31] *Ibid.* s.81.
[32] *Ibid.* s.11.
[33] *Ibid.* s.12.
[34] *Ibid.* s.13 conferring in present circumstances with the privatised water authorities under the Water Act 1989.
[35] *Ibid.* s.21.

land in their area local planning authorities may plant trees. They may carry out works to bring into use or improve the appearance of land which is derelict, neglected or unsightly where the land is owned by them or by some other person with his consent. Powers of compulsory purchase are available.[36]

By-laws

Wide by-law making powers are given to local planning authorities in respect of land in their area and ownership comprised in a National Park, area of outstanding natural beauty or subject to access by the public under Part V of the 1949 Act and for country parks.[37] By-laws may be made for the preservation of order, the prevention of damage and the maintenance of order in the interests of persons resorting to the land.[38] The Minister has default powers to make by-laws when the authority fail to comply with his requirement to make them.[39]

Management agreements

County planning authorities in respect of land in a National Park, the successor authority to the Greater London Council and the London Borough Councils in respect of land in London and local planning authorities for other land, may make management agreements with land owners and occupiers for the purpose of conserving or enhancing the natural beauty or amenity of any land in the countryside and within their area, for promoting its enjoyment by the public.[40] Management agreements may include restrictions on the use of the land by the owner or occupier and may confer power on the local authority to carry out works for the purpose of their functions under the Acts. The Acts contain a number of powers enabling the local planning authorities to give financial assistance to other persons and bodies carrying out work in furtherance of conserving and enhancing natural beauty in the countryside or incidental thereto. This includes making contributions to persons putting up boundary notices, warning notices, displaying maps, and providing public facilities in a National Park.[41]   **8.42**

Facilities and services provided by local authorities under the 1968 Act are to be made available as readily for persons who live outside their areas as for their own residents. They are given powers to make reasonable charges for facilities and services which they provide and may authorise   **8.43**

---

[36] National Parks and Access to the Countryside Act 1949, s.89.
[37] *Ibid.* s.90 as amended by s.130 of the Environmental Protection Act 1990.
[38] Countryside Act 1968, s.41. The Litter Act 1983 reinforces such by-laws in one respect.
[39] National Parks and Access to the Countryside Act 1949, s.91 and Wildlife and Countryside Act 1981, s.49.
[40] Wildlife and Countryside Act 1981, s.39.
[41] National Parks and Access to the Countryside Act 1949, ss.82 and 99; Countryside Act 1968, s.20; and Wildlife and Countryside Act 1981, s.44.

other persons providing facilities and services for the authority to make reasonable charges.[42]

E. FOOTPATHS

8.44 Found in public parks, National Parks and generally throughout any open air recreational area, footpaths are one important part of the law of highways. For the purposes of this work, we shall deal with their nature, the ways in which they come into existence, how to divert them, how to close them and, finally, how to deal with questions of their maintenance and obstruction.

1. **Nature**

A footpath is a highway on which the public can pass and repass on foot. This distinguishes the footway from highways on which vehicles may freely move[43]; it also implies a distinction from the bridleway, which is a highway for use by foot and by horse and, since the Countryside Act 1968, also by pedal bicycle.[44] Cyclists are, by the terms of the above Act, to give way to pedestrians and to persons on horseback.

The law has, in the Rights of Way Act 1990, for the first time introduced dimensions for the minimum width of a footpath[45]; it does not, however, prescribe the nature of its surface. The fact that footpaths serve an infinite variety of terrain is a good reason for that measure of restraint. All that the law requires is that the way should be reasonably passable.

2. **Origins**

8.45 Public footpaths may come into existence because they have been clearly dedicated for use in that way. Another method is for them to be presumed to be public footpaths after 20 years enjoyment as such by the public.[46] Thirdly, a statutory record of these and other rights of way has been brought into existence since 1949 and appearance on that record will produce evidence of the footpath in law.[47]

One way in which direct dedication occurs is when a new highway is made, perhaps in the course of creating a turning circle for buses or simply

---

[42] Countryside Act 1968, s.43.

[43] Known since the Wildlife and Countryside Act 1981 s.54 as 'byways'—"a byway open to all traffic" is a classification for a road used as a public path without a made up carriageway. The section provides that the old expression—"road used as a public path"—shall not be used for such highways.

[44] Countryside Act 1968, s.30.

[45] See Rights of Way Act 1990, s.12A where for a field-edge footpath the figure for minimum width is 1.5m, otherwise 1m; and for a field-edge bridleway 3m, otherwise 2m. This applies on restoration after disturbance by, *e.g.* ploughing and is, says the Act, to be indicated "so that it is apparent to members of the public wishing to use it" Highways Act 1980, s.134 and Rights of Way Act 1990, s.1 (*supra*).

[46] Highways Act 1980, s.31.

[47] Wildlife and Countryside Act 1981, s.56(1).

to serve newly built houses. There is no place for argument or inference: there is a document which supplies the evidence that the owner intended to create that highway as a new footpath, the work was done, and by usage the new way came into being.[48]

There are many footpaths, however, where things are not as simple. For them the Highways Act 1980 provides a statutory presumption that a way actually enjoyed by the public as of right and without interruption for a full period of 20 years is deemed to have been dedicated as a highway, unless there is sufficient evidence that there was no intention during that period to dedicate it.[49]

Such a contrary intent would be the placing of a chain or some other physical form of closure annually by the landowner to prevent the 20 year period from running. Again the placing of a notice at the end of the footpath bearing words such as "Private Path. No public right of way" would serve the landowner's purpose of preventing the above statutory presumption from operating.[50]

The third way is the definitive map and statement. A record by map **8.46** and by written statement was required of local authorities under the National Parks and Access to the Countryside Act 1949. This was to show all public rights of way. It was comprehensive, almost a Domesday Book approach to this important element in knowledge of the use of the land. But it broke down because of the weight of work it imposed at certain critical points, for instance on the Ministry in dealing with objections and on the local authorities, in organising periodic reviews. The Act was amended and simplified. Definitive maps are now prepared and these can be modified to keep them up to date with known changes. The reason for referring to this system as a third way in which footpaths come into being, is that the immense community research, by specialist societies and in town halls at officer and member level, has revealed footpaths and the history of footpaths that were not hitherto known. In so far as that was its aim, it succeeded.[51]

---

[48] Highways Act 1980, s.25, for district councils, county councils, the National Park Planning Board, or a London Borough Council. Highways Act 1980, s.30 for local councils. The document may be a Public Path Creation Agreement under this section. Alternatively, it may be a builder's agreement with the local authority, under s.38 of the 1980 Act, whereby the carriageways and footways on the new estate become maintainable public highways. The same Act, s.26, deals with creation orders, when compulsory powers are used to create a footpath.

[49] Highways Act 1980, s.31.

[50] Also s.31(6); somewhat academic and little used. It allows a landowner to deposit with the highway authority a map and statement of the ways over his land which he admits are public highways. It is renewable every six years. On this and many practical details, the new, book *Rights of Way* by P. Clayden and J. Trevelyan (Ramblers Association and Open Spaces Society (1983)) is helpful.

[51] It was then the role of county and county borough councils. The Countryside Act 1968, Sched. 3, was one effort to speed the process. The Wildlife and Countryside Act 1981 contains the method now in use. S.53 shows the way modifications are made to a definitive map. S.54 relates to the duty in relation to footpaths, and the Wildlife and Countryside (Definitive Maps and Statements) Regulations 1983 (S.I. 1983 No. 21) have the detail.

3. **Diversion and Closure**

8.47　Diversion of a public footpath may be required for the convenience of the owner of nearby property. A farmer may be putting up a new barn, a new highway may cross the existing footpath, a new building in the village may be better sited if the footpath were re-routed.

There are three legal procedures available for this common situation. One is under the Town and Country Planning Act 1971, and is by way of an Order made by the local planning authority to facilitate development. It will be done when the alternative route is agreed and the land of that route can be dedicated as a footpath. It will also take into account the physical work in constructing the new footpath and responsibility for paying for that work.[52]

The second legal method is by a magistrate's court order under the Highways Act 1980. As the statute says that the diverted way is to be "more commodious to the public," this condition may in the circumstances be an obstacle to using that method.[53] The section sets out other details of the procedure, concerning public notice in various forms. If for one reason or another, this method is inappropriate, then thirdly, the local authority may turn to a Public Path Diversion Order, under another section of the Highways Act 1980.[54] This is slightly more intricate and the legal requirements for confirmation of such an Order by the Secretary of State, when objection has been raised, are a little more formidable. There are, in substance, four of them, namely:

  (a) The diversion is expedient.

  (b) The path will not be substantially less convenient to the public in consequence of the diversion.

  (c) Consideration has been given to the effect the diversion would have on public enjoyment of the path as a whole, and

  (d) Consideration has been given both to the effect the diversion will have on the old route and land held with it and also to the new route and land held with it. (This last point is one that might be seen in the light of arrangements made for payments by or between the landowner and the local authority.)

The procedure for confirmation of such an Order is in the Sixth Schedule to the Highways Act 1980 and may involve a local inquiry to hear objections.

8.48　The procedure for the closing of a public path is similar to that described above for its diversion. Thus an extinguishment order under the Town and Country Planning Act 1971 is available. When there are no objections to the public notices, the local authority may make the Order; when objections appear, the draft Order goes to the Secretary of State. Again, under the Highways Act 1980, closure may be made after application to the magistrates court for an order. This is available only if the

---

[52] Town and Country Planning Act 1971, s.210.

[53] Highways Act 1980, s.116.

[54] *Ibid.* s.119. DOE Circular 1/83 *Public Rights of Way* para. 21, encourages the use of ss.118, 119 and 120, rather than s.116.

court is satisfied that the path to be closed is "unnecessary." This unvarnished word has been the stumbling block for not a few applications. So, if the interested parties turn to the third possibility, a public path extinguishment order, they meet a form of words in the Statute to the effect that it is "expedient" that the path be stopped up on the ground that it is "not needed for public use." The procedure is as indicted for the diversion order.[55]

4. Maintenance and Obstruction

Under the Highways Act 1980, the highway authority are under a duty to **8.49** maintain a highway maintainable at the public expense.[56] This is a duty that a district council can undertake, in place of the county council, the highway authority.[57] Apart from that possibility, the duty is one that can be enforced by court order.[58] Adequacy of maintenance is occasionally a matter for argument; suffice it to say that the standard will be that appropriate to the locality and user.

Obstruction of a footpath is common. Again, as with maintenance, the highway authority has a duty to prevent an obstruction and this duty is enforceable against that authority.[59] A temporary obstacle is unlikely to be accepted by the courts as an obstruction within the Highways Act meaning. "Anything which substantially prevents the public from having free access over the whole of the highway, which is not purely temporary in nature, is an unlawful obstruction" were the words of Parker L.C.J. in *Seekings* v. *Clarke*.[60]

If a growing crop encroaches on an adjacent highway to reduce its apparent width to less than the minimum width[61] then the Rights of Way Act 1990 creates an offence.[62]

5. Danger from Bulls

In Part III of the last major Act to deal with public rights of way, *i.e.* the **8.50** Wildlife and Countryside Act 1981, is a section which deals with the situation when a bull is in a field crossed by a public footpath.

It is made an offence to keep a bull at large in such a field and this is punishable by fine in a magistrates' court.[63] However, the action is subject to certain important exceptions:

(a) Bulls less than 10 months old.

[55] Highways Act 1980, s.120.
[56] *Ibid.* s.41.
[57] *Ibid.* s.42.
[58] *Ibid.* s.56.
[59] *Ibid.* s.130(3).
[60] (1961) 59 L.G.R. 268.
[61] See para 8.44 *supra.*
[62] Highways Act 1980, s.137A and Rights of Way Act 1990, s.1.
[63] Wildlife and Countryside Act 1981, s.59.

(b) A bull which is not of a recognised dairy breed and is at large with cows or heifers. (The breeds in question are Ayrshire, British Friesian, British Holstein, Dairy Shorthorn, Guernsey, Jersey and Kerry.)

F. Picnic Sites

8.51   The provision of picnic sites is now an authorised function of local planning authorities and district councils. They may "provide in their area . . . picnic sites for motorists and others using the roads, with space for parking vehicles and a means of access to and from the road."[64]

Additionally, these authorities may do anything appearing to them to be desirable in connection with the provision of such a site, especially "services or facilities for their health or convenience."[65]

Since land is needed, the councils are empowered to acquire land, compulsorily if necessary, that is required for this service. They may take the site on lease or lease it to someone to act as the council's agent in providing the service.[66]

Lastly, they can charge for the service or they can permit their lessee to charge similarly.

This is a summary of the simple legal code associated with the provision of these sites. The policy, the planning scene, the design skill and the practical common sense in managing them are touched on in the Sandford Committee report on National Parks and government circulars on the same wide subject.[67]

G. Litter

8.52   The law formerly in the Litter Act 1983 has been recast by Part IV of the Environmental Protection Act 1990. In place of a simple offence of leaving litter in a public place and a fine of £400, the 1990 Act provides a comprehensive set of offences, duties, a Code of Practice and a penalty for breaches that has risen to £1,000. Managers of leisure facilities, from beaches to sports centre car parks, should also be aware that those areas of land are just what may be designated as Litter Control Areas.[68] Complaints to magistrates courts about litter in such areas can give rise to abatement notices and potential penalties for breach.

Those interested in further detail will wish to study the Act and especially the Code of Practice[69] which classifies locations into four grades, discusses cleaning frequencies and is a most important document.

---

[64] Countryside Act 1968, s.10.

[65] *Ibid.*

[66] *Ibid.* s.43.

[67] See below n.70. They would seem to be prime candidates, scheduled as an area group, for the Litter Control Areas now permitted by the Environmental Protection Act 1990, s.90.

[68] Enviromental Protection Act 1990, s.90.

[69] Issued November 1990 under Enviromental Protection Act 1990, s.89.

The thrust of the new Act can be gauged perhaps by its resolute definition of the primary offence. It is now a catch-all: "throws down, drops, . . . deposits . . . so as to cause, or contribute to, or tend to lead to . . . the defacement by litter . . . "

Relevant enforcement local authorities include county and district councils, London borough councils and the Common Council. Others may be designated by the Minister.

We leave the subject noting that, just as the title of this chapter, so this legislation is still about open air activity.

H. CARAVANS

1. Site Licensing

Caravan sites came of legal age in 1960, when the Caravan Sites and Control of Development Act 1960 introduced legal site licensing. Previously there had allegedly been 3,000 unlicensed sites in this country and some form of regulation was needed.   **8.53**

Caravans have become a feature of national parks and they are discussed in recent authoritative documents on that subject.[70]

The main features of the regulatory system contained in the above Act of 1960[71] are as follows.

A caravan site licence always follows the grant of planning pemission for that use.[72] Indeed, without planning permission, a site licence must not be issued. A second recognition of the close relation between these two legal steps is the provision that if the planning permission is limited in time, then the site licence will lapse at the same time.[73] Apart from this, a caravan site licence is not to be issued for a limited period only.

A site licence is issued by a local authority, which for this purpose is a district council, a London borough council or the Common Council of the City of London.[74]

The site licence is primarily about the internal management of the cara-   **8.54**
van site. The planning permission deals with the prior question of its suitability for use by caravans. All site licences will not be in the same terms; they must be appropriate for the particular site. The Act of 1960 suggests the following subjects as those that might be considered by those responsible for drawing up the site licence[75]:

(a) A time limit for caravans on the site.

---

[70] The Sandford Committee Report 1974 (National Park Policies Review Committee) and DOE Circular 4/76 (see especially paras. 41–46).
[71] Pt. I is about caravans; Pt. II, now repealed, was about general development control. For definition, sometimes subtle, see s.29 of the Act of 1960 and amendment in Countryside Act 1968, s.13.
[72] Caravan Sites and Control of Development Act 1960, s.3(3).
[73] *Ibid.* s.4.
[74] *Ibid.* s.29.
[75] *Ibid.*

(b) A limit on the total number of caravans on the site.
(c) Control over the types of caravans permitted, though not about the materials of which those caravans are made.[76]
(d) The position of the caravans on the site and restraints on the positions of tents, vehicles and other structures.
(e) The amenity of the site, including the planting of bushes and trees.
(f) Fire fighting. This important subject is amplified in the Model Standards issued by the Department of the Environment.[77]
(g) Sanitary arrangements.
(h) The display of the licence on the site.[78]

8.55   The case of *Esdell Caravan Parks Ltd*. v. *Hemel Hempstead Urban District Council*,[79] provided useful guidance on the extent to which site licence conditions could go. A challenge to a limit of 24 caravans in the licence, was made by a site occupier, who wanted to have 78 caravans on the site. He lost. The court accepted the view that educational, transport and shopping aspects of the caravan population in relation to the locality, were reasonable matters to be considered. The court did not favour restricting conditions on a site licence to public health ones, or what Winn L.J. called "the meretriciously simple test" of "an inward looking view."[80]

Again, the case of *Mixnam's Properties* v. *Chertsey Urban District Council*[81] in the House of Lords, shows that conditions about the rent for the caravan sites, the security of tenure of the occupants, and their personal and social activities, were too wide to go into site licence conditions. They were all held *ultra vires*. Lord Radcliffe said "permissible conditions must relate to the user of the licensed site, not to the user of the licensee's legal powers of letting or licensing caravan spaces." Lord Upjohn found that the conditions in question involved "oppressive and gratuitous interference with the rights of the occupier." They were, he said, "wholly unnecessary for the good governance of the site."

As these cases show, the site owner has a right of appeal against conditions in the site licence. That appeal goes to a magistrates court, which has the limited duty of considering whether the condition in question is "unduly burdensome."[82] The local authority, for its part, may alter the

---

[76] Caravan Sites and Control of Development Act 1960, s.5(2). There is an interesting legal stipulation in s.5(5), that a condition is valid notwithstanding that it requires the site owner to do something which he cannot do "as of right." This might conceivably involve obtaining an easement from the adjoining owner.

[77] (1965) 3 All E.R. 737. See also Act of 1960, ss.3A and 3B, added by the Local Government (Miscellaneous Provisions) Act 1982, s.8.

[78] *Ibid.* at p.752B. Caravan Sites and Control of Development Act 1960, s.5(3). "The (caravan site) licensing authority cannot pull chestnuts out of the fire for the planning authority"—Harvey L.J., in the *Esdell* case.

[79] [1965] A.C. 735.

[80] *Ibid.* at p. 752B.

[81] See also *Babbage* v. *North Norfolk District Council* [1990] 1 P.L.R. 65, C.A. for examples of conditions held *ultra vires*.

[82] Caravan Sites and Control of Development Act 1960, s.7. The case of *Llanfyllain Rural District Council* v. *Holland* (1964) 62 L.G.R. 459, illustrates justices allowing an appeal on this statutory ground, when they agreed that a site licence condition about drainage connections to individual caravan standings was unreasonable. The High Court upheld the justices on appeal by the local authority, since they had applied the right test.

conditions, provided that it gives the site owner an opportunity to make representations on the matter before a decision is reached.[83]

A local authority can send its officers to inspect a site, but must give 24 hours prior notice. It is an offence to obstruct the officers in their reasonable task.[84] **8.56**

Breaches of conditions in a site licence can be prosecuted by a local authority and a third conviction of such an offence can give rise to revocation of the site licence. In so far as a condition requires works to be done, the local authority may carry out those works, in default of compliance by the site owner. The cost of such work can then be recovered by the local authority.[85]

The Act of 1960 provides for the transfer of site licences when the legal occupier of the site changes. The local authority must be informed and its consent is needed for the transfer to be lawful.

2. Exemptions

There are a number of situations where a site licence is not needed. (It should be noted that planning permission for these cases is a separate question. The General Development Order does grant such permission for many but not all of these cases.) They are listed in the First Schedule to the Act of 1960 and are as follows: **8.57**

(a) When the caravan is sited within the curtilage of a dwellinghouse and is incidental to the enjoyment of that use.

(b) Use of land for not more than two nights when travelling with a caravan. This is subject to that land not being used for more than 28 days in the twelve month period, which ends on the day on which the caravan is brought onto the land.[86]

(c) When a site not exceeding *five* acres does not have more than *three* caravans in total thereon for more than *28* days in a year. (These three numbers are variable by Order of the Secretary of State.)

(d) Sites occupied and supervised by exempted organisations.[87]

(e) A site which is duly certified by such an exempted organisation for not more than five caravans and for not more than one year.

(f) Meetings by such exempted organisations for not more than five days.

(g) Agricultural and forestry workers, engaged on such work on land in the same occupation.

(h) Caravans on building and engineering sites, occupied by persons employed on those sites.

---

[83] Caravan Sites and Control of Development Act 1960, s.8.
[84] *Ibid.* s.26.
[85] *Ibid.* s.9.
[86] s.12 of the Act should be studied by any concerned with a breach of his licence or tenancy by a tenant in letting a caravan site develop on his land. This is essentially a landlord and tenant dispute.
[87] At the time of going to press, there are 11 of these, listed in DOE Circ. 17/65, *e.g.* Caravan Club, Boy Scouts and Girl Guides Assocations, Caravan Tourists Association.

(i) Travelling showmen, accompanying their equipment and transports.
(j) Sites occupied by the licensing authority itself.
(k) Sites occupied by a county council as accommodation for gypsies.
(l) There is a reserve power to deal with an individual site by Order of the Secretary of State, on the application of a local authority.

3. General

8.58 The Act has several provisions about existing, *i.e.* pre-1960, sites.

Local authorities are required to keep registers of site licences and these must be open for public inspection.[88] The Act applies to land normally considered as Crown land, when the occupier is not the Crown.[89] A district council can make an Order in relation to a Common in their area, prohibiting wholly or partly the stationing of caravans upon it for the purposes of human habitation.[90] It is an offence to contravene that Order. There are certain legal formalities to be complied with in taking such a step, in connection with consultation, and public notice and hearing representations.[91]

It should be said that the 1960 Act gives specific power for local authorities to provide and manage caravan sites or lease them.[92] The Broads Authority is a local authority for this purpose.[93] Protection for residents on caravan sites in the form of length of notice, no harassment and suspension of eviction orders, are contained in the Caravan Sites Act 1968.

The Mobile Homes Acts of 1975 and 1983 come into play where a caravan is to be the "only or main residence." Minimum standards can be prescribed.[94]

I. Skiing

8.59 Legal hazards lie in wait at the end of every ski run. Fortunately most people enjoying this popular sport never encounter them.[95] The important legal aspects of the sport would appear to this non-skier to be as follows[96]:
(a) The principle of *volenti non fit injuria* applies to all participants. They must expect no recompense from anyone else for injuries inevitable in a sport, in this respect no different from many others, which carries an element of danger.
(b) The accident due to the negligence of the lift company may none-

[88] Caravan Sites and Control of Development Act 1960, s.25.
[89] *Ibid.* s.28.
[90] *Ibid.* s.23.
[91] *Ibid.* See Sched. 2.
[92] *Ibid.* s.24.
[93] Norfolk & Suffolk Broads Act 1988.
[94] *Adams & Adams* v. *Watkins* (1990) 22 H.L.R. 107.
[95] Though a friend losing a ski on the slopes in Italy was only able to lodge a claim for replacement value through the organisers by completing an affidavit in a two hour session with local police.
[96] The writer acknowledges considerable indebtedness to Mr. P. C. Maxlow-Tomlinson, Solicitor, of Exeter.

theless give rise to a claim which will be resolved on the basis of the laws of contract and tort for the country in question. A strict liability is frequently imposed on such lift operators, so that negligence does not have to be proved by a claimant for damages.

(c) A 10 point Code of Conduct is set out below.[97] This bears the authority of the international controlling body, Fédération Internationale de Ski (F.I.S.). As with Highway and other Codes, it lacks the force of law but its breach is referred to in European courts and is regarded as prima facie evidence of negligence.

(d) In Austria, to take one example, and perhaps some of the states in the United States, criminal proceedings might arise for negligence giving rise to death or serious personal injury, especially by a hit and run skier. They could be followed by civil proceedings.

(e) The physical reality of the ski slope has its bearings on the legal relations of the various parties. For instance the skier, as he is carried uphill, usually has every opportunity to see the state of the snow and the existence of potential hazards such as rocks or trees. It may affect the application of the *volenti* rule.

Experts consider this a growth area for litigation, especially since the package holiday operator based in Britain has a contract which covers most factors, such as instructors, ski hire, lift tickets and thus can give rise to litigation in British courts.

1. **Code of conduct**

(i) *Respect for others*

A skier must behave in such a way that he does not endanger or prejudice others.

(ii) *Control of speed and skiing*

A skier must ski in control. He must adapt his speed and manner of skiing to his personal ability and to the prevailing conditions of terrain, snow and weather as well as to the density of traffic.

(iii) *Choice of route*

A skier coming from behind must choose his route in such a way that he does not endanger skiers ahead.

(iv) *Overtaking*

A skier may overtake another skier above or below and to the right or to the left, provided that he leaves enough space for the overtaken skier to make any voluntary or involuntary movement.

---

[97] It was updated in 1990 from a 1967 version.

(v) *Entering and starting*

A skier entering a marked run or starting again after stopping must look up and down the run to make sure that he can do so without endangering himself or others.

(vi) *Stopping on the piste*

Unless absolutely necessary, a skier must avoid stopping on the piste in narrow places where visibility is restricted. After a fall in such a place, a skier must move clear of the piste as soon as possible.

(vii) *Climbing and descending on foot*

Both a skier climbing or descending on foot must keep to the side of the piste.

(viii) *Respect for signs and marking*

A skier must respect all signs and markings.

(ix) *Assistance*

At accidents, every skier is duty-bound to assist.

(x) *Identification*

Every skier and witness, whether a responsible party or not, must exchange names and addresses following an accident.

J. Car Races in Towns

In 1986 Birmingham became the first town in this country to run international motor racing along its streets. The event has considerable community interest and implications.

Our limited approach is to take note only of the legal framework within which the event was possible. This is a Local Act of 1985 and its main terms were to permit the closure to other traffic on two occasions in each year, for a first trial period of five years, of all the streets required for the 2.4 miles superprix as it is known in the city.

The event was successful but a later attempt to obtain Parliamentary powers for greater flexibility with the race days and duration of each race was unsuccessful. The local authority has currently paused in efforts for renewed promotion of this sport since the first five year period finished its course.[98]

---

[98] Birmingham City Council Act 1985. The Act covered also the making of by-laws, the issue of a code of practice, compensation for damage (with a set off for benefits from the racing) and a strict liability was imposed on the Council for damages for personal injury or damage to buildings (s.20).

It is perhaps worth mentioning that the City of Hull, again by Local Act, promotes an annual go-kart race in its city centre. The Isle of Mull is the other United Kingdom area with this sport in its quiverful of leisure services.

CHAPTER 9

AVAILABILITY OF FINANCE

"For the purposes of this Schedule nil may be an appropriate number"
Local Authorities (Miscellaneous Provisions) Act 1982, Sched. 1, para. 12(4)

INTRODUCTION

9.01 The public and private leisure services, as surveyed in this book, have a strong base in the local authorities of this country. They are not, however, confined to those authorities but extend at the public service level into a series of public boards, commissions, trusts and quangos. This chapter considers the finance available for the public leisure services and begins with local authorities. The finances available from non-local-authority sources are, nevertheless, of considerable practical interest.

The first edition devoted a considerable amount of space in the comparable chapter to the details of local authority finance, to show how that portion was controlled which became available for spending on the public leisure services. However, the last six years have seen a significant series of ever more detailed statutes which complicate that subject even further; more importantly it has become a field for specialists and we have decided that it ceases to warrant space in this book. We must nevertheless take account of a number of specific grants of interest to the leisure services. Then, turning from local government, we deal with the relation to both the public and the private leisure services of the Tourist Board, the Arts Council and the Sports Council and the role of private trusts.

By selecting this context, it is hoped to portray realistically the portfolio of financial aid that is available for all the leisure services.

A. SPECIFIC GRANTS

9.02 In our first edition we picked out five specific grants that could assist leisure services promoters. These related to caravan sites for gypsies, National Parks, local lotteries, derelict land and National Parks and grants under the Countryside Act of 1968.

A revised list seven years on suggests the following as relevant:
  (a) Countryside Commission
  (b) National Parks
  (c) Derelict Land
  (d) The European Commission

318

The most important replacement to our earlier list is the European Commission.

1. **Countryside**

The Countryside Act 1968 still provides the legal framework for important **9.03** grants to support the main aims of that Act and the preceding National Parks and Access to the Countryside Act 1949. These include facilities for enjoyment of the countryside, conserving and enhancing its beauty and amenities, and helping public access for the purpose of open air recreation.[1] The above Act of 1949 places emphasis on these aims within National Parks and adds "study of nature" to them. One of the main recent changes is that these grants are not limited to public bodies but are available for "any persons."[2] The actual facilities which can benefit from these extensive powers are very wide. In addition to making grants the Commission can make loans.

2. **Derelict Land and National Parks**

Under the Derelict Land Act 1982,[3] the Secretary of State can make a **9.04** grant for expenditure to reclaim or improve land which is derelict, neglected or unsightly.[4] If the land is in a development or intermediate area and a local authority is the applicant, the grant is 100 per cent. Otherwise it is 80 per cent. This grant can also be made to bring such land into use. An additional final category of land for which these grants are available is that which passes into one of these classes by an actual or apprehended collapse of the surface associated with mining operations.[5]

Where the land in question is in a National Park, or in an area of outstanding natural beauty, and the applicant for grant is a local authority, the government grant is to be 75 per cent. of the approved expenditure. In other circumstances it is to be 50 per cent. of that expenditure.[6]

3. **The European Commission**

The European Commission has become an increasingly important source **9.05** of finance for some local authority sponsored projects. It is commonplace to see the blue and gold sign of the EEC mounted on these sites to publicise the fact of EC support. Since this resource is hemmed about with

---

[1] Local Government Act 1974, s.9 implants this power and the Environmental Protection Act 1990, s.130 has added its quota of support in definition and qualification.

[2] Countryside Act 1968, s.1.

[3] ss.1 and 5.

[4] Perhaps an example helps. The new Eureka National Children's Museum at Halifax has attracted finance from this source. This is because it occupies a large, formerly unsightly site near the railway station and promises to be a significant tourist attraction.

[5] See definition in s.1(11) *ibid.*

[6] *Ibid.* s.1(6). (This general provision was initially in the National Parks and Access to the Countryside Act 1949, s.97, and amended by the Countryside Act 1968, s.36.) See important Circular DLGA. 1 of May 1991.

qualifications, it may be useful to itemise some of these. The foundation document is Council Regulation (EEC) No. 2052/88[7] on the tasks of the so-called Structural Funds. The two most relevant Funds are the European Regional Development Fund and the European Social Fund. The former is to help to redress imbalances in the regions and the latter is to combat long-term unemployment and "facilitate" the "occupational integration of young people."

The above Regulation sets out five objectives, two of which include:

9.06   (a) Promoting the development of rural areas; and

         (b) Converting the regions, including employment areas, and urban communities seriously affected by industrial decline. Assisted Areas has become a term of art for those areas which are accepted by the EEC as coming within this objective.

In these areas, the Community's Structural Funds—specifically the European Regional Development Fund—are allowed to participate in the co-financing of productive investment to enable the creation or maintenance of permanent jobs. The projects have to satisfy a number of eligibility criteria specified in regional programmes administered by the Department of the Environment or by the DTI. It is important to note that the funds are for regional development: projects are thus expected to provide regional benefits. This usually disqualifies local leisure developments, even if they can be shown to create or maintain jobs. Tourism projects, on the other hand, may attract a grant if they meet the EC tourism eligibility criteria. The most important of these is a demonstration that the project will attract a certain level of visitors from outside the region, or, alternatively, the project should be located in a recognised tourist area.[8]

4. Miscellaneous

9.07 Other grants are tailored to different situations in varying localities. The Regional Museum Councils are sometimes able to assist. For a developer of a football ground the Football Grounds Improvement Trust should be contacted. Coast protection works can imaginatively be seen as enhancement of leisure facilities, perhaps with golf links, and there can be grants in this field.[9] The London scene is dealt with specifically in the next chapter but, illustratively, includes a grant-making power in relation to voluntary organisations.[10]

B. FEES AND CHARGES

9.08 The impact of fees and charges as a useful form of revenue must never be overlooked. With some popular seaside resorts, for instance, this can be a very significant figure.

---

[7] June 24, 1988.

[8] Both derive from the duties of the Commission in Article 130 of the Treaty of Rome. This précis should not be allowed to shield readers from the awesome fact that this Regulation has at least 124 paragraphs, many of considerable complexity.

[9] Local Government Act 1972, s.29.

[10] Local Government Act 1985, s.48.

C. Non-Local-Authority Finance

1. **The Arts Council**

The Arts Council of Great Britain is an important grant-making body for   **9.09**
those engaged in the public leisure services. It was founded by Royal
Charter in 1946. In a recent operating year, the Arts Council made grants
of some £145 million to a considerable range of persons and societies in the
fields of arts and culture. It is not surprising that the organisation through
which such a large sum is dispensed is complex; this note simply indicates
the broad picture of an important component of the British public leisure
services scene.

(1) *Aims and Objects*

The objects for which the Arts Council of Great Britain is established are   **9.10**
(i) to develop and improve the knowledge, understanding and practice of
the arts; (ii) to increase the accessibility of the arts to the public throughout Great Britain; (iii) to co-operate with government departments, local
authorities and other bodies to achieve these ends.[11]

(2) *Organisation*

The central Council consists of a Chairman and not more than 18 others.   **9.11**
The Vice-Chairman is chosen from those others and the Chairman is
appointed by the Secretary of State for Education and Science. The Secretary of State for Education and Science is the point of liaison with the
Government; he has an assessor attached to the Council. The Treasury
are involved in appointments. The Secretary of State for Wales is the
point of liaison for the Welsh Arts Council, which interlocks with the
British one.[12]
  There are now 10 Regional Arts Boards through which the national
Council works. The Arts Council also has its own framework of advisory
panels, groups or committees, on drama, arts films, photography, art,
dance, housing the arts, literature, music, and training. In Wales, some of
these arts are also represented by specialist groups; in addition, there is a
group to advise on crafts.

(3) *Grant-Aided Leisure Services*

In a recent year the divisions of the beneficiaries were as follows: **9.12**
   (a) Five national companies: the English National Opera, National
       Theatre Board, Royal Opera House Covent Garden Limited, the
       Royal Shakespeare Theatre and South Bank Board
   (b) Ten Regional Arts Associations

[11] Article 17 of the Charter of Incorporation of February 7, 1967.
[12] There is also a Scottish Arts Council, of which the Chairman too is a member of the
British Arts Council.

(c) Music
(d) Touring
(e) Drama
(f) Dance
(g) Visual Arts
(h) Literature
(i) Film, Video and Broadcasting

To gauge the range of Arts Council grants, it should be noted that within the above totals is a block grant to the 1,200-strong National Federation of Music Societies, which distributes to its members. It has been further estimated that the 10 Regional Arts Associations make grants to some 7,000 separate persons or societies or local authorities.

The address of the Arts Council is 14 Great Peter Street, London SW1P 3NQ.

2. **The Sports Council**

9.13 This also is an important grant-making body in the field of public leisure services. One of its annual reports affords evidence of the large number of activities it supports and the considerable benefit it provides for participants in over 60 sports and pastimes.

(1) *Aims*

Founded by Royal Charter in 1972, the primary aims and legal objects of the Sports Council are "fostering the knowledge and practice of sport and physical education among the public at large and the provision of facilities therefor."

The Charter also enjoins the Council to "encourage the attainment of high standards in conjunction with governing bodies of sport and physical recreation."

These broad objects have led over the years to detailed projects, targets and schemes for the various sports in which the Council is involved.

(2) *Grants*

9.14 The figures taken from a recent annual report[13] show that the main areas through which the Sports Council channelled its financial support, in the form of grants and loans, were as follows:

   (a) Nationally, to governing bodies of sport for administration, coaching, competitions and other ongoing commitments—£22.9 million.
   (b) Regionally, grant aid for regional and local facilities—£12.6 million.
   (c) Revenue and capital support for the five national sports centres of the Sports Council—£3.6 million.[14] These are Bisham Abbey, Lilleshall Hall, Plas y Brenin, Crystal Palace and Holme Pierrepont,

---

[13] Annual report of the Sports Council for the year 1990/1991.
[14] *Ibid.* at p. 32.

situated and designed to provide emphasis on climbing, athletics, tennis or other sports but not limited by that speciality; they provide a stimulus for the whole country and are being regularly developed to meet changing fashions and needs.

(3) *Organisation*

The Sports Council devolves detailed grant making for certain levels to its Regional Councils, of which there are 10. It attaches great importance to the national sports centres, each of which has its own managing committee. **9.15**

The Regional Councils are paralleled by regional conferences for sport and recreation. The Council has 10 panels and groups attached to it in order to receive specialist advice on areas of activity. These include trade and industry, coaches, drug abuse, physical education, fitness and health, medical services, sports science, recreation management and community sports leadership training. There is a separate Sports Council for Wales.

(4) *Conclusion*

There is ongoing research into the provision of artificial pitches, into golf courses, the low-cost provision of swimming pools and, finally, on the capacity, playing quality and soil characteristics of a range of sporting pitches; in fact, the Sports Council provides a stimulus for many of the public leisure pursuits dealt with in this work. Apart from the Safety of Sports Grounds Act 1975,[15] it is difficult to identify items of statute law, still less cases in the courts, in which the Council, as distinct from players, clubs, coaches and referees and associated sports supporters of all kinds, has been involved. The address of the Sports Council is 16 Upper Woburn Place, London WC1H 0QP. **9.16**

3. **The Tourist Board**

The public leisure services are all, to a greater or lesser degree, involved in this country's tourist trade. This makes them a natural partner of the British Tourist Authority and associated Tourist Boards, which legally and in every other way have a prime role in this field. As the Tourist Authority has power to provide financial assistance for suitable projects, a note about its legal status is appropriate. **9.17**

(1) *The Development of Tourism Act* 1969

This Act establishes the British Tourist Authority and the English, Scottish and Welsh Tourist Boards. The chairmen of the three national Boards are on the board of the British Tourist Authority, together with six others appointed by the Secretary of State for Trade.[16]

---

[15] See Chapter 6.
[16] Development of Tourism Act 1969, s.1 and the Secretary of State (New Departments) Order 1974 (S.I. 1974 No. 692).

    (a) The function of all four bodies is to encourage people to visit Great Britain and people living in Great Britain to take their holidays there; and

    (b) encourage the provision and improvement of tourist amenities and facilities in Great Britain."

"Tourist amenities and facilities" are, "in relation to any country, amenities and facilities for visitors to that country and for other people travelling within it on business or pleasure."[17]

9.18   The British Tourist Authority may "prepare schemes for the giving of financial assistance (by the above three national Boards) for the carrying out of projects of such classes as may be specified in the schemes, being schemes which will, in the opinion of the Authority, provide or improve tourist amenities or facilities in Great Britain."[18] Assistance is by a grant or loan or by a combination of those methods.[19] A scheme is to be submitted to the Department of Trade, who may "by order confirm it with or without modification" and if a scheme is so confirmed, it shall thereupon have effect.[20] Any Order made by the Department of Trade, approving such a scheme, is to be by statutory instrument. The Order requires Treasury consent and a draft to be approved by each House of Parliament.[21]

In addition to the above procedure about schemes, a Tourist Board has power to give financial assistance for a project which will improve or provide tourist amenities or facilities in the country for which the Tourist Board is responsible.

The relevant Minister and the Treasury must approve; the assistance may be in the form of a grant, a loan or by subscribing to or otherwise acquiring shares or stock in a company if the project is to be carried out by a company incorporated in Great Britain.[22]

(2) *Local Authorities*

9.19   The Local Government Act 1972 included a provision to stimulate tourism through initiatives by the local authority. Local authorities, alone or jointly with some other person, might "encourage persons, by advertisement or otherwise, to visit their area for recreation, for health purposes, or to hold conferences, trade fairs and exhibitions in their area and provide and improve facilities for these purposes."[23]

Fourteen years later[24] the word "recreation" was removed from the three purposes. This followed the much wider concept of recreation

---

[17] Development of Tourism Act 1969, s.2(9).

[18] *Ibid.* s.3(1). The annual report of the B.T.A. for 1991 says that 251 joint promotions, pump-primed by the Authority, were then running. Sched. 2 to the Act of 1969 sets out the conditions to be attached to a grant pursuant to s.3 schemes.

[19] *Ibid.* s.3(3).

[20] *Ibid.* s.3(2).

[21] *Ibid.* s.3(6).

[22] *Ibid.* s.4.

[23] s.144.

[24] Local Government (Miscellaneous Provisions) Act 1976, s.81(1), Sched. 2.

embodied in the Local Government (Miscellaneous Provisions) Act 1976 and in respect of which wide new powers were conferred on local authorities.

The Local Government Act 1972 also empowered local authorities to contribute to any organisation approved by the Secretary of State for the purposes of the section, as stated above, and being an organisation established for the purpose of encouraging persons to visit the United Kingdom or any part thereof. The address of the British Tourist Authority is Thames Tower, Black's Road, London W6 9EL.

4. **Private Trust Funds**

The leading directory of charitable trusts in this country, with some 2,500 **9.20** entries, shows a significant proportion with powers to assist the leisure services in all their range.[25]

Music and the arts, physical fitness, the preservation of the environment and the architectural heritage, the promotion of recreation, all figure in the quoted items of reference of many of the listed trusts

It is true that these bodies vary greatly in their resources and some confine their donations to certain parts of the country. Additionally, the current edition of the directory indicates that some trusts can take no new applications for the time being, being committed with existing assistance for some time to come.

Having made these qualifications, it is evident that many hundreds of trusts have resources to deploy in the field covered by this book. They thus furnish another avenue for financial assistance to those leisure services with funding difficulties for new projects.[26]

---

[25] *Directory of Grant-Making Trusts* 1991. (Published by Charities Aid Foundation, Tonbridge).

[26] By way of example, in the Environmental Class, £4.3 million was distributed in 1,651 grants in the preceding year and £78 million went via the Humanities umbrella, for art, drama and associated recreations, via 1,200 grants.

CHAPTER 10

LONDON LEISURE SERVICES

"The clearer a thing is, the more difficult it is to find any express authority or any dictum exactly to the point."

James L.J. in *Panama and South Pacific Telegraph Company* v. *India Rubber, Gutta Pecha and Telegraph Works Company* (1875) 10 Ch.App. 515, 526.

INTRODUCTION

10.01   The aim of this chapter is to pick out the differences in the legal powers available to the local authorities in Greater London from local authorities in the remainder of the country. Where appropriate, non-local-authority providers of such services are also considered.

Not the least of the difficulties for a writer on this subject is the inconsistent treatment of the law for London in Acts of Parliament. The Greater London Council was abolished in April 1986. Before then the last great reorganisation of London local government was in 1964, following a Royal Commission. There was a plethora of special London legislation and the reorganisation, encouraged by that Royal Commission, began the process of bringing local London legislation into line with the rest of the country. Subsequently, some statutes have referred to "local authorities" and this has included those in London; sometimes, there have been special London provisions.[1] There is a strong tradition in London of annual "General Powers" Acts, promoted by the old London County Council and the Greater London Council, dealing with problems peculiar to the metropolis and, often, paving the way for later national legislation.

The London Government Act 1963 is the present Act of Parliament, which lays down the framework of local authorities for Greater London, as there defined. The City of London, 32 London Borough Councils, and the strange historic survival, the Inner and Middle Temples, comprise the unique group of 35 local authorities for that great metropolitan area.

1. **Historic Buildings, Statues and Monuments**

10.02   Listed Buildings in need of repair can be acquired by the Historic Buildings and Monuments Commission for England ("the Commission") and

---

[1] The Royal Commission Report, a comprehensive, even inspiring, document on the place of London local government in the national scene, is Cmnd. 1164, Report on Local Government in Greater London. The chairman was Sir Edwin Herbert.

326

by the London Borough Councils (in this chapter "the Boroughs"), with the use of compulsory powers.[2]

When a building is of special architectural or historical interest it may be acquired by agreement by the Boroughs.

The Commission and Boroughs, with the owner's consent, put plaques **10.03** on buildings, in their areas, to indicate "an event of public interest."[3]

The relevant London authority, the Common Council and the Boroughs are local authorities for the purposes of the Ancient Monuments and Archaeological Areas Act 1979.[4]

The Common Council, the Boroughs and the Temples, for their respective areas, are authorised to provide and maintain public clocks, statues and monuments in streets and public places.[5]

The obelisk adjoining Westminster Bridge, known as Cleopatra's **10.04** Needle, is under the care of the relevant London authority. An initial list of 15 statues compiled in 1854, including Nelson's Column, has been added to over the years. All those statues became publicly repairable.[6] The Boroughs have the powers of local authorities in relation to war memorials.[7] Under the Roosevelt Memorial Act 1946, a statue of President Roosevelt was erected in Grosvenor Square, at the instance of the Pilgrim's Society, by the Department of the Environment.

2. Open Spaces and Recreation

(1) *London Borough Councils*[8]

The Boroughs have the powers available under the Open Spaces Act **10.05** 1906, and also powers in relation to Open Space and Recreation from a Local Act, the Ministry of Housing and Local Government Provisional Order Confirmation (Greater London Parks and Open Spaces) Act 1967. The extended powers in this Local Act of 1967 may be summarised in this way.

"Open space" for this purpose means land under the control of a local authority, being a public park, heath, common, recreation

---

[2] Planning (Listed Buildings and Conservation Areas) Act 1990, ss.47–50.

[3] Local Government Act 1985, Sched. 2, para. 4. This Act generally transferred to the Commission the powers of the former Greater London Council relating to listed buildings and ancient monuments. The 12 inner London boroughs are: City of Westminster, Camden, Islington, Hackney, Tower Hamlets, Greenwich, Lewisham, Southwark, Lambeth, Wandsworth, Hammersmith and the Royal Borough of Kensington and Chelsea. The 20 outer London Boroughs are: Hounslow, Hillingdon, Ealing, Brent, Harrow, Barnet, Haringey, Enfield, Waltham Forest, Redbridge, Havering, Barking, Newham, Bexley, Bromley, Croydon, Sutton, Merton, Richmond and the Royal Borough of Kingston upon Thames.

[4] s.61.

[5] Public Health Act 1875, s.165; Public Health Acts Amendment Act 1890, ss.42 and 46; London Government Act 1963, s.40; Local Government Act 1972, s.180.

[6] Public Statutes (Metropolis) Act 1854, ss.5 and 7.

[7] War Memorials (Local Authorities' Powers) Act 1923, s.4 and London Government Act 1963, s.4(4)(a).

[8] London Government Act 1963, s.58.

ground, pleasure ground, garden, walk, ornamental enclosure or disused burial ground.[9]

Powers to provide for recreation

In relation to such open spaces, there are seven powers[10]:

(a) To provide facilities of all kinds for swimming and open air recreation, including golf courses, gymnasia and rifle ranges, indoor
recreational facilities of all kinds, and centres for the use of clubs,
and organisations of a social, recreational and educational nature.
Such indoor centres must not unfairly restrict the space available
to the public for open air recreation on that particular open space.

(b) Amusement fairs, entertainments, bands of music, concerts, cinematographic exhibitions, pageants.

(c) In the winter season, the provision of ice-skating on created ice
rinks.

(d) Meals and refreshments for sale.

(e) All supporting equipment in the form of lockers, conveniences,
clothing, apparatus, including swings and platforms.

(f) The erection and maintenance of associated buildings and structures to afford accommodation.

(g) The right to set apart portions of the available open space for use in
connection with the above.

10.06   The following three limits to the use of these powers are contained in
the Act of 1967:

(a) Persons must not be excluded from the open space not specially
laid out, whilst games are not taking place.

(b) In any event, the amount specially set apart for the above facilities should not exceed one acre or one-tenth, whichever is the
greater.

(c) Entertainments in the form of a cinematographic film are to be for
the advancement of art, education, drama, science, music or literature.

They are not to be films normally shown on the commercial circuit,
within 12 months of their general release in Great Britain. When the time
for local authority showing arrives, there is to be a charge for customers
which is not less than the comparable charge in local cinemas. An exception to this charging stipulation is allowed when the show is for charitable,
educational, cultural, social or public purposes.[11]

Powers of letting

10.07   The local authorities may, by licence or letting, grant to other persons
the right of exercising the powers set out above; open space land or buildings of the authority may be included in those agreements. The authority
may contribute directly or indirectly to the expenses of providing the

[9] London Government Act 1963, s.6.
[10] *Ibid.* s.7.
[11] *Ibid.* s.7.

entertainment in question.[12] Vegetation on an open space may be enclosed, to ensure its cultivation or preservation, in the interests of amenity or of public safety, for such periods and on such conditions as may be deemed expedient.[13]

There is a flexible power for authorities to charge for the facilities provided as described above. This is subject to a limit for reading rooms.[14] **10.08**

The Act then sets out certain limitations to be observed by local authorities which use the extensive powers described above. There are four of these:

(a) Not to override a person's legal rights, other than as a member of the public, except with his consent.

(b) Not, by use of its powers, to deny members of the public access, without charge, to some part of each plot of open space land.[15]

(c) Not to conflict with the terms of a trust relating to such land, unless an appropriate order, allowing a departure from the terms of that trust, has been obtained from the High Court or Charity Commissioners, or, alternatively, by obtaining the consent of a person who is in a position to enforce that trust.[16]

(d) Not to violate any building by-law, town planning or other relevant legal requirement, in relation to the buildings or enclosures or methods employed to use its powers.[17]

Competitions

Local authorities are granted wide powers of running competitions in relation to "any recreation," provided that they do not, if setting aside land in an open space for spectators at a competition, enclose more than one acre or one-tenth of that open space, whichever is the greater.[18] **10.09**

Transfers among local authorities

Local authorities may transfer open space between themselves, if it will thereby provide a more convenient exercise of their functions. In so doing, they must not depart from private legal trusts or covenants affecting the land in question. If the transfer involves assignment of a lessee's interest in a lease, then the lessor's consent to such an assignment must be obtained in the usual way.[19] **10.10**

---

[12] London Government Act 1963, s.8.

[13] *Ibid.* s.9.

[14] *Ibid.* s.10.

[15] *Ibid.* s.11. A special legal protection for Paddington Recreation Ground is contained in this section.

[16] *Ibid.* s.11. A trust under s.10 of the Open Spaces Act 1906 is an exception to this provision.

[17] *Ibid.* s.11(4).

[18] *Ibid.* s.13. "Recreation" is widely defined as any activity for which a local authority have power to provide facilities in an open space (s.13(1)).

[19] *Ibid.* s.14. This section also preserves the positions under the London Squares (Preservation) Act 1931 and s.16 of the Open Spaces Act 1906, should they be relevant to the site.

Land exchanges

There is, lastly, a useful power of effecting an exchange of land in an open space with other land or enlargement adjacent but outside the open space, when an improvement or enlargement of the open space will result.[20] One plot will lose its open space character: the other will acquire it.

To facilitate the development of open space, local authorities are empowered to enter into agreements with the owners of land, to secure for the local authority the first refusal to acquire that land, when the owner decides to sell his estate or interest in the land.

The circumstances[21] in which part of an open space may be used for street improvements are naturally[22] somewhat complex. The power is nonetheless available.

Local authorities may appoint staff to supervise open space land, in order to secure compliance by the public with by-laws or regulations. The staff can only act as constables if duly sworn in and then in uniform or provided with a warrant.[23]

10.11   In an earlier Act, the London Council (General Powers) Act 1890, it was provided that any by-law which prohibits military drill on a heath or common is ineffective unless approved by the Secretary of State for Defence. Even then such a by-law is not to restrain the right and powers of that Secretary of State over parks and gardens or other open space in any case of national danger or emergency.[24]

10.12   A power to close public parks on three Sundays in a calendar year is held by the relevant London authority, contrary to the position in the rest of the country.[25] The same authority has legal powers in a number of local Acts in relation to two special estates affording open space facilities to the public: Holland House in Kensington[26] (used by the Greater London Council successor authority as a hostel and its grounds as open space), and Crystal Palace (vested in the Greater London Council successor authority to be used for the purposes of education, recreation, and the promotion of industry, commerce and art).[27]

---

[20] London Government Act 1963, s.15. Compensation may be paid for rights extinguished in such a transaction (s.15(2)).

[21] *Ibid.* s.16.

[22] *Ibid.* s.17.

[23] *Ibid.* s.18.

[24] London Council (General Powers) Act 1890, s.16.

[25] The Greater London Council (General Powers) Act 1978, s.12. Prior notice of such closures is necessary. The same Act incorporates a slight variation in relation to other park closures. Instead of the permitted six consecutive days, (excluding Sundays), under s.44 of the Public Health Acts Amendment Act 1890, and Public Health Act 1961, s.53, the Boroughs may close their parks for six consecutive days, including Sundays.

[26] See London County Council (Holland House) Act 1952.

[27] London County Council (Crystal Palace) Act 1951, and London Government Act 1963, s.57(2)(*e*).

(2) *The Common Council of the City of London*

The Corporation of the City of London, by ancient tradition and sanction **10.13**
from Parliament, manages a number of famous London open spaces that
lie outside its administrative area.

Epping Forest

The City of London (Various Powers) Act 1977 contains a number of
provisions about this forest. Compensation became payable to all persons
who had pastured their cattle in the Forest during the previous 10 years
and who, in view of the new condition, stood to lose their right of pastur-
age.[28]

The ancient name for the legal managers of Epping Forest was the Conservators. By the Act of 1977, the City of London Corporation, acting
through its Epping Forest Committee, were the Conservators. Under this
Act of 1977, the above Committee assessed the number of cattle pastured
in the open space and thus assessed the compensation under the above
provision. There was statutory arbitration where the parties did not agree
the amount.[29]

In order to regenerate the Forest and protect it as an open space for the
recreation of the public, the Conservators were authorised to take areas of
the open space, one by one, none exceeding 100 acres, and by enclosing
them, exclude the public.[30] These powers of closure should not close public footpaths nor bridleways. If they interfered with the latter, the Conservators must provide an alternative route. Lastly, these enclosure powers
were not to interfere with the apparatus of statutory undertakers.

The Act of 1977 further empowered the Corporation to provide facilities **10.14**
by way of refreshments, car parks, public conveniences and shelters. They
could charge for use of these facilities and might also authorise other persons, by agreement, to provide the facilities in question.[31]

Fines for offences under the Epping Forest Act 1878 or those contained
in by-laws made under the Corporation of London (Open Spaces) Act
1878 have recently been increased.[32] The lands of the Conservators have
been redefined in the City of London (Various Powers) Act 1956.[33] The
by-laws making powers of the Conservators in relation to deer sanctuaries
in Epping Forest are now to be found in the City of London (Various
Powers) Act 1959.[34] The City of London (Various Powers) Act 1967 contains authority for the Conservators to provide buildings suitable for the

---

[28] s.5.
[29] ss.5 and 6.
[30] s.7.
[31] s.8. The Act includes the common qualification that meals and refreshments are not to be
provided by the public body, *i.e.* the Common Council, unless the existing provision in the
neighbourhood of the Forest is unsatisfactory.
[32] City of London (Various Powers) Act 1977. The maximum fine for both classes of offence
was raised to £200.
[33] s.10. The City of London (Various Powers) Act 1967, ss.26–27, related also to the total
City land ownership in this forest.
[34] s.17.

teaching of biology, ecology, and allied subjects and for the instruction of children and also the public generally in the natural history of the Forest and its conservation.[35] In the City of London (Various Powers) Act 1971 are to be found powers recently taken by the Conservators to regulate horse-riding in Epping Forest.[36]

Burnham Beeches, Spring Park, West Wickham, West Wickham Common, and Coulsdon Commons

10.15   The City of London (Various Powers) Act 1977 contains powers for the provision in these open spaces of similar facilities, and subject to the same qualifications as are set out in relation to Epping Forest.[37]

Highgate Wood, Queens Park in Kilburn, West Ham Park

These are examples of other open spaces which are maintained by the Common Council of the City of London. These activities of the Common Council proceed from a power contained in the Corporation of London (Open Spaces) Act 1878 to acquire open spaces within 25 miles of the City boundaries and to make agreements "for the assertion and protection" of rights over such spaces.

Hampstead Heath

This resulted from the London Government Reorganisation (Hampstead Heath) Order 1989 (S.I. 1989 No. 304), made during post 1985 arrangements.

3. **Land**

10.16   Under the City of London (Various Powers) Act 1958, the Common Council is empowered not only to acquire and dispose of land for its various functions but also to acquire land in advance of requirements.[38] The Greater London Council inherited the powers and duties of the former Middlesex and London County Councils in relation to Green Belt land.[39] This was initially dealt with in the Green Belt (London and Home Counties) Act 1938 and involves a detailed framework of powers for the designation and protection of lands falling within the huge open spaces known as the Green Belt. The areas include parts of Essex, Hertford, Kent, Surrey, Buckingham and Greater London. The powers now allow the Boroughs to acquire land,[40] enter into covenants with owners to preserve the Green Belt status, and compensate for the imposition of restrictions on

[35] s.27.
[36] Pt. IV.
[37] s.9.
[38] ss.7–10.
[39] London Government Act 1963, s.59.
[40] Green Belt (London and Home Counties) Act 1938, s.3.

building, adverse use or alienation.[41] Recreation, camping and agriculture are three uses which are encouraged by owners or, if the land is owned by a London Borough, by letting.[42]

4. **Commons**

In Chapter 2 we considered the legal framework within which commons **10.17** fall to be managed in the remainder of this country. In the Greater London area metropolitan commons have been the subject of legislation for more than a century; there are interesting differences between the making of Schemes for the management of such commons and those outside London, and these legal differences can usefully be tabulated:

The Commons Act 1899	The Metropolitan Commons Acts 1866–1899[43]
1. The Scheme is made by the local authority.	1. The Scheme is made also by the commoners or the Lord of the Manor.
2. The procedure begins with a draft prepared, published and submitted to the Department of the Environment.	2. The procedure begins with a memorial presented by one of the bodies in 1. (above) to the Commons Commissioners.
3. The period for objections is three months.	3. The comparable period is two months.
4. If the Lord of the Manor or one third of the commoners object, the Scheme cannot go ahead.	4. There is no such built-in power of objection. The inquiry into objections is in respect of their merits.
5. Confirmation by the above Department is the final step before implementation.	5. A Scheme for the management of a metropolitan common requires confirmation by Parliament.

The Boroughs are the registration authorities for commons under the **10.18** Commons Registration Act 1965.[44] They can make agreements with the Ministry of Agriculture, Fisheries and Food, for the surrender of land from a common for the purposes of a highway improvement. Any land given in exchange becomes part of the common.[45]

Commons are protected against encroachment by buildings or enclos-

---

[41] Green Belt (London and Home Counties) Act 1938, ss.3 and 5.
[42] *Ibid.* s.27.
[43] Commons Act 1899, ss.1 and 2; Metropolitan Commons Act 1866, ss.6–10.
[44] s.2.
[45] London County Council (General Powers) Act 1960, s.10, as amended by the Local Law (G.L.C. and Inner London Boroughs) Order 1965 (S.I. 1965 No. 540).

ures, by provisions in the Act of 1967 discussed in relation to Open Spaces above. Before such encroachment can proceed, Ministerial consent, if necessary after a public inquiry, is required.[46]

A power in the Countryside Act 1968 is available for the relevant London authority, the Common Council and the Boroughs to provide facilities for a common on land "in the neighbourhood of a common." These include car parks, refreshments, conveniences and shelters. Compulsory powers are available to obtain such adjacent land.[47]

10.19 Two cases relating to the validity of by-laws for London commons are of interest:

Mitcham Common Conservators v. *Cox*; *The same* v. *Cole*[48]

A golf club formed two courses, with the agreement and under a letting from the Conservators of Mitcham Common. The Conservators acted under a Local Act which allowed a Scheme to be made under the Metropolitan Commons Act of 1866 and 1869; by-laws were then made, duly confirmed by the Local Government Board, followed by regulations, which were not deemed to require such confirmation. Schemes, by-laws and regulations formed the legal framework for management of the two golf clubs and cases came before the King's Bench Divisional Court to challenge some of these regulations. The court decided:

 (a) A regulation that no one should play, unless accompanied by a caddie approved by the club, was upheld.

 (b) However, a regulation was held void which limited those who could play to members of the club and inhabitants of Mitcham.

 (c) Similarly, the court held void a regulation which said that no non-members could play on Saturdays. This was "partial," within the principles laid down in *Kruse* v. *Johnson*.[49]

de Morgan v. *Metropolitan Board of Works*[50]

This concerned a by-law which regulated the holdings of meetings on Clapham Common. Speakers had to obtain prior approval from the Board and, in this case, the plaintiff preached a sermon without seeking such permission. He was prosecuted and convicted, and challenged the by-law. The court upheld the by-law; it was a reasonable way of maintaining limits on the time and space occupied by speakers on a public common.

It is sometimes a surprise to learn how many commons there are in Greater London; the concept of a built-up metropolis does not always allow for this element in the total London scene. It should be remarked

---

[46] See s.12 of Act referred to in n. 53.
[47] s.6(1), s.9 and Sched. 2.
[48] [1911] 2 K.B. 854. A case heard shortly afterwards, *Harris* v. *Harrison* (1914) 111 L.T. 534, shows that the club altered its rules, giving preference for club members for limited times only and the court upheld that amended rule.
[49] [1898] 2 Q.B. 91. See Chap. 4.
[50] (1880) 5 Q.B. 155.

that commons are inherited by the modern community: they are not created by them.

5. **Squares**

London squares as open spaces have been the subject of legislation and, in particular, the Metropolis Management Act 1855, and the Town Gardens Protection Act 1863. The aim of this legislation is to facilitate the formation for each square of a committee of the householders whose premises front on to the square. The committees were empowered to raise moneys to maintain the physical amenities of the square, failing which the local authority would assume that responsibility. **10.20**

The Common Council and the two Temples are the relevant local authorities for squares in their territories.[51]

6. **Libraries and Museums**

Whilst the Boroughs and the Common Council are the library authorities,[52] they are local authorities for the purposes of the Public Libraries and Museums Act 1964.[53] In addition to books, articles which may be provided and repaired for a library include statuary, sculpture, models "and other articles of a similar nature."[54] **10.21**

A division of responsibility was made in the Local Government Act 1985 in respect of five famous museums and stately homes until then managed by the Greater London Council.

The statutory powers of management are unchanged for all five and these are to provide for the accommodation, exhibition, and preservation of works of art or objects of historical, antiquarian or other public interest. The premises now vested in the Inner London Education Authority are the Horniman Museum and the Geffrye Museum. Then it is the Historic Buildings and Monuments Commission in which are vested Kenwood House, Marble Hill House, Twickenham and Rangers House, Greenwich,[55] sometimes known as the Historic House Museums.

The London Boroughs and Common Council have powers not only to acquire but to commission works of art and then to erect, maintain and contribute to the maintenance of works of art.[56] They also may make contributions to any society providing a public service by means of cultural activities in the area.[57] The Common Council has power to receive on

---

[51] Background on these squares is to be found in the report of the Royal Commission on London Squares, Cmnd. 3196 of 1928. The London Squares Preservation Act 1931 is also of interest, in providing the powers to preserve squares from development.

[52] Local Government Act 1972, s.206. The Common Council is the library authority, not only in the City but also in the two Temples: Temples Order 1971 (S.I. 1971 No. 1732), art. 5.

[53] Public Libraries and Museums Act 1964, s.25.

[54] London County Council (General Powers) Act 1947, s.36.

[55] Local Government Act 1985, ss.44 and 45.

[56] *Ibid.* Pt. II.

[57] London County Council (General Powers) Act 1947, s.59.

deposit, or acquire, or commission and erect and maintain, or contribute to the cost of, pictures, sculptures or works of art.[58]

7. The Royal Parks

10.22   The Crown Lands Act 1851 lays on Commissioners of Works the duty to manage the royal parks. These are St. James's and Hyde and Green Park, Kensington Gardens, Chelsea Gardens, the Treasury Garden, Parliament Square Garden, Regents Park, Primrose Hill, Victoria Park, Battersea Park, Greenwich Park, Kew Gardens Pleasure Grounds and Green, Kew and Richmond Roads, Hampton Court Gardens, Green and Road, Hampton Court Park, Richmond Park and Green, and Bushey Park.

Regulations govern the conduct of visitors to the parks and constables are used for enforcement. The Acts under which the royal parks are managed are the Parks Regulation Act 1872, the Parks Regulation (Amendment) Act 1926, and the Parks Regulation (Amendment) Act 1974.

8. Entertainment and Licensing

10.23   The London Boroughs are the licensing authorities in Greater London for many forms of public entertainment, including:

     (a) Betting tracks.[59]
     (b) Public boxing and wrestling.
     (c) Entertainment licences, which include the former music, singing and dancing licences.[60]
     (d) Theatres.[61]
     (e) Cinemas.[62]
     (f) Private places of entertainment.[63]
     (g) Exhibitions and displays at the Alexandra Palace, the Central Hall Westminster, Earl's Court, Olympia, the Royal Festival Hall, the Royal Horticultural Halls and Seymour Hall.[64]

Sex establishments are licensed by the Boroughs and Common Council after a resolution of the relevant council so to do.[65]

It being "deemed expedient" as the preamble to the Greater London Council (General Powers) Act 1986 said, to have greater control over a separate class of these premises, "sex encounter establishments," another legal code was devised, adoptable in London by the Boroughs and Com-

---

[58] City of London (Various Powers) Act 1962, s.5.
[59] Local Government Act 1963, s.53.
[60] Local Government (Miscellaneous Provisions) Act 1982. The Common Council is the licensing authority in its own area for these licences, also theatres, arenas and private places of entertainment.
[61] Theatres Act 1968, ss.12–14 and s.28.
[62] Cinematograph Act 1909 and London Government Act 1963, s.52.
[63] Private Places of Entertainment Act 1967, s.7; Local Government (Miscellaneous Provisions) Act 1982, Sched. 2.
[64] Greater London Council (General Powers) Act 1966, s.21.
[65] Local Government (Miscellaneous Provisions) Act 1982, s.2.

mon Council.[66] A recent decision of the House of Lords on this code, *McMonagle* v. *Westminster City Council*,[67] proved to be even more revealing in law than the premises in question were designed to be in fact. The House held certain words "which are not unlawful" to be not merely surplusage but the product of an "unusual degree of ineptitude" by draftsmen. They reached back to precedents in Natal and a Water Act a century ago to justify treating these positive words as otiose. They had been the basis of a submission, characterised as "startling and unedifying" that a prosecution should eliminate by evidence four more serious offences as ones a defendant had *not* committed, in order to satisfy a court of the one under this Act which he was alleged to have transgressed. The House would have none of this: the offence was simple and straightforward. The case is an important chapter in legal history.

9. Recreation and Sport

(1) *The Thames Region*

The National Rivers Authority is now responsible for this large area, dealing with it as the Thames Region. The Water Resources Act of 1991 contains an identical set of provisions to that within the new domestic water legislation, now the Water Industry Act 1991.[68] This embodies firm duties in relation to preserving natural beauty, conserving flora, fauna and geological features of special interest. Amenity and recreation for the public are touched on in these Acts. **10.24**

The only distinctive legislation for the Thames Region is in the old Thames Conservancy Acts. These private Acts give the power under which various sets of by-laws have been made to safeguard the extensive navigation on the river, in the interests of boat users, fishermen, river bank enjoyment, and general amenity.

(2) *The Lee Valley*

The Lee Valley Regional Park Authority was set up to develop and improve, preserve and manage an area (partly in Greater London) near the river Lee as a place for leisure, recreation, sport, games, amusements, the provision of nature reserves and the provision and enjoyment of entertainments.[69] **10.25**

With a governing body comprising representatives from the relevant neighbouring authorities, the Authority was empowered to make by-laws, to enter into agreements to eliminate restrictive covenants[70] and, among many other powers, to remove houseboats which had become "seriously injurious to the amenity of the waterways."[71]

[66] s.12.
[67] [1990] 1 All E.R. 993.
[68] ss.16, 17 and 18.
[69] See Lee Valley Regional Park Act 1966.
[70] *Ibid.* s.26.
[71] *Ibid.* s.38.

10. **The Countryside**

10.26   A Farm Interpretation Centre at Park Lodge Farm, Hillingdon is to be used "for the purposes of education, recreation and leisure."[72] It is now managed by the London Borough of Hillingdon.

Allotments

London Boroughs are smallholding authorities[73] and each of the London Boroughs is also an allotments authority.[74] A significant difference from the rest of the country is made by the London Government Act 1963, under which the provision of allotments is a power and not a duty.[75]

---

[72] Greater London Council (General Powers) Act 1974, ss.3–6. The statutory purposes are unchanged.

[73] Agriculture Act 1970, s.38.

[74] Small-Holdings and Allotments Act 1908, s.23.

[75] s.55(4). This also eliminates the right contained in our general laws for six ratepayers as currently described in law to request consideration of their desire for allotments. (See Chap. 8.)

Index

References throughout are to paragraph numbers.
Those followed by "n" (e.g. 2.09n.) are to footnotes.

INDEX